A
RED and **ROVER**

Cartoon Collection by Brian Basset

Andrews McMeel
Publishing®

Kansas City • Sydney • London

Other Books by Brian Basset

Life in the Fast Food Lane

Life Begins at 6:40

Minivanity

Bless This Home Office . . . With Tax Credits

Café Adam

Red and Rover

This book is dedicated to all the selfless individuals who have *dedicated* themselves to the welfare and humane treatment of animals everywhere.

Red and Rover® is syndicated by Universal Uclick.

Andrews McMeel Publishing, LLC
an Andrews McMeel Universal company
1130 Walnut Street, Kansas City, Missouri 64106

www.andrewsmcmeel.com

ISBN: 978-0-7407-4133-3

Library of Congress Control Number: 2003111160

www.gocomics.com

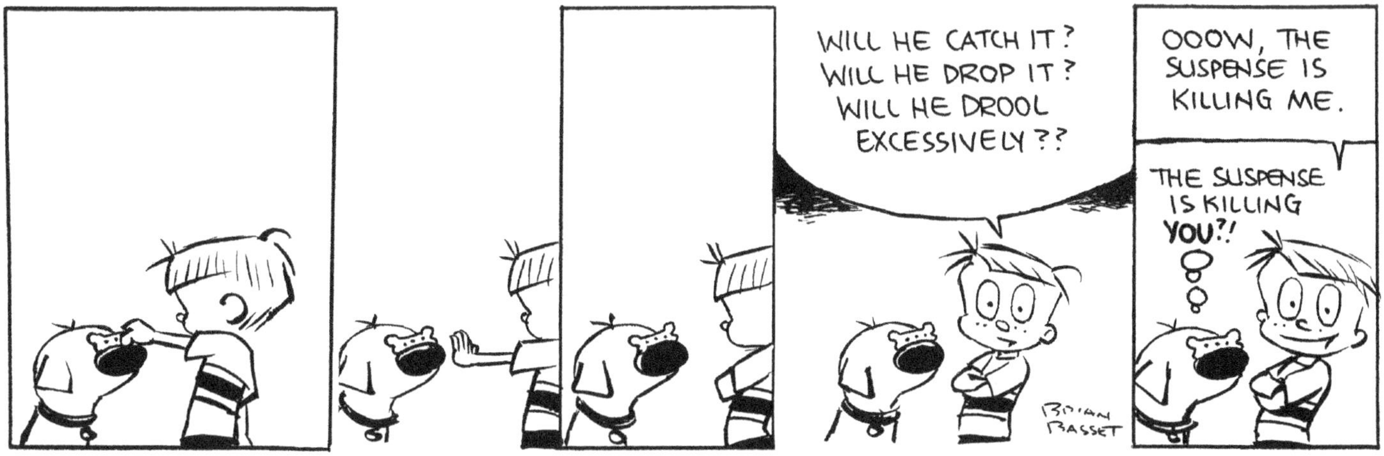
WILL HE CATCH IT? WILL HE DROP IT? WILL HE DROOL EXCESSIVELY??
OOOW, THE SUSPENSE IS KILLING ME.
THE SUSPENSE IS KILLING **YOU**?!
BRIAN BASSET

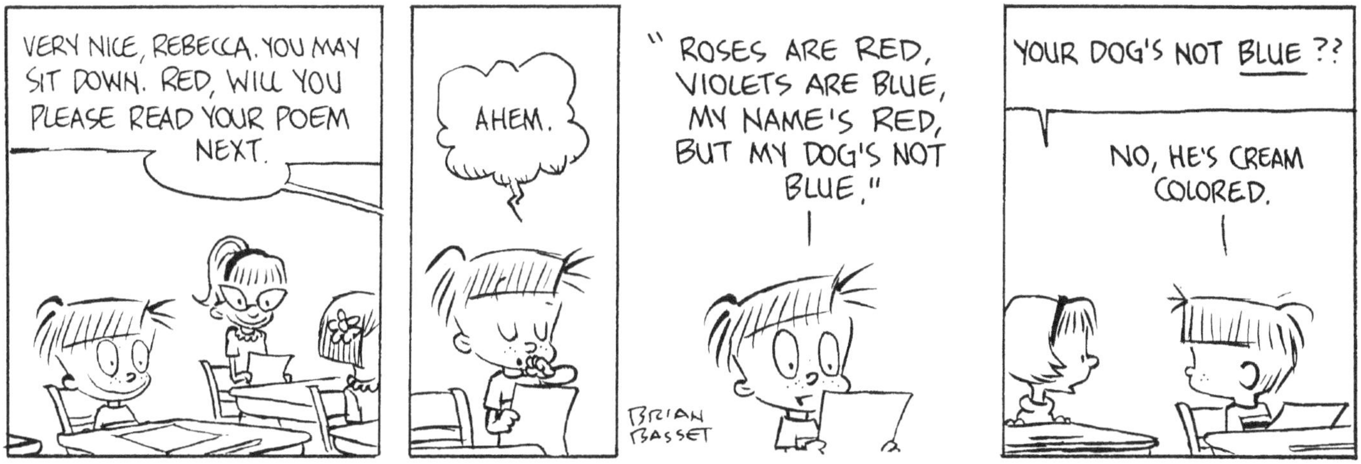
VERY NICE, REBECCA. YOU MAY SIT DOWN. RED, WILL YOU PLEASE READ YOUR POEM NEXT.
AHEM.
"ROSES ARE RED, VIOLETS ARE BLUE, MY NAME'S RED, BUT MY DOG'S NOT BLUE."
YOUR DOG'S NOT BLUE??
NO, HE'S CREAM COLORED.
BRIAN BASSET

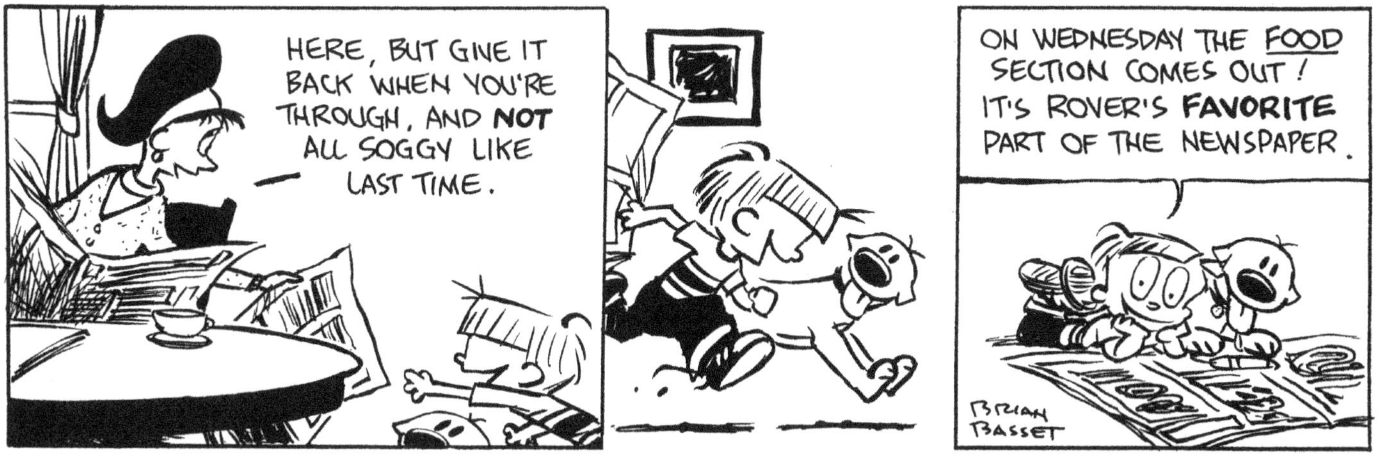
HERE, BUT GIVE IT BACK WHEN YOU'RE THROUGH, AND **NOT** ALL SOGGY LIKE LAST TIME.
ON WEDNESDAY THE FOOD SECTION COMES OUT! IT'S ROVER'S **FAVORITE** PART OF THE NEWSPAPER.
BRIAN BASSET

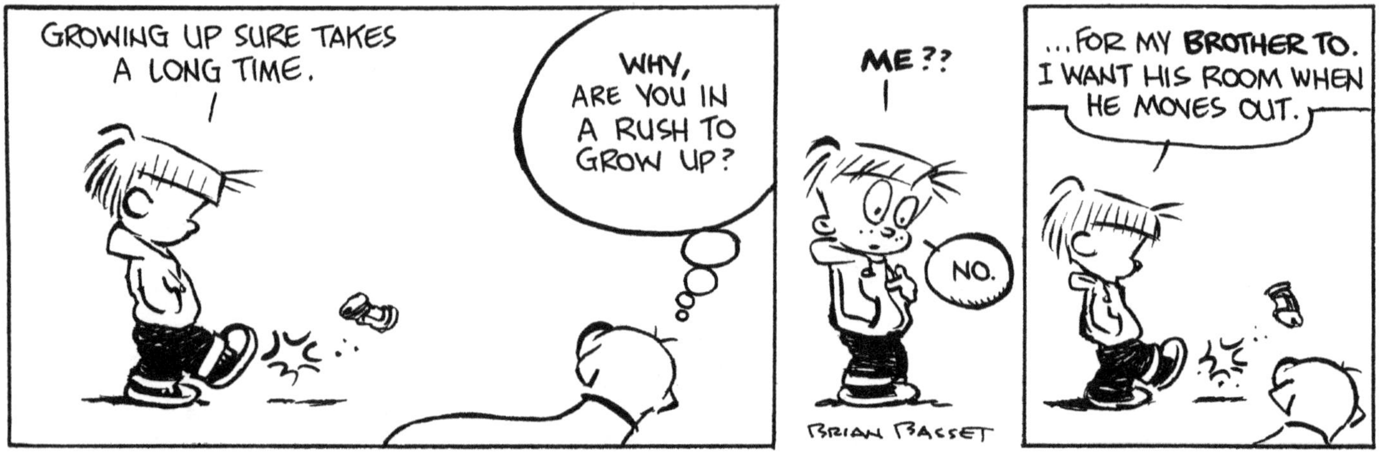
GROWING UP SURE TAKES A LONG TIME.
WHY, ARE YOU IN A RUSH TO GROW UP?
ME??
NO.
BRIAN BASSET
...FOR MY **BROTHER TO.** I WANT HIS ROOM WHEN HE MOVES OUT.

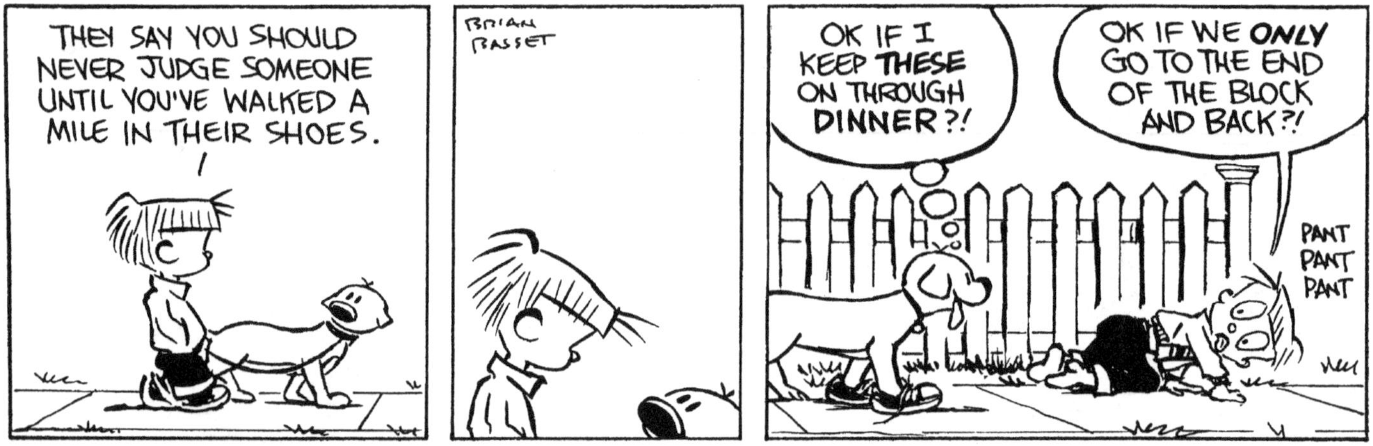
THEY SAY YOU SHOULD NEVER JUDGE SOMEONE UNTIL YOU'VE WALKED A MILE IN THEIR SHOES.
BRIAN BASSET
OK IF I KEEP **THESE** ON THROUGH **DINNER**?!
OK IF WE **ONLY** GO TO THE END OF THE BLOCK AND BACK?!
PANT
PANT
PANT

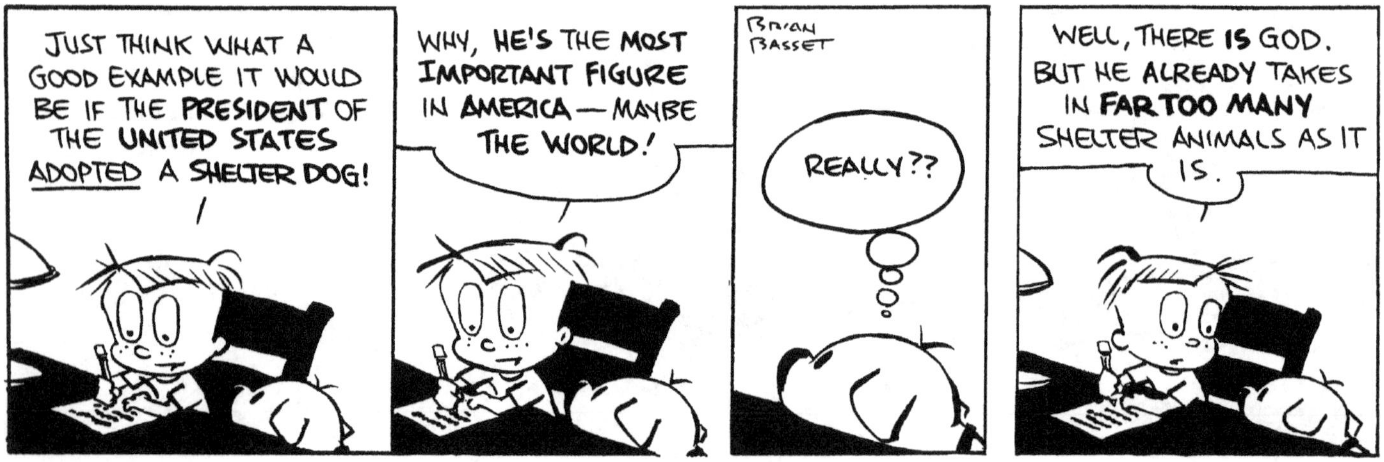
JUST THINK WHAT A GOOD EXAMPLE IT WOULD BE IF THE **PRESIDENT** OF THE **UNITED STATES** ADOPTED A **SHELTER DOG**!
WHY, **HE'S** THE **MOST IMPORTANT FIGURE** IN **AMERICA** — MAYBE **THE WORLD**!
BRIAN BASSET
REALLY??
WELL, THERE **IS** GOD. BUT HE **ALREADY** TAKES IN **FAR TOO MANY** SHELTER ANIMALS AS IT IS.

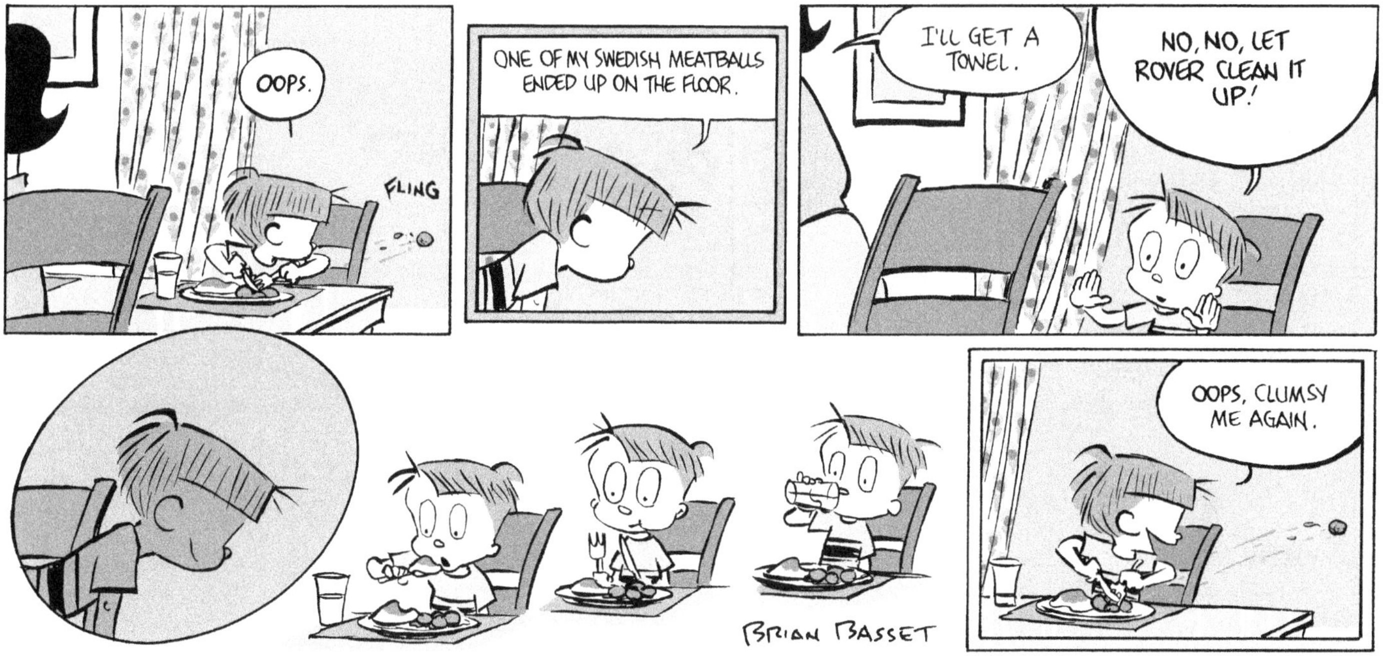
OOPS.
FLING
ONE OF MY SWEDISH MEATBALLS ENDED UP ON THE FLOOR.
I'LL GET A TOWEL.
NO, NO, LET ROVER CLEAN IT UP!
BRIAN BASSET
OOPS, CLUMSY ME AGAIN.

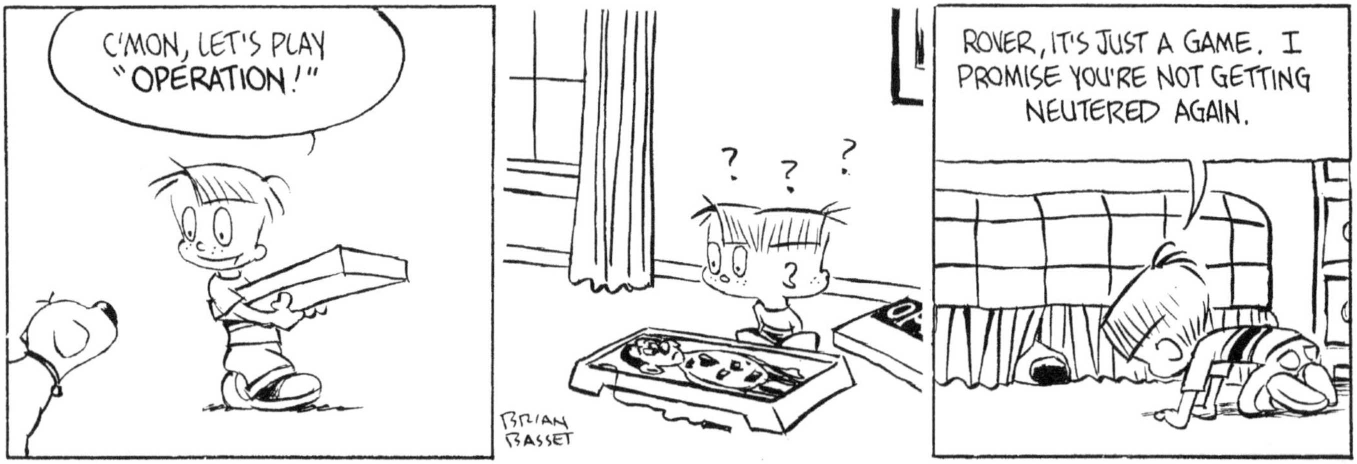
C'MON, LET'S PLAY "OPERATION!"
? ? ?
?
BRIAN BASSET
ROVER, IT'S JUST A GAME. I PROMISE YOU'RE NOT GETTING NEUTERED AGAIN.

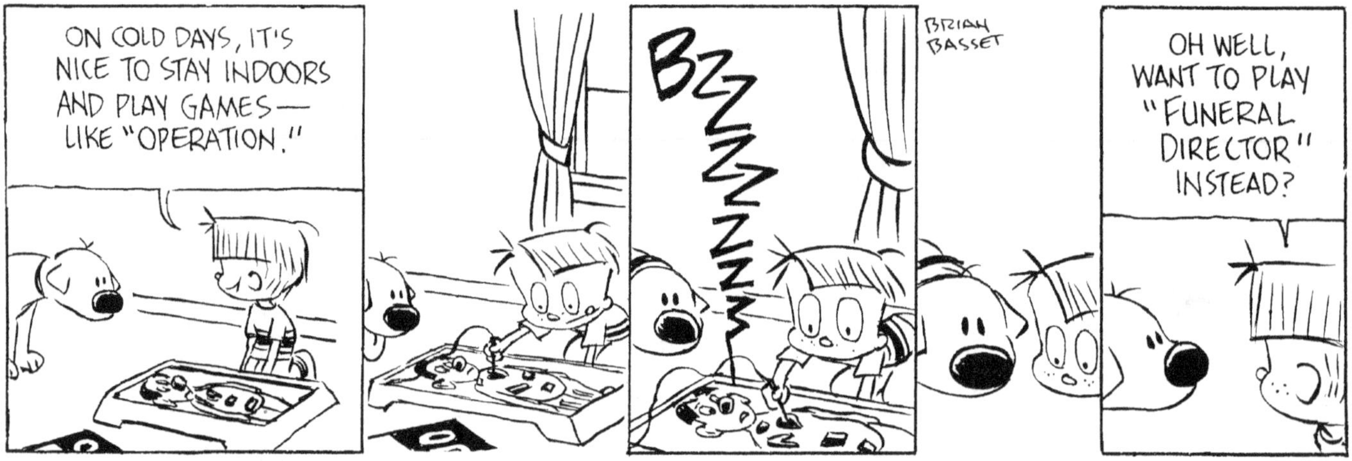
ON COLD DAYS, IT'S NICE TO STAY INDOORS AND PLAY GAMES— LIKE "OPERATION."
BZZZZZZZZ
BRIAN BASSET
OH WELL, WANT TO PLAY "FUNERAL DIRECTOR" INSTEAD?

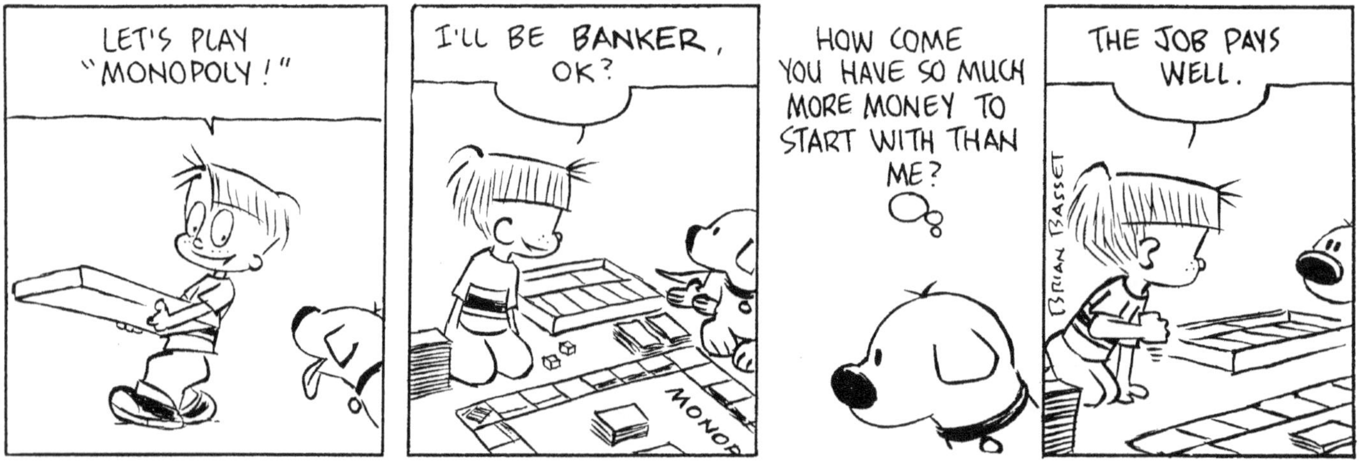
LET'S PLAY "MONOPOLY!"
I'LL BE BANKER, OK?
HOW COME YOU HAVE SO MUCH MORE MONEY TO START WITH THAN ME?
BRIAN BASSET
THE JOB PAYS WELL.

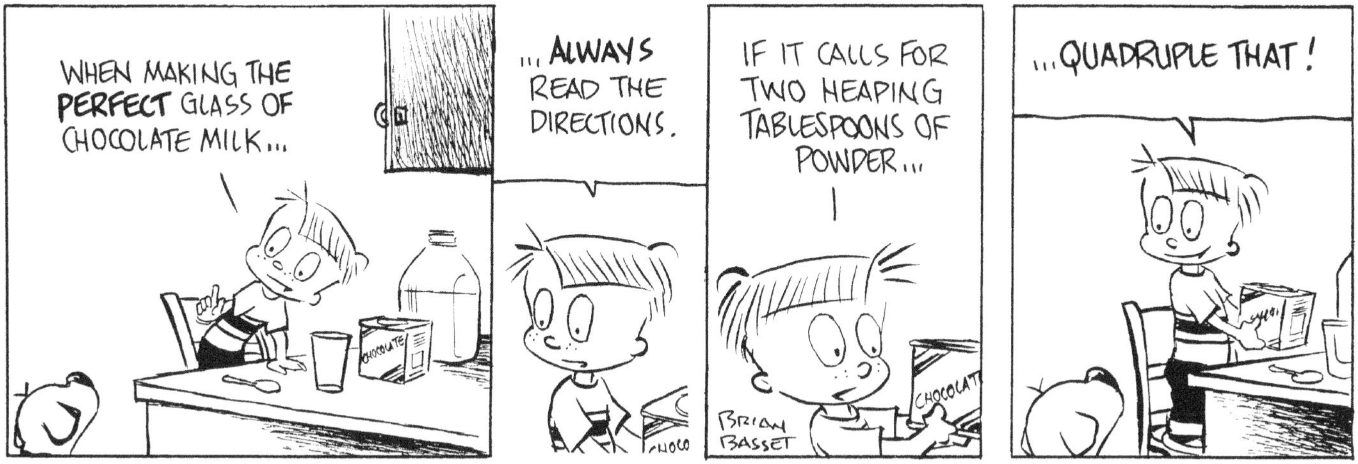
WHEN MAKING THE PERFECT GLASS OF CHOCOLATE MILK...
...ALWAYS READ THE DIRECTIONS.
IF IT CALLS FOR TWO HEAPING TABLESPOONS OF POWDER...
...QUADRUPLE THAT!
BRIAN BASSET

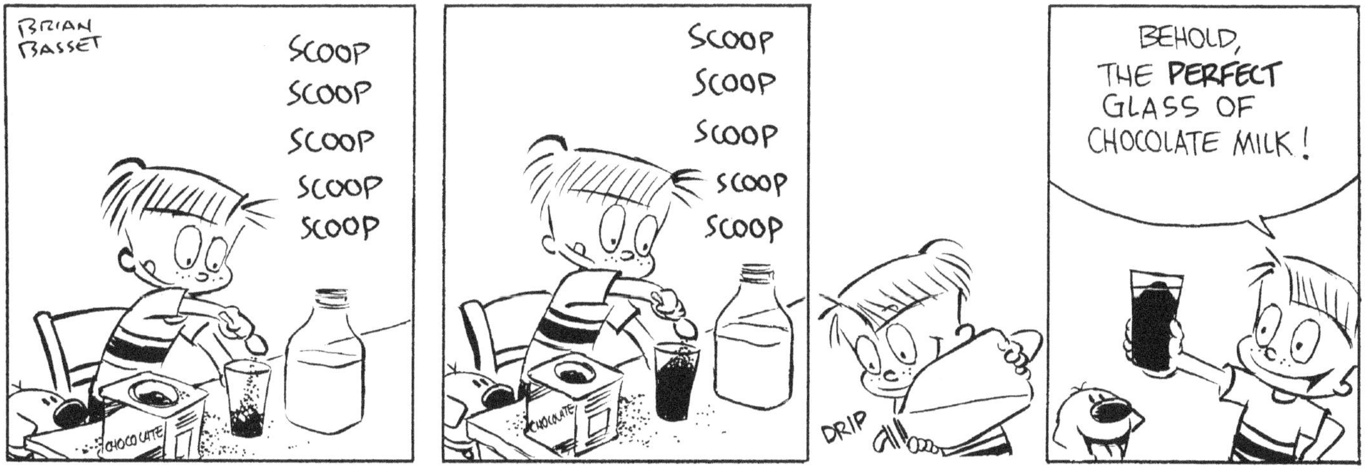
BRIAN BASSET
SCOOP SCOOP SCOOP SCOOP SCOOP
SCOOP SCOOP SCOOP SCOOP SCOOP
DRIP
BEHOLD, THE PERFECT GLASS OF CHOCOLATE MILK!

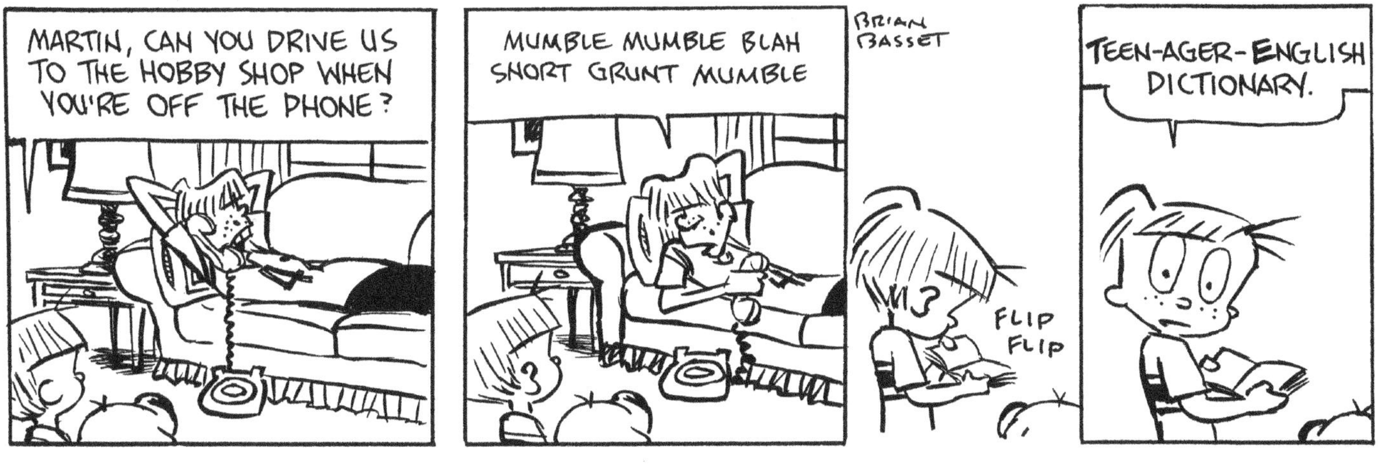
MARTIN, CAN YOU DRIVE US TO THE HOBBY SHOP WHEN YOU'RE OFF THE PHONE?
MUMBLE MUMBLE BLAH SNORT GRUNT MUMBLE
BRIAN BASSET
FLIP FLIP
TEEN-AGER-ENGLISH DICTIONARY.

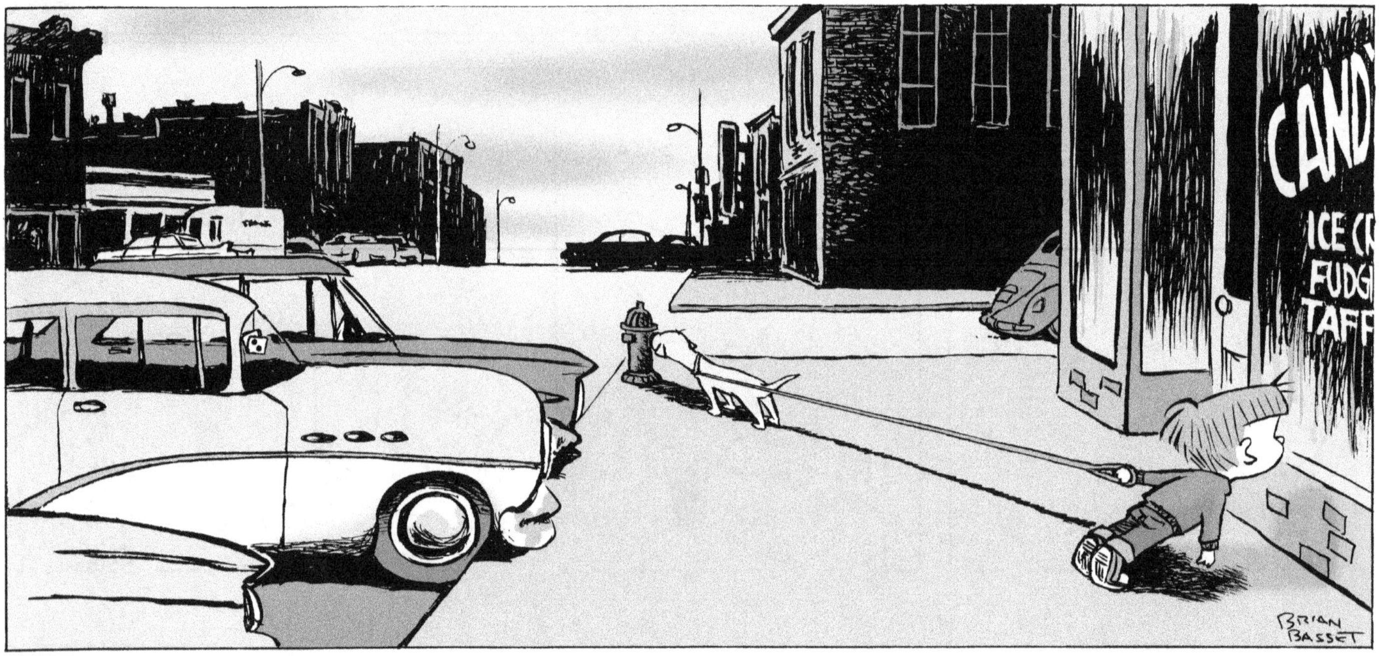
CAND
ICE CR
FUDG
TAFF
BRIAN BASSET

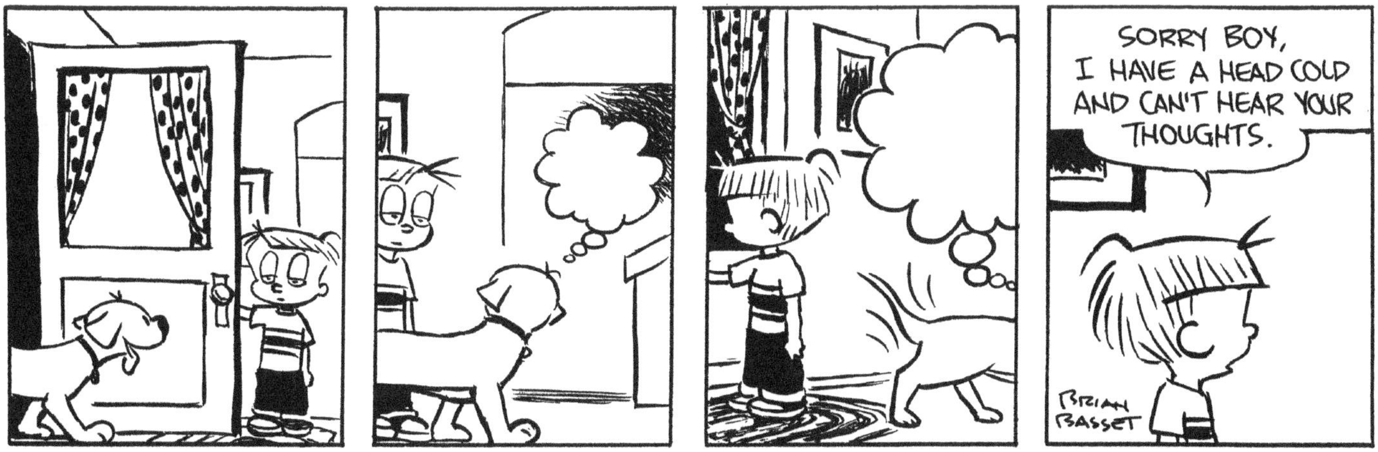
SORRY BOY, I HAVE A HEAD COLD AND CAN'T HEAR YOUR THOUGHTS.
BRIAN BASSET

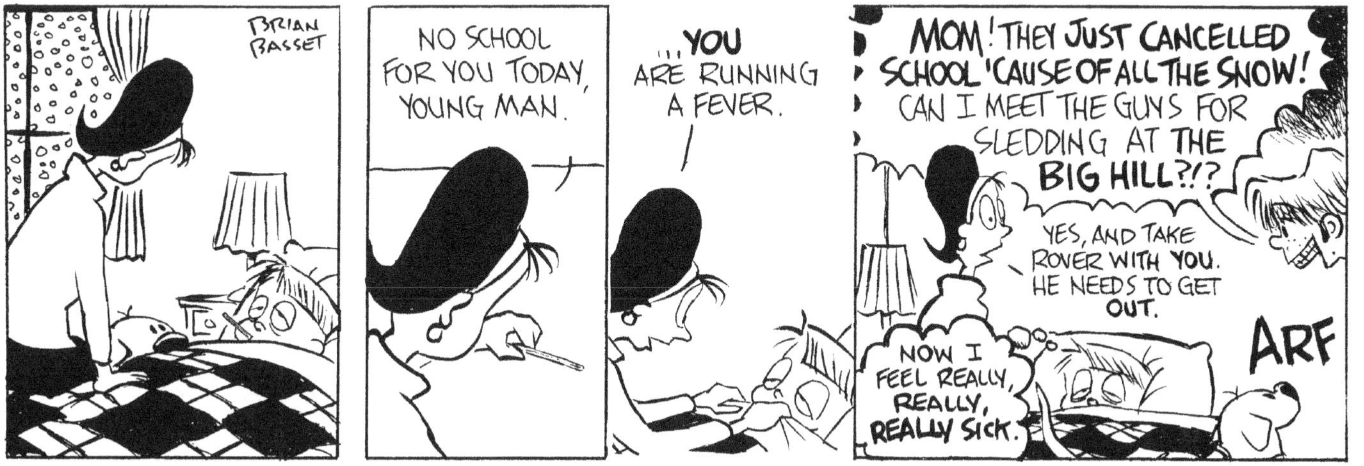
BRIAN BASSET
NO SCHOOL FOR YOU TODAY, YOUNG MAN.
...YOU ARE RUNNING A FEVER.
MOM! THEY JUST CANCELLED SCHOOL 'CAUSE OF ALL THE SNOW! CAN I MEET THE GUYS FOR SLEDDING AT THE BIG HILL?!?
YES, AND TAKE ROVER WITH YOU. HE NEEDS TO GET OUT.
ARF
NOW I FEEL REALLY, REALLY, REALLY SICK.

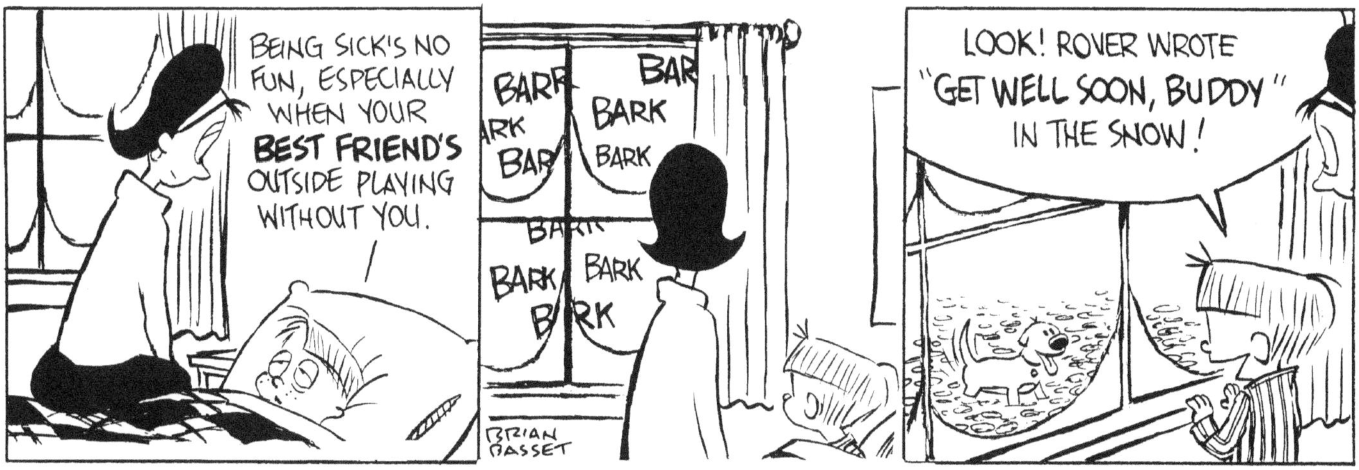
BEING SICK'S NO FUN, ESPECIALLY WHEN YOUR BEST FRIEND'S OUTSIDE PLAYING WITHOUT YOU.
BARK
BARK
BARK
BARK
BRIAN BASSET
LOOK! ROVER WROTE "GET WELL SOON, BUDDY" IN THE SNOW!

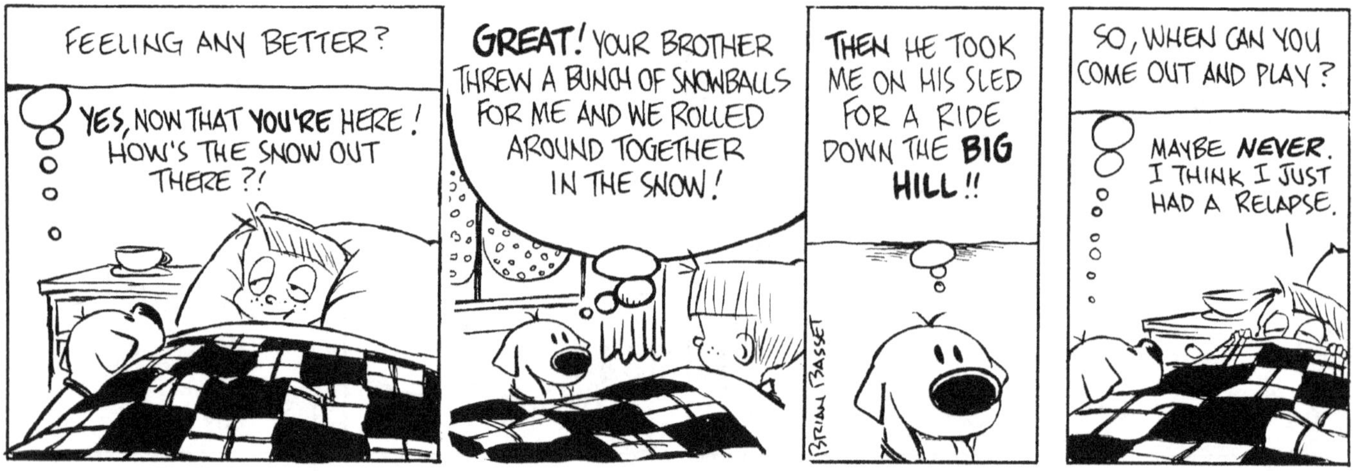
FEELING ANY BETTER?
YES, NOW THAT YOU'RE HERE! HOW'S THE SNOW OUT THERE?!
GREAT! YOUR BROTHER THREW A BUNCH OF SNOWBALLS FOR ME AND WE ROLLED AROUND TOGETHER IN THE SNOW!
THEN HE TOOK ME ON HIS SLED FOR A RIDE DOWN THE BIG HILL!!
BRIAN BASSET
SO, WHEN CAN YOU COME OUT AND PLAY?
MAYBE NEVER. I THINK I JUST HAD A RELAPSE.

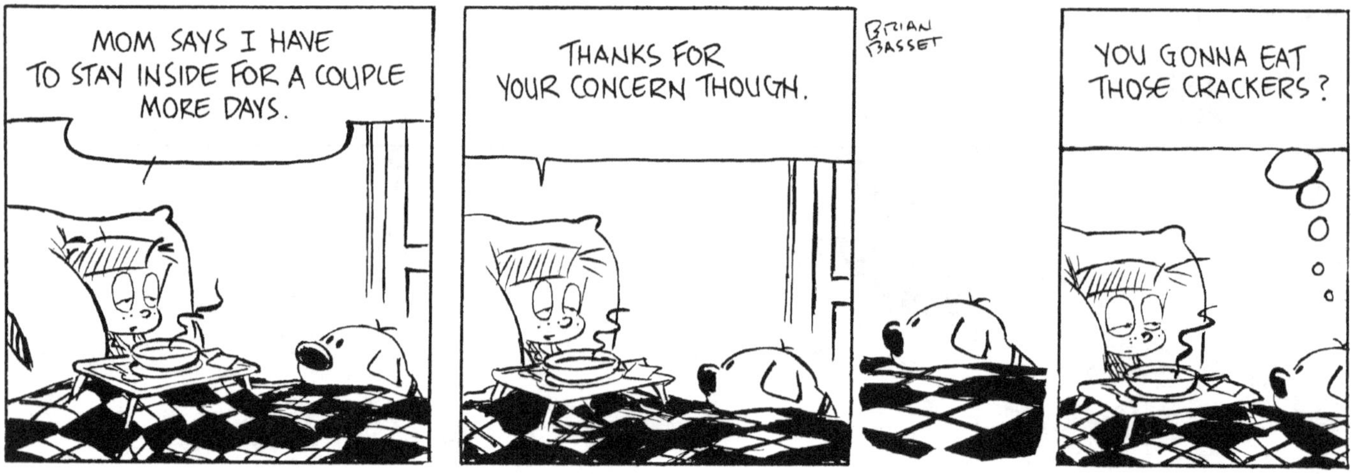
MOM SAYS I HAVE TO STAY INSIDE FOR A COUPLE MORE DAYS.
THANKS FOR YOUR CONCERN THOUGH.
BRIAN BASSET
YOU GONNA EAT THOSE CRACKERS?

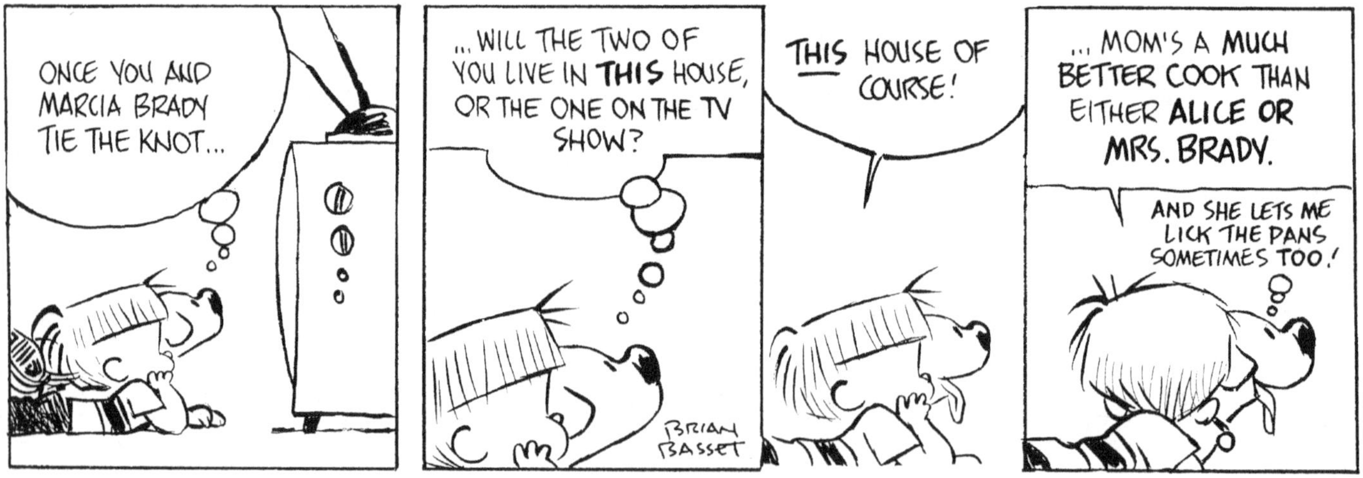
ONCE YOU AND MARCIA BRADY TIE THE KNOT...
...WILL THE TWO OF YOU LIVE IN THIS HOUSE, OR THE ONE ON THE TV SHOW?
BRIAN BASSET
THIS HOUSE OF COURSE!
...MOM'S A MUCH BETTER COOK THAN EITHER ALICE OR MRS. BRADY.
AND SHE LETS ME LICK THE PANS SOMETIMES TOO!

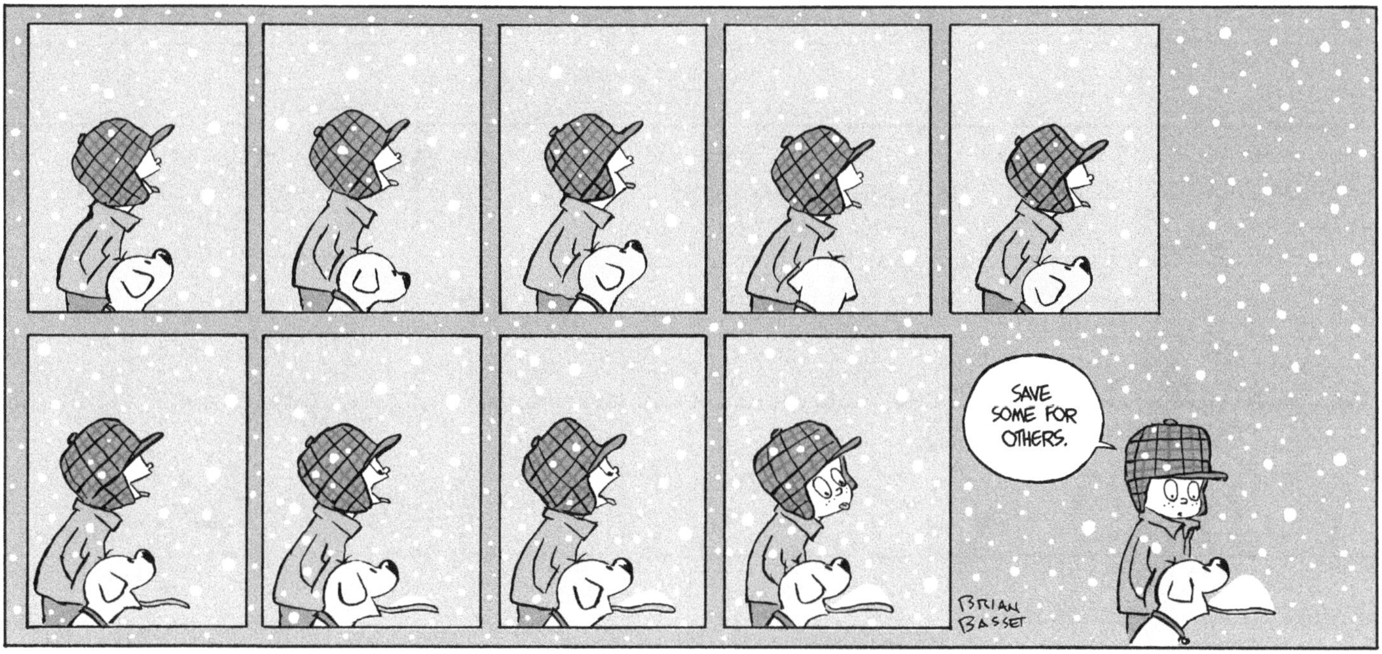
SAVE SOME FOR OTHERS.
BRIAN BASSET

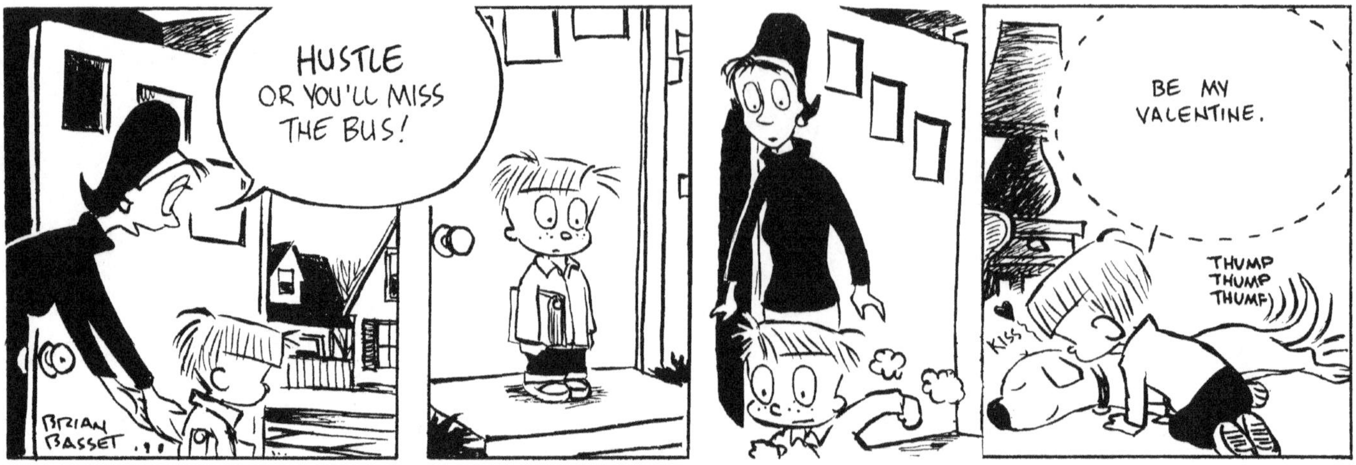
HUSTLE OR YOU'LL MISS THE BUS!
BRIAN BASSET
BE MY VALENTINE.
KISS
THUMP THUMP THUMP

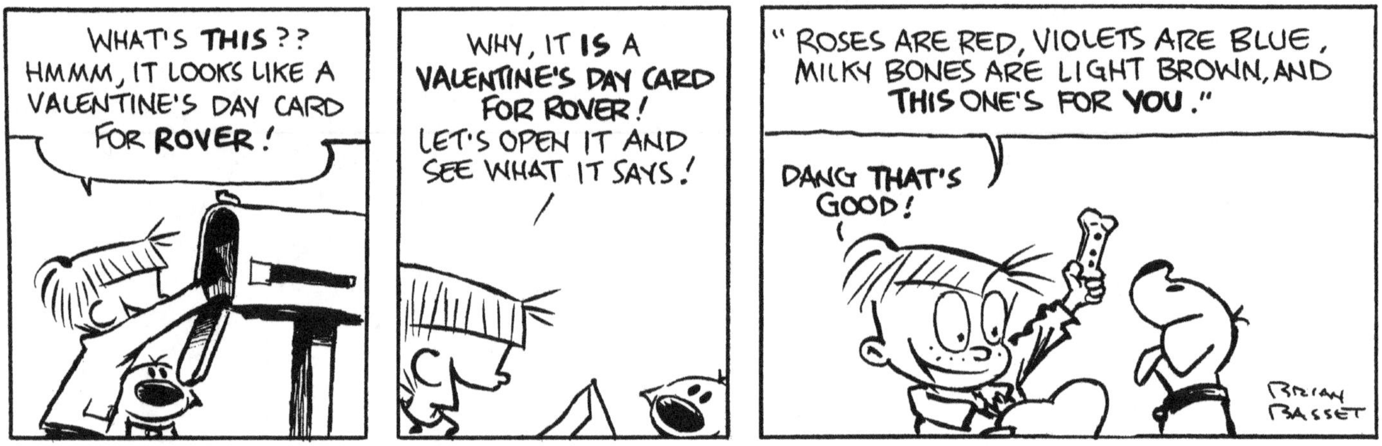
WHAT'S THIS?? HMMM, IT LOOKS LIKE A VALENTINE'S DAY CARD FOR ROVER!
WHY, IT IS A VALENTINE'S DAY CARD FOR ROVER! LET'S OPEN IT AND SEE WHAT IT SAYS!
"ROSES ARE RED, VIOLETS ARE BLUE, MILKY BONES ARE LIGHT BROWN, AND THIS ONE'S FOR YOU."
DANG THAT'S GOOD!
BRIAN BASSET

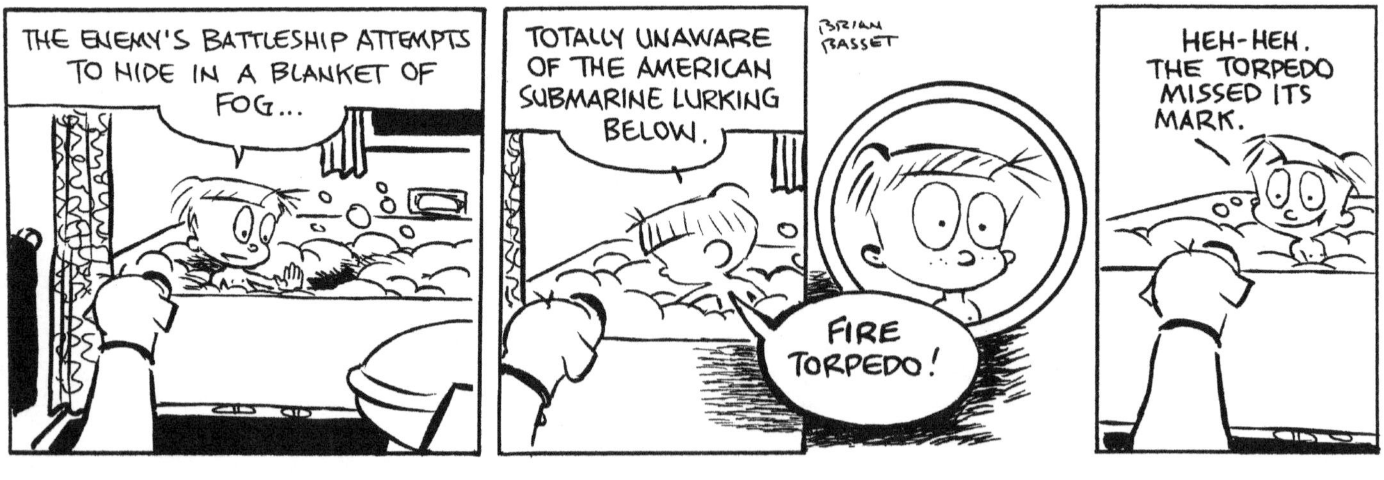
THE ENEMY'S BATTLESHIP ATTEMPTS TO HIDE IN A BLANKET OF FOG...
TOTALLY UNAWARE OF THE AMERICAN SUBMARINE LURKING BELOW.
BRIAN BASSET
FIRE TORPEDO!
HEH-HEH. THE TORPEDO MISSED ITS MARK.

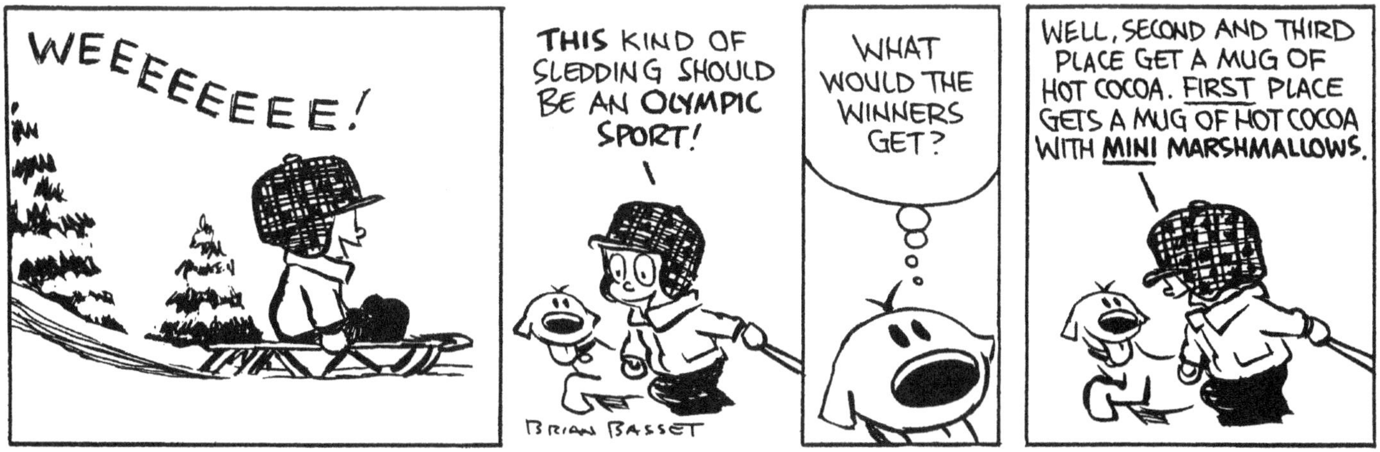
WEEEEEEEEE!
THIS KIND OF SLEDDING SHOULD BE AN OLYMPIC SPORT!
BRIAN BASSET
WHAT WOULD THE WINNERS GET?
WELL, SECOND AND THIRD PLACE GET A MUG OF HOT COCOA. FIRST PLACE GETS A MUG OF HOT COCOA WITH MINI MARSHMALLOWS.

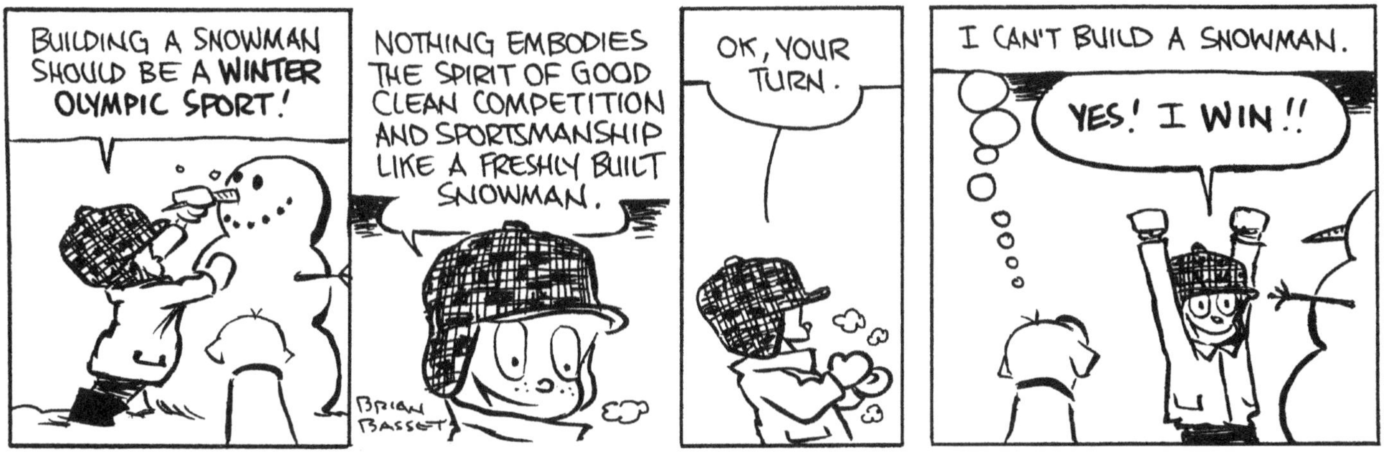
BUILDING A SNOWMAN SHOULD BE A WINTER OLYMPIC SPORT!
NOTHING EMBODIES THE SPIRIT OF GOOD CLEAN COMPETITION AND SPORTSMANSHIP LIKE A FRESHLY BUILT SNOWMAN.
BRIAN BASSET
OK, YOUR TURN.
I CAN'T BUILD A SNOWMAN.
YES! I WIN!!

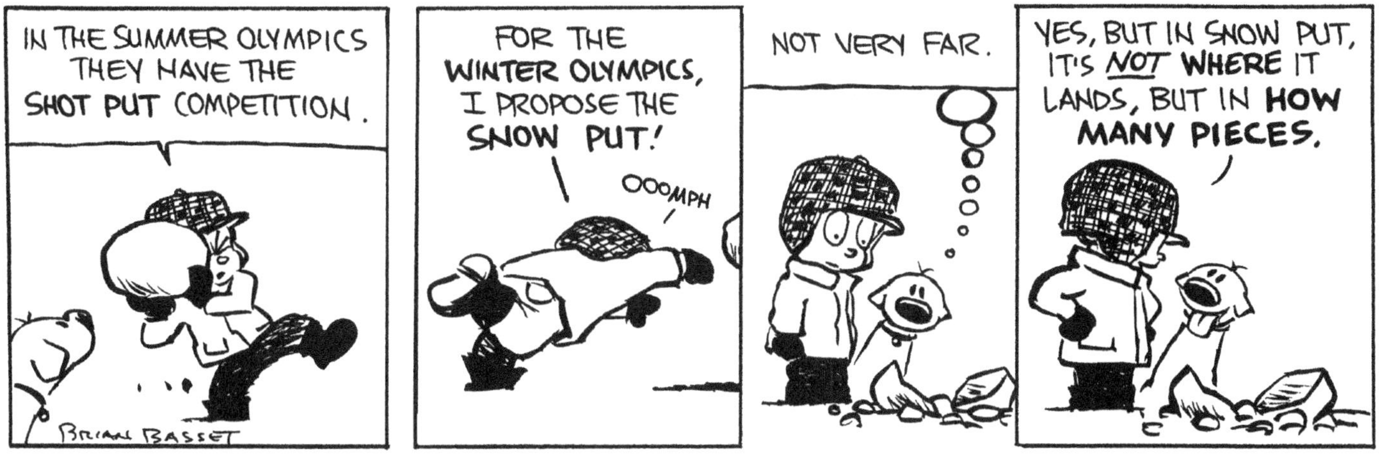
IN THE SUMMER OLYMPICS THEY HAVE THE SHOT PUT COMPETITION.
BRIAN BASSET
FOR THE WINTER OLYMPICS, I PROPOSE THE SNOW PUT!
OOOMPH
NOT VERY FAR.
YES, BUT IN SNOW PUT, IT'S NOT WHERE IT LANDS, BUT IN HOW MANY PIECES.

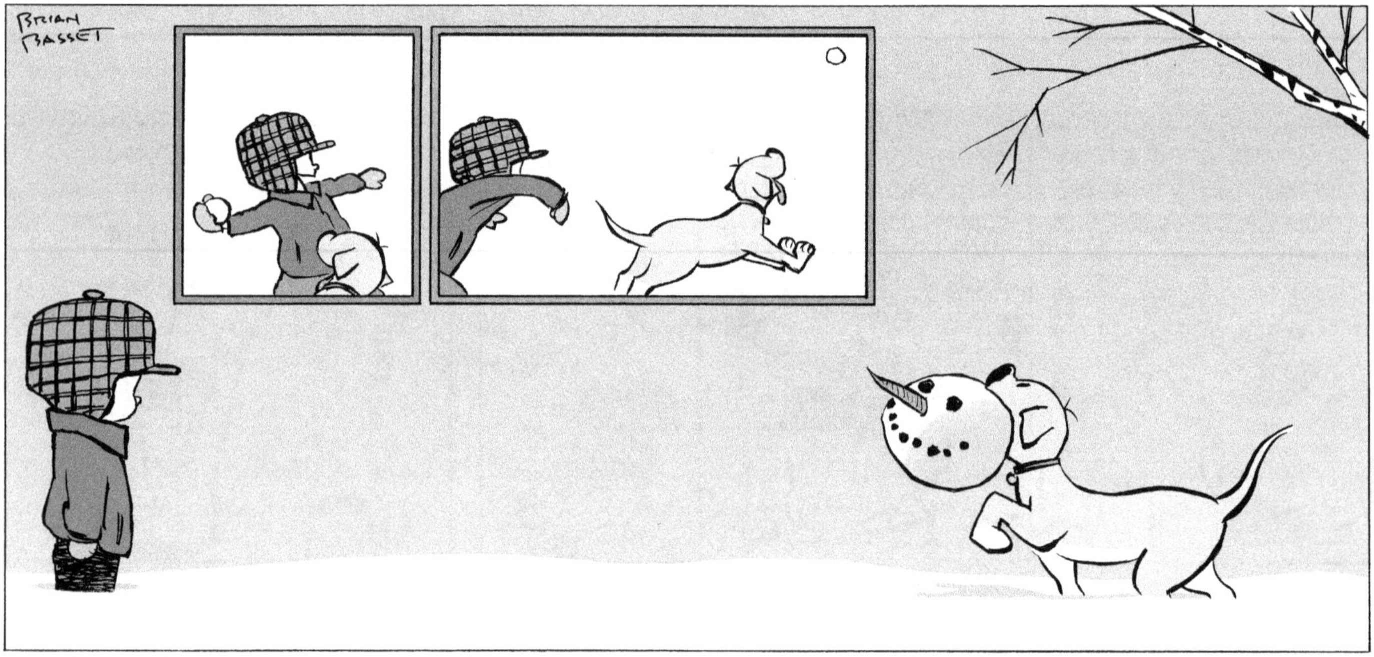
BRIAN
BASSET

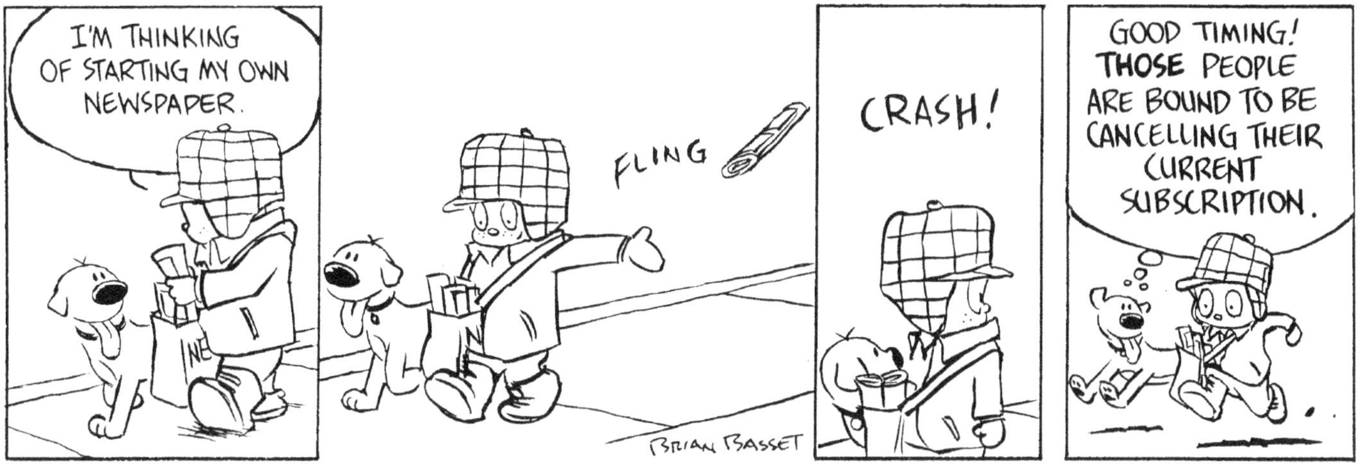
I'M THINKING OF STARTING MY OWN NEWSPAPER.
FLING
BRIAN BASSET
CRASH!
GOOD TIMING! THOSE PEOPLE ARE BOUND TO BE CANCELLING THEIR CURRENT SUBSCRIPTION.

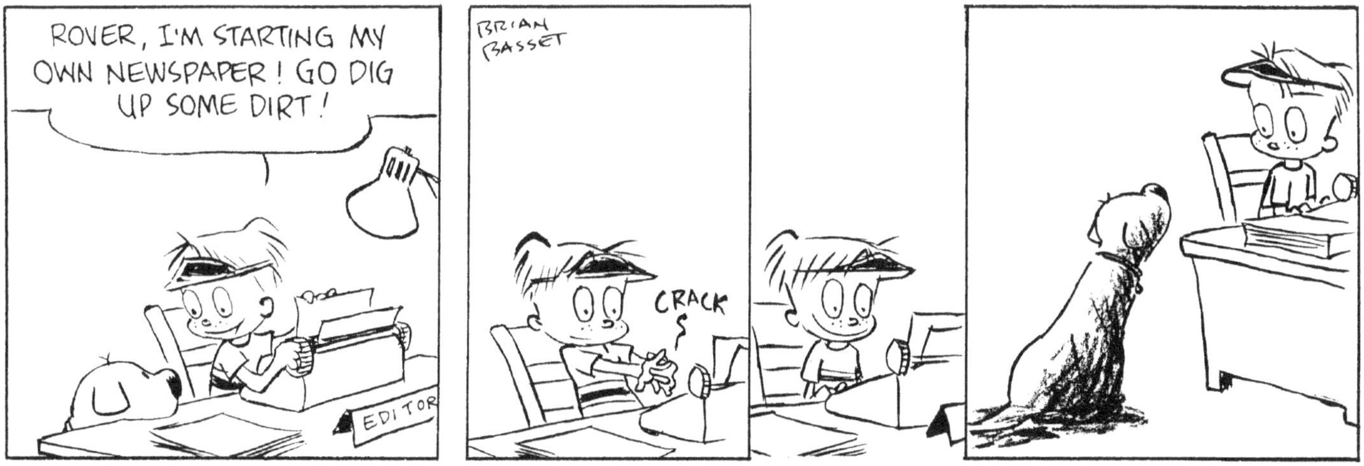
ROVER, I'M STARTING MY OWN NEWSPAPER! GO DIG UP SOME DIRT!
EDITOR
BRIAN BASSET
CRACK

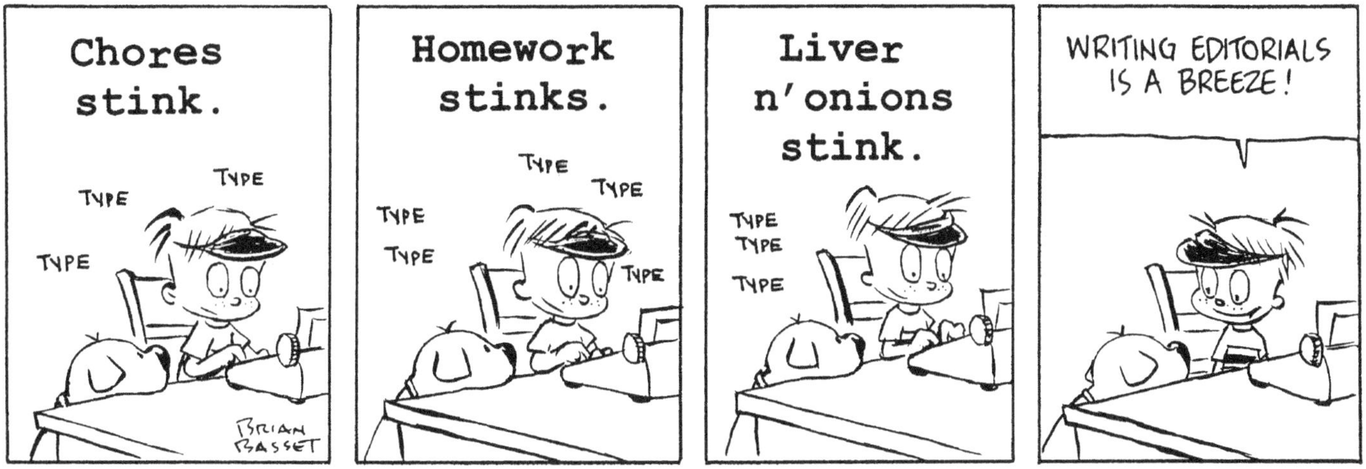
Chores stink.
TYPE
TYPE
TYPE
BRIAN BASSET
Homework stinks.
TYPE
TYPE
TYPE
TYPE
TYPE
Liver n'onions stink.
TYPE
TYPE
TYPE
WRITING EDITORIALS IS A BREEZE!

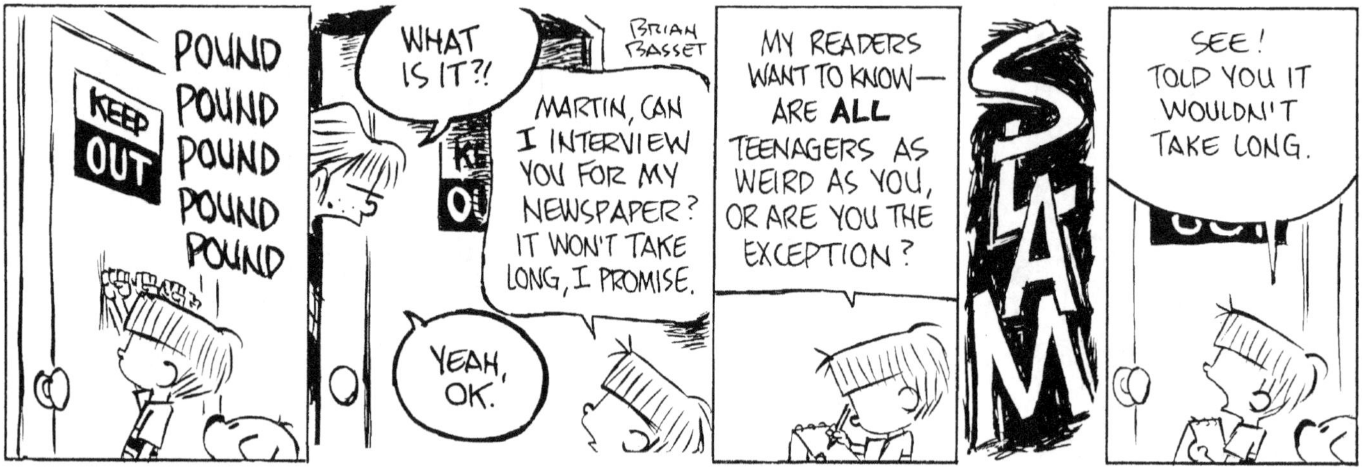
KEEP OUT
POUND POUND POUND POUND POUND
WHAT IS IT?!
BRIAN BASSET
MARTIN, CAN I INTERVIEW YOU FOR MY NEWSPAPER? IT WON'T TAKE LONG, I PROMISE.
YEAH, OK.
MY READERS WANT TO KNOW— ARE **ALL** TEENAGERS AS WEIRD AS YOU, OR ARE YOU THE EXCEPTION?
SLAM
SEE! TOLD YOU IT WOULDN'T TAKE LONG.

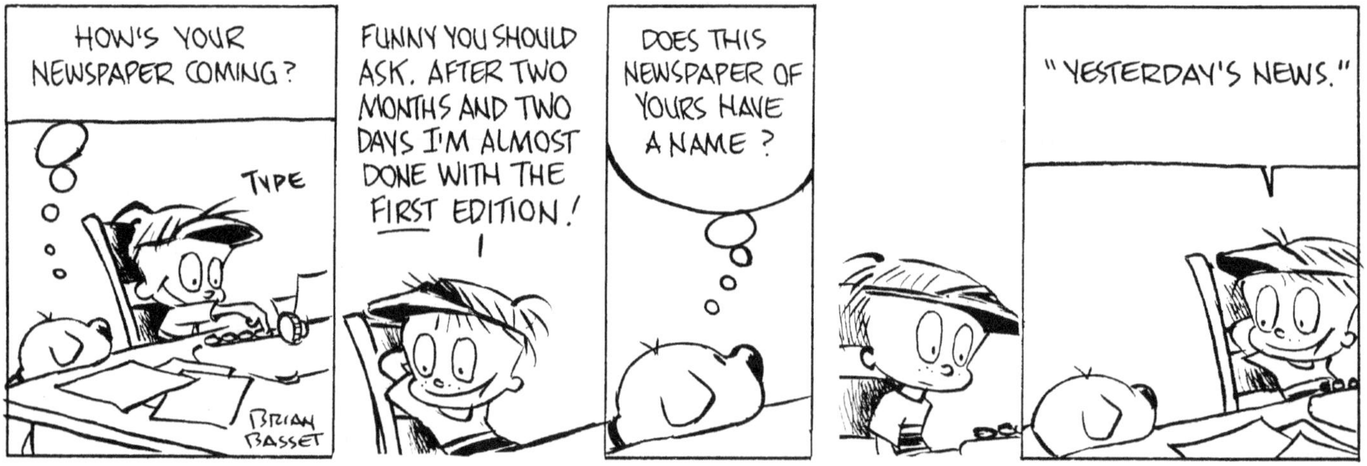
HOW'S YOUR NEWSPAPER COMING?
TYPE
BRIAN BASSET
FUNNY YOU SHOULD ASK. AFTER TWO MONTHS AND TWO DAYS I'M ALMOST DONE WITH THE FIRST EDITION!
DOES THIS NEWSPAPER OF YOURS HAVE A NAME?
"YESTERDAY'S NEWS."

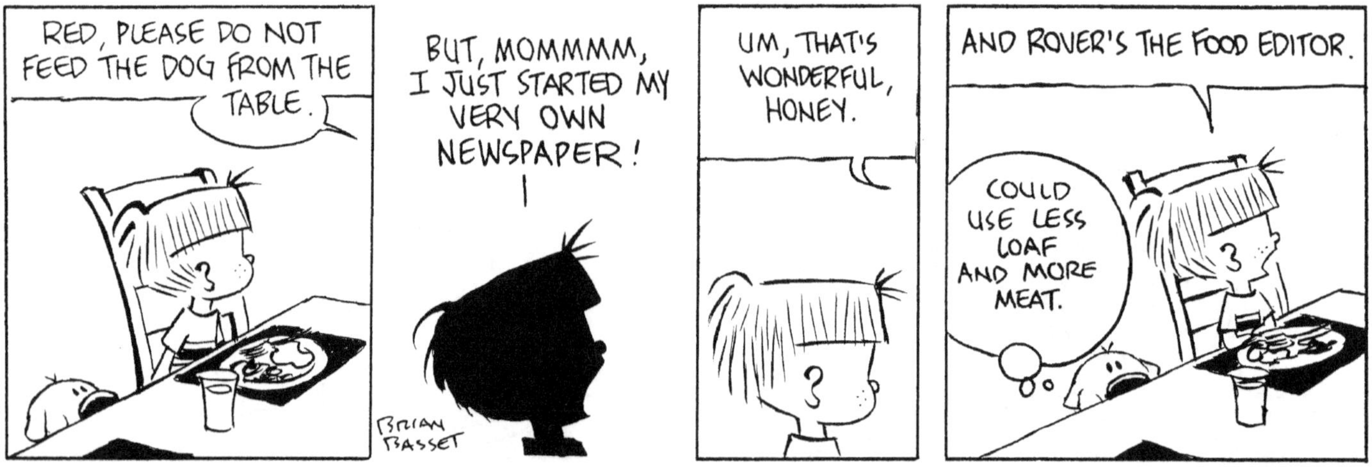
RED, PLEASE DO NOT FEED THE DOG FROM THE TABLE.
BUT, MOMMMM, I JUST STARTED MY VERY OWN NEWSPAPER!
BRIAN BASSET
UM, THAT'S WONDERFUL, HONEY.
AND ROVER'S THE FOOD EDITOR.
COULD USE LESS LOAF AND MORE MEAT.

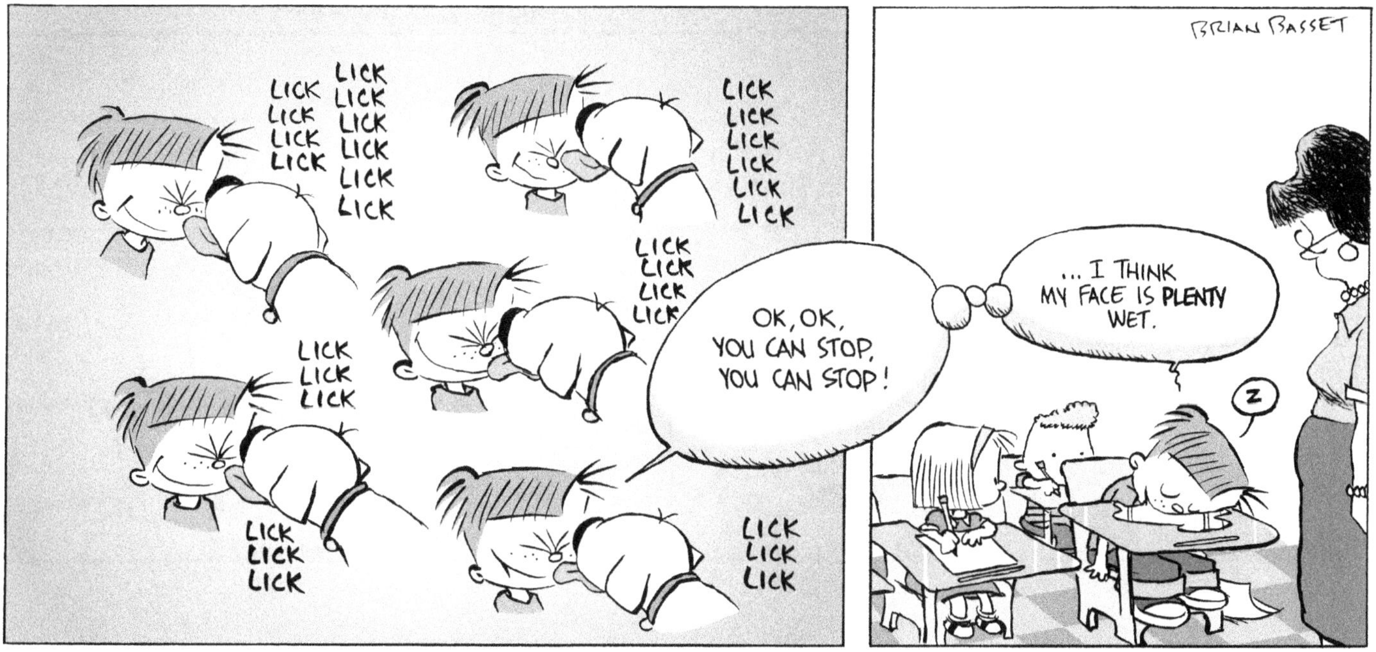
BRIAN BASSET
LICK LICK LICK LICK
LICK LICK LICK LICK LICK LICK
LICK LICK LICK LICK LICK LICK
LICK LICK LICK LICK
LICK LICK LICK
LICK LICK LICK
LICK LICK LICK
OK, OK, YOU CAN STOP, YOU CAN STOP!
... I THINK MY FACE IS PLENTY WET.
Z

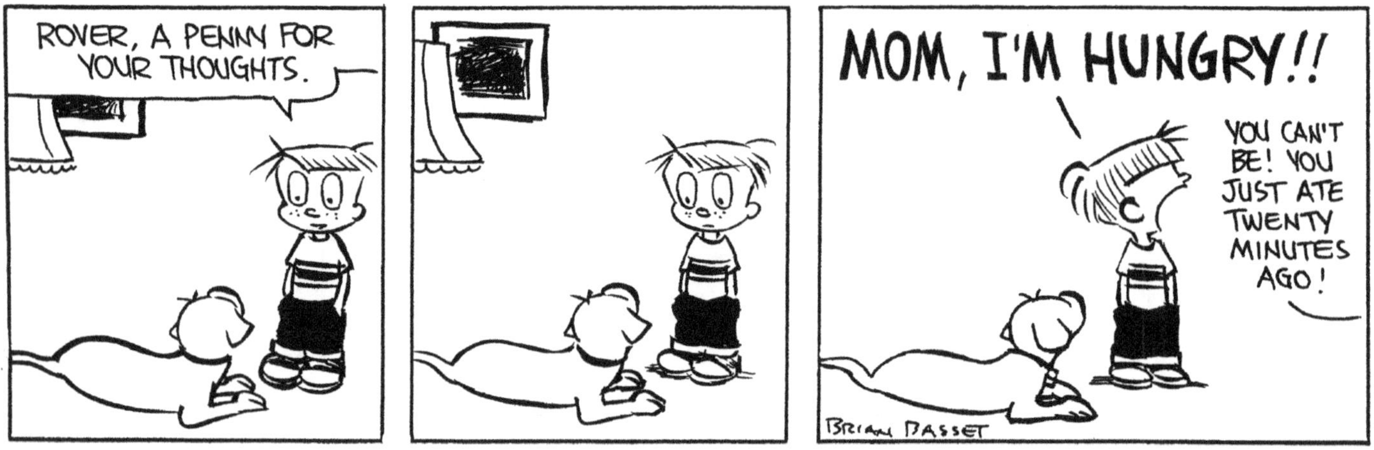
ROVER, A PENNY FOR YOUR THOUGHTS.
MOM, I'M HUNGRY!!
YOU CAN'T BE! YOU JUST ATE TWENTY MINUTES AGO!
BRIAN BASSET

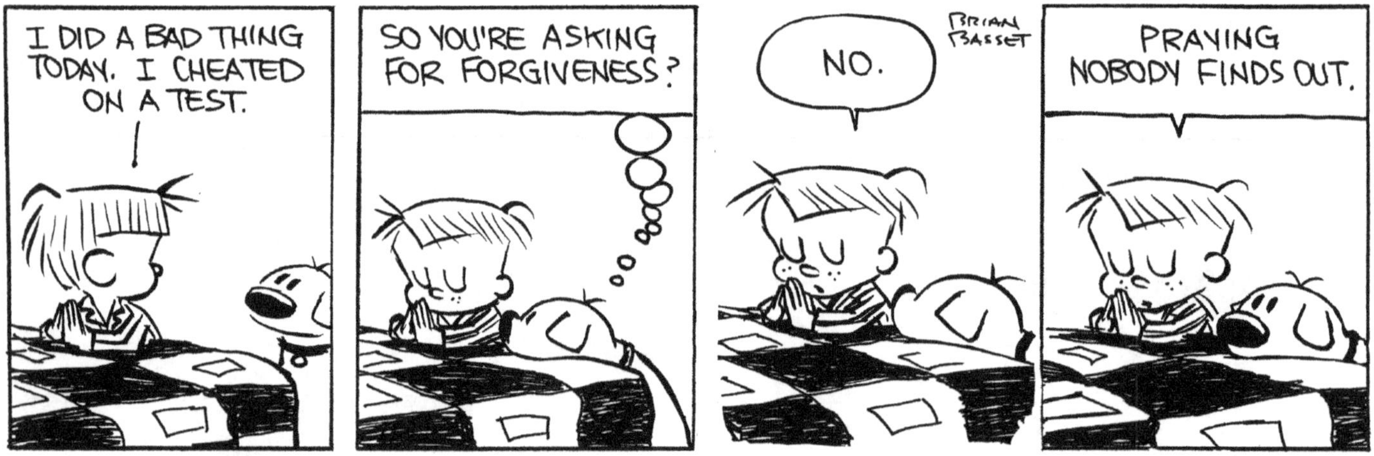
I DID A BAD THING TODAY. I CHEATED ON A TEST.
SO YOU'RE ASKING FOR FORGIVENESS?
NO.
BRIAN BASSET
PRAYING NOBODY FINDS OUT.

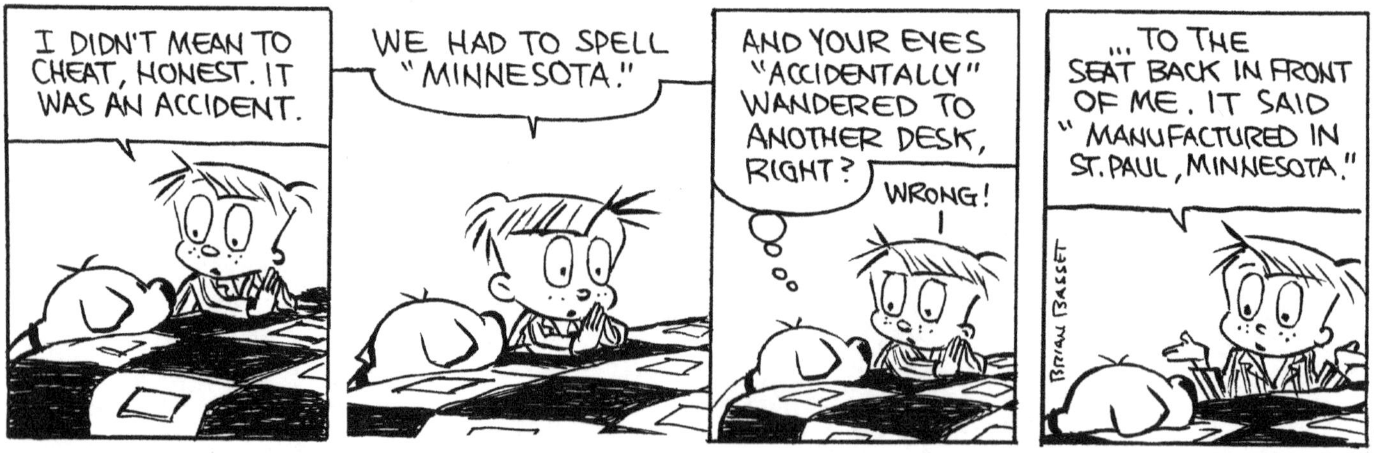
I DIDN'T MEAN TO CHEAT, HONEST. IT WAS AN ACCIDENT.
WE HAD TO SPELL "MINNESOTA."
AND YOUR EYES "ACCIDENTALLY" WANDERED TO ANOTHER DESK, RIGHT?
WRONG!
... TO THE SEAT BACK IN FRONT OF ME. IT SAID "MANUFACTURED IN ST. PAUL, MINNESOTA."
BRIAN BASSET

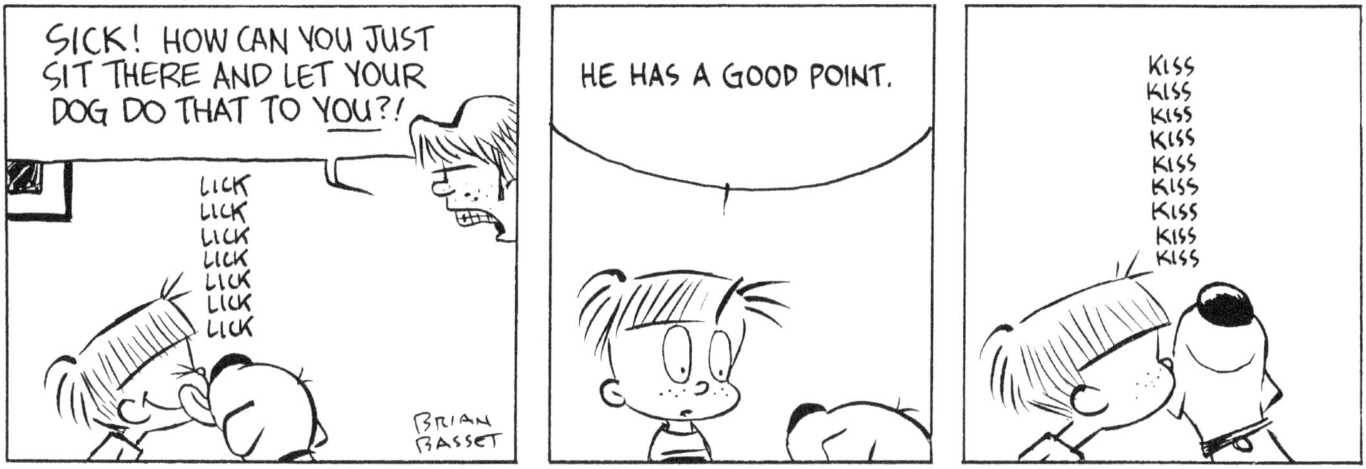
SICK! HOW CAN YOU JUST SIT THERE AND LET YOUR DOG DO THAT TO YOU?!
LICK LICK LICK LICK LICK LICK LICK
BRIAN BASSET
HE HAS A GOOD POINT.
KISS KISS KISS KISS KISS KISS KISS KISS KISS

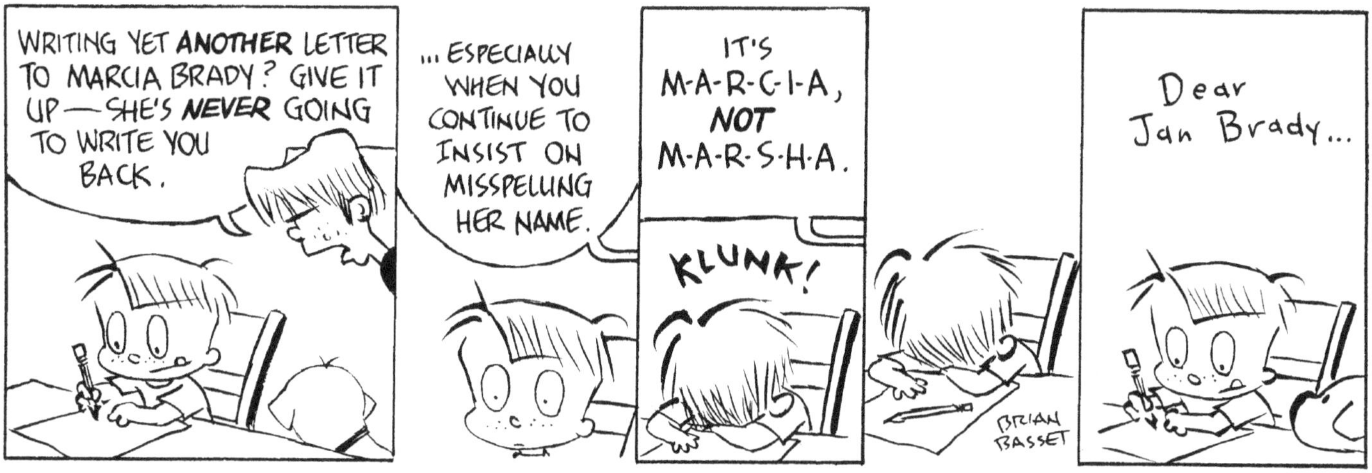
WRITING YET ANOTHER LETTER TO MARCIA BRADY? GIVE IT UP—SHE'S NEVER GOING TO WRITE YOU BACK.
...ESPECIALLY WHEN YOU CONTINUE TO INSIST ON MISSPELLING HER NAME.
IT'S M-A-R-C-I-A, NOT M-A-R-S-H-A.
KLUNK!
BRIAN BASSET
Dear Jan Brady...

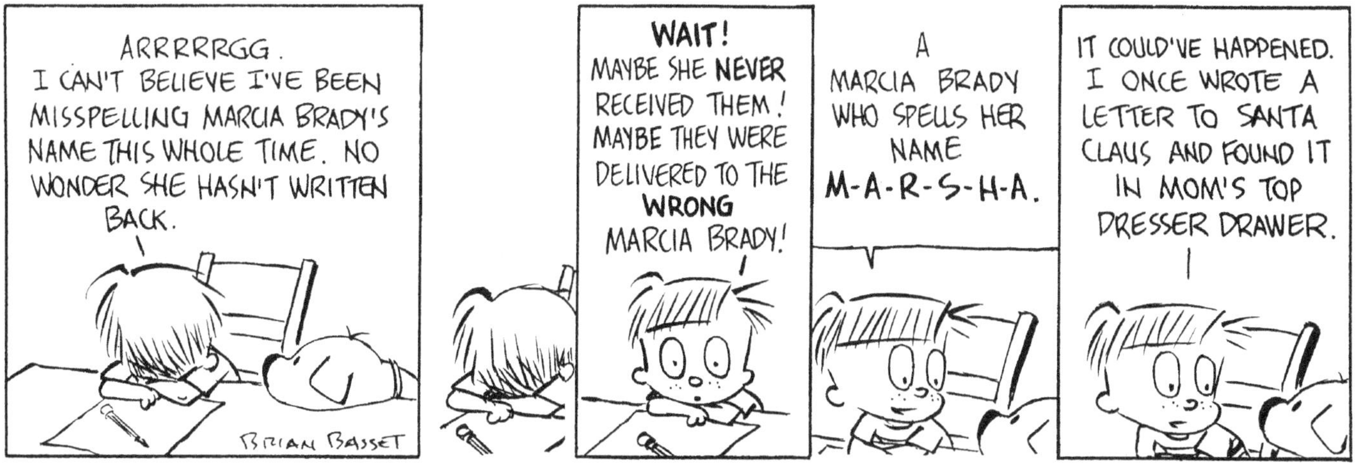
ARRRRRGG. I CAN'T BELIEVE I'VE BEEN MISSPELLING MARCIA BRADY'S NAME THIS WHOLE TIME. NO WONDER SHE HASN'T WRITTEN BACK.
BRIAN BASSET
WAIT! MAYBE SHE NEVER RECEIVED THEM! MAYBE THEY WERE DELIVERED TO THE WRONG MARCIA BRADY!
A MARCIA BRADY WHO SPELLS HER NAME M-A-R-S-H-A.
IT COULD'VE HAPPENED. I ONCE WROTE A LETTER TO SANTA CLAUS AND FOUND IT IN MOM'S TOP DRESSER DRAWER.

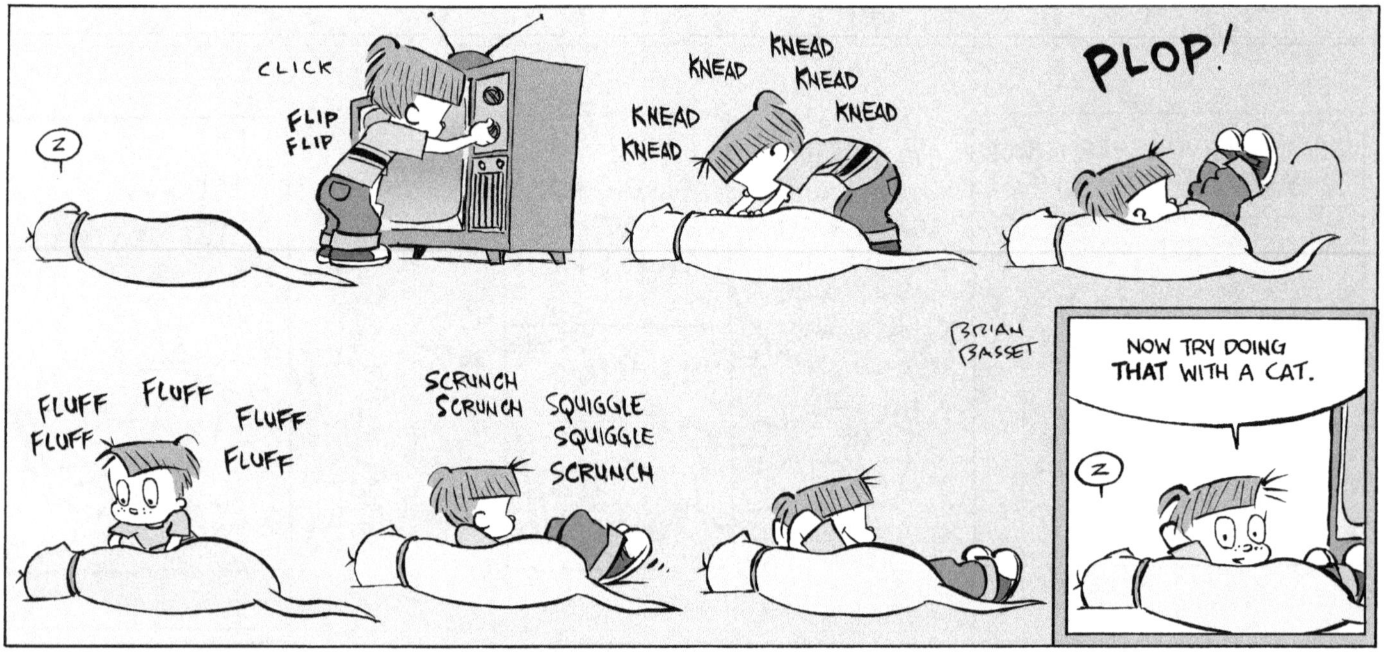
Z
CLICK
FLIP
FLIP
KNEAD
KNEAD
KNEAD
KNEAD
KNEAD
KNEAD
PLOP!
FLUFF
FLUFF
FLUFF
FLUFF
FLUFF
SCRUNCH
SCRUNCH
SQUIGGLE
SQUIGGLE
SCRUNCH
BRIAN BASSET
NOW TRY DOING **THAT** WITH A CAT.
Z

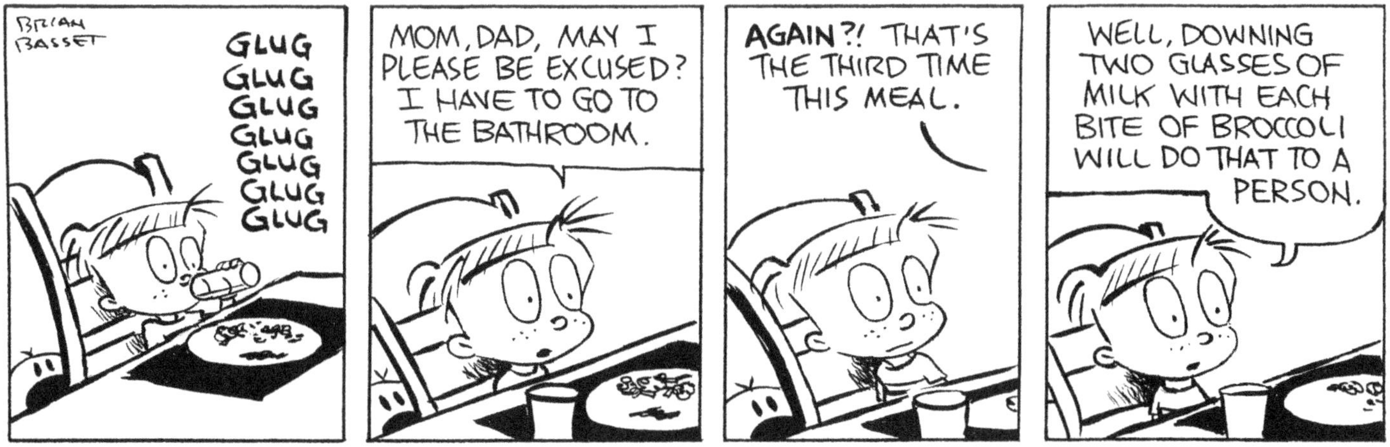
BRIAN BASSET
GLUG GLUG GLUG GLUG GLUG GLUG GLUG
MOM, DAD, MAY I PLEASE BE EXCUSED? I HAVE TO GO TO THE BATHROOM.
AGAIN?! THAT'S THE THIRD TIME THIS MEAL.
WELL, DOWNING TWO GLASSES OF MILK WITH EACH BITE OF BROCCOLI WILL DO THAT TO A PERSON.

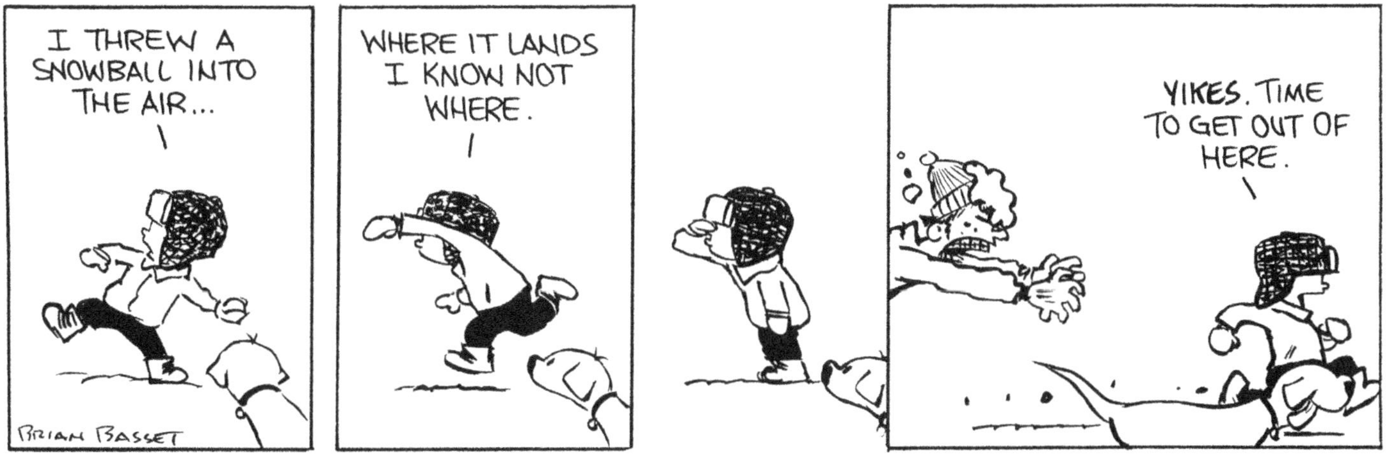
I THREW A SNOWBALL INTO THE AIR...
BRIAN BASSET
WHERE IT LANDS I KNOW NOT WHERE.
YIKES. TIME TO GET OUT OF HERE.

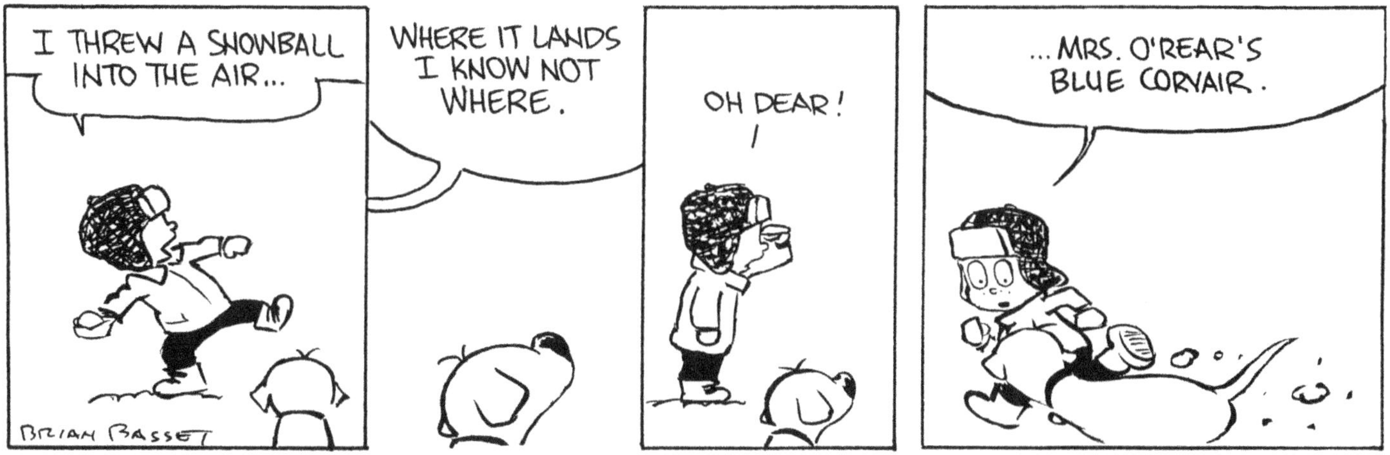
I THREW A SNOWBALL INTO THE AIR...
BRIAN BASSET
WHERE IT LANDS I KNOW NOT WHERE.
OH DEAR!
...MRS. O'REAR'S BLUE CORVAIR.

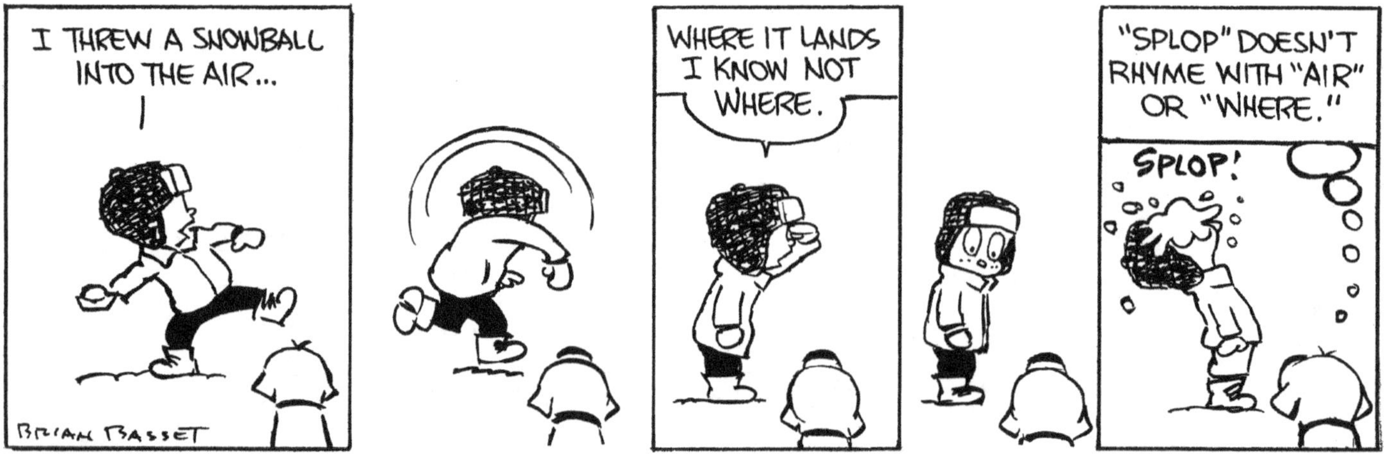
I THREW A SNOWBALL INTO THE AIR...
BRIAN BASSET
WHERE IT LANDS I KNOW NOT WHERE.
"SPLOP" DOESN'T RHYME WITH "AIR" OR "WHERE."
SPLOP!

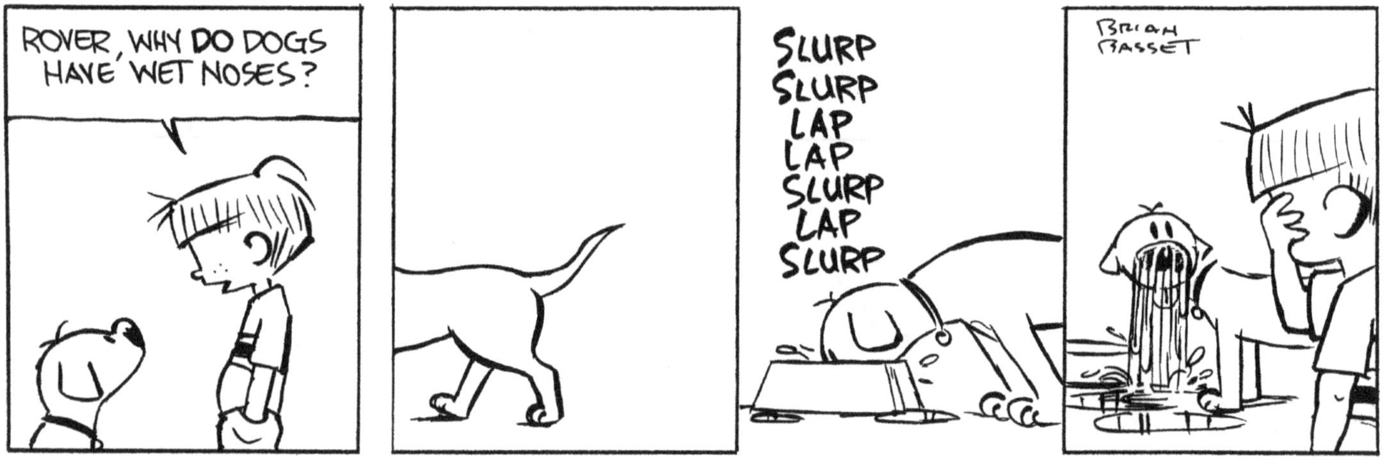
ROVER, WHY DO DOGS HAVE WET NOSES?
SLURP
SLURP
LAP
LAP
SLURP
LAP
SLURP
BRIAN BASSET

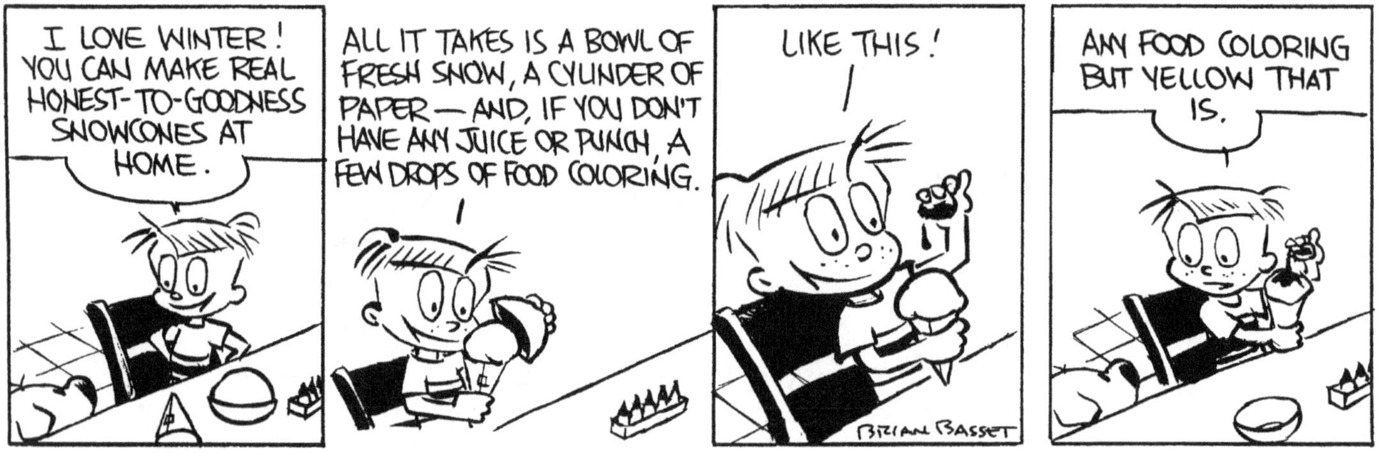
I LOVE WINTER! YOU CAN MAKE REAL HONEST-TO-GOODNESS SNOWCONES AT HOME.
ALL IT TAKES IS A BOWL OF FRESH SNOW, A CYLINDER OF PAPER — AND, IF YOU DON'T HAVE ANY JUICE OR PUNCH, A FEW DROPS OF FOOD COLORING.
LIKE THIS!
BRIAN BASSET
ANY FOOD COLORING BUT YELLOW THAT IS.

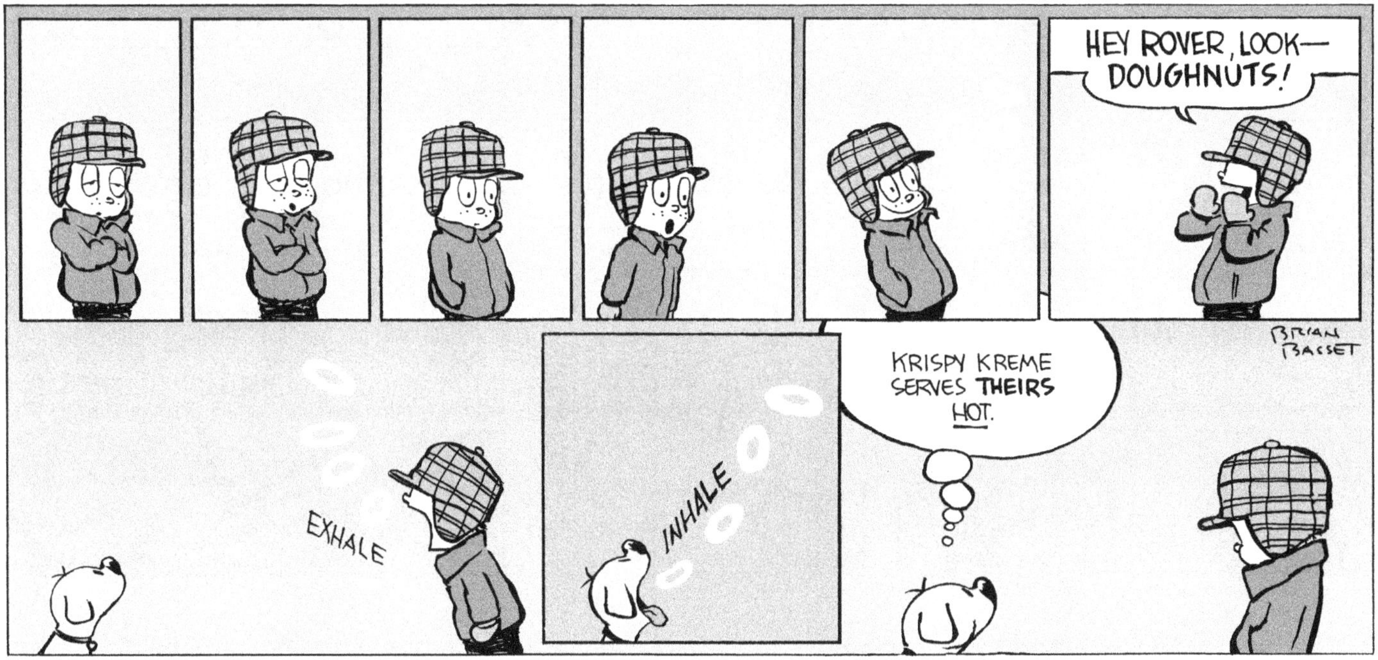
HEY ROVER, LOOK—
DOUGHNUTS!
BRIAN BASSET
EXHALE
INHALE
KRISPY KREME SERVES **THEIRS** HOT.

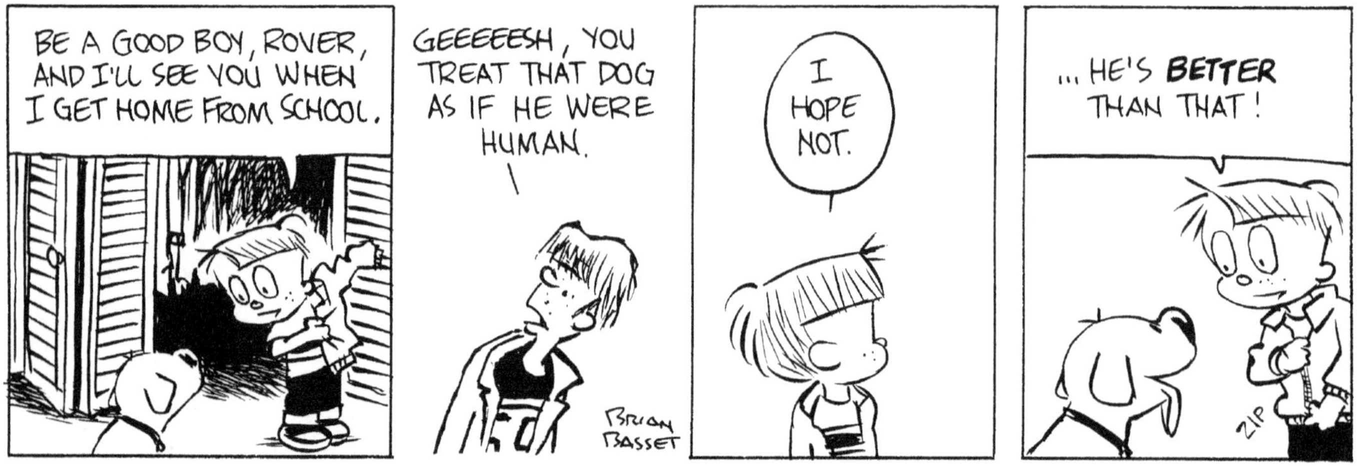
BE A GOOD BOY, ROVER, AND I'LL SEE YOU WHEN I GET HOME FROM SCHOOL.
GEEEEEESH, YOU TREAT THAT DOG AS IF HE WERE HUMAN.
BRIAN BASSET
I HOPE NOT.
...HE'S BETTER THAN THAT!
ZIP

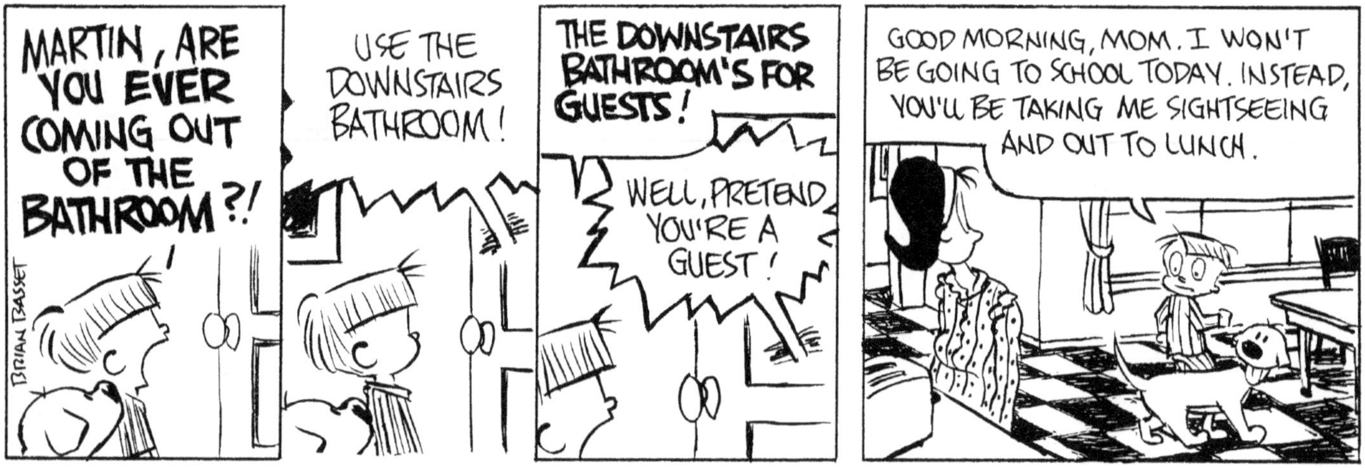
MARTIN, ARE YOU EVER COMING OUT OF THE BATHROOM?!
BRIAN BASSET
USE THE DOWNSTAIRS BATHROOM!
THE DOWNSTAIRS BATHROOM'S FOR GUESTS!
WELL, PRETEND YOU'RE A GUEST!
GOOD MORNING, MOM. I WON'T BE GOING TO SCHOOL TODAY. INSTEAD, YOU'LL BE TAKING ME SIGHTSEEING AND OUT TO LUNCH.

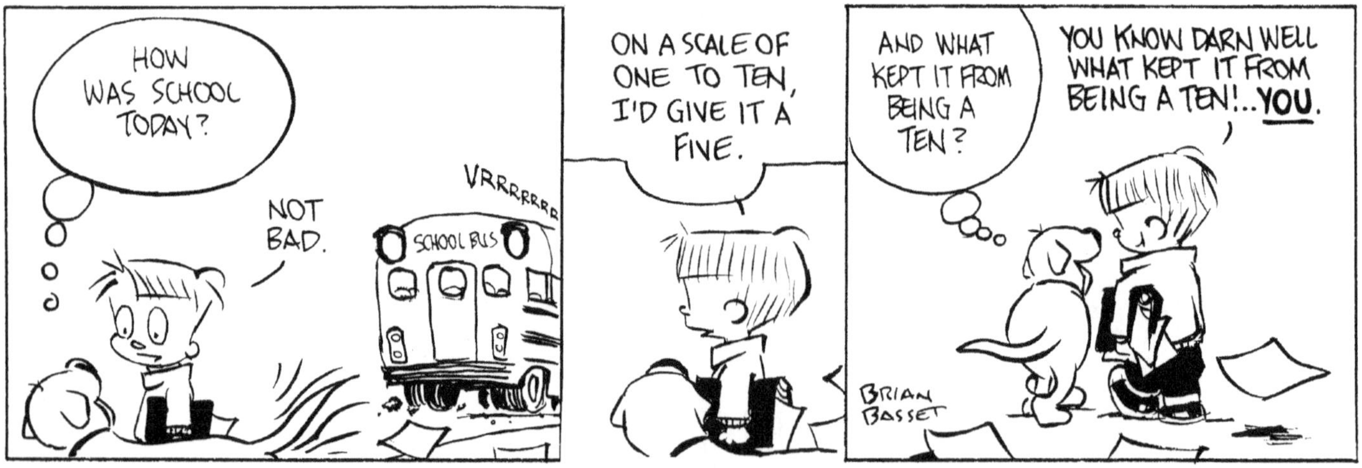
HOW WAS SCHOOL TODAY?
NOT BAD.
VRRRRRRR
SCHOOL BUS
ON A SCALE OF ONE TO TEN, I'D GIVE IT A FIVE.
AND WHAT KEPT IT FROM BEING A TEN?
YOU KNOW DARN WELL WHAT KEPT IT FROM BEING A TEN!...YOU.
BRIAN BASSET

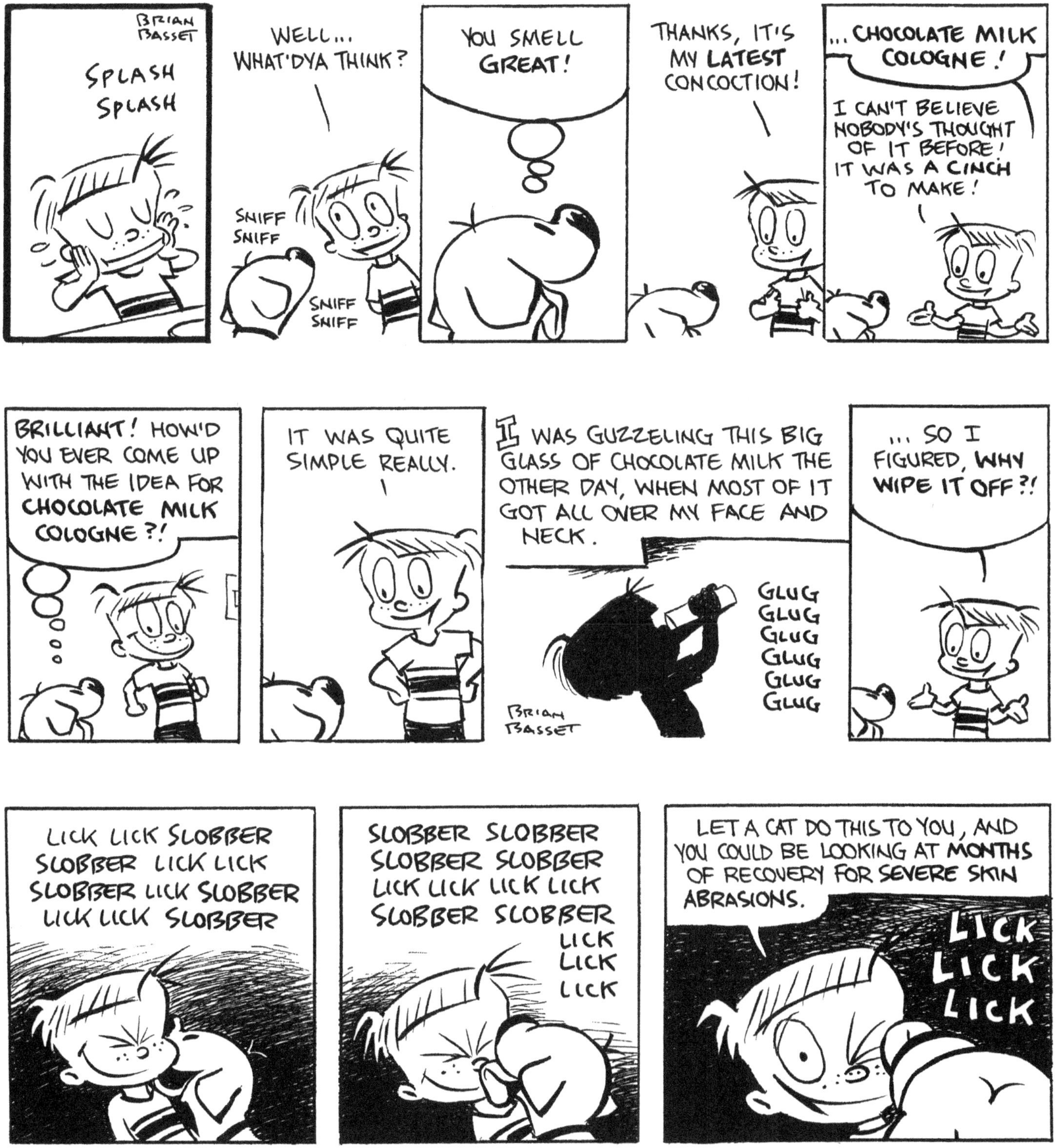
BRIAN BASSET
SPLASH SPLASH
WELL... WHAT'DYA THINK?
SNIFF SNIFF
SNIFF SNIFF
YOU SMELL GREAT!
THANKS, IT'S MY LATEST CONCOCTION!
... CHOCOLATE MILK COLOGNE!
I CAN'T BELIEVE NOBODY'S THOUGHT OF IT BEFORE! IT WAS A CINCH TO MAKE!
BRILLIANT! HOW'D YOU EVER COME UP WITH THE IDEA FOR CHOCOLATE MILK COLOGNE?!
IT WAS QUITE SIMPLE REALLY.
I WAS GUZZELING THIS BIG GLASS OF CHOCOLATE MILK THE OTHER DAY, WHEN MOST OF IT GOT ALL OVER MY FACE AND NECK.
GLUG GLUG GLUG GLUG GLUG GLUG
BRIAN BASSET
... SO I FIGURED, WHY WIPE IT OFF?!
LICK LICK SLOBBER SLOBBER LICK LICK SLOBBER LICK SLOBBER LICK LICK SLOBBER
SLOBBER SLOBBER SLOBBER SLOBBER LICK LICK LICK LICK SLOBBER SLOBBER
LICK LICK LICK
LET A CAT DO THIS TO YOU, AND YOU COULD BE LOOKING AT MONTHS OF RECOVERY FOR SEVERE SKIN ABRASIONS.
LICK LICK LICK

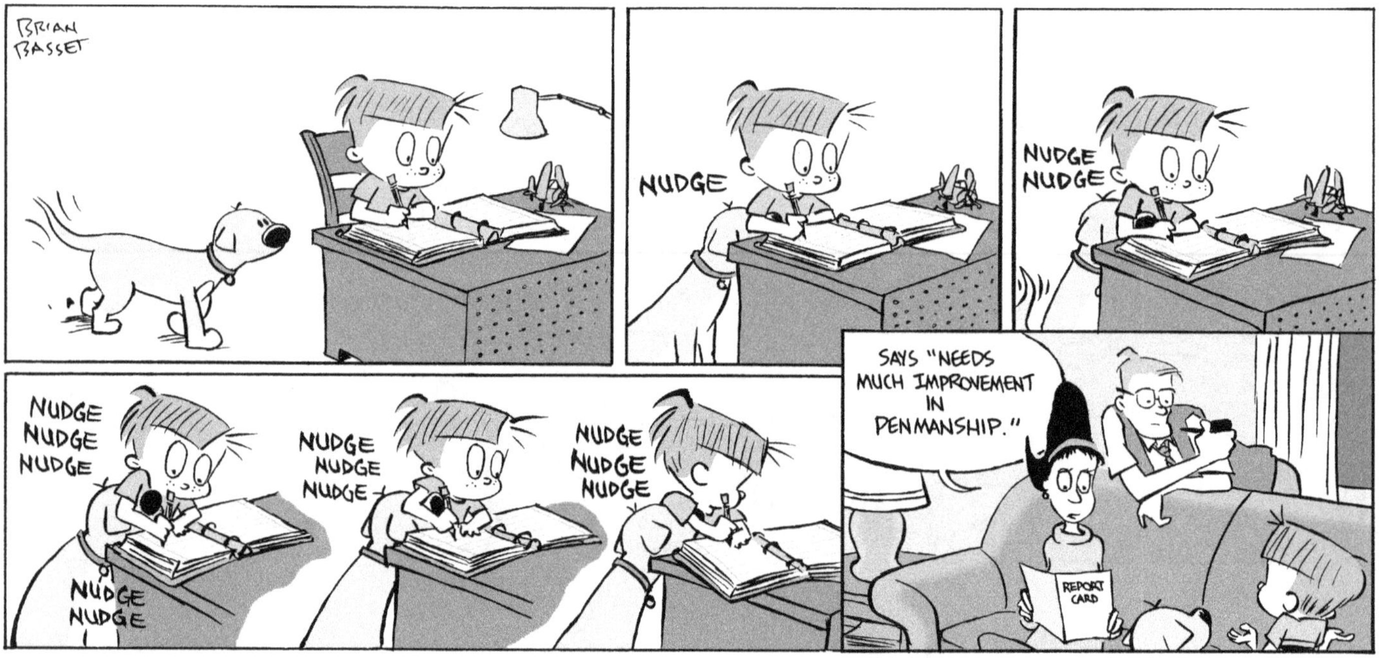
BRIAN BASSET
NUDGE
NUDGE NUDGE
NUDGE NUDGE NUDGE
NUDGE NUDGE
NUDGE NUDGE NUDGE
NUDGE NUDGE NUDGE
SAYS "NEEDS MUCH IMPROVEMENT IN PENMANSHIP."
REPORT CARD

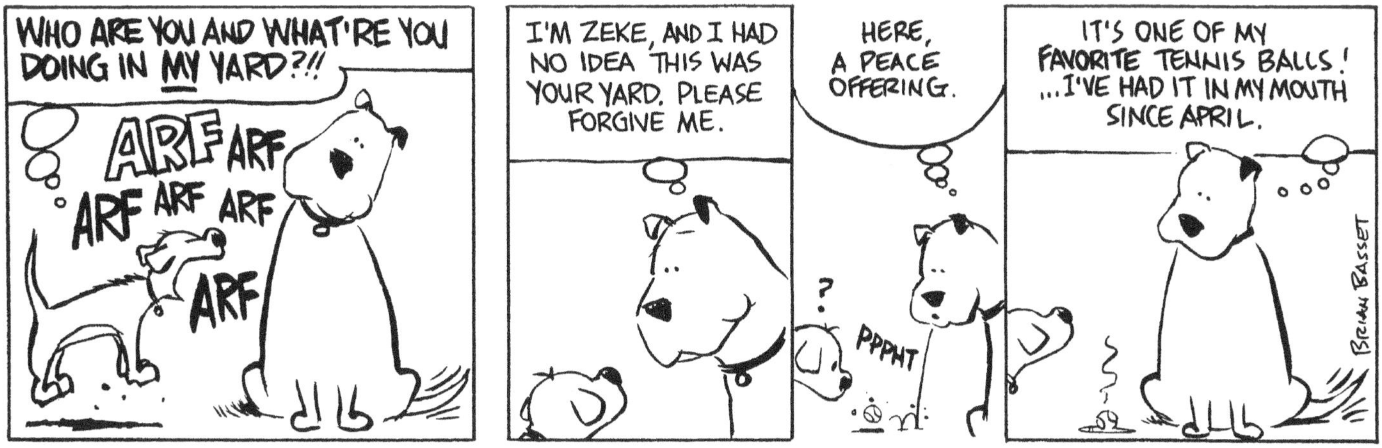

WHO ARE YOU AND WHAT'RE YOU DOING IN MY YARD?!!
ARF ARF ARF ARF ARF ARF
I'M ZEKE, AND I HAD NO IDEA THIS WAS YOUR YARD. PLEASE FORGIVE ME.
HERE, A PEACE OFFERING.
?
PPPHT
IT'S ONE OF MY FAVORITE TENNIS BALLS! ...I'VE HAD IT IN MY MOUTH SINCE APRIL.
BRIAN BASSET

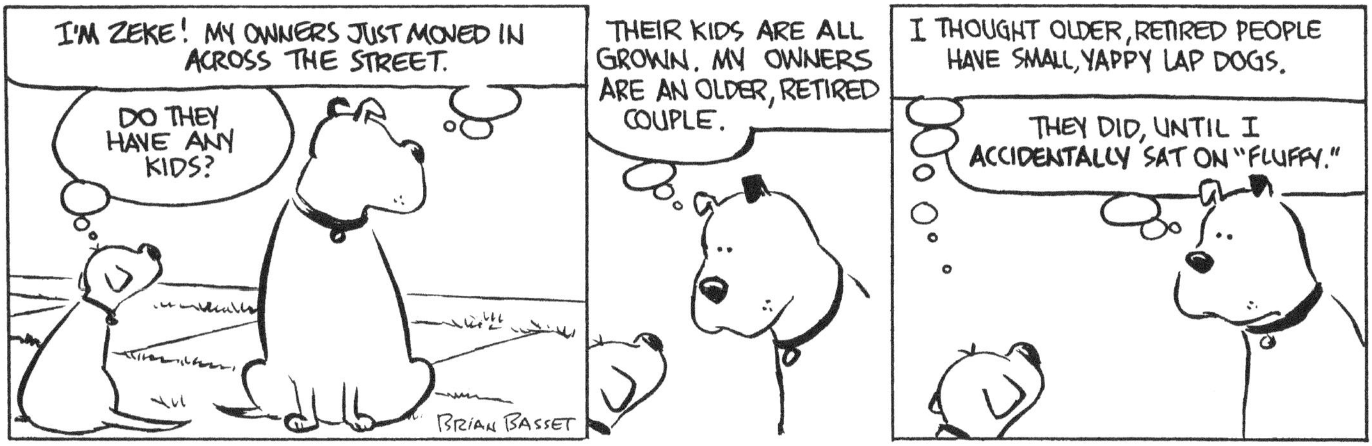

I'M ZEKE! MY OWNERS JUST MOVED IN ACROSS THE STREET.
DO THEY HAVE ANY KIDS?
BRIAN BASSET
THEIR KIDS ARE ALL GROWN. MY OWNERS ARE AN OLDER, RETIRED COUPLE.
I THOUGHT OLDER, RETIRED PEOPLE HAVE SMALL, YAPPY LAP DOGS.
THEY DID, UNTIL I ACCIDENTALLY SAT ON "FLUFFY."

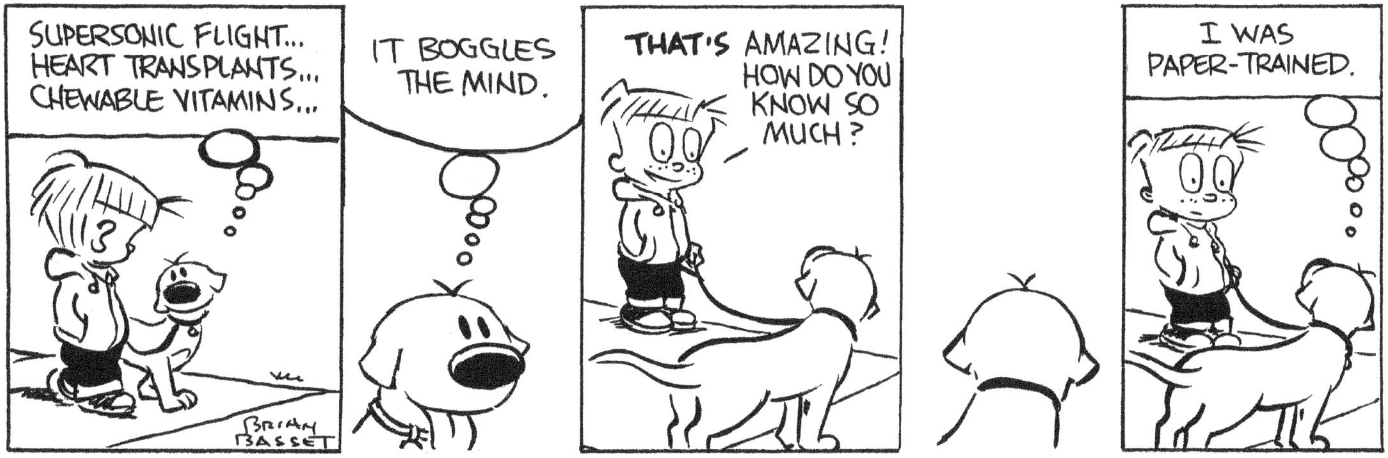

SUPERSONIC FLIGHT... HEART TRANSPLANTS... CHEWABLE VITAMINS...
BRIAN BASSET
IT BOGGLES THE MIND.
THAT'S AMAZING! HOW DO YOU KNOW SO MUCH?
I WAS PAPER-TRAINED.

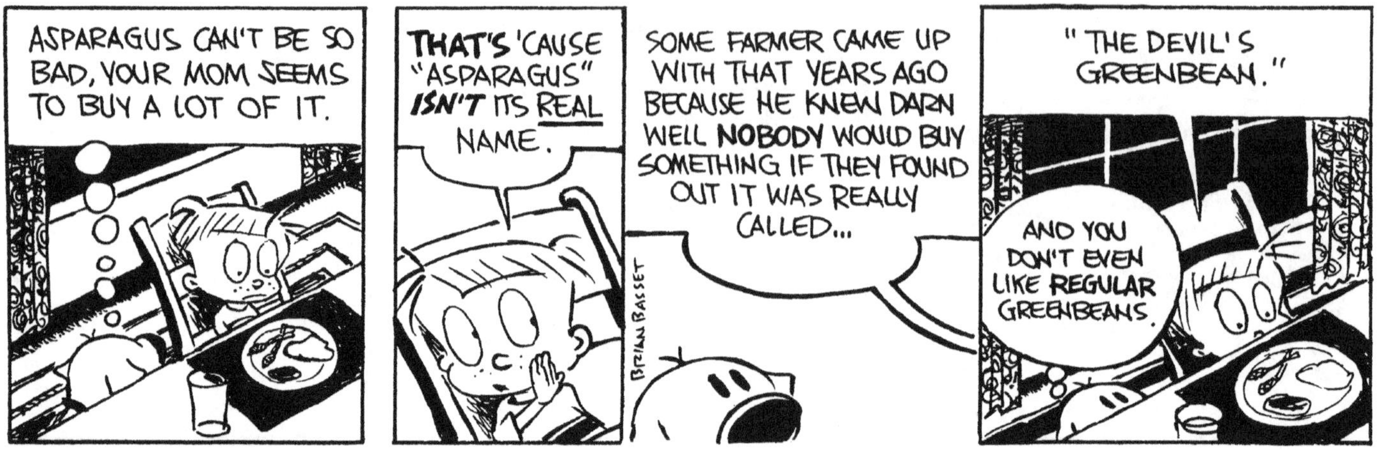
ASPARAGUS CAN'T BE SO BAD, YOUR MOM SEEMS TO BUY A LOT OF IT.
THAT'S 'CAUSE "ASPARAGUS" ***ISN'T*** ITS REAL NAME.
SOME FARMER CAME UP WITH THAT YEARS AGO BECAUSE HE KNEW DARN WELL **NOBODY** WOULD BUY SOMETHING IF THEY FOUND OUT IT WAS REALLY CALLED...
BRIAN BASSET
"THE DEVIL'S GREENBEAN."
AND YOU DON'T EVEN LIKE **REGULAR** GREENBEANS.

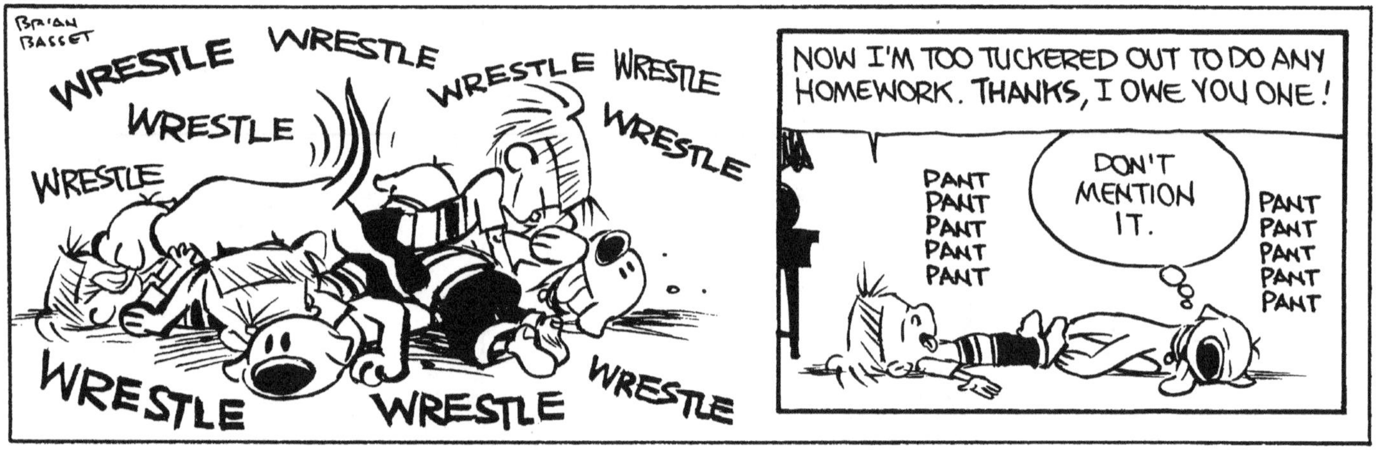
BRIAN BASSET
WRESTLE WRESTLE WRESTLE WRESTLE WRESTLE WRESTLE WRESTLE WRESTLE WRESTLE WRESTLE
NOW I'M TOO TUCKERED OUT TO DO ANY HOMEWORK. **THANKS,** I OWE YOU ONE!
PANT PANT PANT PANT PANT
DON'T MENTION IT.
PANT PANT PANT PANT PANT

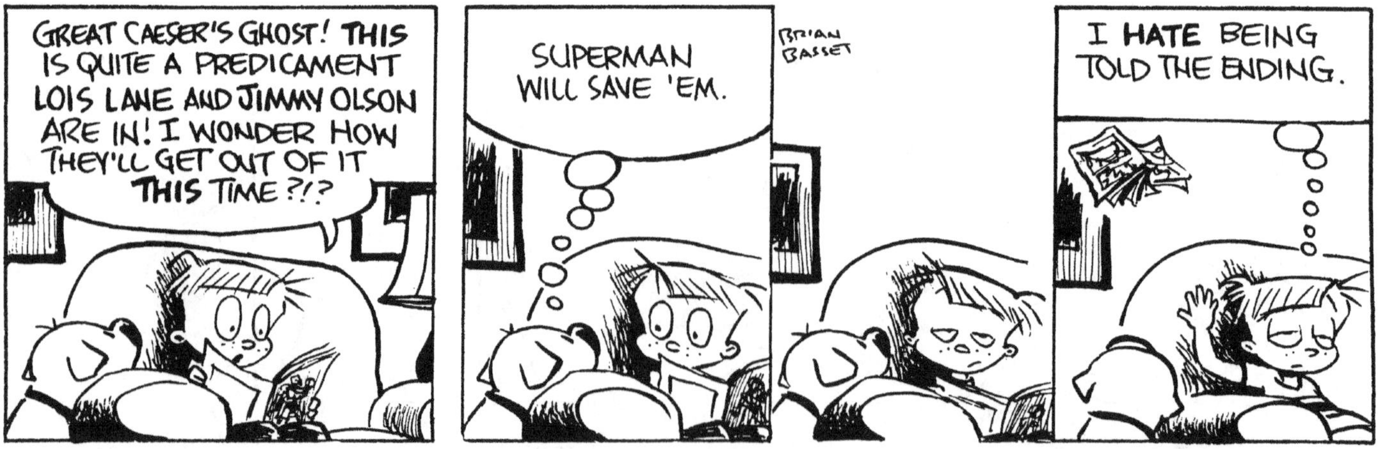
GREAT CAESER'S GHOST! **THIS** IS QUITE A PREDICAMENT **LOIS LANE** AND **JIMMY OLSON** ARE IN! I WONDER HOW THEY'LL GET OUT OF IT **THIS** TIME ?!?
SUPERMAN WILL SAVE 'EM.
BRIAN BASSET
I **HATE** BEING TOLD THE ENDING.

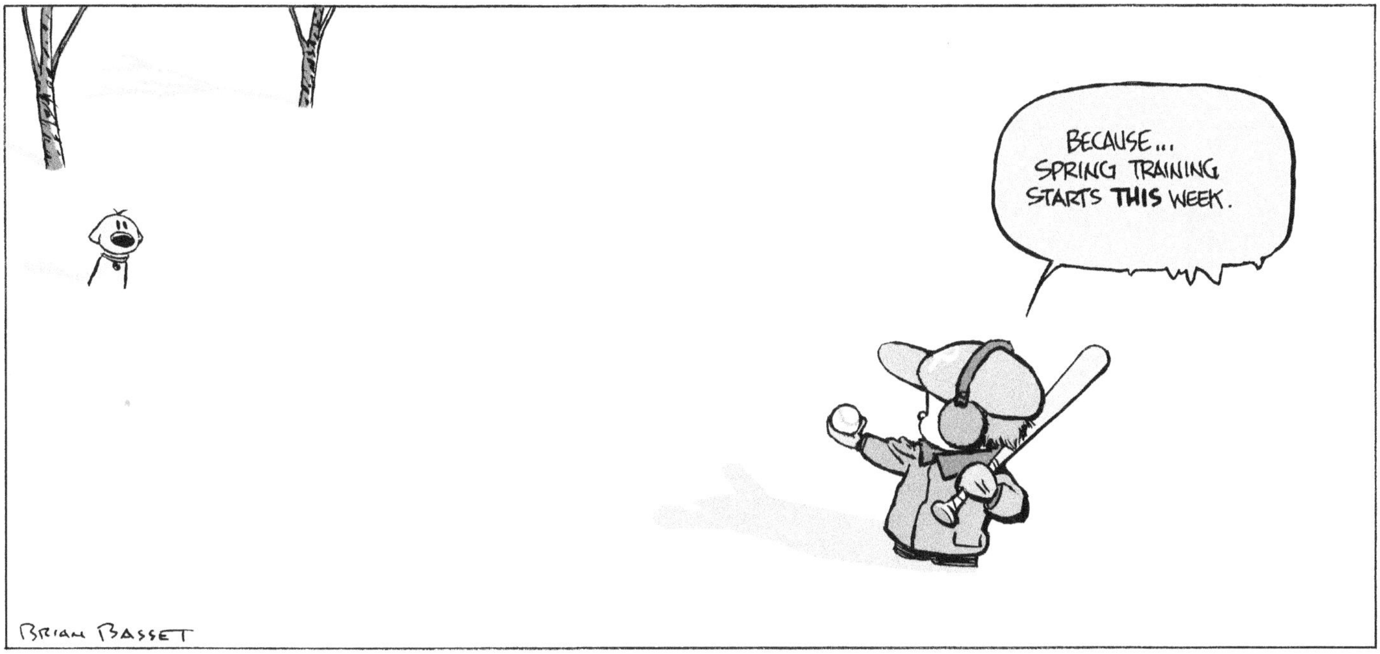
BECAUSE... SPRING TRAINING STARTS **THIS** WEEK.
BRIAN BASSET

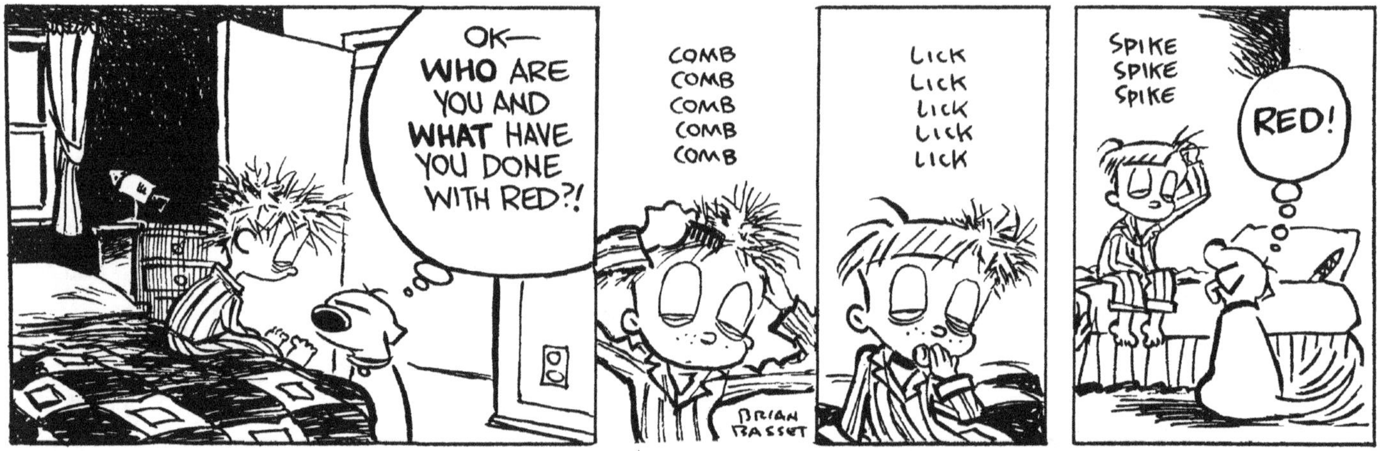
OK— WHO ARE YOU AND WHAT HAVE YOU DONE WITH RED?!
COMB COMB COMB COMB COMB
BRIAN BASSET
LICK LICK LICK LICK LICK
SPIKE SPIKE SPIKE
RED!

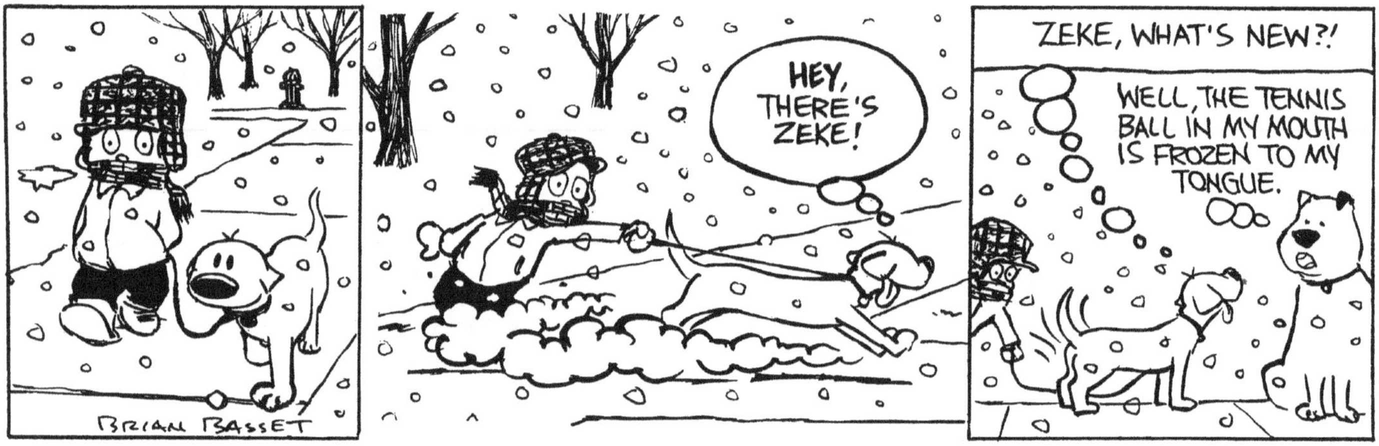
BRIAN BASSET
HEY, THERE'S ZEKE!
ZEKE, WHAT'S NEW?!
WELL, THE TENNIS BALL IN MY MOUTH IS FROZEN TO MY TONGUE.

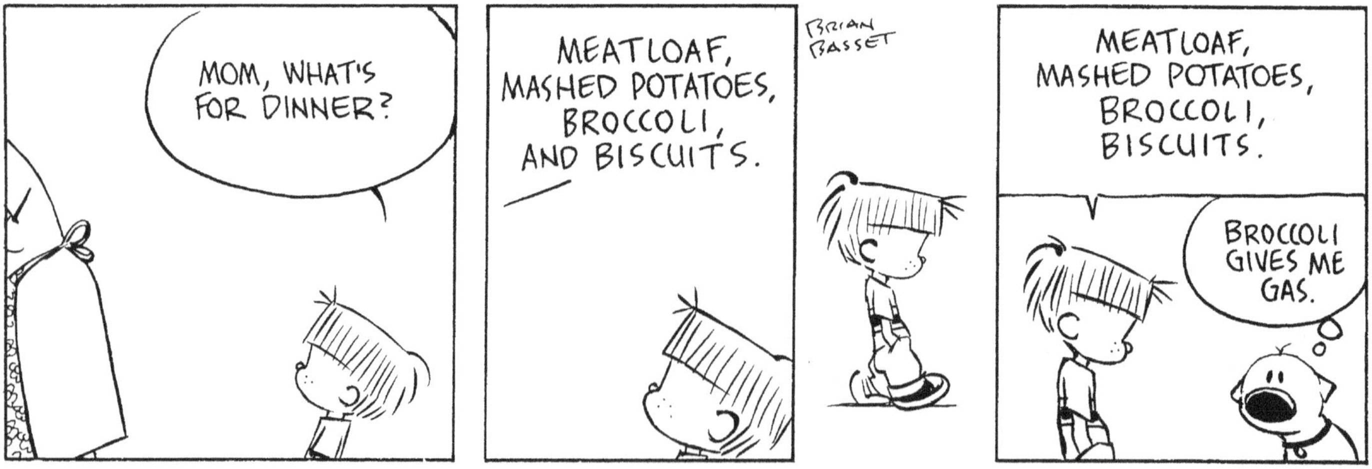
MOM, WHAT'S FOR DINNER?
MEATLOAF, MASHED POTATOES, BROCCOLI, AND BISCUITS.
BRIAN BASSET
MEATLOAF, MASHED POTATOES, BROCCOLI, BISCUITS.
BROCCOLI GIVES ME GAS.

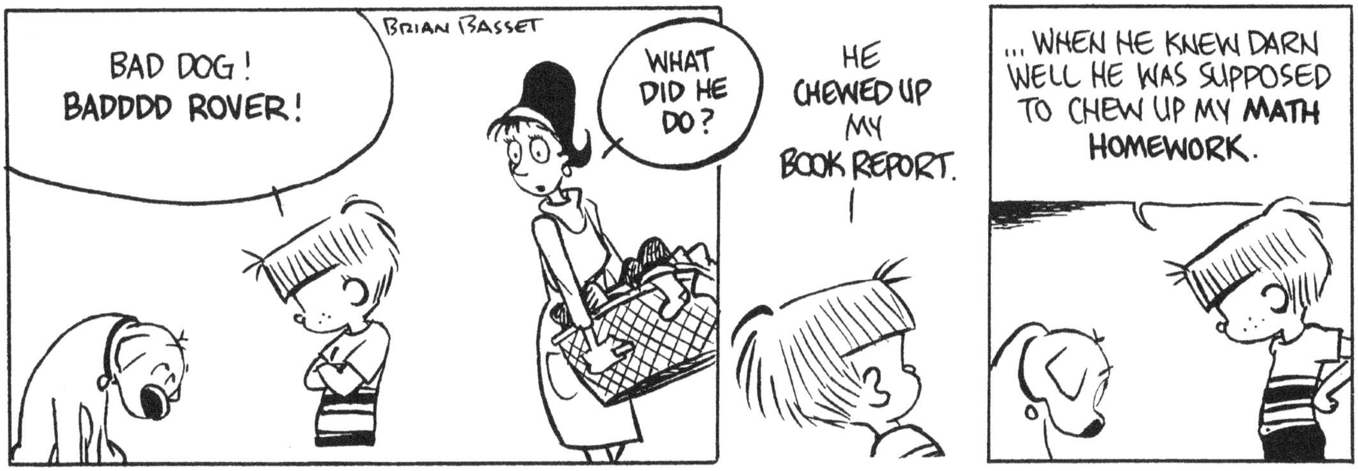
BRIAN BASSET
BAD DOG! BADDDD ROVER!
WHAT DID HE DO?
HE CHEWED UP MY BOOK REPORT.
... WHEN HE KNEW DARN WELL HE WAS SUPPOSED TO CHEW UP MY MATH HOMEWORK.

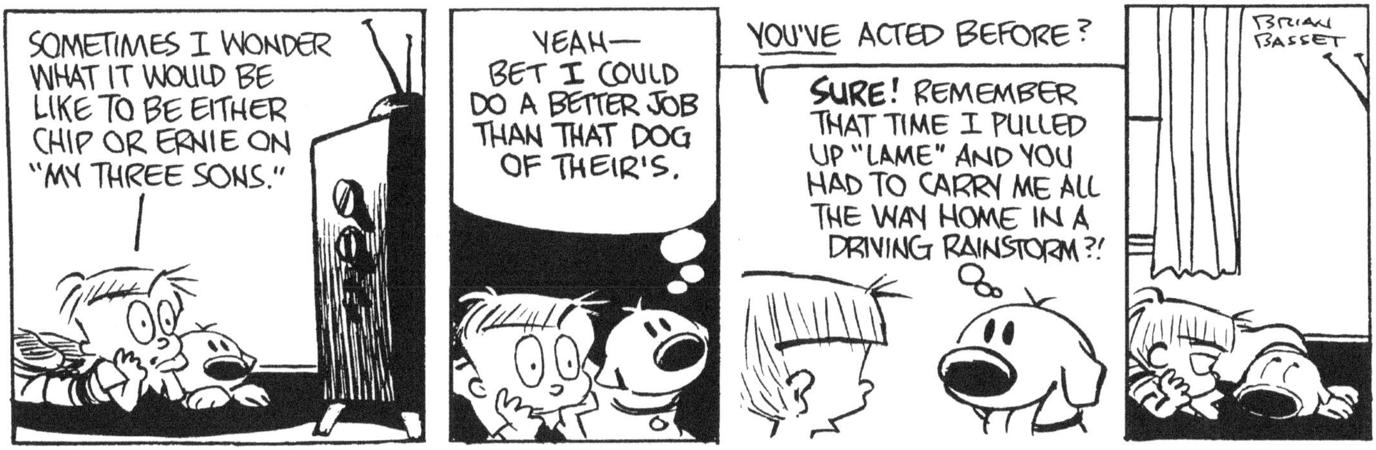
SOMETIMES I WONDER WHAT IT WOULD BE LIKE TO BE EITHER CHIP OR ERNIE ON "MY THREE SONS."
YEAH— BET I COULD DO A BETTER JOB THAN THAT DOG OF THEIR'S.
YOU'VE ACTED BEFORE?
SURE! REMEMBER THAT TIME I PULLED UP "LAME" AND YOU HAD TO CARRY ME ALL THE WAY HOME IN A DRIVING RAINSTORM?!
BRIAN BASSET

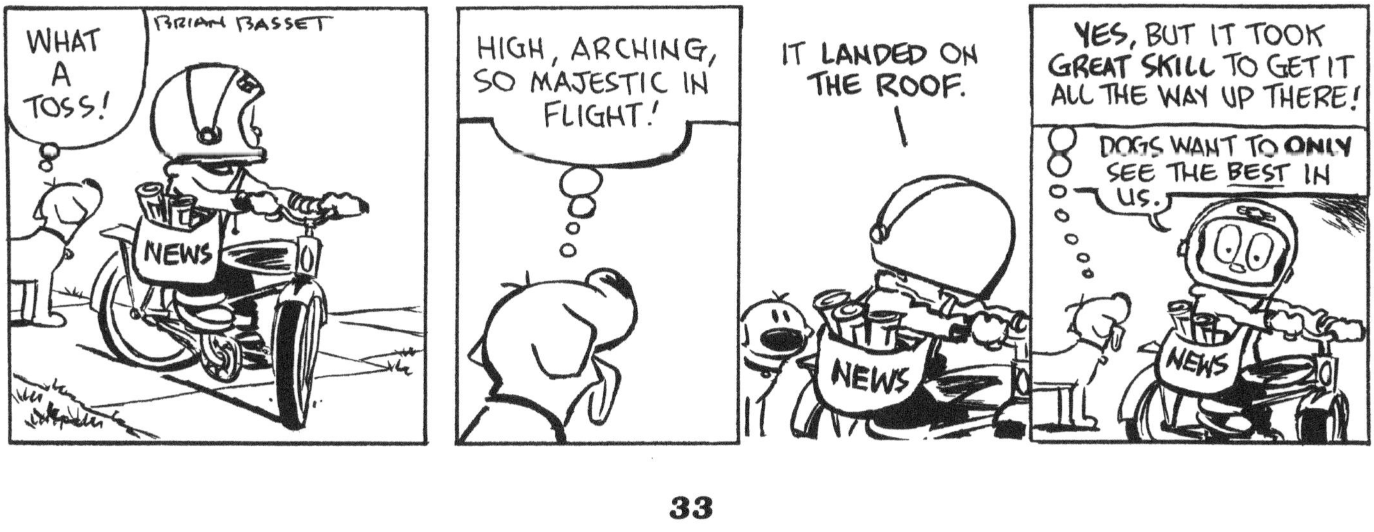
BRIAN BASSET
WHAT A TOSS!
NEWS
HIGH, ARCHING, SO MAJESTIC IN FLIGHT!
IT LANDED ON THE ROOF.
NEWS
YES, BUT IT TOOK GREAT SKILL TO GET IT ALL THE WAY UP THERE!
DOGS WANT TO ONLY SEE THE BEST IN US.
NEWS

WANNA PLAY CATCH?
SURE!
SKIP SKIP
E-MAIL REDANDROVER@AOL.COM
©2002 DIST. BY WASHINGTON POST WRITERS GROUP
HEADS UP!
4/7
BRIAN BASSET
I GOT IT! I GOT IT!
SNATCH!
YOU REALLY DREAMED WE WERE IN THE SUNDAY FUNNIES?!
YEAH. PRETTY SILLY, HUH?

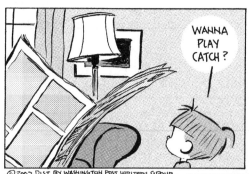

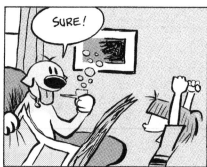

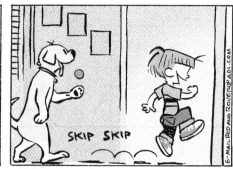

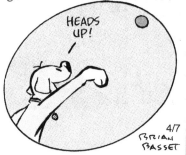

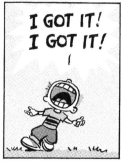

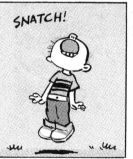

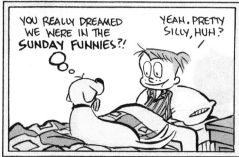

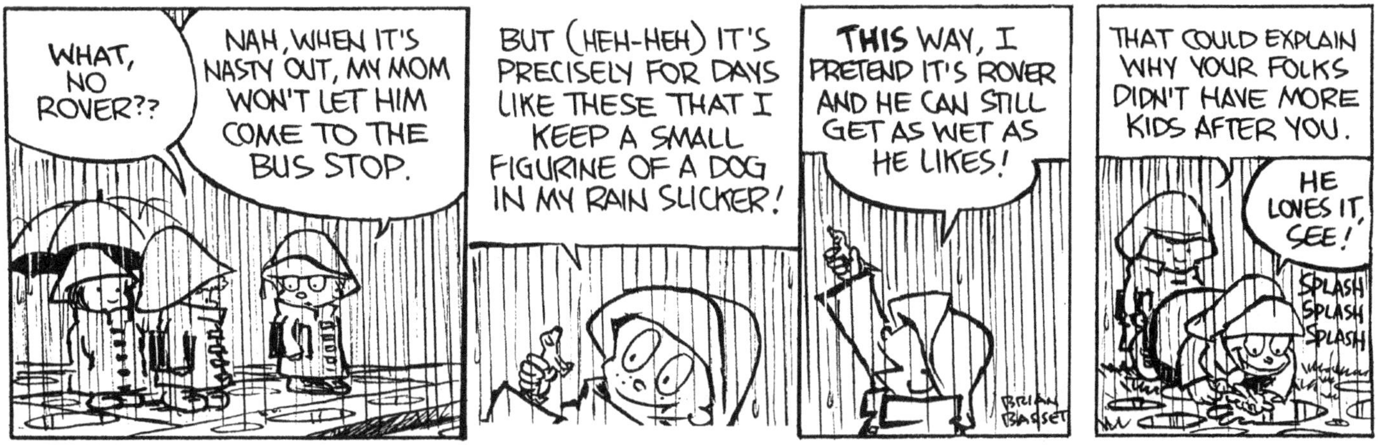
WHAT, NO ROVER??
NAH, WHEN IT'S NASTY OUT, MY MOM WON'T LET HIM COME TO THE BUS STOP.
BUT (HEH-HEH) IT'S PRECISELY FOR DAYS LIKE THESE THAT I KEEP A SMALL FIGURINE OF A DOG IN MY RAIN SLICKER!
THIS WAY, I PRETEND IT'S ROVER AND HE CAN STILL GET AS WET AS HE LIKES!
BRIAN BASSET
THAT COULD EXPLAIN WHY YOUR FOLKS DIDN'T HAVE MORE KIDS AFTER YOU.
HE LOVES IT, SEE!
SPLASH SPLASH SPLASH

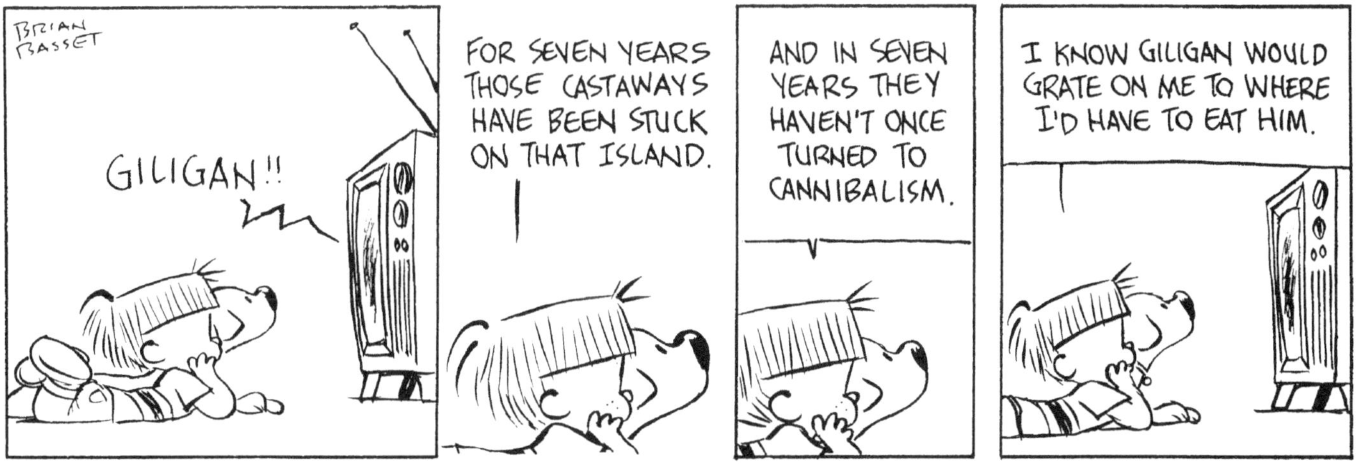
BRIAN BASSET
GILIGAN!!
FOR SEVEN YEARS THOSE CASTAWAYS HAVE BEEN STUCK ON THAT ISLAND.
AND IN SEVEN YEARS THEY HAVEN'T ONCE TURNED TO CANNIBALISM.
I KNOW GILIGAN WOULD GRATE ON ME TO WHERE I'D HAVE TO EAT HIM.

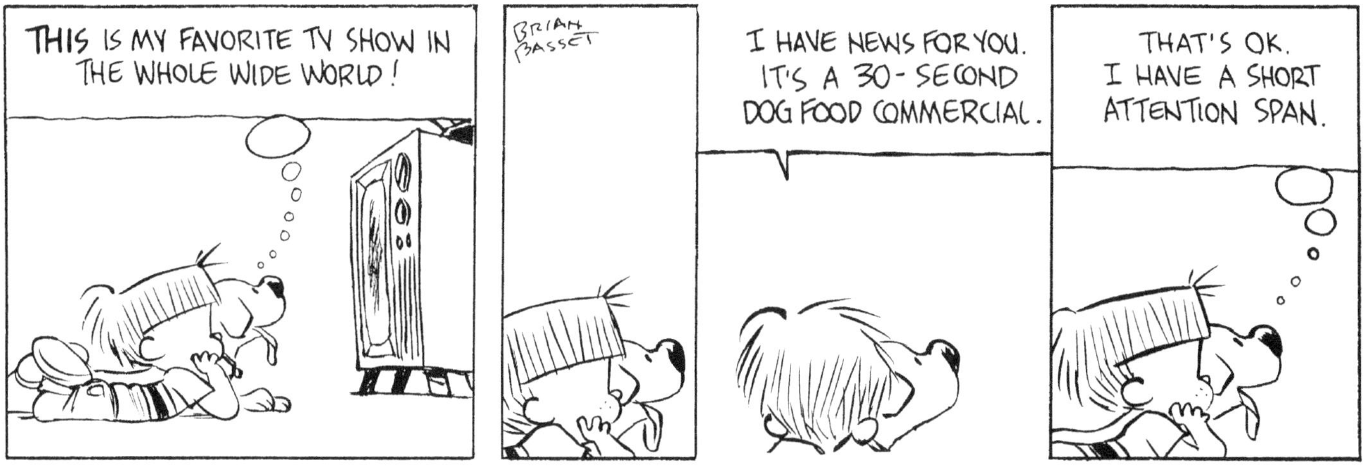
THIS IS MY FAVORITE TV SHOW IN THE WHOLE WIDE WORLD!
BRIAN BASSET
I HAVE NEWS FOR YOU. IT'S A 30-SECOND DOG FOOD COMMERCIAL.
THAT'S OK. I HAVE A SHORT ATTENTION SPAN.

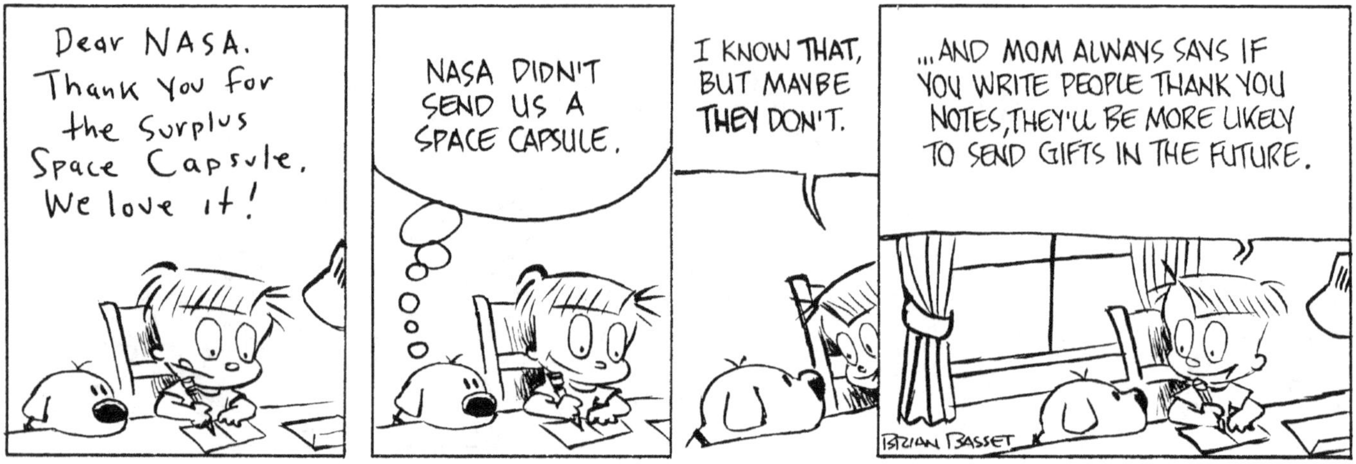
Dear NASA. Thank You for the Surplus Space Capsule. We love it!
NASA DIDN'T SEND US A SPACE CAPSULE.
I KNOW THAT, BUT MAYBE THEY DON'T.
...AND MOM ALWAYS SAYS IF YOU WRITE PEOPLE THANK YOU NOTES, THEY'LL BE MORE LIKELY TO SEND GIFTS IN THE FUTURE.
BRIAN BASSET

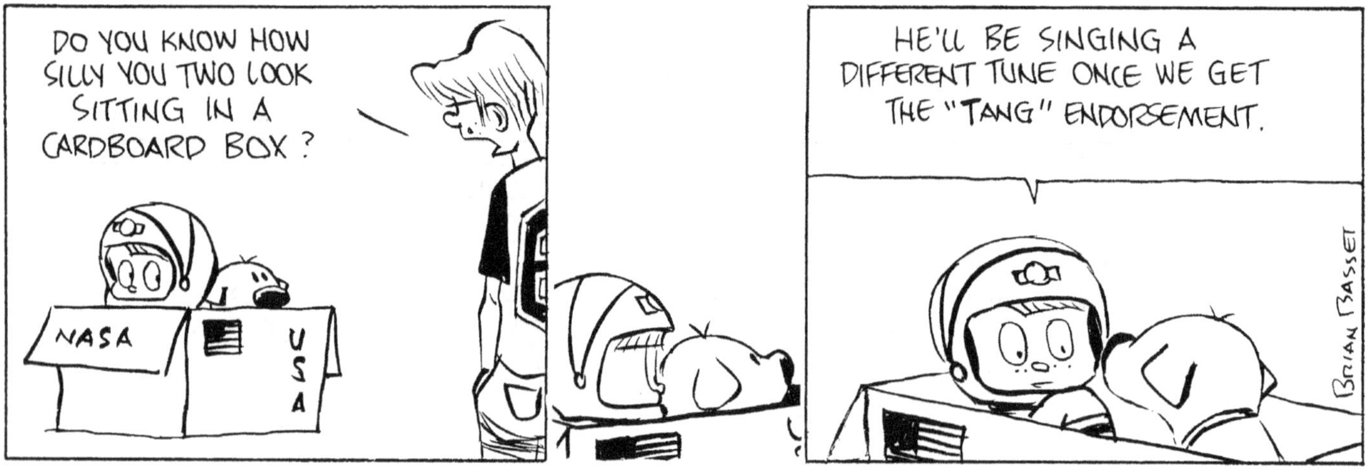
DO YOU KNOW HOW SILLY YOU TWO LOOK SITTING IN A CARDBOARD BOX?
NASA
USA
HE'LL BE SINGING A DIFFERENT TUNE ONCE WE GET THE "TANG" ENDORSEMENT.
BRIAN BASSET

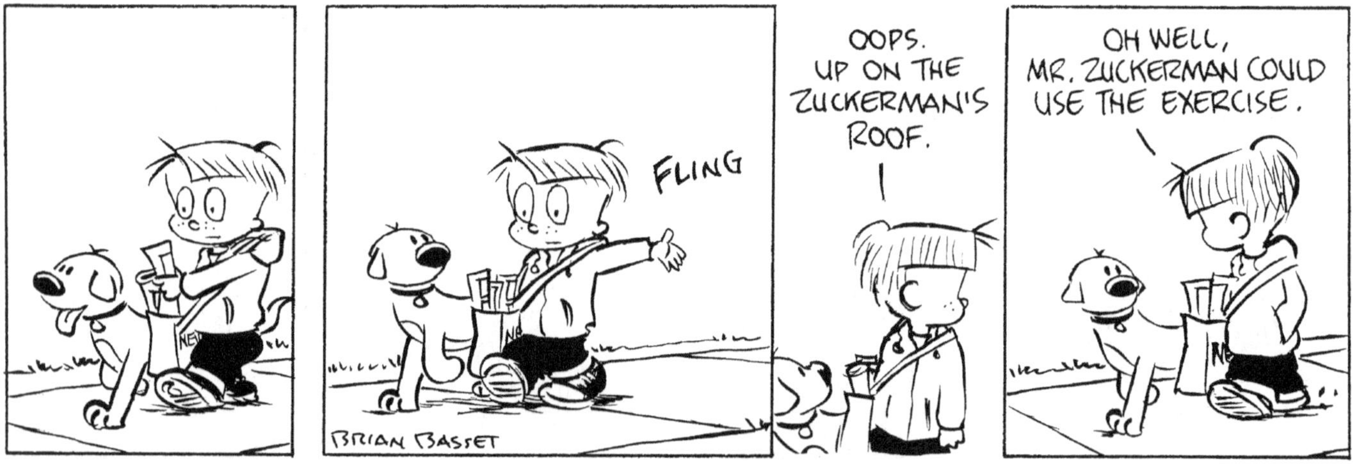
FLING
BRIAN BASSET
OOPS. UP ON THE ZUCKERMAN'S ROOF.
OH WELL, MR. ZUCKERMAN COULD USE THE EXERCISE.

The many
hats worn
by kids

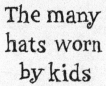
Scout

Astronaut

Baseball player

Arctic explorer

Weatherman

BRIAN
BASSET

Construction
worker

Caring pet owner

37

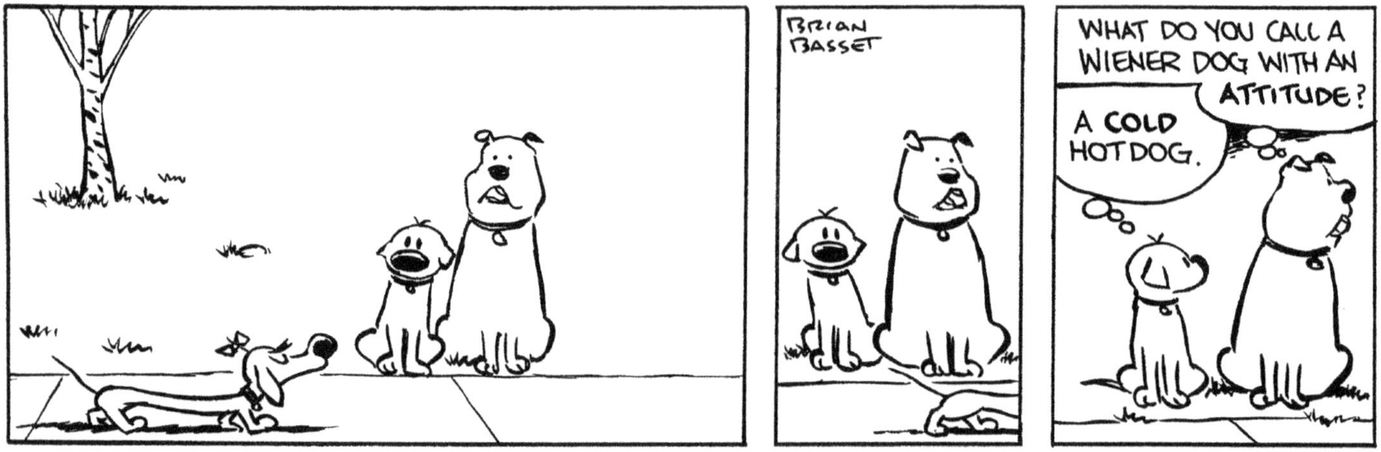
BRIAN BASSET
WHAT DO YOU CALL A WIENER DOG WITH AN ATTITUDE?
A COLD HOTDOG.

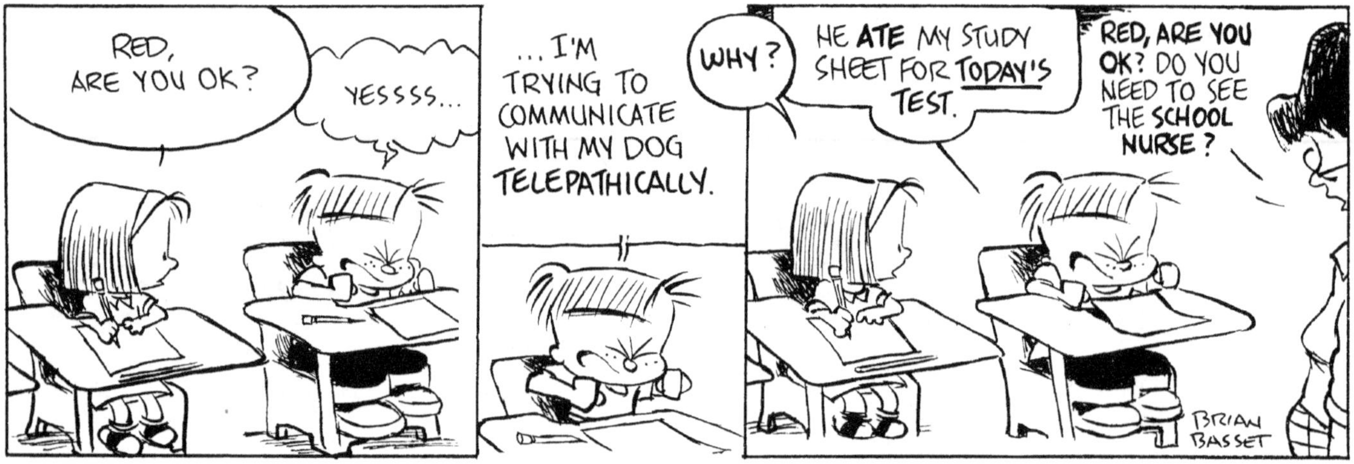
RED, ARE YOU OK?
YESSSS...
... I'M TRYING TO COMMUNICATE WITH MY DOG TELEPATHICALLY.
WHY?
HE ATE MY STUDY SHEET FOR TODAY'S TEST.
RED, ARE YOU OK? DO YOU NEED TO SEE THE SCHOOL NURSE?
BRIAN BASSET

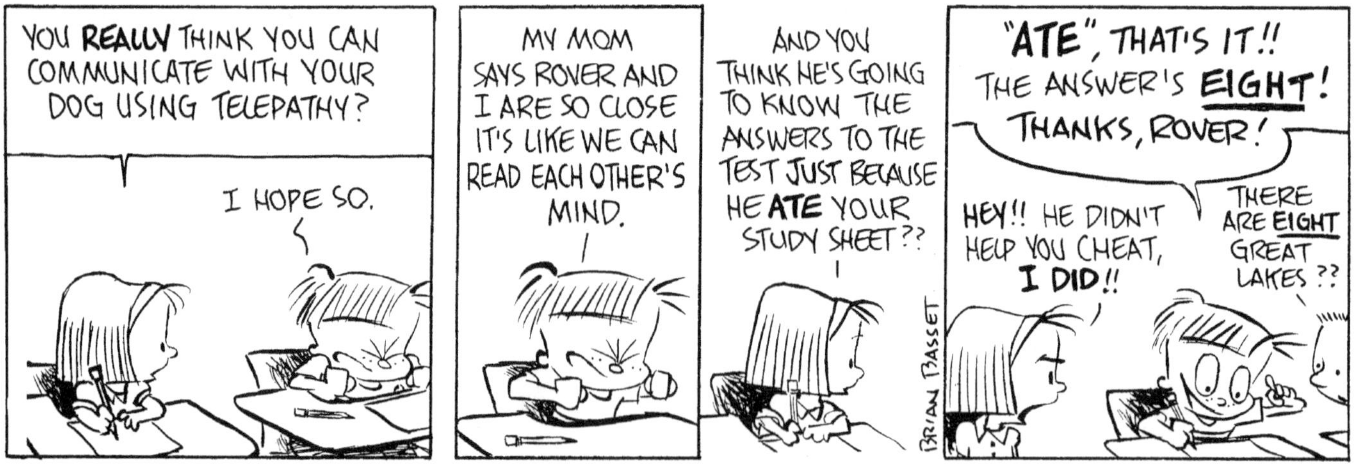
YOU REALLY THINK YOU CAN COMMUNICATE WITH YOUR DOG USING TELEPATHY?
I HOPE SO.
MY MOM SAYS ROVER AND I ARE SO CLOSE IT'S LIKE WE CAN READ EACH OTHER'S MIND.
AND YOU THINK HE'S GOING TO KNOW THE ANSWERS TO THE TEST JUST BECAUSE HE ATE YOUR STUDY SHEET??
BRIAN BASSET
"ATE", THAT'S IT!! THE ANSWER'S EIGHT! THANKS, ROVER!
HEY!! HE DIDN'T HELP YOU CHEAT, I DID!!
THERE ARE EIGHT GREAT LAKES??

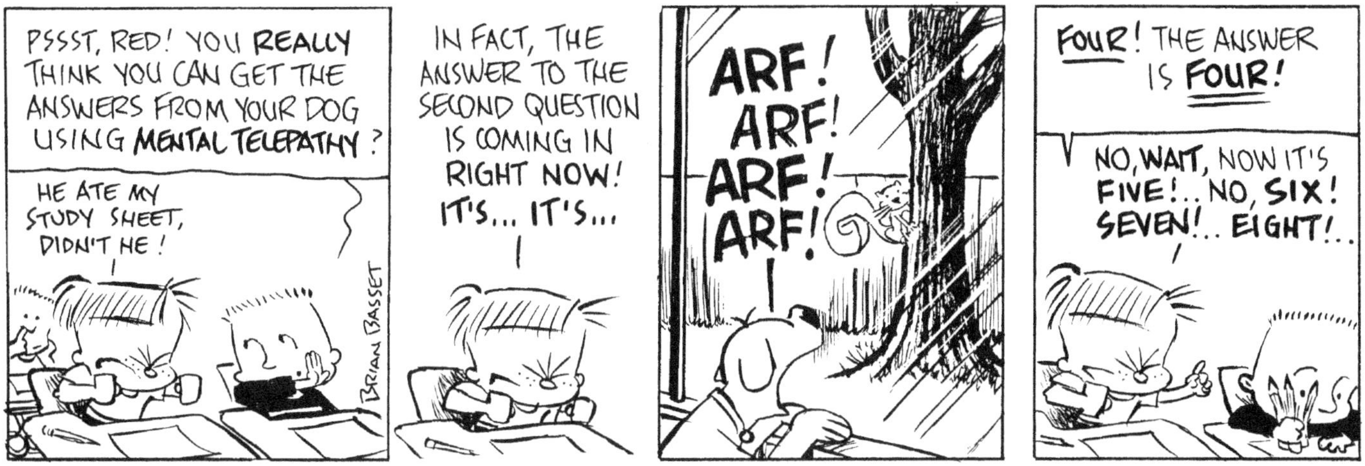
PSSST, RED! YOU REALLY THINK YOU CAN GET THE ANSWERS FROM YOUR DOG USING MENTAL TELEPATHY?
HE ATE MY STUDY SHEET, DIDN'T HE!
BRIAN BASSET
IN FACT, THE ANSWER TO THE SECOND QUESTION IS COMING IN RIGHT NOW! IT'S... IT'S...
ARF! ARF! ARF! ARF!
FOUR! THE ANSWER IS FOUR!
NO, WAIT, NOW IT'S FIVE!.. NO, SIX! SEVEN!.. EIGHT!..

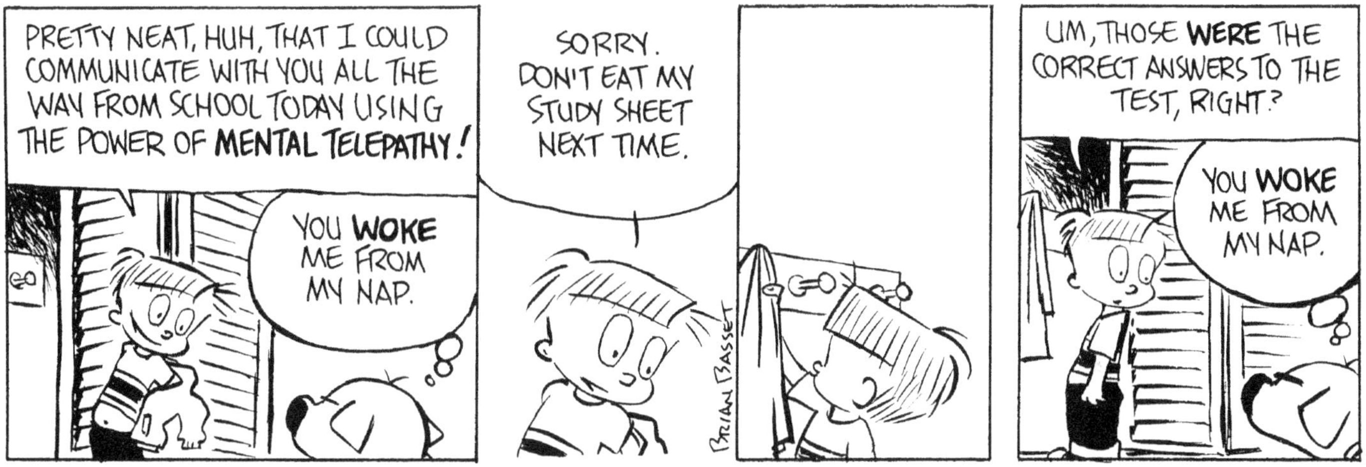
PRETTY NEAT, HUH, THAT I COULD COMMUNICATE WITH YOU ALL THE WAY FROM SCHOOL TODAY USING THE POWER OF MENTAL TELEPATHY!
YOU WOKE ME FROM MY NAP.
SORRY. DON'T EAT MY STUDY SHEET NEXT TIME.
BRIAN BASSET
UM, THOSE WERE THE CORRECT ANSWERS TO THE TEST, RIGHT?
YOU WOKE ME FROM MY NAP.

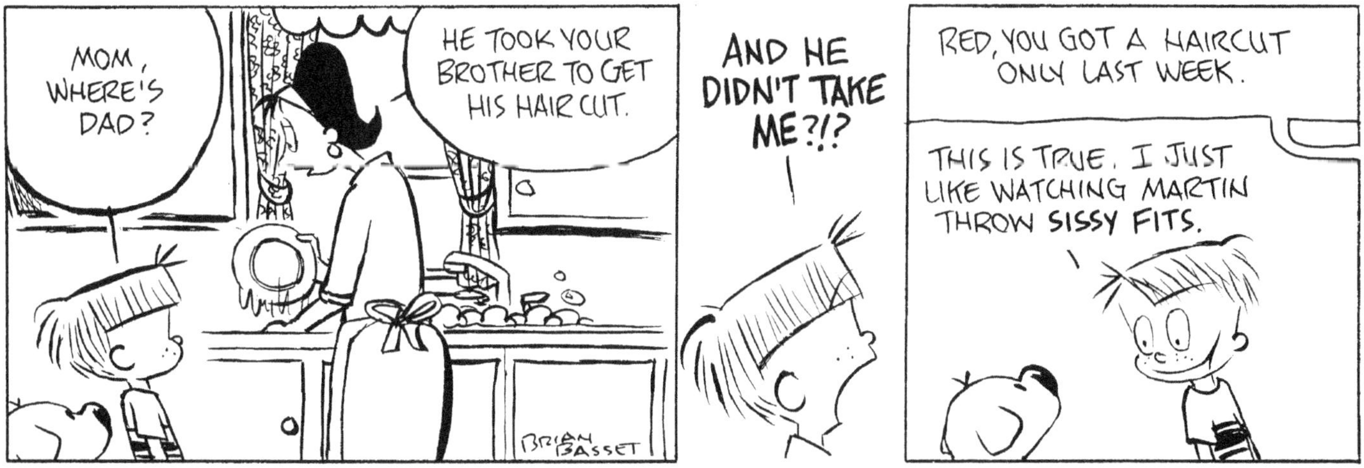
MOM, WHERE'S DAD?
HE TOOK YOUR BROTHER TO GET HIS HAIR CUT.
BRIAN BASSET
AND HE DIDN'T TAKE ME?!?
RED, YOU GOT A HAIRCUT ONLY LAST WEEK.
THIS IS TRUE. I JUST LIKE WATCHING MARTIN THROW SISSY FITS.

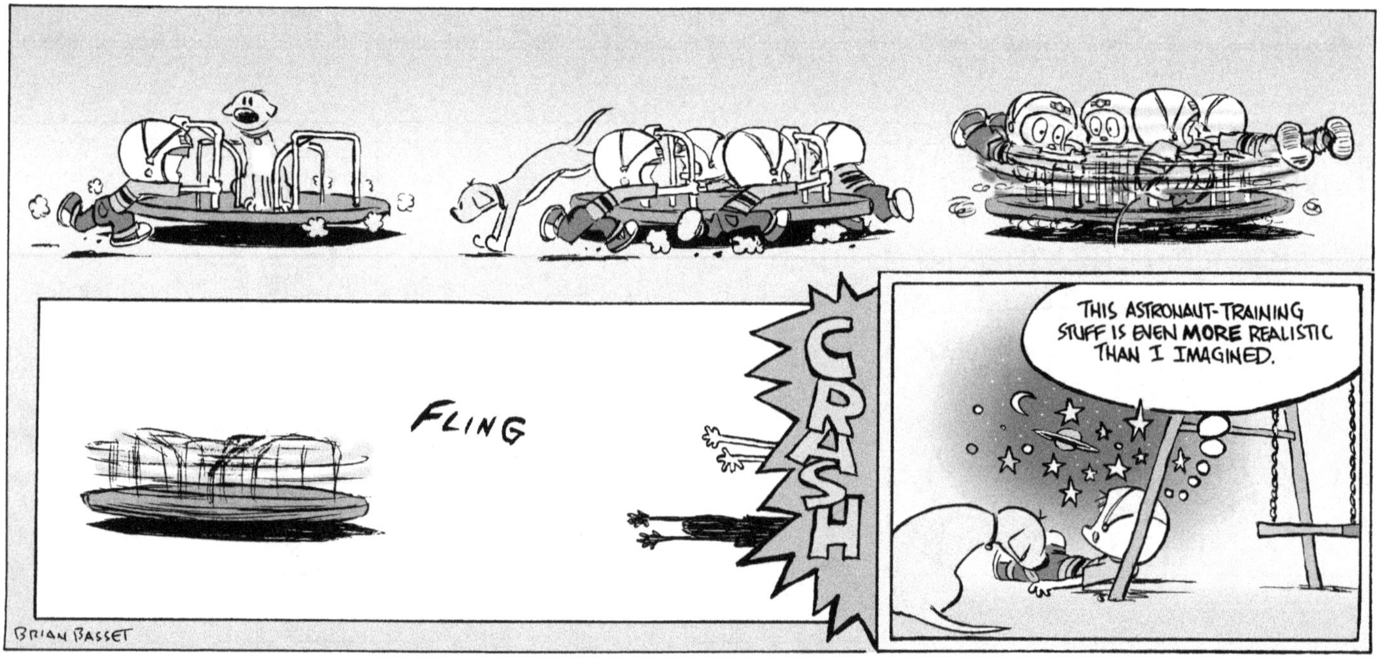
FLING
CRASH
THIS ASTRONAUT-TRAINING STUFF IS EVEN MORE REALISTIC THAN I IMAGINED.
BRIAN BASSET

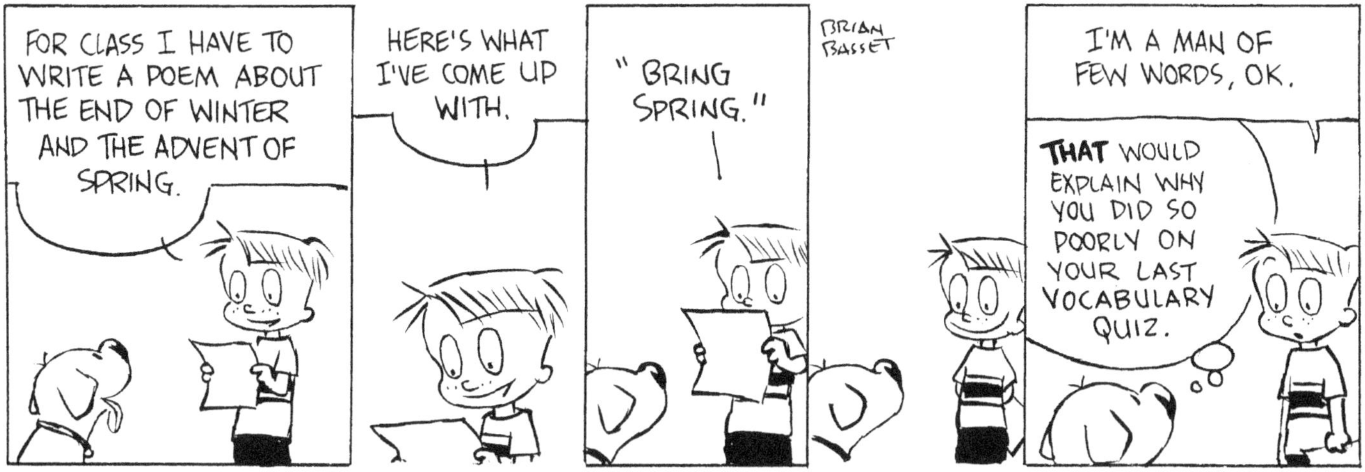
FOR CLASS I HAVE TO WRITE A POEM ABOUT THE END OF WINTER AND THE ADVENT OF SPRING.
HERE'S WHAT I'VE COME UP WITH.
"BRING SPRING."
BRIAN BASSET
I'M A MAN OF FEW WORDS, OK.
THAT WOULD EXPLAIN WHY YOU DID SO POORLY ON YOUR LAST VOCABULARY QUIZ.

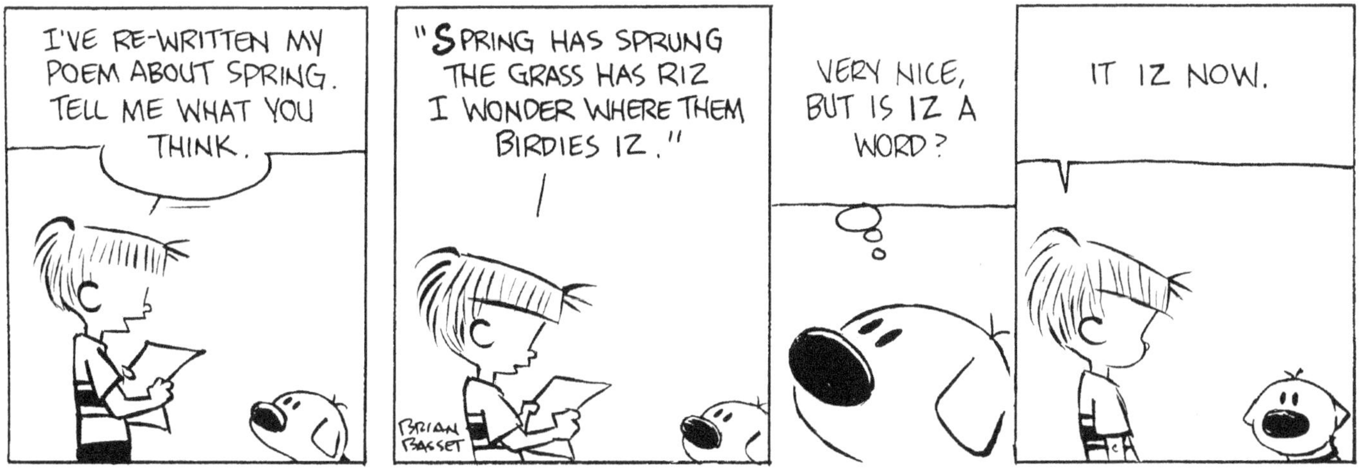
I'VE RE-WRITTEN MY POEM ABOUT SPRING. TELL ME WHAT YOU THINK.
"SPRING HAS SPRUNG THE GRASS HAS RIZ I WONDER WHERE THEM BIRDIES IZ."
BRIAN BASSET
VERY NICE, BUT IS IZ A WORD?
IT IZ NOW.

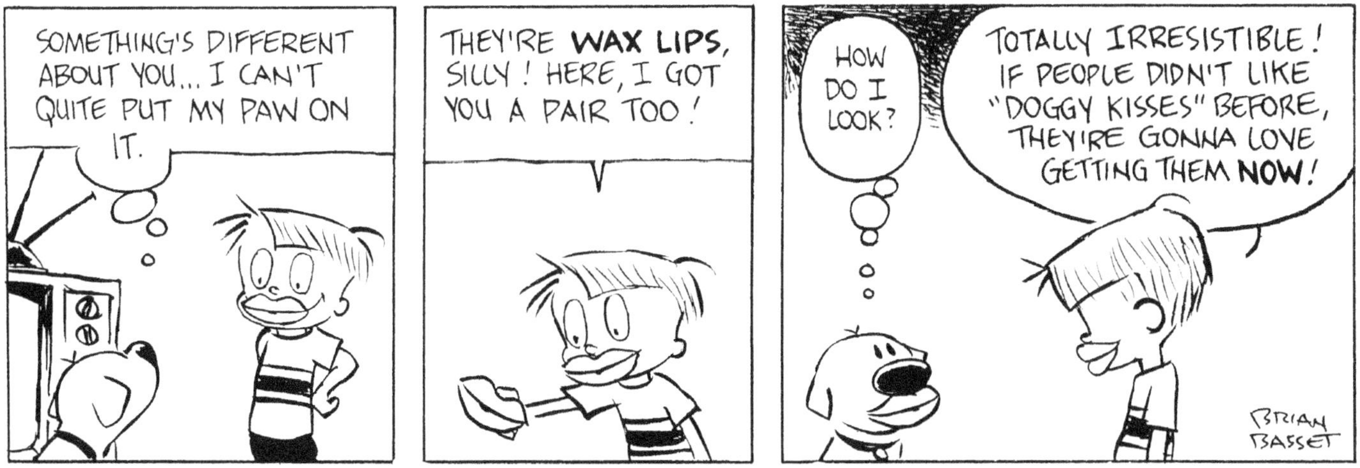
SOMETHING'S DIFFERENT ABOUT YOU... I CAN'T QUITE PUT MY PAW ON IT.
THEY'RE WAX LIPS, SILLY! HERE, I GOT YOU A PAIR TOO!
HOW DO I LOOK?
TOTALLY IRRESISTIBLE! IF PEOPLE DIDN'T LIKE "DOGGY KISSES" BEFORE, THEY'RE GONNA LOVE GETTING THEM NOW!
BRIAN BASSET

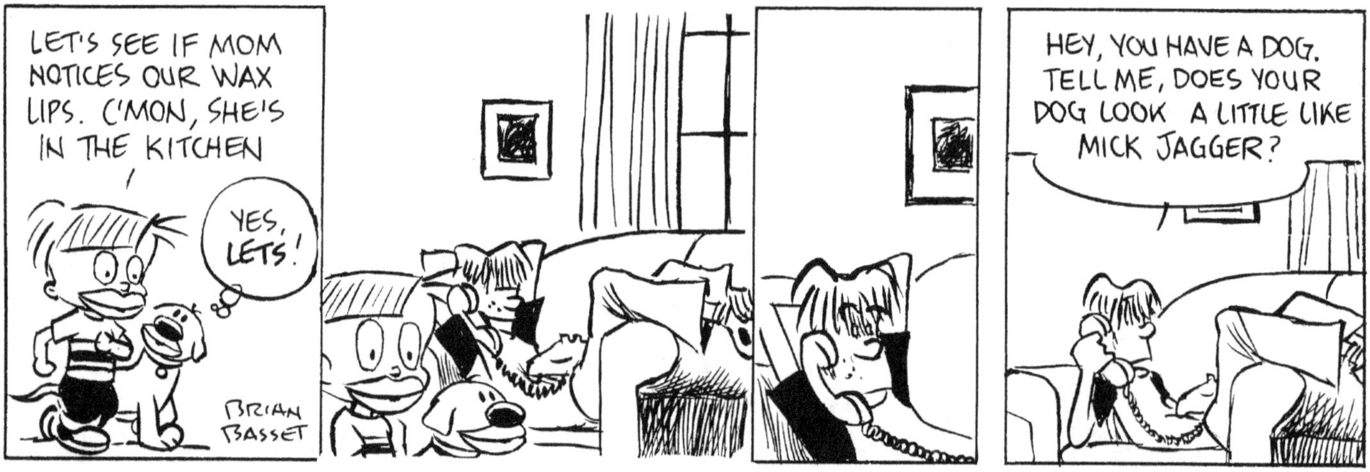
LET'S SEE IF MOM NOTICES OUR WAX LIPS. C'MON, SHE'S IN THE KITCHEN
YES, LETS!
BRIAN BASSET
HEY, YOU HAVE A DOG. TELL ME, DOES YOUR DOG LOOK A LITTLE LIKE MICK JAGGER?

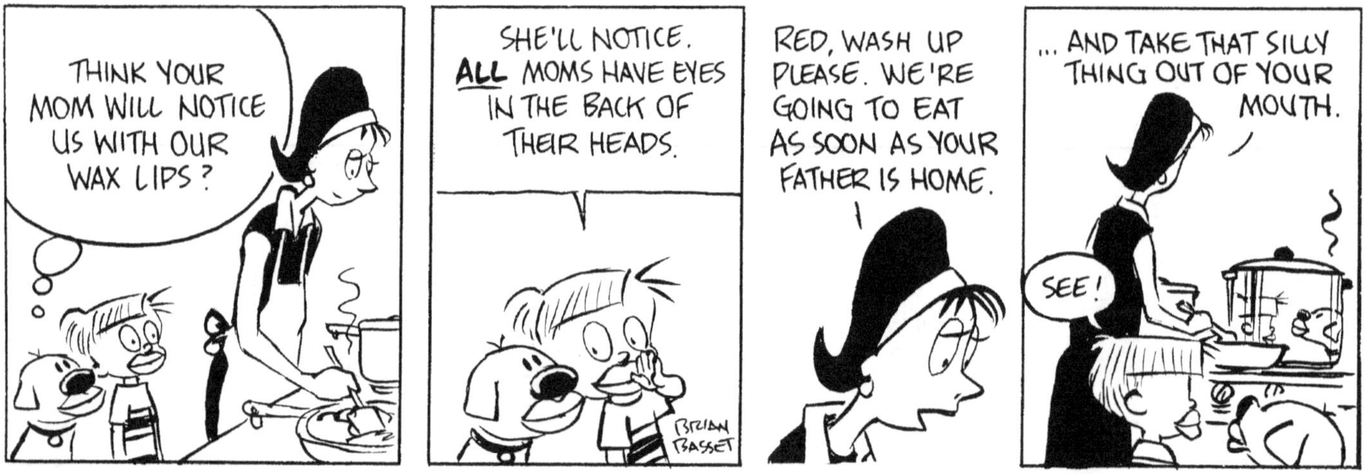
THINK YOUR MOM WILL NOTICE US WITH OUR WAX LIPS?
SHE'LL NOTICE. ALL MOMS HAVE EYES IN THE BACK OF THEIR HEADS.
BRIAN BASSET
RED, WASH UP PLEASE. WE'RE GOING TO EAT AS SOON AS YOUR FATHER IS HOME.
... AND TAKE THAT SILLY THING OUT OF YOUR MOUTH.
SEE!

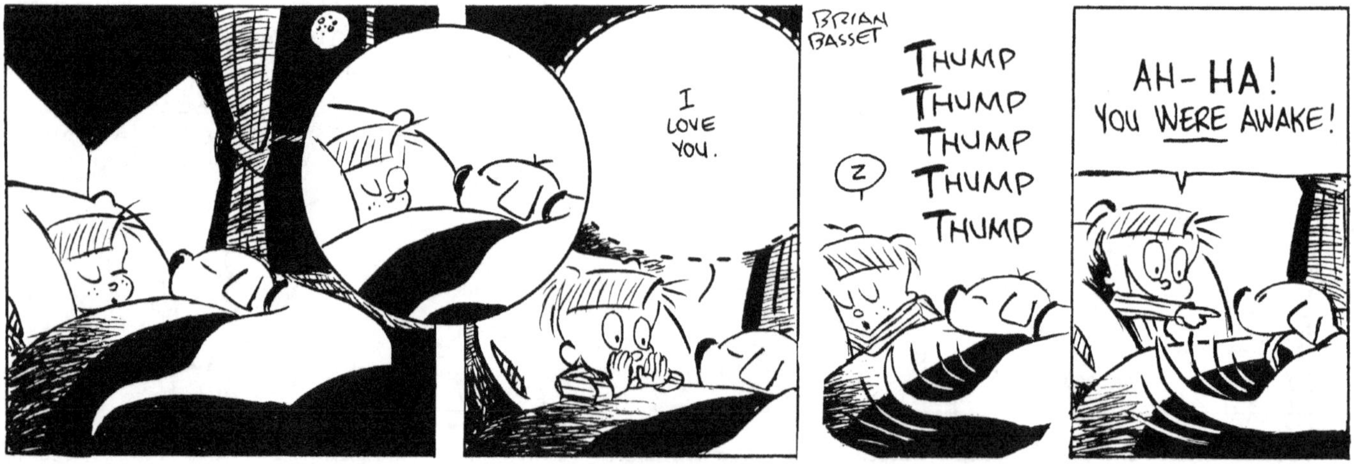
I LOVE YOU.
BRIAN BASSET
THUMP
THUMP
THUMP
THUMP
THUMP
Z
AH-HA! YOU WERE AWAKE!

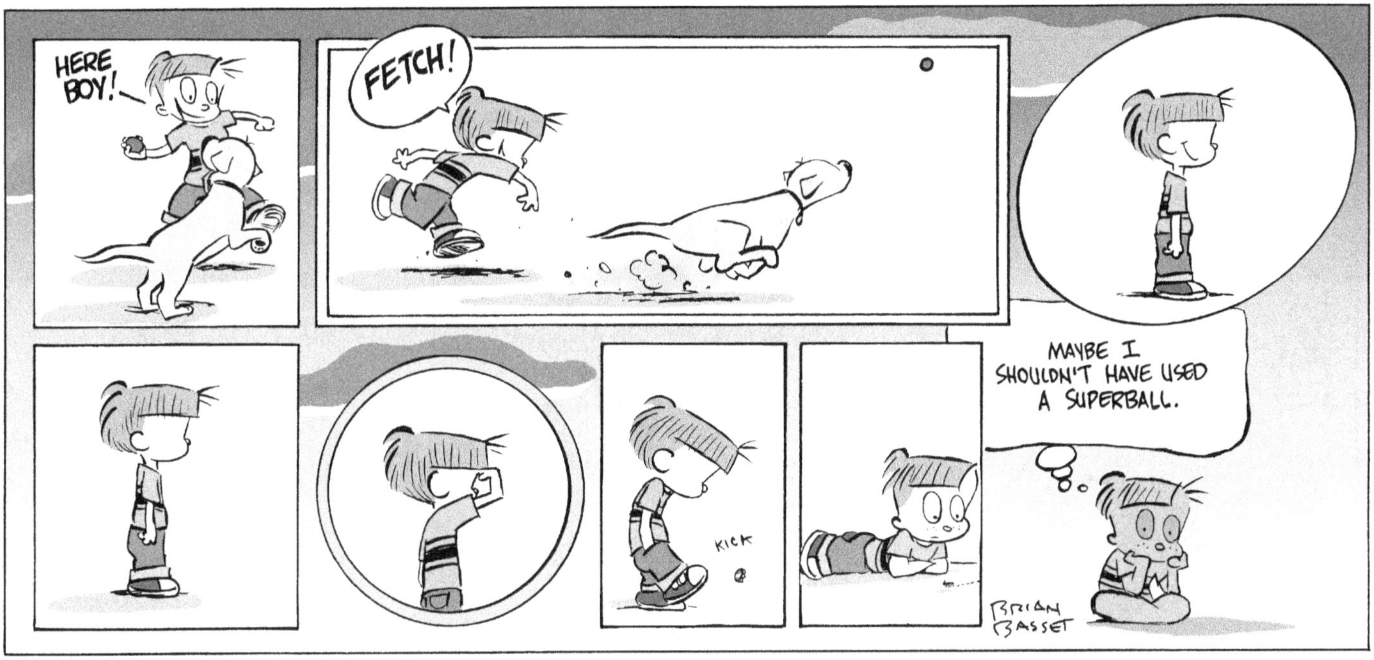

HERE BOY!
FETCH!
KICK
MAYBE I SHOULDN'T HAVE USED A SUPERBALL.
BRIAN BASSET

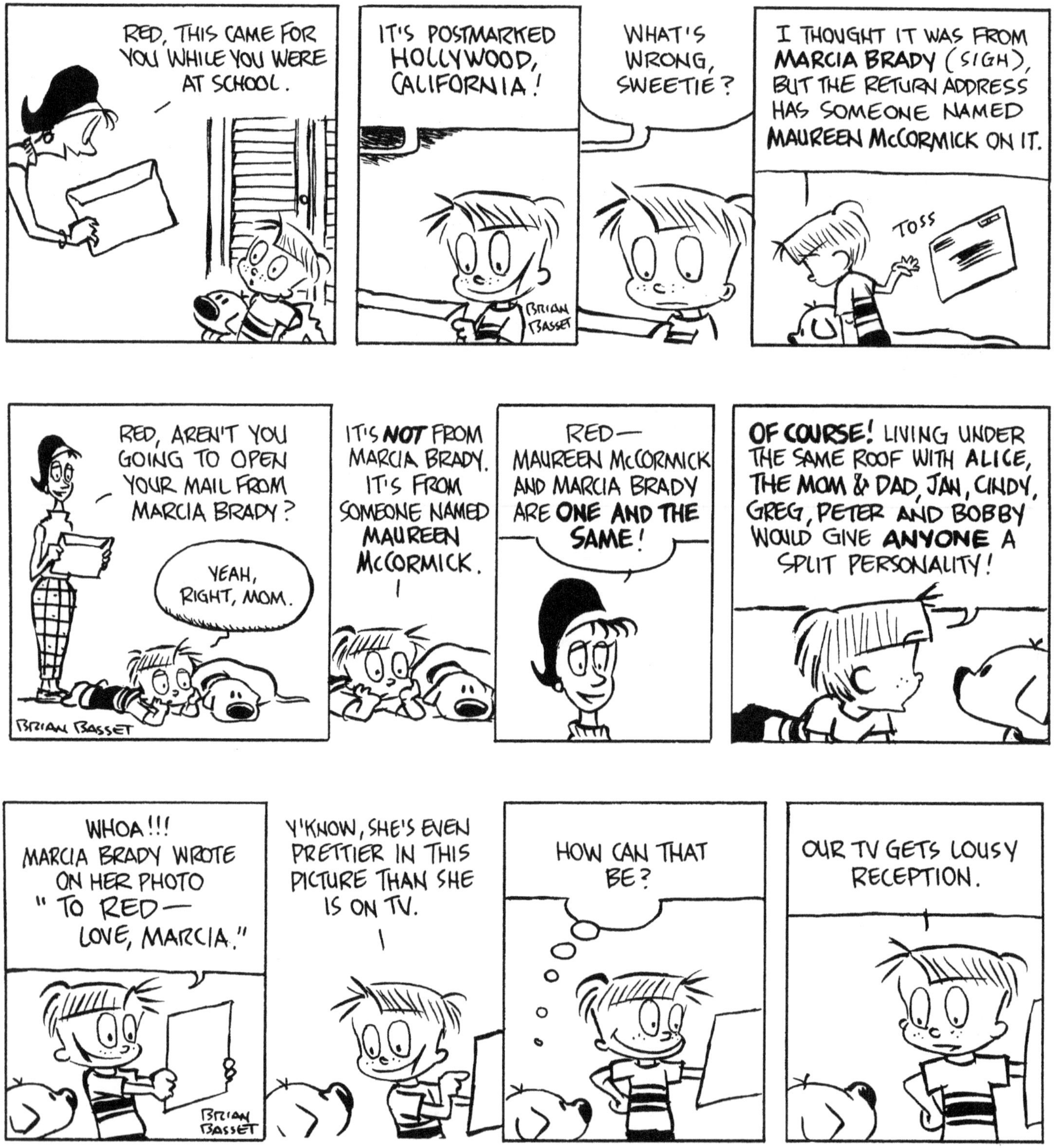
RED, THIS CAME FOR YOU WHILE YOU WERE AT SCHOOL.
IT'S POSTMARKED HOLLYWOOD, CALIFORNIA!
BRIAN BASSET
WHAT'S WRONG, SWEETIE?
I THOUGHT IT WAS FROM MARCIA BRADY (SIGH), BUT THE RETURN ADDRESS HAS SOMEONE NAMED MAUREEN McCORMICK ON IT.
TOSS
RED, AREN'T YOU GOING TO OPEN YOUR MAIL FROM MARCIA BRADY?
YEAH, RIGHT, MOM.
BRIAN BASSET
IT'S NOT FROM MARCIA BRADY. IT'S FROM SOMEONE NAMED MAUREEN McCORMICK.
RED— MAUREEN McCORMICK AND MARCIA BRADY ARE ONE AND THE SAME!
OF COURSE! LIVING UNDER THE SAME ROOF WITH ALICE, THE MOM & DAD, JAN, CINDY, GREG, PETER AND BOBBY WOULD GIVE ANYONE A SPLIT PERSONALITY!
WHOA!!! MARCIA BRADY WROTE ON HER PHOTO "TO RED— LOVE, MARCIA."
BRIAN BASSET
Y'KNOW, SHE'S EVEN PRETTIER IN THIS PICTURE THAN SHE IS ON TV.
HOW CAN THAT BE?
OUR TV GETS LOUSY RECEPTION.

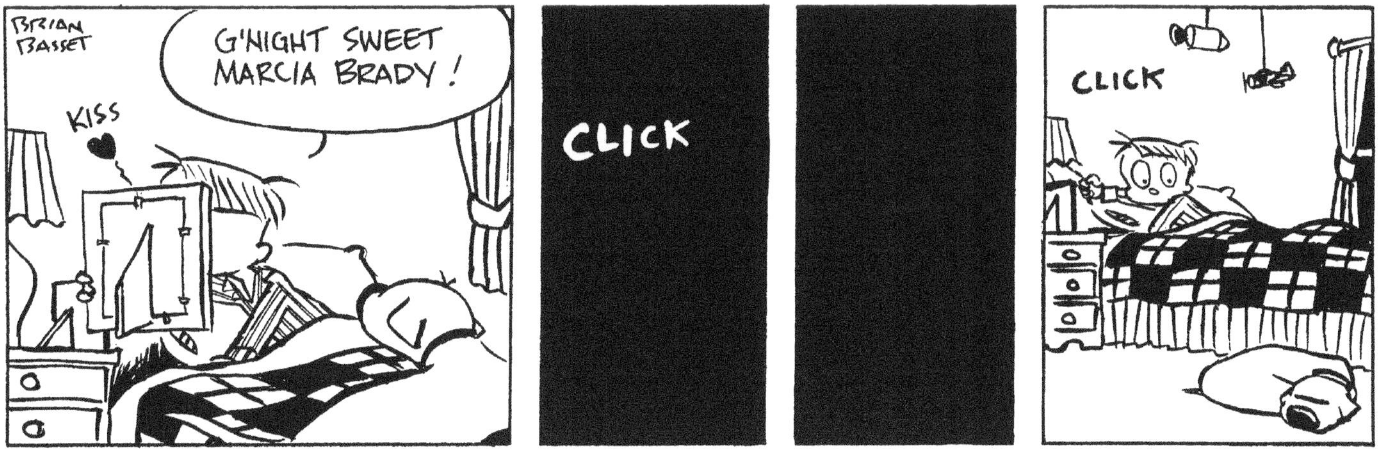
BRIAN BASSET
G'NIGHT SWEET MARCIA BRADY!
KISS
CLICK
CLICK

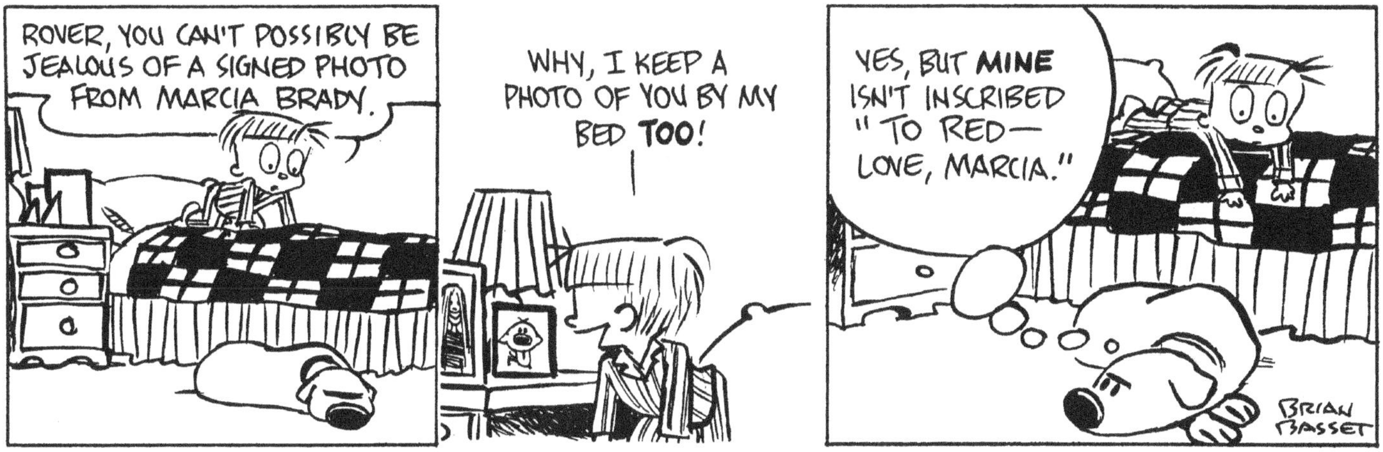
ROVER, YOU CAN'T POSSIBLY BE JEALOUS OF A SIGNED PHOTO FROM MARCIA BRADY.
WHY, I KEEP A PHOTO OF YOU BY MY BED **TOO**!
YES, BUT **MINE** ISN'T INSCRIBED "TO RED— LOVE, MARCIA."
BRIAN BASSET

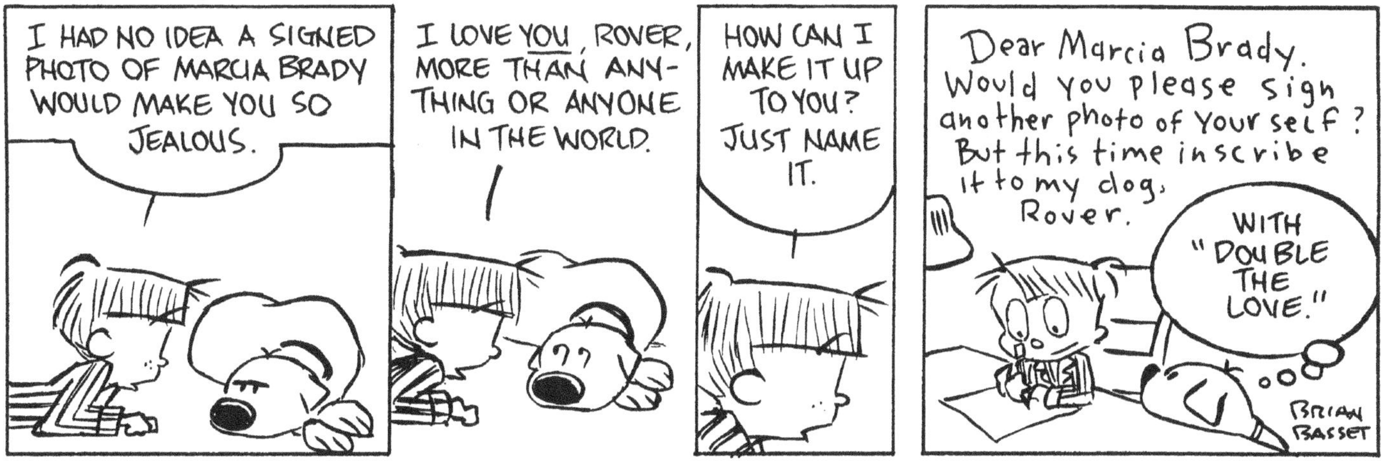
I HAD NO IDEA A SIGNED PHOTO OF MARCIA BRADY WOULD MAKE YOU SO JEALOUS.
I LOVE YOU, ROVER, MORE THAN ANYTHING OR ANYONE IN THE WORLD.
HOW CAN I MAKE IT UP TO YOU? JUST NAME IT.
Dear Marcia Brady. Would you please sign another photo of yourself? But this time inscribe it to my dog, Rover.
WITH "DOUBLE THE LOVE."
BRIAN BASSET

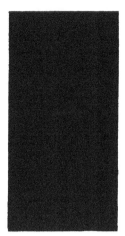

PANT
PANT
PANT
PANT
PANT

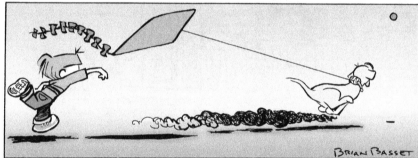

BRIAN BASSET

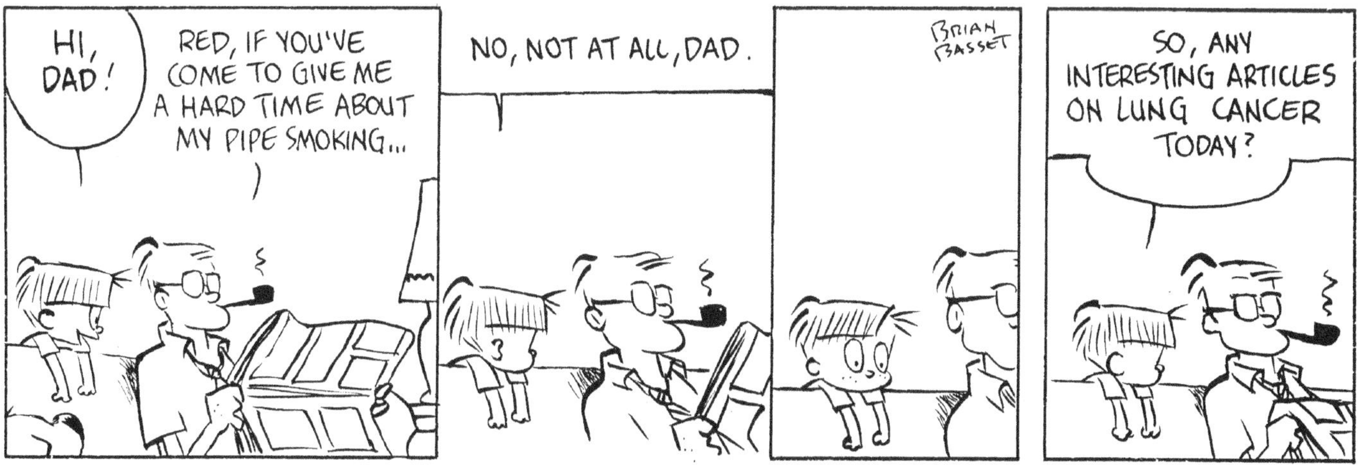
HI, DAD!
RED, IF YOU'VE COME TO GIVE ME A HARD TIME ABOUT MY PIPE SMOKING...
NO, NOT AT ALL, DAD.
BRIAN BASSET
SO, ANY INTERESTING ARTICLES ON LUNG CANCER TODAY?

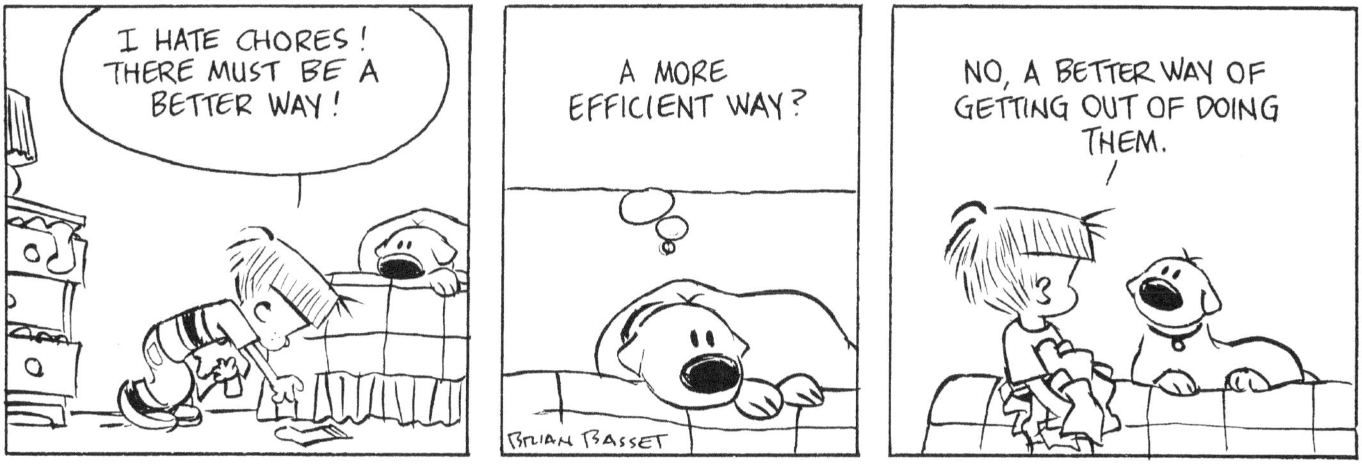
I HATE CHORES! THERE MUST BE A BETTER WAY!
A MORE EFFICIENT WAY?
BRIAN BASSET
NO, A BETTER WAY OF GETTING OUT OF DOING THEM.

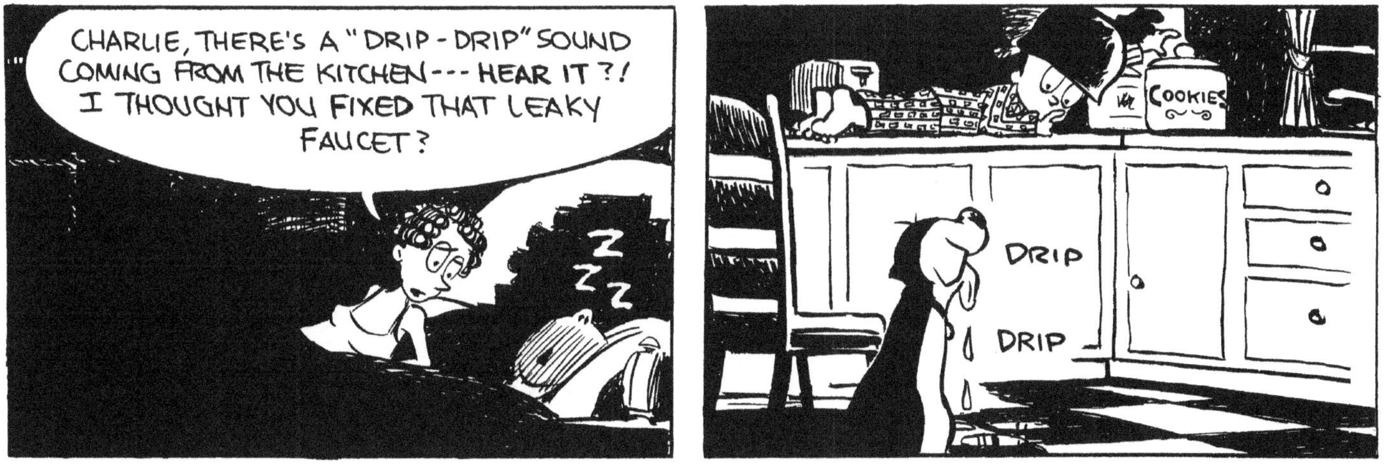
CHARLIE, THERE'S A "DRIP-DRIP" SOUND COMING FROM THE KITCHEN--- HEAR IT?! I THOUGHT YOU FIXED THAT LEAKY FAUCET?
Z
Z
Z
COOKIES
DRIP
DRIP

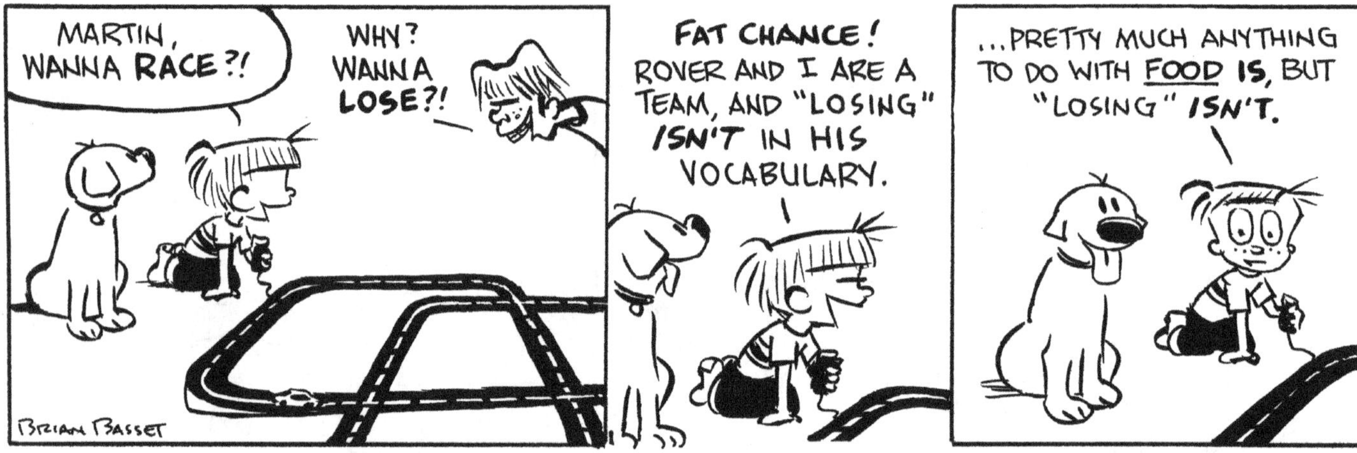
MARTIN, WANNA RACE?!
WHY? WANNA LOSE?!
BRIAN BASSET
FAT CHANCE! ROVER AND I ARE A TEAM, AND "LOSING" ISN'T IN HIS VOCABULARY.
...PRETTY MUCH ANYTHING TO DO WITH FOOD IS, BUT "LOSING" ISN'T.

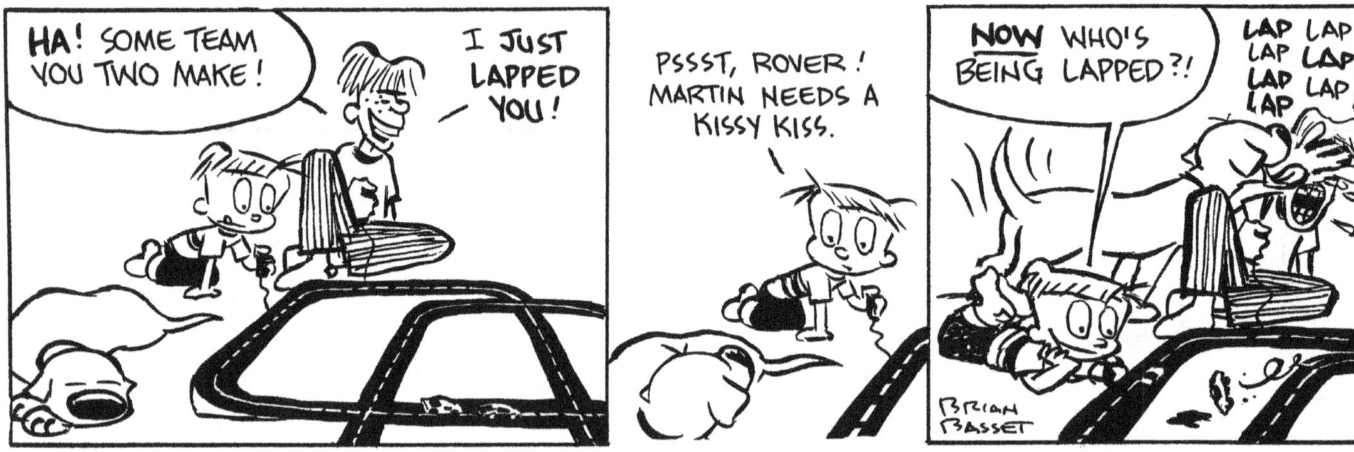
HA! SOME TEAM YOU TWO MAKE!
I JUST LAPPED YOU!
PSSST, ROVER! MARTIN NEEDS A KISSY KISS.
NOW WHO'S BEING LAPPED?!
LAP LAP LAP LAP LAP LAP LAP LAP LAP
BRIAN BASSET

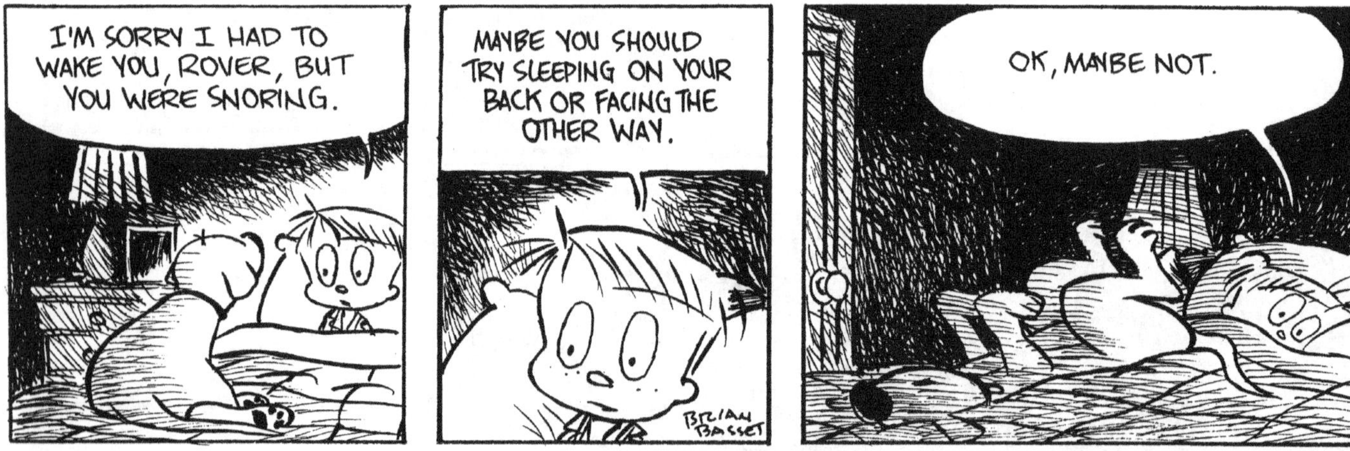
I'M SORRY I HAD TO WAKE YOU, ROVER, BUT YOU WERE SNORING.
MAYBE YOU SHOULD TRY SLEEPING ON YOUR BACK OR FACING THE OTHER WAY.
BRIAN BASSET
OK, MAYBE NOT.

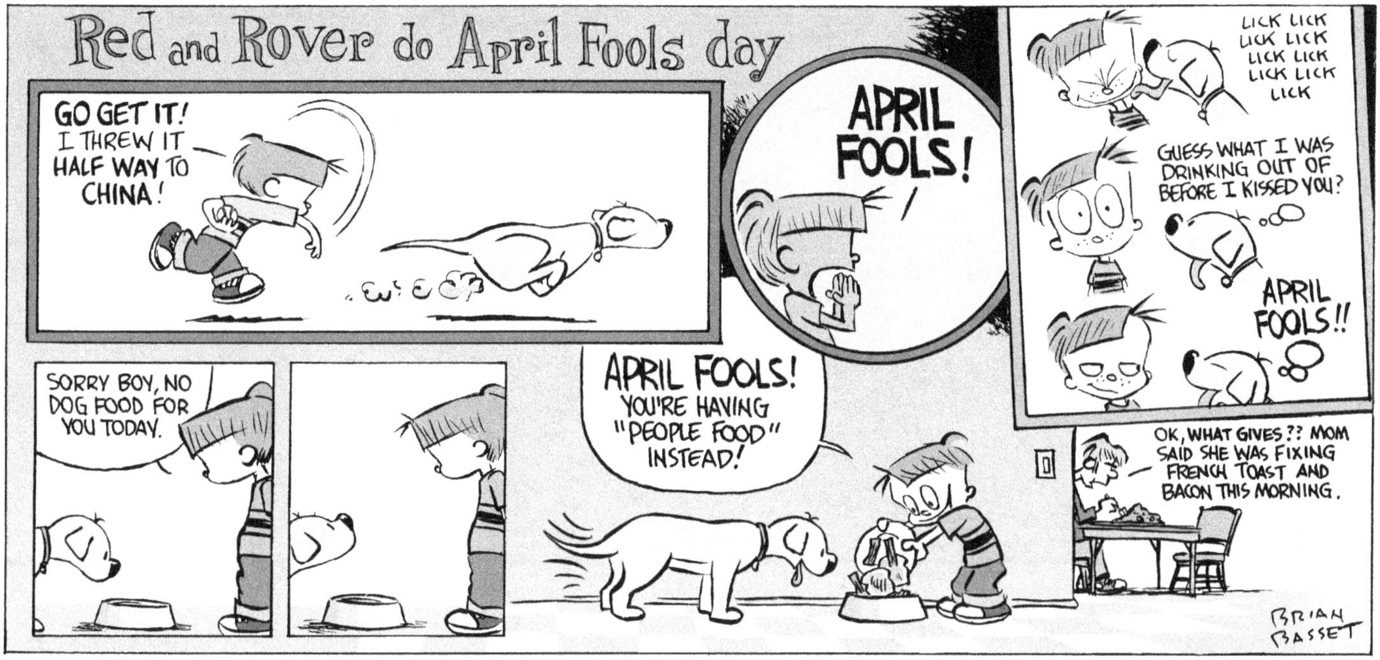
Red and Rover do April Fools day
GO GET IT! I THREW IT HALF WAY TO CHINA!
APRIL FOOLS!
LICK LICK LICK LICK LICK LICK LICK LICK LICK
GUESS WHAT I WAS DRINKING OUT OF BEFORE I KISSED YOU?
APRIL FOOLS!!
SORRY BOY, NO DOG FOOD FOR YOU TODAY.
APRIL FOOLS! YOU'RE HAVING "PEOPLE FOOD" INSTEAD!
OK, WHAT GIVES?? MOM SAID SHE WAS FIXING FRENCH TOAST AND BACON THIS MORNING.
BRIAN BASSET

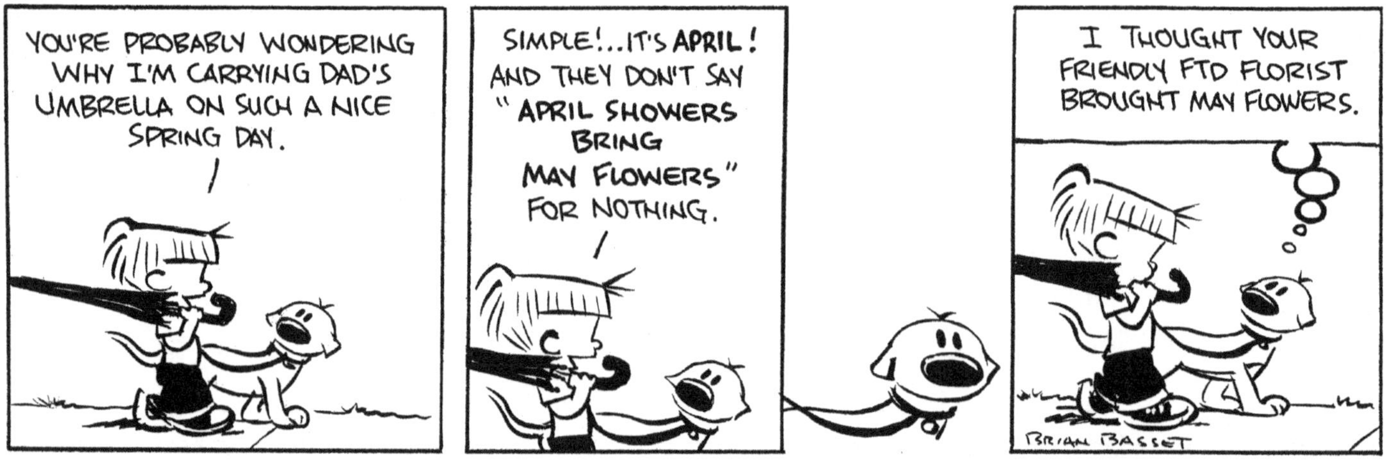
YOU'RE PROBABLY WONDERING WHY I'M CARRYING DAD'S UMBRELLA ON SUCH A NICE SPRING DAY.
SIMPLE!...IT'S APRIL! AND THEY DON'T SAY "APRIL SHOWERS BRING MAY FLOWERS" FOR NOTHING.
I THOUGHT YOUR FRIENDLY FTD FLORIST BROUGHT MAY FLOWERS.
BRIAN BASSET

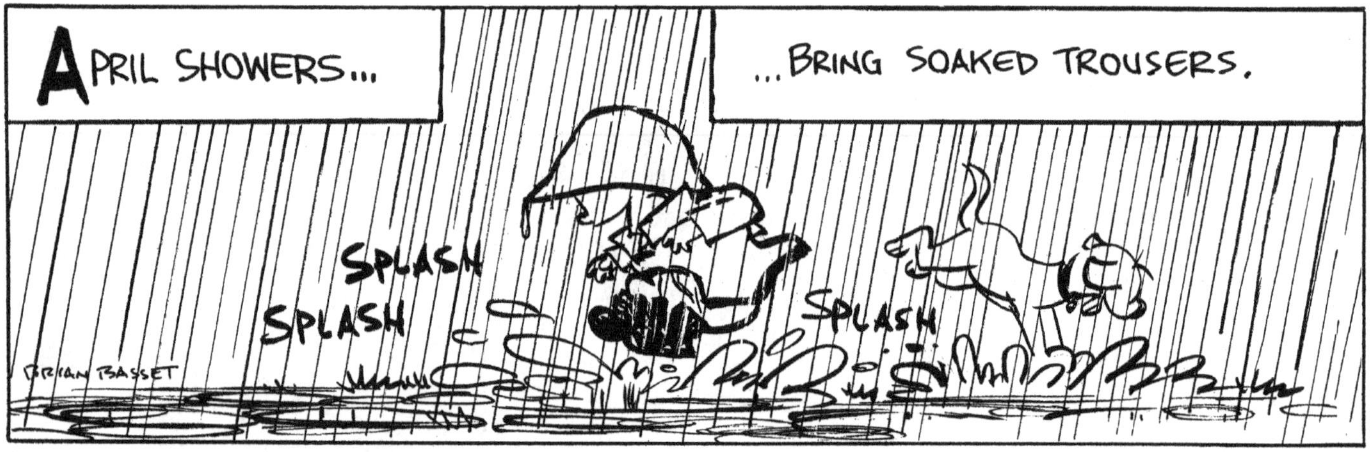
APRIL SHOWERS...
...BRING SOAKED TROUSERS.
SPLASH
SPLASH
SPLASH
BRIAN BASSET

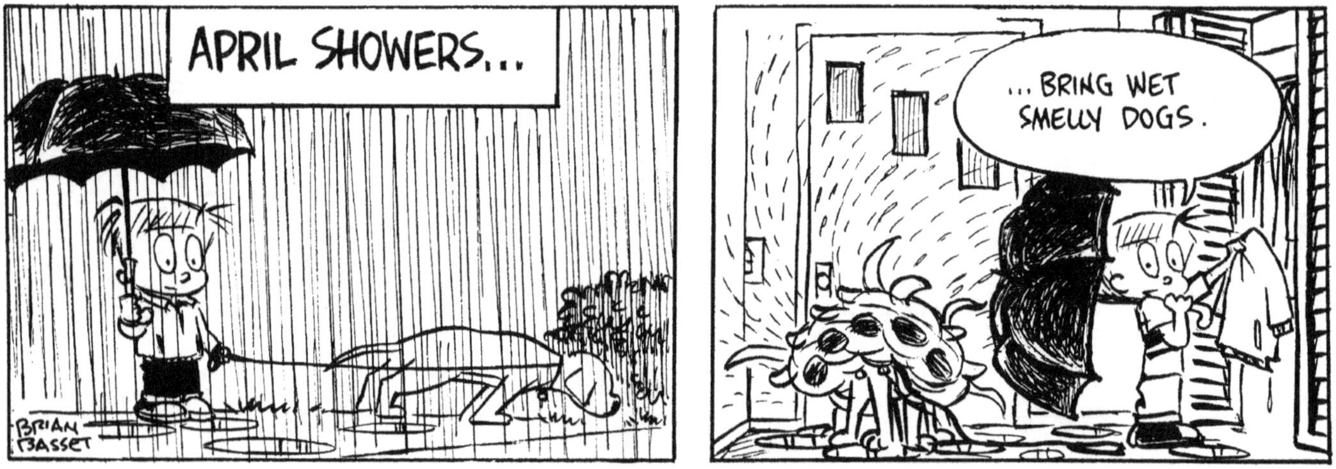
APRIL SHOWERS...
BRIAN BASSET
...BRING WET SMELLY DOGS.

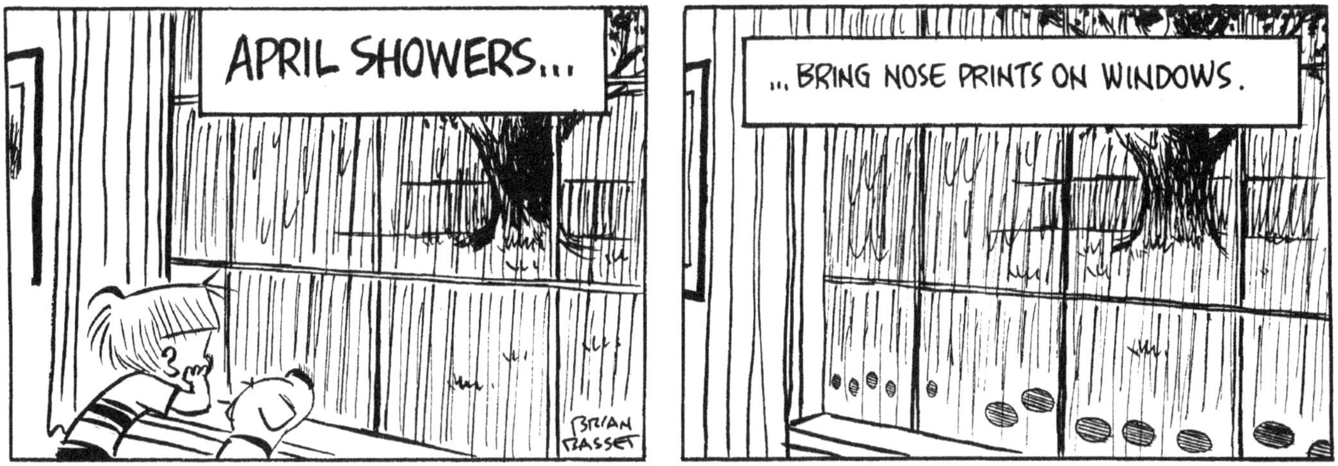
APRIL SHOWERS...
BRIAN BASSET
... BRING NOSE PRINTS ON WINDOWS.

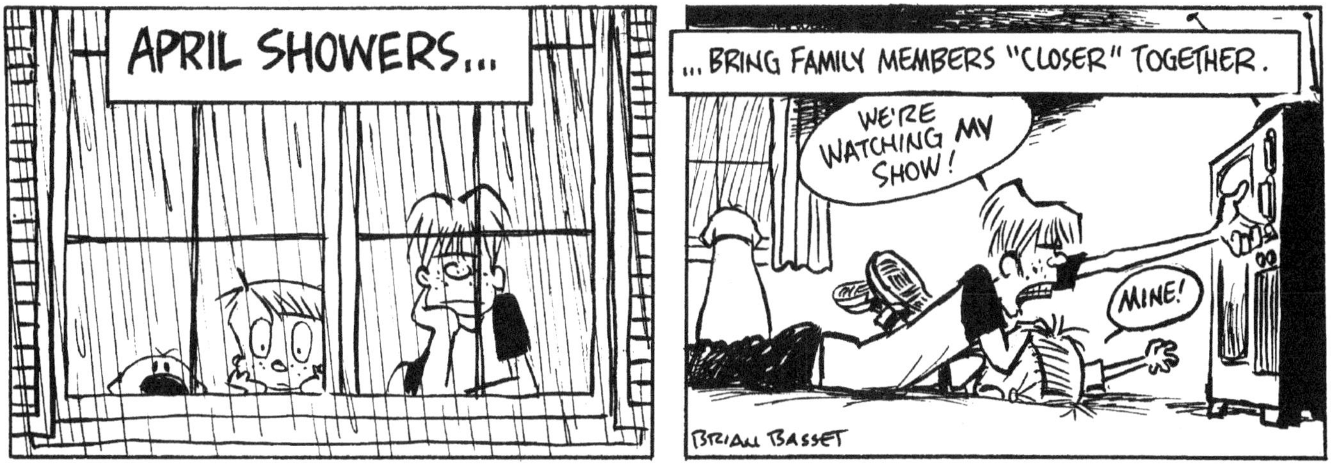
APRIL SHOWERS...
... BRING FAMILY MEMBERS "CLOSER" TOGETHER.
WE'RE WATCHING MY SHOW!
MINE!
BRIAN BASSET

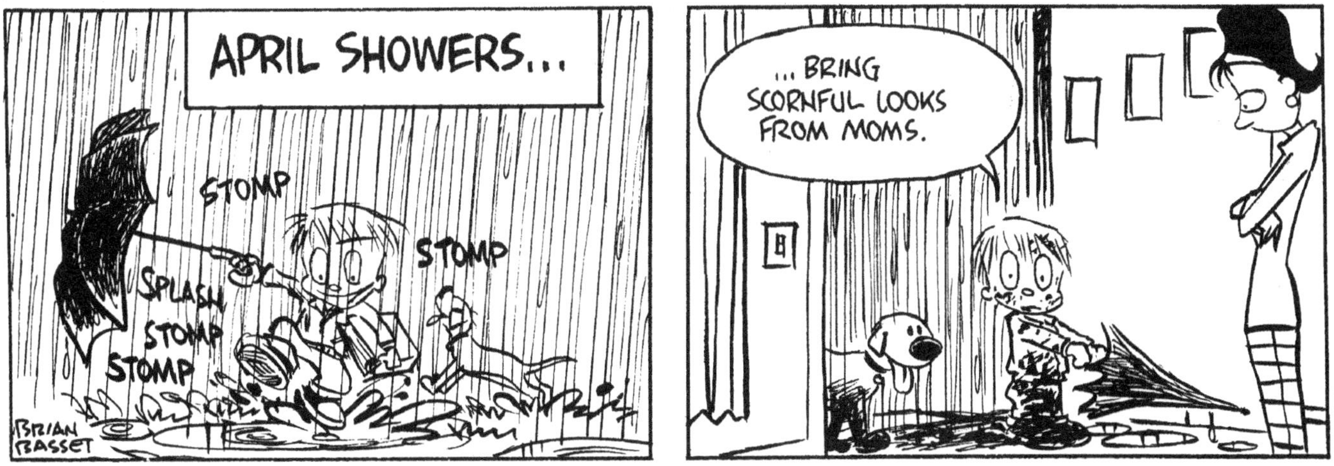
APRIL SHOWERS...
STOMP
STOMP
SPLASH
STOMP
STOMP
BRIAN BASSET
... BRING SCORNFUL LOOKS FROM MOMS.

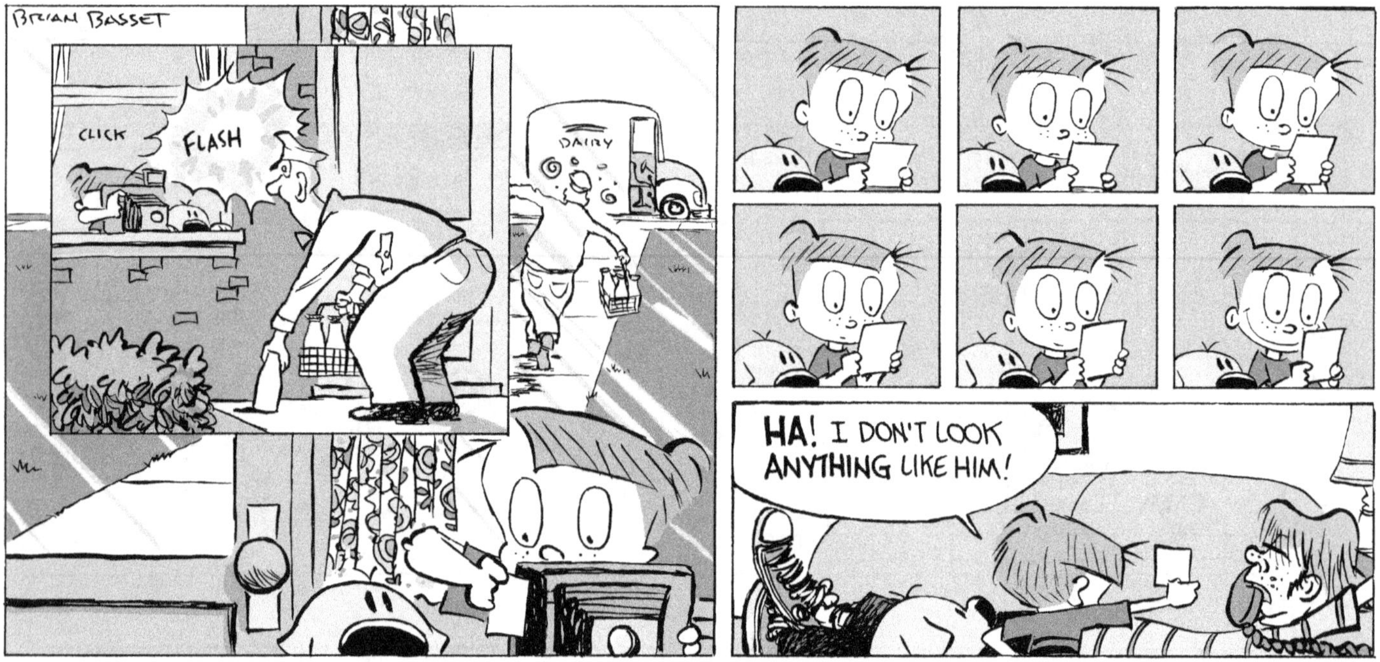
BRIAN BASSET
CLICK
FLASH
DAIRY
HA! I DON'T LOOK ANYTHING LIKE HIM!

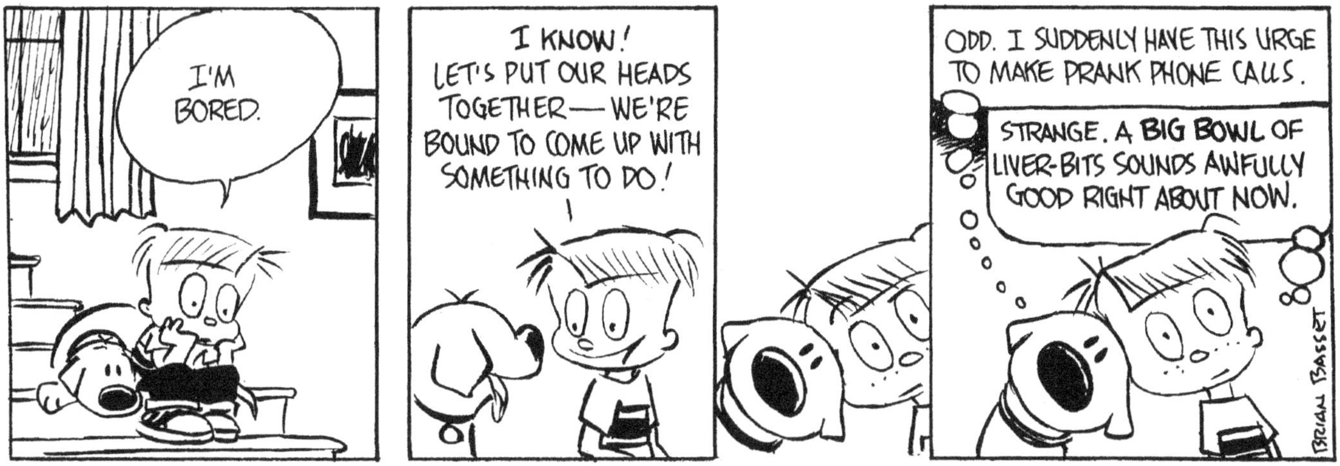
I'M BORED.
I KNOW! LET'S PUT OUR HEADS TOGETHER— WE'RE BOUND TO COME UP WITH SOMETHING TO DO!
ODD. I SUDDENLY HAVE THIS URGE TO MAKE PRANK PHONE CALLS.
STRANGE. A BIG BOWL OF LIVER-BITS SOUNDS AWFULLY GOOD RIGHT ABOUT NOW.
BRIAN BASSET

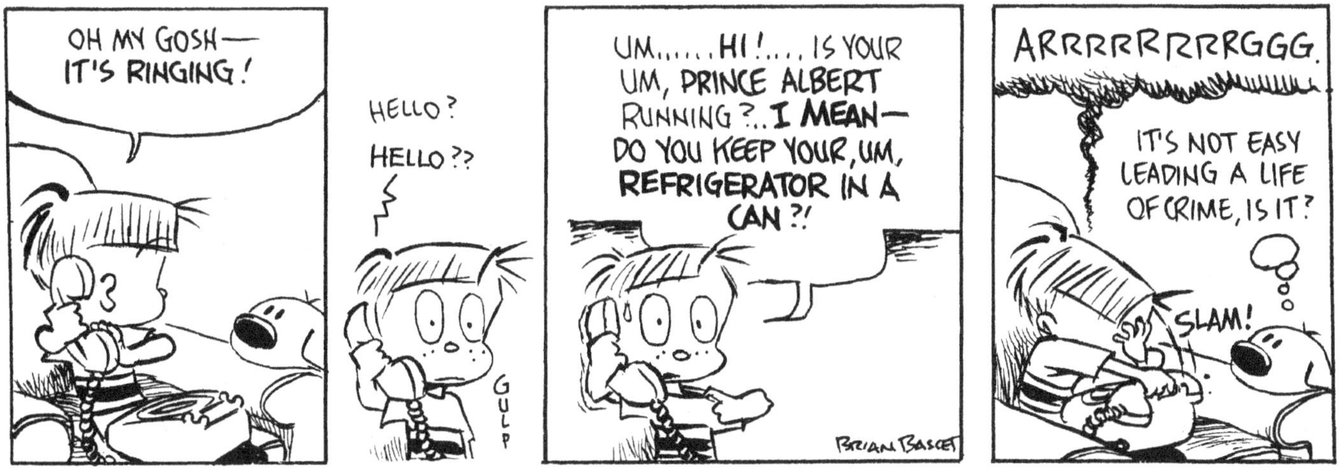
OH MY GOSH— IT'S RINGING!
HELLO?
HELLO??
GULP
UM......HI!.... IS YOUR UM, PRINCE ALBERT RUNNING?.. I MEAN— DO YOU KEEP YOUR, UM, REFRIGERATOR IN A CAN?!
BRIAN BASSET
ARRRRRRRRGGG.
IT'S NOT EASY LEADING A LIFE OF CRIME, IS IT?
SLAM!

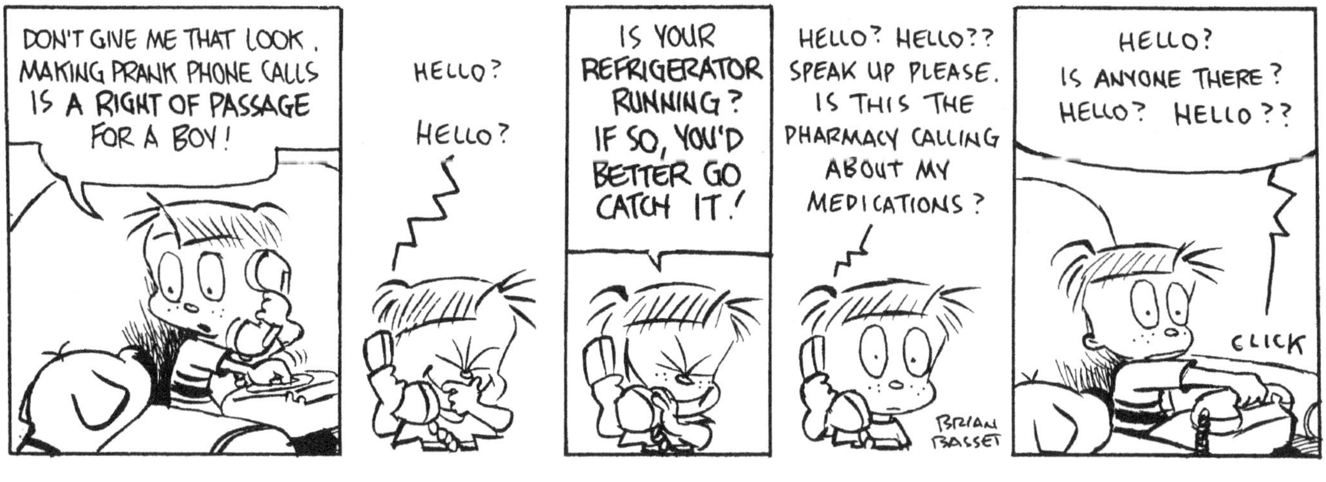
DON'T GIVE ME THAT LOOK. MAKING PRANK PHONE CALLS IS A RIGHT OF PASSAGE FOR A BOY!
HELLO?
HELLO?
IS YOUR REFRIGERATOR RUNNING? IF SO, YOU'D BETTER GO CATCH IT!
HELLO? HELLO?? SPEAK UP PLEASE. IS THIS THE PHARMACY CALLING ABOUT MY MEDICATIONS?
BRIAN BASSET
HELLO? IS ANYONE THERE? HELLO? HELLO??
CLICK

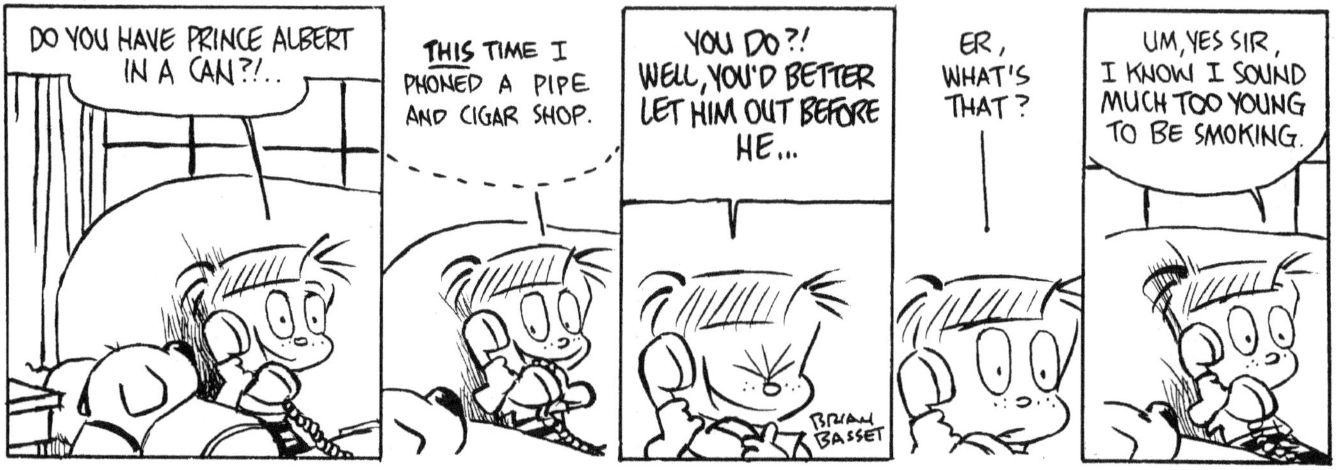
DO YOU HAVE PRINCE ALBERT IN A CAN?!..
THIS TIME I PHONED A PIPE AND CIGAR SHOP.
YOU DO?! WELL, YOU'D BETTER LET HIM OUT BEFORE HE...
BRIAN BASSET
ER, WHAT'S THAT?
UM, YES SIR, I KNOW I SOUND MUCH TOO YOUNG TO BE SMOKING.

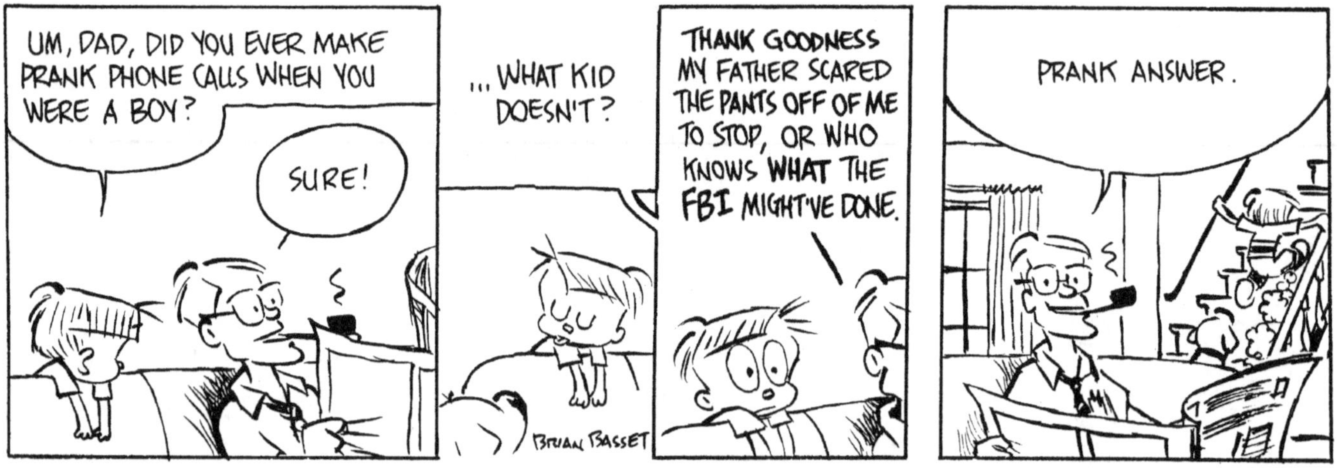
UM, DAD, DID YOU EVER MAKE PRANK PHONE CALLS WHEN YOU WERE A BOY?
SURE!
... WHAT KID DOESN'T?
BRIAN BASSET
THANK GOODNESS MY FATHER SCARED THE PANTS OFF OF ME TO STOP, OR WHO KNOWS WHAT THE FBI MIGHT'VE DONE.
PRANK ANSWER.

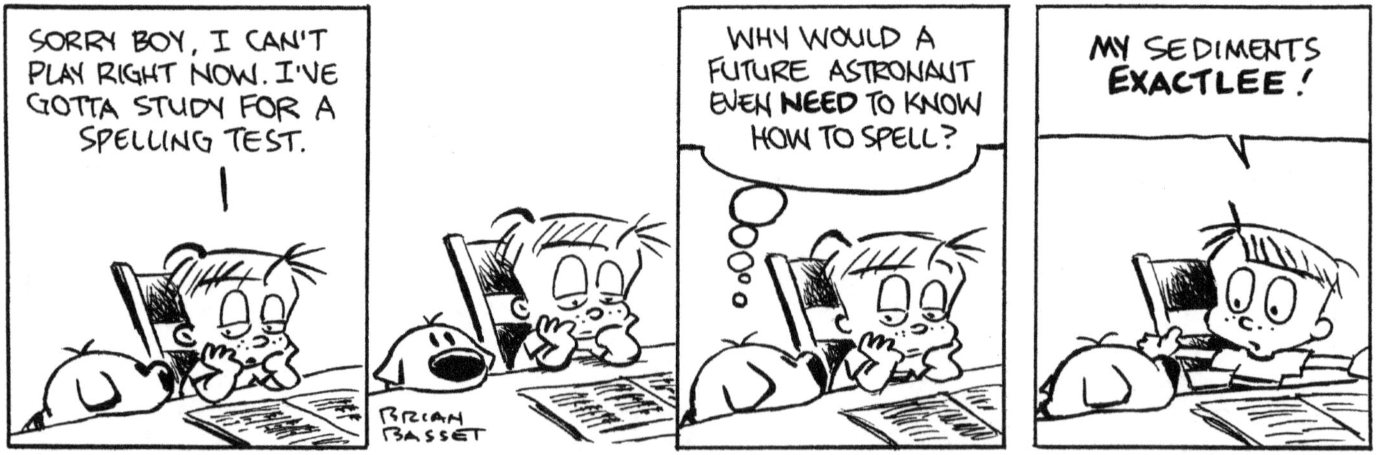
SORRY BOY, I CAN'T PLAY RIGHT NOW. I'VE GOTTA STUDY FOR A SPELLING TEST.
BRIAN BASSET
WHY WOULD A FUTURE ASTRONAUT EVEN NEED TO KNOW HOW TO SPELL?
MY SEDIMENTS EXACTLEE!

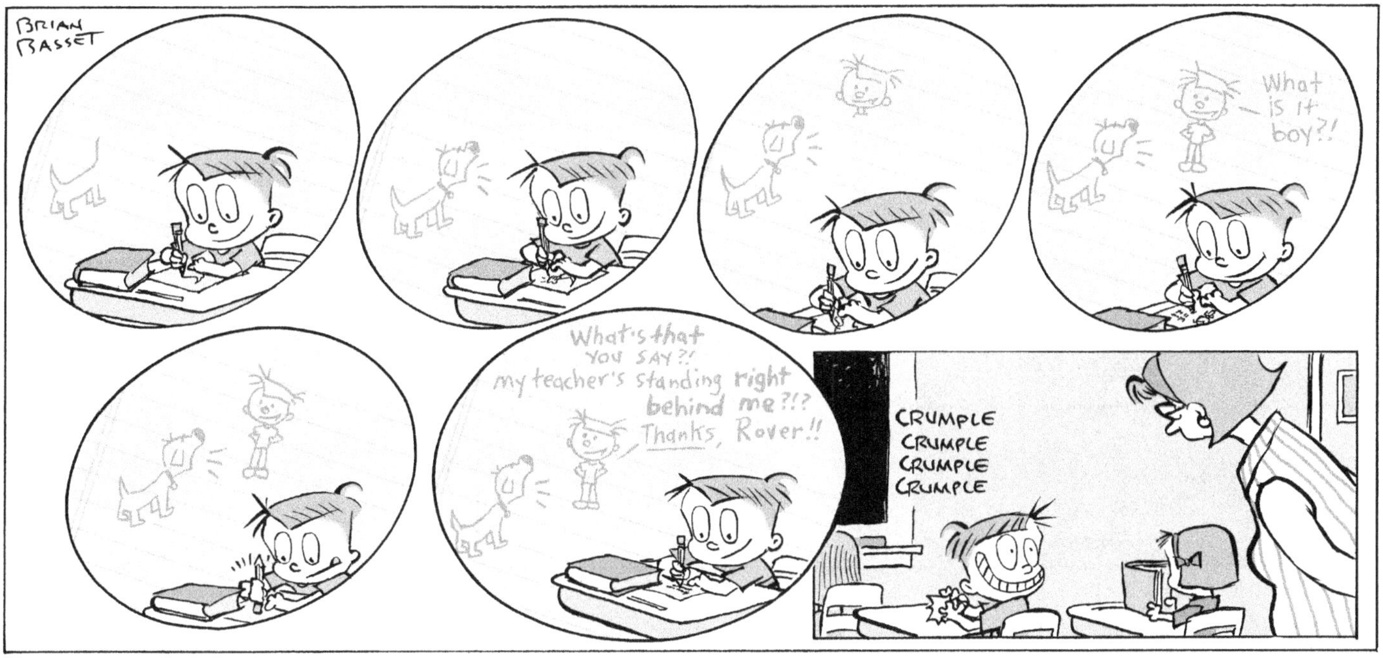
BRIAN BASSET
What is it boy?!
What's that YOU SAY?!
my teacher's standing right behind me?!?
Thanks, Rover!!
CRUMPLE
CRUMPLE
CRUMPLE
CRUMPLE

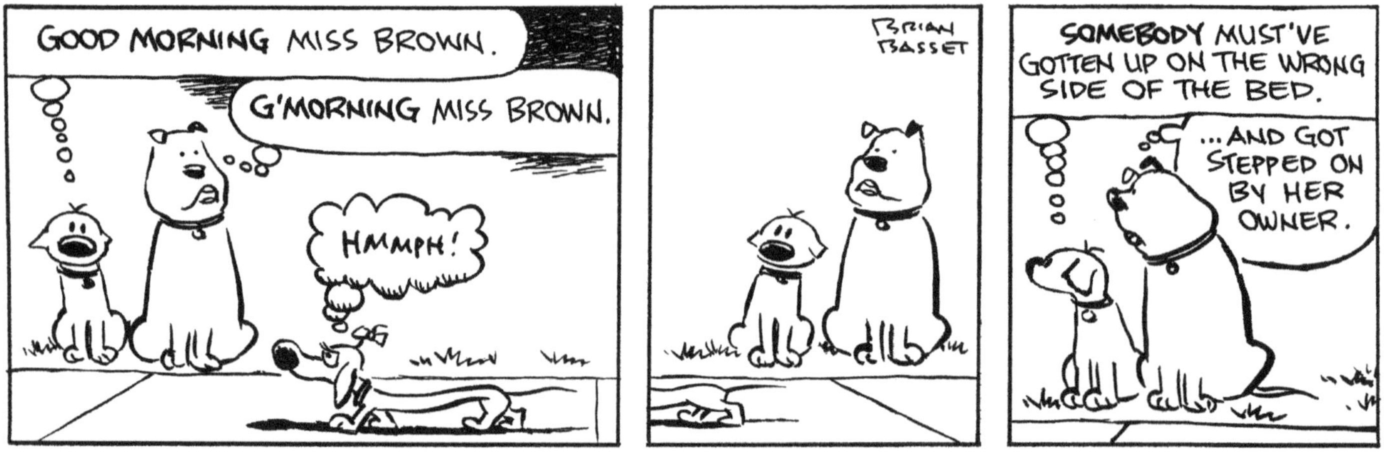
GOOD MORNING MISS BROWN.
G'MORNING MISS BROWN.
HMMPH!
BRIAN BASSET
SOMEBODY MUST'VE GOTTEN UP ON THE WRONG SIDE OF THE BED.
...AND GOT STEPPED ON BY HER OWNER.

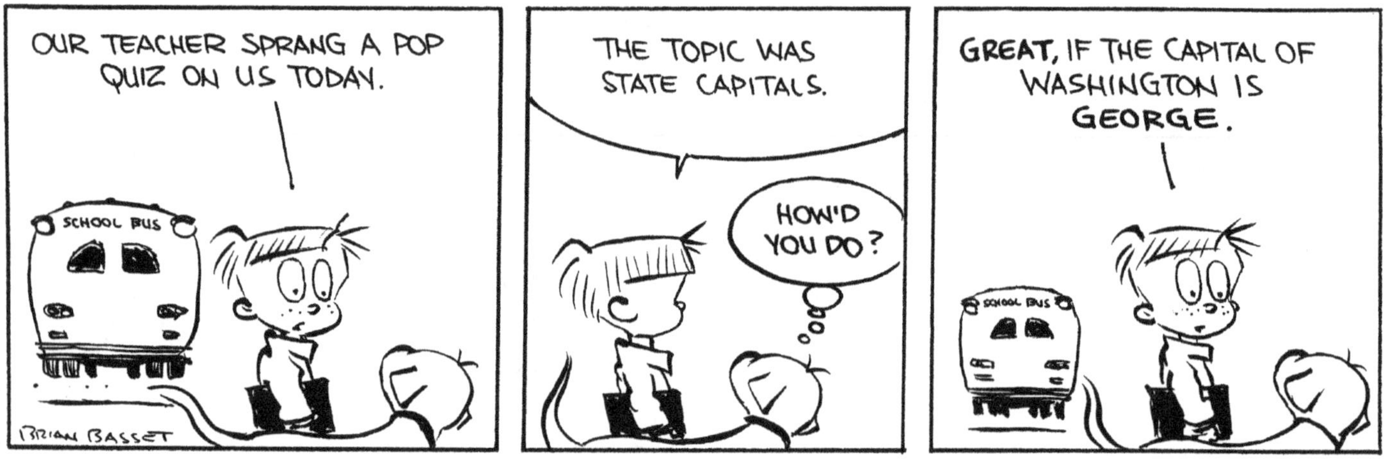
OUR TEACHER SPRANG A POP QUIZ ON US TODAY.
SCHOOL BUS
BRIAN BASSET
THE TOPIC WAS STATE CAPITALS.
HOW'D YOU DO?
GREAT, IF THE CAPITAL OF WASHINGTON IS GEORGE.
SCHOOL BUS

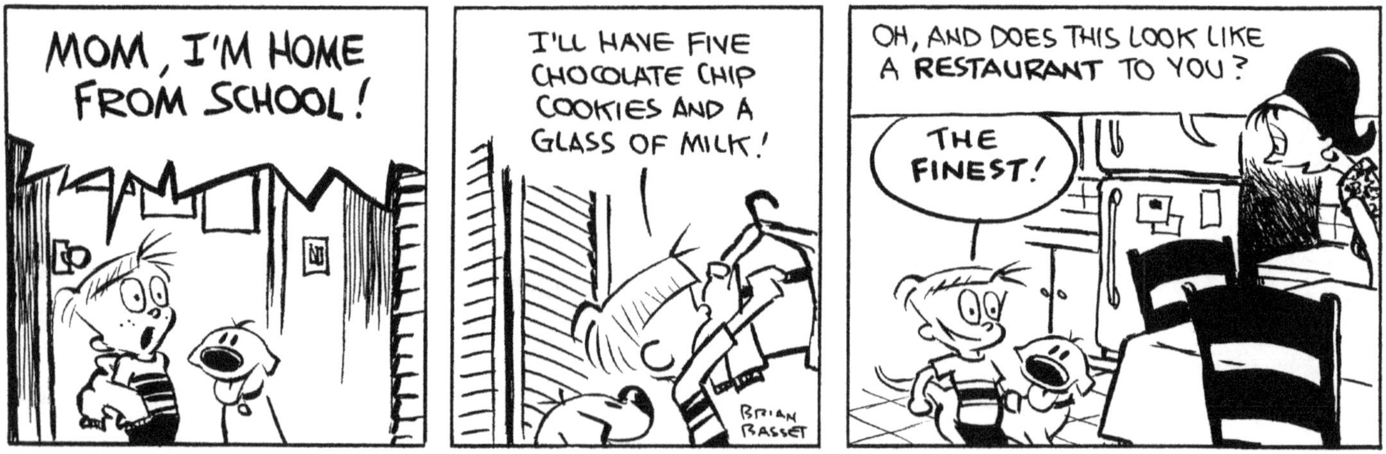
MOM, I'M HOME FROM SCHOOL!
I'LL HAVE FIVE CHOCOLATE CHIP COOKIES AND A GLASS OF MILK!
BRIAN BASSET
OH, AND DOES THIS LOOK LIKE A RESTAURANT TO YOU?
THE FINEST!

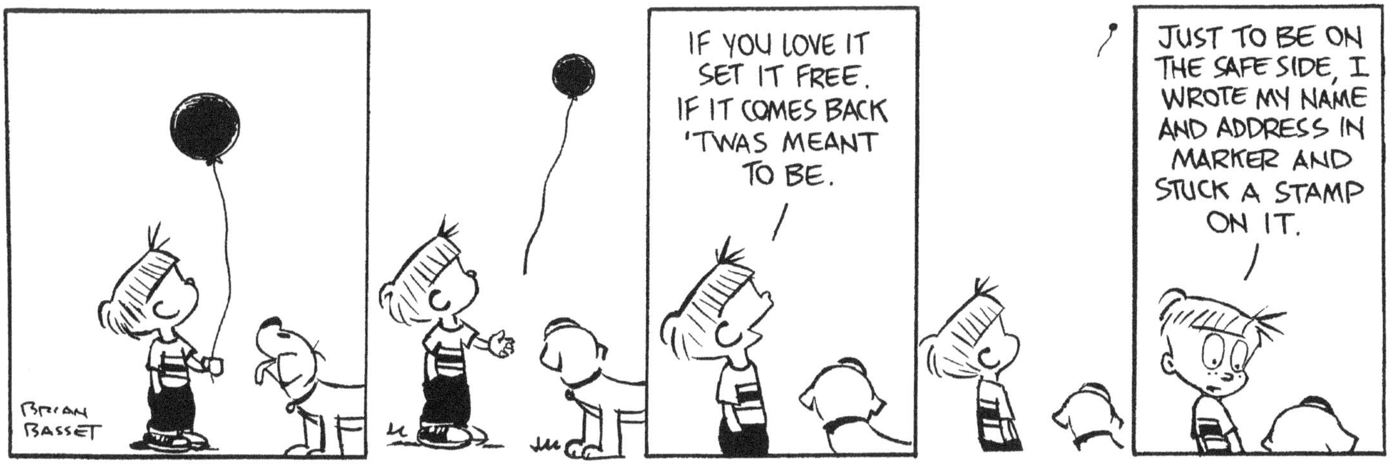
BRIAN BASSET
IF YOU LOVE IT SET IT FREE. IF IT COMES BACK 'TWAS MEANT TO BE.
JUST TO BE ON THE SAFE SIDE, I WROTE MY NAME AND ADDRESS IN MARKER AND STUCK A STAMP ON IT.

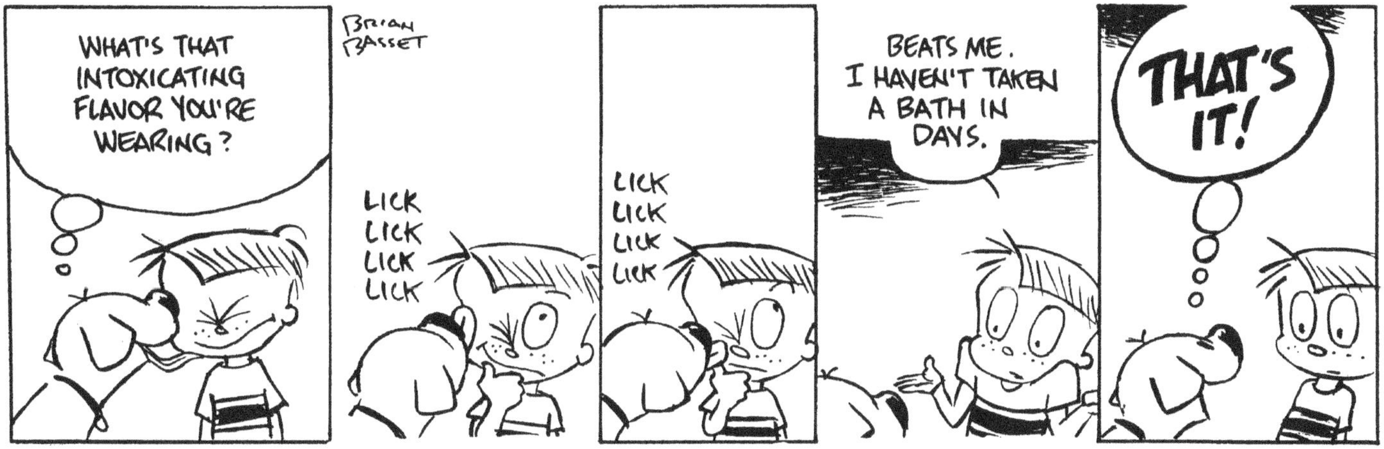
WHAT'S THAT INTOXICATING FLAVOR YOU'RE WEARING?
BRIAN BASSET
LICK LICK LICK LICK
LICK LICK LICK LICK
BEATS ME. I HAVEN'T TAKEN A BATH IN DAYS.
THAT'S IT!

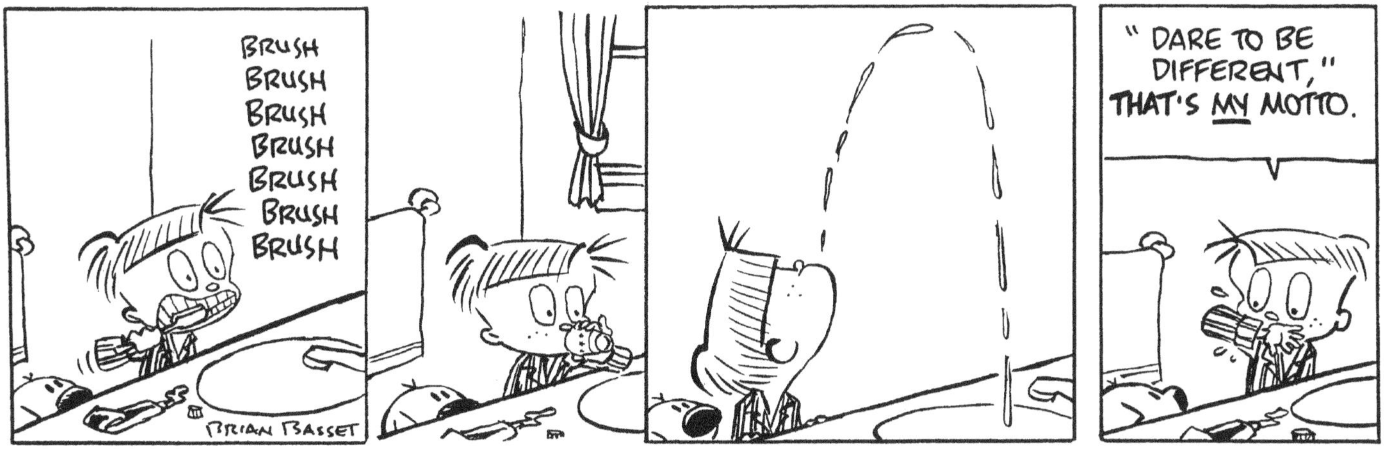
BRUSH BRUSH BRUSH BRUSH BRUSH BRUSH BRUSH
BRIAN BASSET
"DARE TO BE DIFFERENT," THAT'S MY MOTTO.

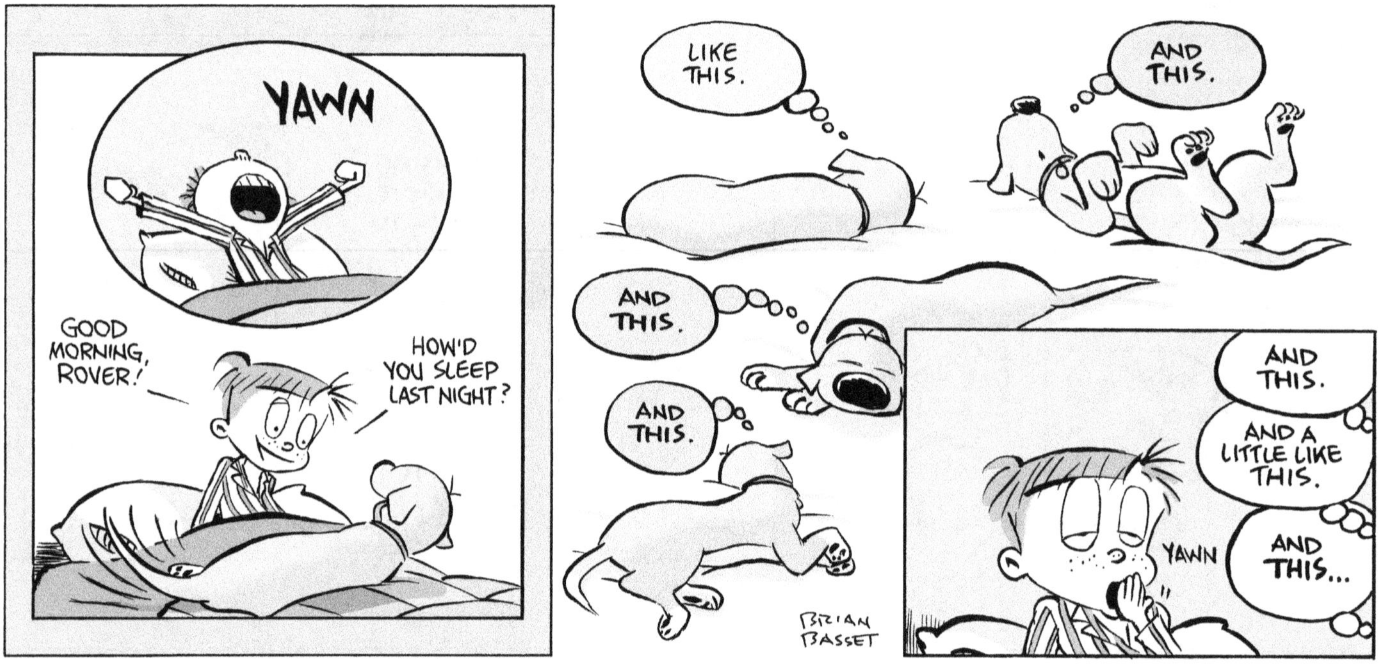
YAWN
GOOD MORNING, ROVER!
HOW'D YOU SLEEP LAST NIGHT?
LIKE THIS.
AND THIS.
AND THIS.
AND THIS.
AND THIS.
AND A LITTLE LIKE THIS.
YAWN
AND THIS...
BRIAN BASSET

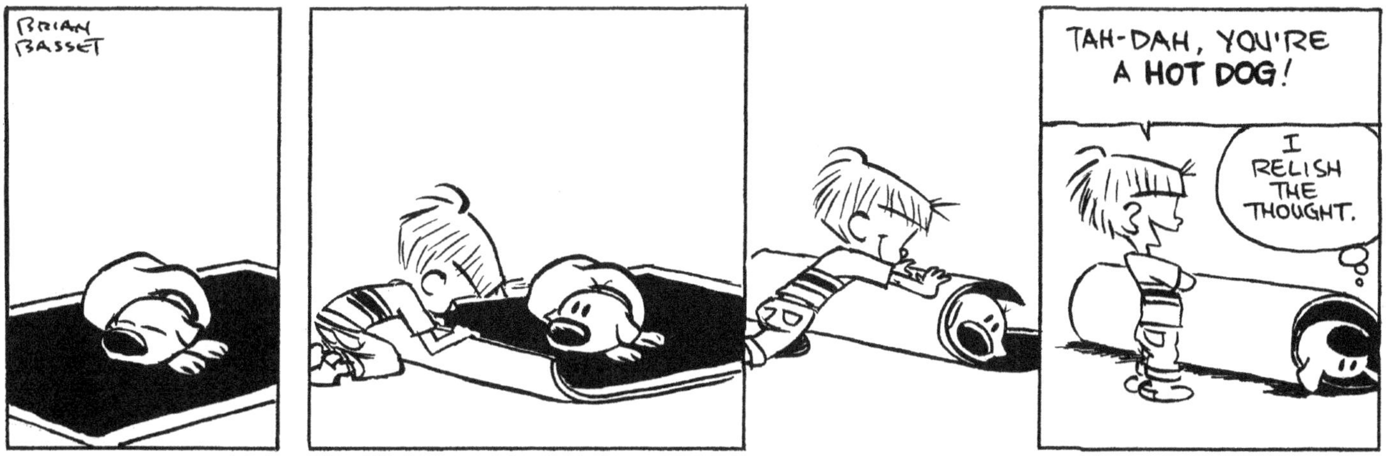
BRIAN BASSET
TAH-DAH, YOU'RE A **HOT DOG**!
I RELISH THE THOUGHT.

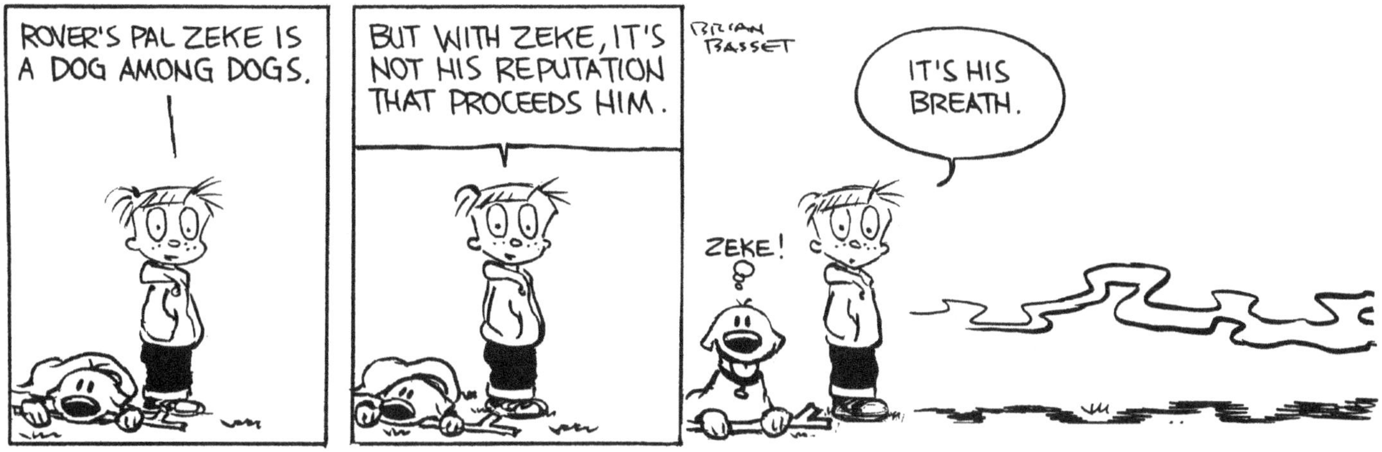
ROVER'S PAL ZEKE IS A DOG AMONG DOGS.
BUT WITH ZEKE, IT'S NOT HIS REPUTATION THAT PROCEEDS HIM.
BRIAN BASSET
IT'S HIS BREATH.
ZEKE!

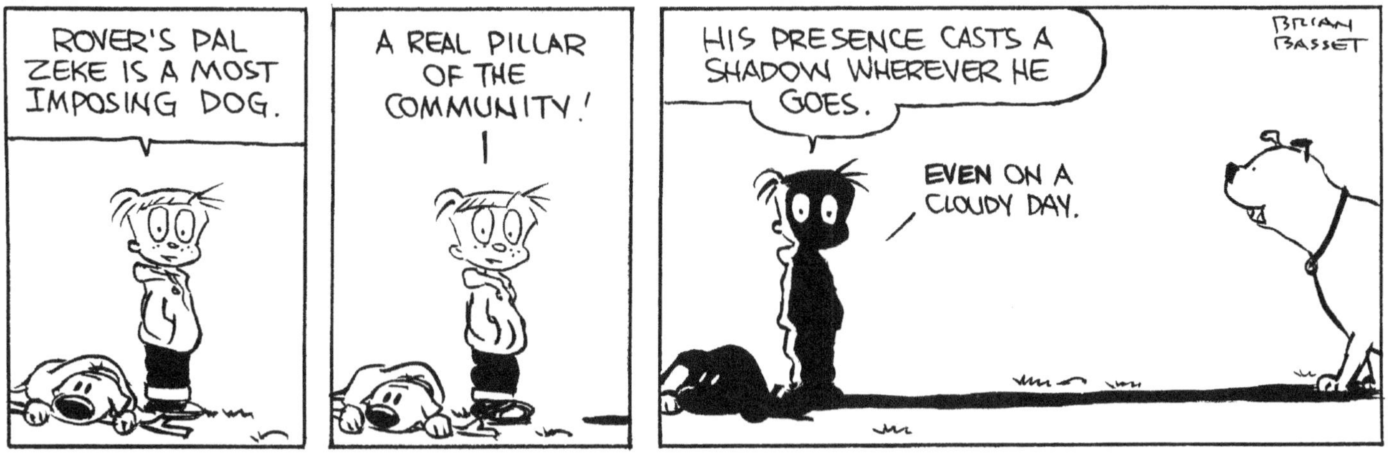
ROVER'S PAL ZEKE IS A MOST IMPOSING DOG.
A REAL PILLAR OF THE COMMUNITY!
HIS PRESENCE CASTS A SHADOW WHEREVER HE GOES.
BRIAN BASSET
EVEN ON A CLOUDY DAY.

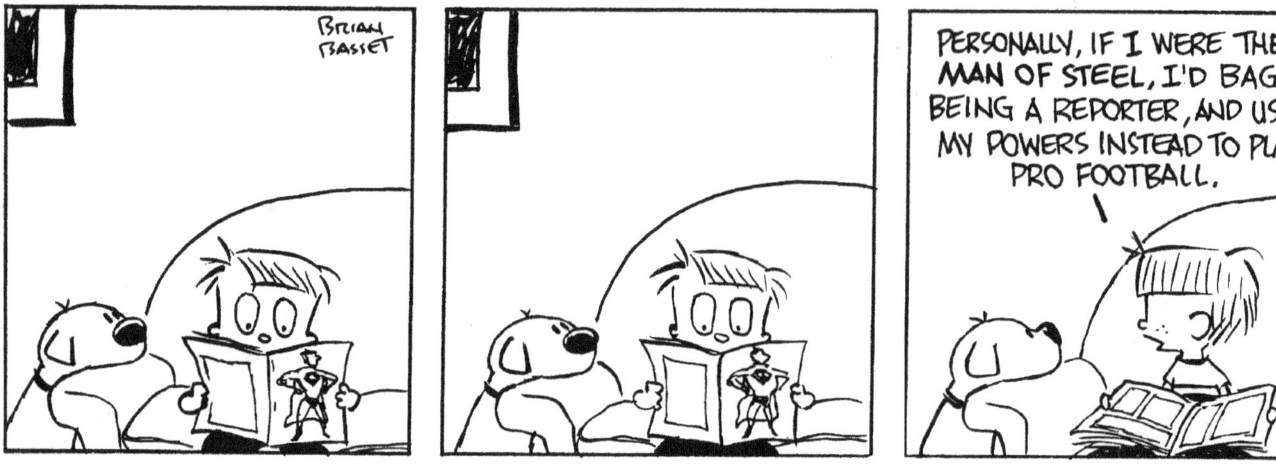
BRIAN BASSET
PERSONALLY, IF I WERE THE **MAN OF STEEL**, I'D BAG BEING A REPORTER, AND USE MY POWERS INSTEAD TO PLAY PRO FOOTBALL.

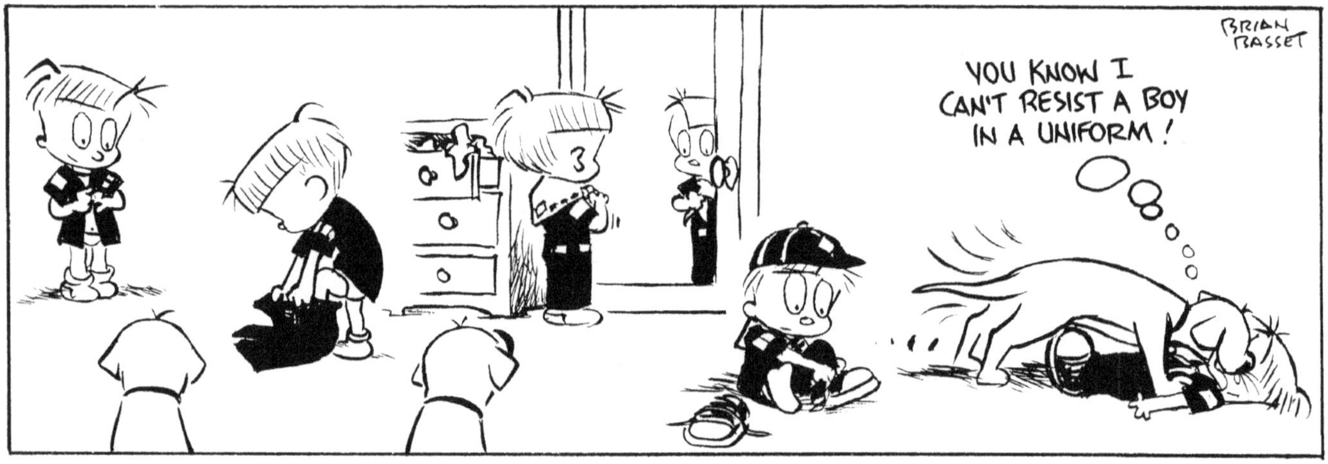
BRIAN BASSET
YOU KNOW I CAN'T RESIST A BOY IN A UNIFORM!

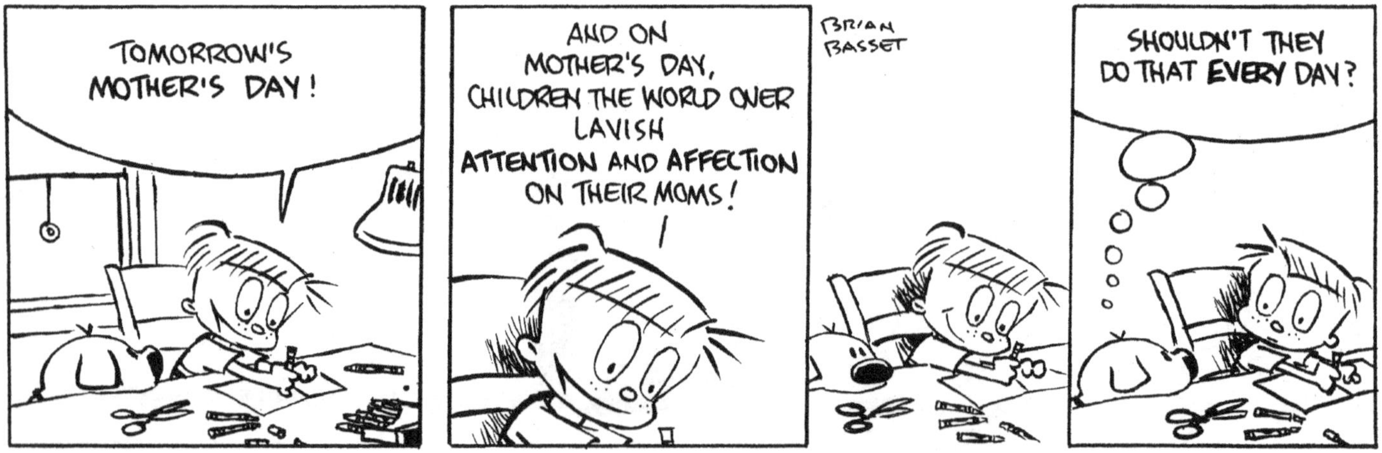
TOMORROW'S MOTHER'S DAY!
AND ON MOTHER'S DAY, CHILDREN THE WORLD OVER LAVISH **ATTENTION AND AFFECTION** ON THEIR MOMS!
BRIAN BASSET
SHOULDN'T THEY DO THAT **EVERY** DAY?

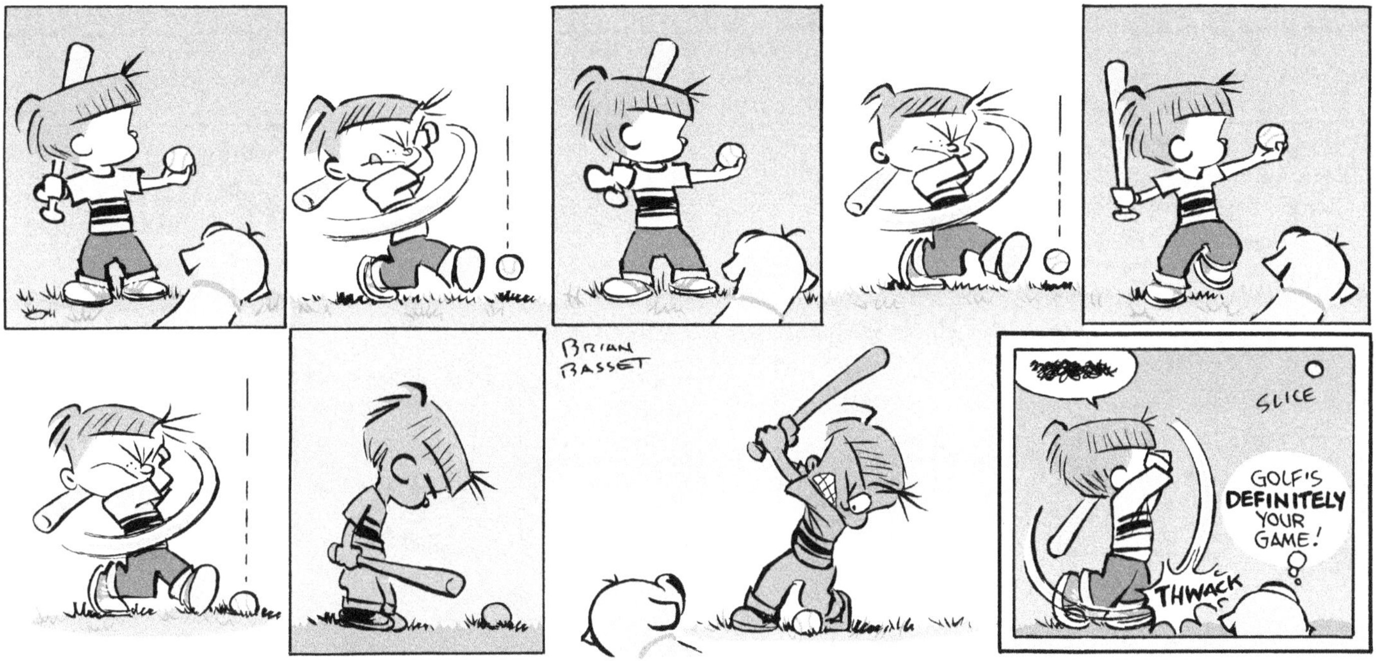
BRIAN BASSET
THWACK
SLICE
GOLF'S DEFINITELY YOUR GAME!

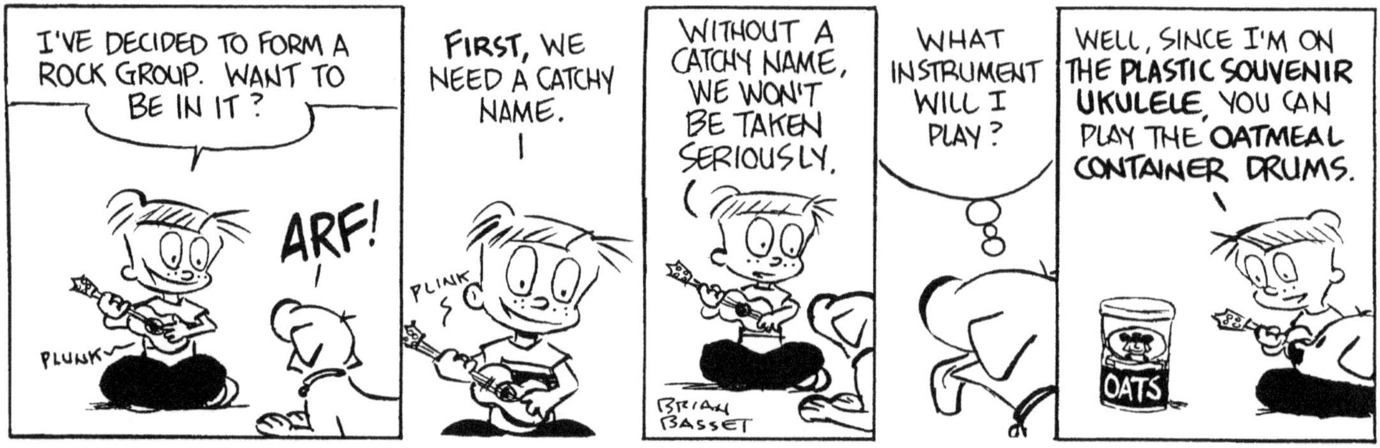
I'VE DECIDED TO FORM A ROCK GROUP. WANT TO BE IN IT?
ARF!
PLUNK
FIRST, WE NEED A CATCHY NAME.
PLINK
WITHOUT A CATCHY NAME, WE WON'T BE TAKEN SERIOUSLY.
BRIAN BASSET
WHAT INSTRUMENT WILL I PLAY?
WELL, SINCE I'M ON THE PLASTIC SOUVENIR UKULELE, YOU CAN PLAY THE OATMEAL CONTAINER DRUMS.
OATS

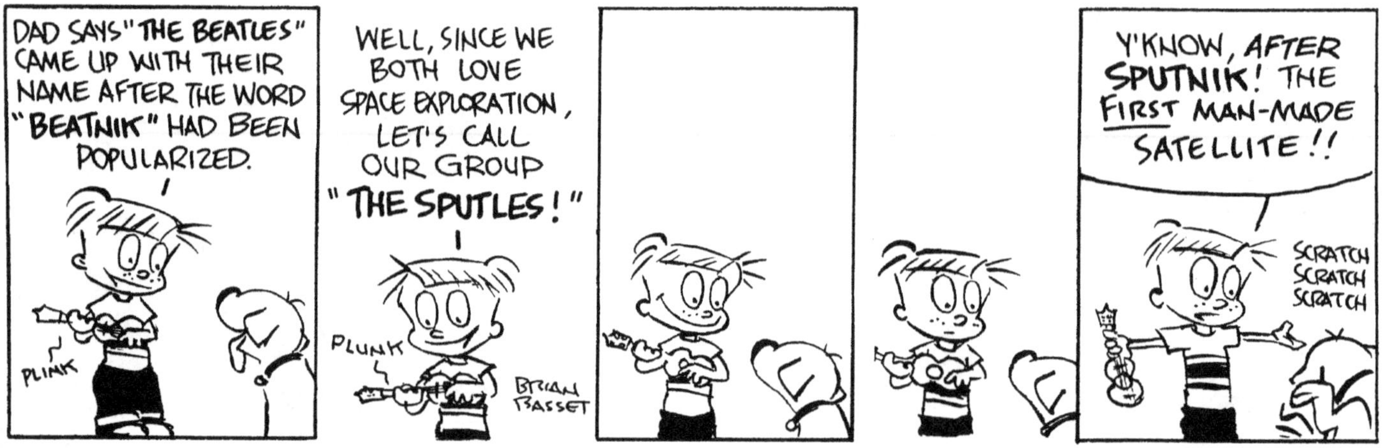
DAD SAYS "THE BEATLES" CAME UP WITH THEIR NAME AFTER THE WORD "BEATNIK" HAD BEEN POPULARIZED.
PLINK
WELL, SINCE WE BOTH LOVE SPACE EXPLORATION, LET'S CALL OUR GROUP "THE SPUTLES!"
PLUNK
BRIAN BASSET
Y'KNOW, AFTER SPUTNIK! THE FIRST MAN-MADE SATELLITE!!
SCRATCH
SCRATCH
SCRATCH

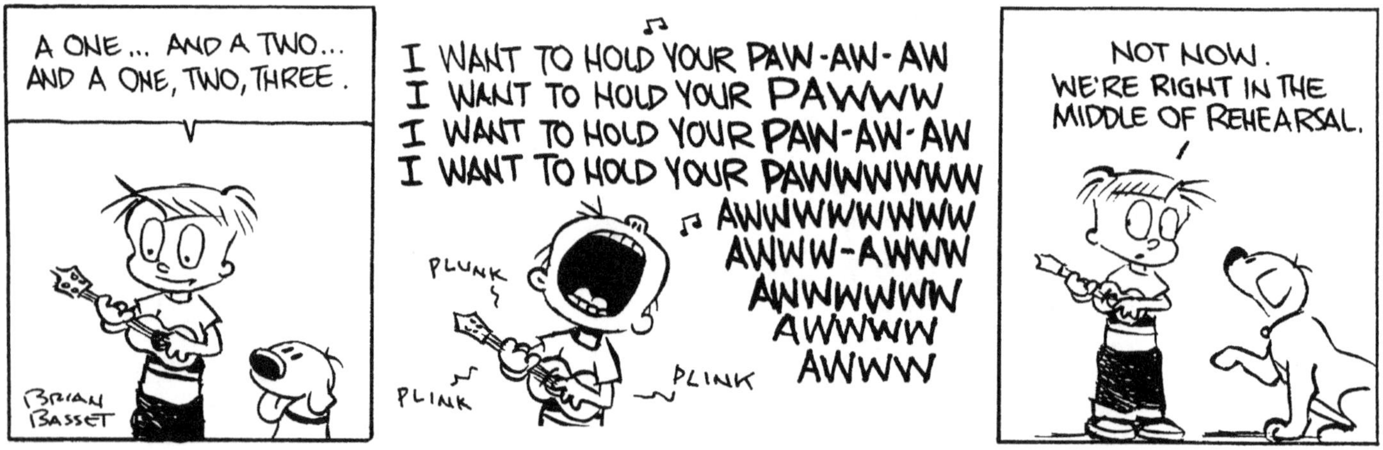
A ONE... AND A TWO... AND A ONE, TWO, THREE.
BRIAN BASSET
I WANT TO HOLD YOUR PAW-AW-AW
I WANT TO HOLD YOUR PAWWW
I WANT TO HOLD YOUR PAW-AW-AW
I WANT TO HOLD YOUR PAWWWWWW
AWWWWWWWW
AWWW-AWWW
AWWWWWW
AWWWW
AWWW
PLUNK
PLINK
PLINK
NOT NOW. WE'RE RIGHT IN THE MIDDLE OF REHEARSAL.

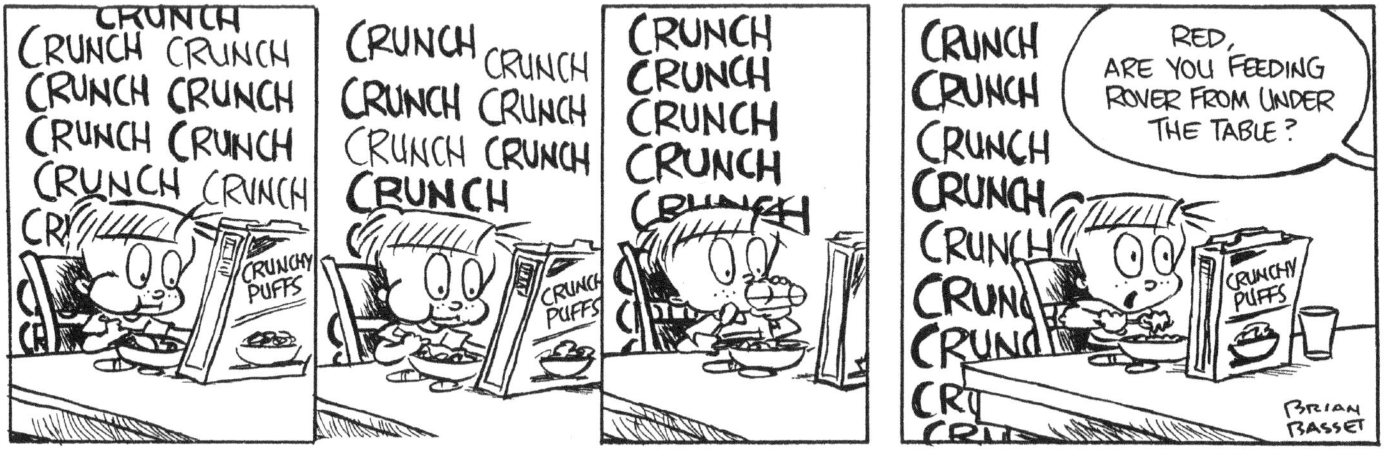
CRUNCH
CRUNCH CRUNCH
CRUNCH CRUNCH
CRUNCH CRUNCH
CRUNCH CRUNCH
CRUNCHY PUFFS
CRUNCH CRUNCH
CRUNCH CRUNCH
CRUNCH CRUNCH
CRUNCH
CRUNCH PUFFS
CRUNCH
CRUNCH
CRUNCH
CRUNCH
CRUNCH
CRUNCH
CRUNCH
CRUNCH
RED, ARE YOU FEEDING ROVER FROM UNDER THE TABLE?
CRUNCHY PUFFS
BRIAN BASSET

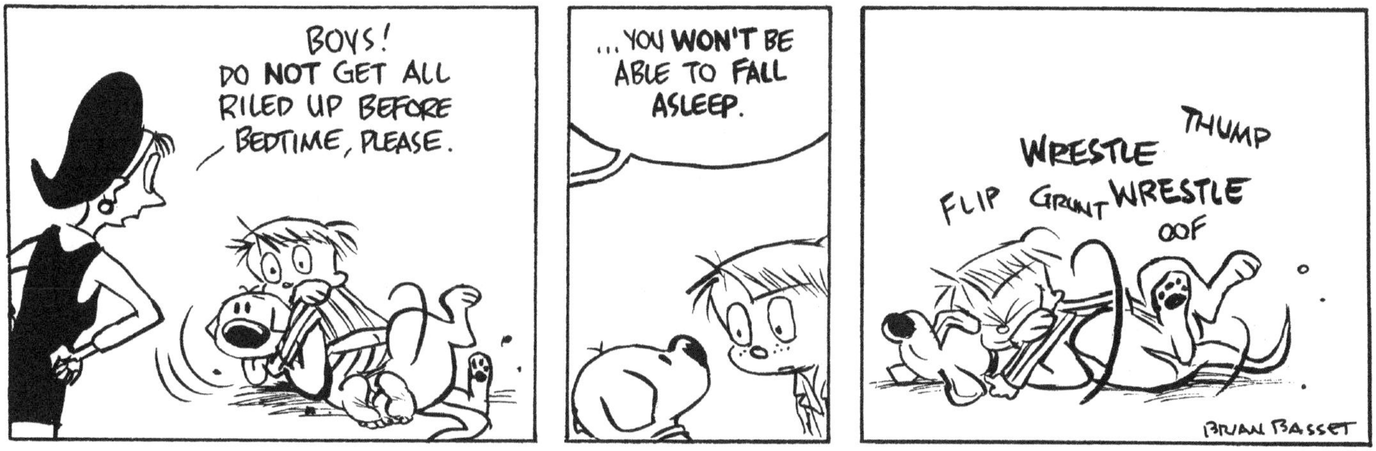
BOYS! DO NOT GET ALL RILED UP BEFORE BEDTIME, PLEASE.
...YOU WON'T BE ABLE TO FALL ASLEEP.
THUMP
WRESTLE
FLIP GRUNT WRESTLE
OOF
BRIAN BASSET

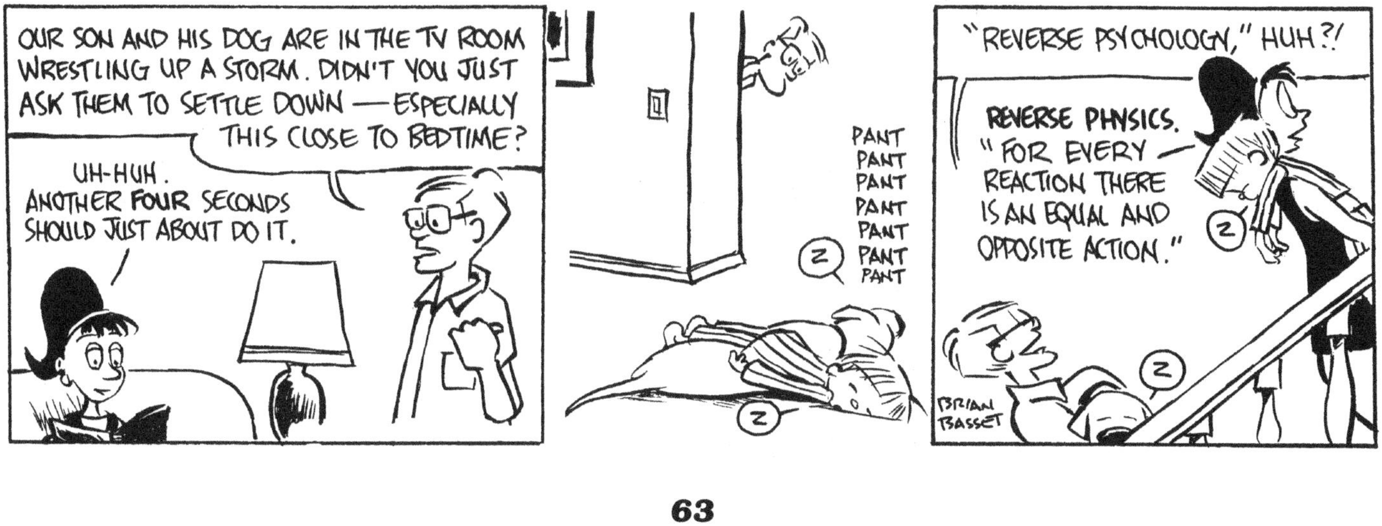
OUR SON AND HIS DOG ARE IN THE TV ROOM WRESTLING UP A STORM. DIDN'T YOU JUST ASK THEM TO SETTLE DOWN — ESPECIALLY THIS CLOSE TO BEDTIME?
UH-HUH. ANOTHER FOUR SECONDS SHOULD JUST ABOUT DO IT.
PANT PANT PANT PANT PANT PANT PANT
Z
Z
"REVERSE PSYCHOLOGY," HUH?!
REVERSE PHYSICS. "FOR EVERY REACTION THERE IS AN EQUAL AND OPPOSITE ACTION."
Z
Z
BRIAN BASSET

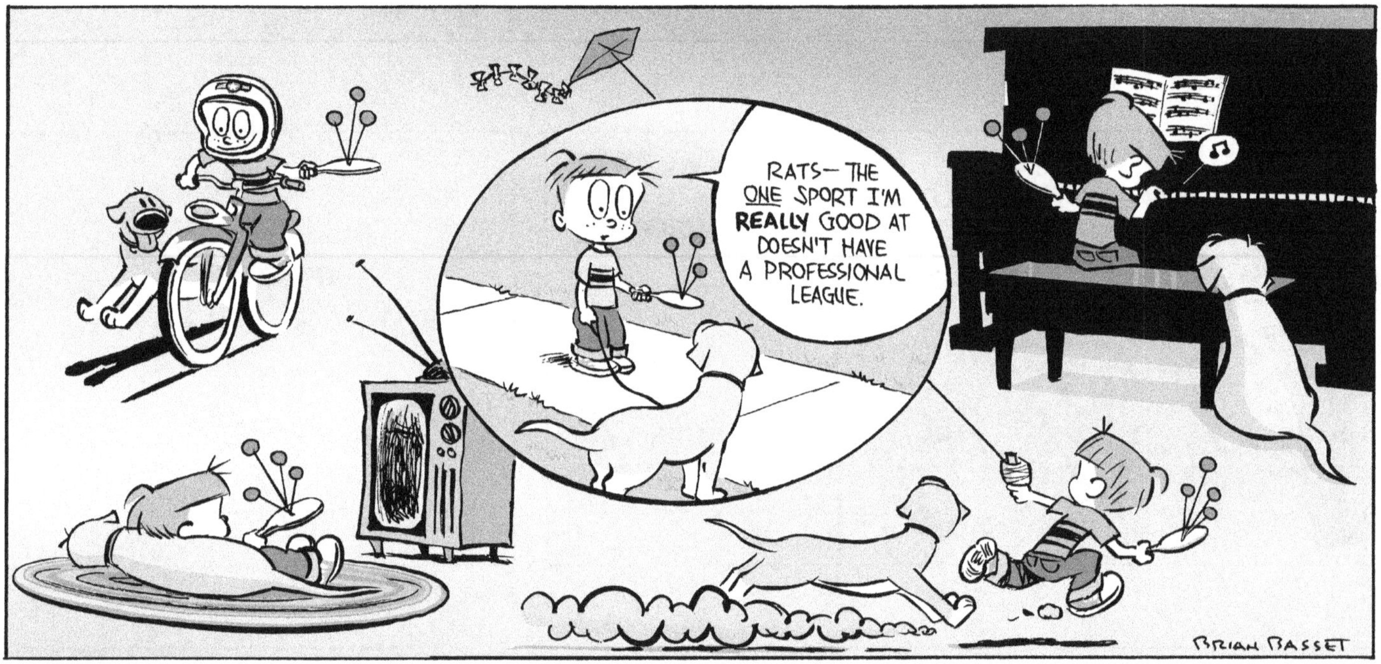
RATS— THE ONE SPORT I'M REALLY GOOD AT DOESN'T HAVE A PROFESSIONAL LEAGUE.
BRIAN BASSET

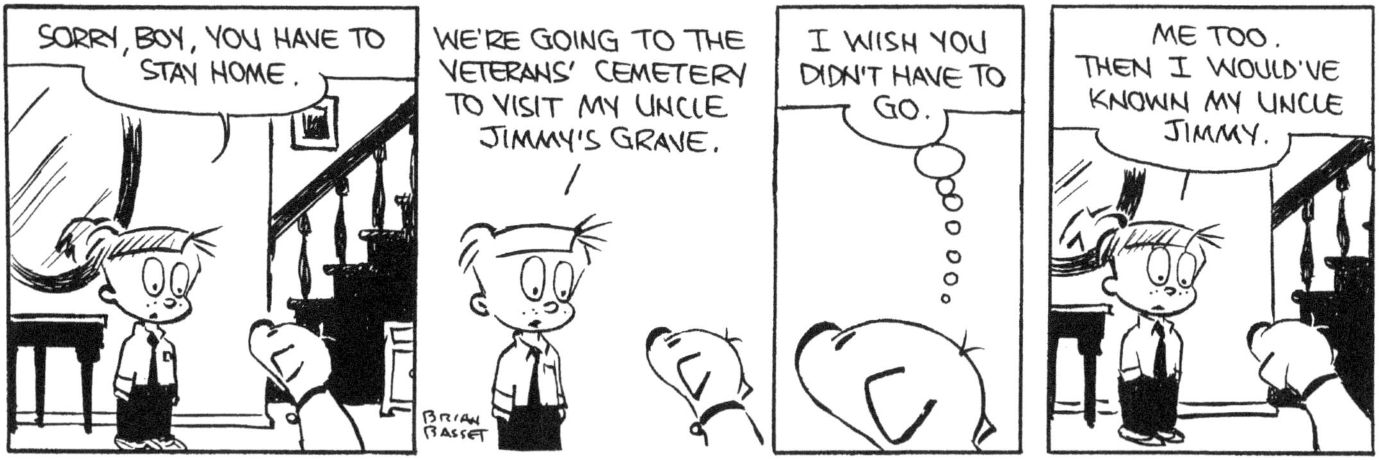
SORRY, BOY, YOU HAVE TO STAY HOME.
WE'RE GOING TO THE VETERANS' CEMETERY TO VISIT MY UNCLE JIMMY'S GRAVE.
BRIAN BASSET
I WISH YOU DIDN'T HAVE TO GO.
ME TOO. THEN I WOULD'VE KNOWN MY UNCLE JIMMY.

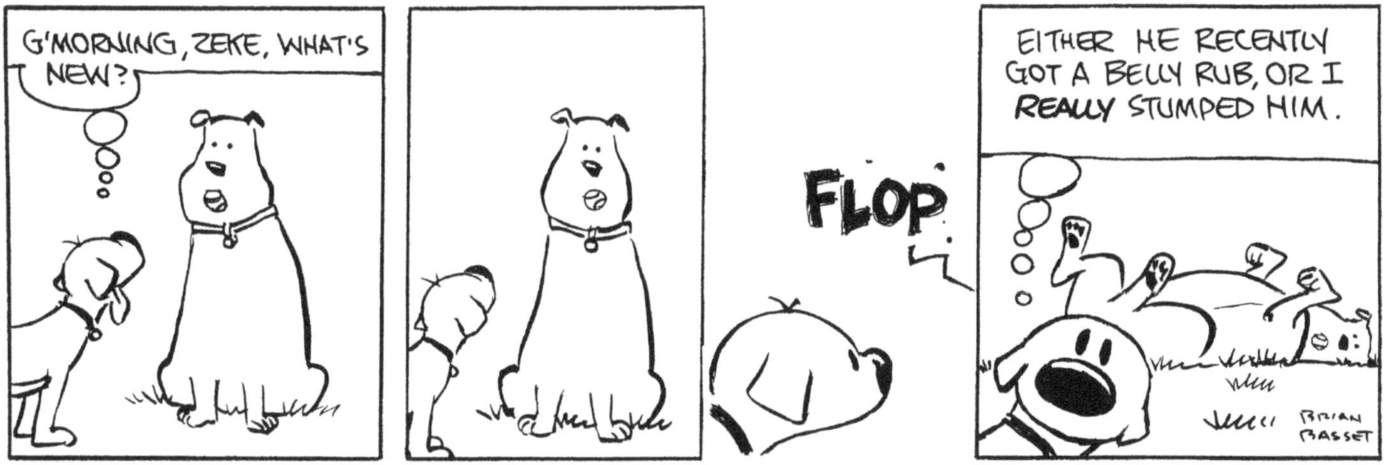
G'MORNING, ZEKE, WHAT'S NEW?
FLOP
EITHER HE RECENTLY GOT A BELLY RUB, OR I REALLY STUMPED HIM.
BRIAN BASSET

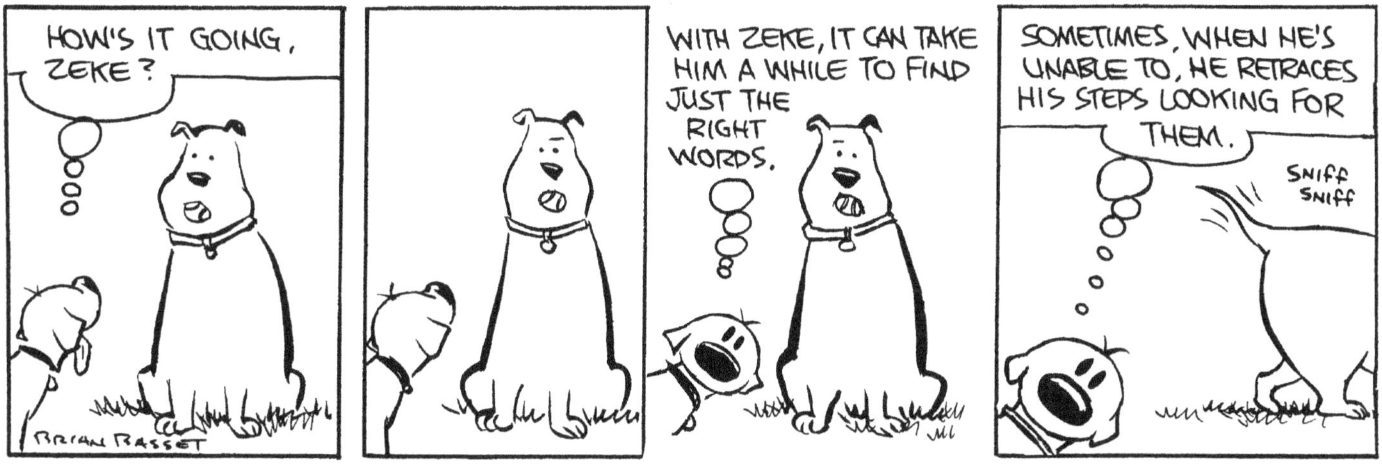
HOW'S IT GOING, ZEKE?
BRIAN BASSET
WITH ZEKE, IT CAN TAKE HIM A WHILE TO FIND JUST THE RIGHT WORDS.
SOMETIMES, WHEN HE'S UNABLE TO, HE RETRACES HIS STEPS LOOKING FOR THEM.
SNIFF SNIFF

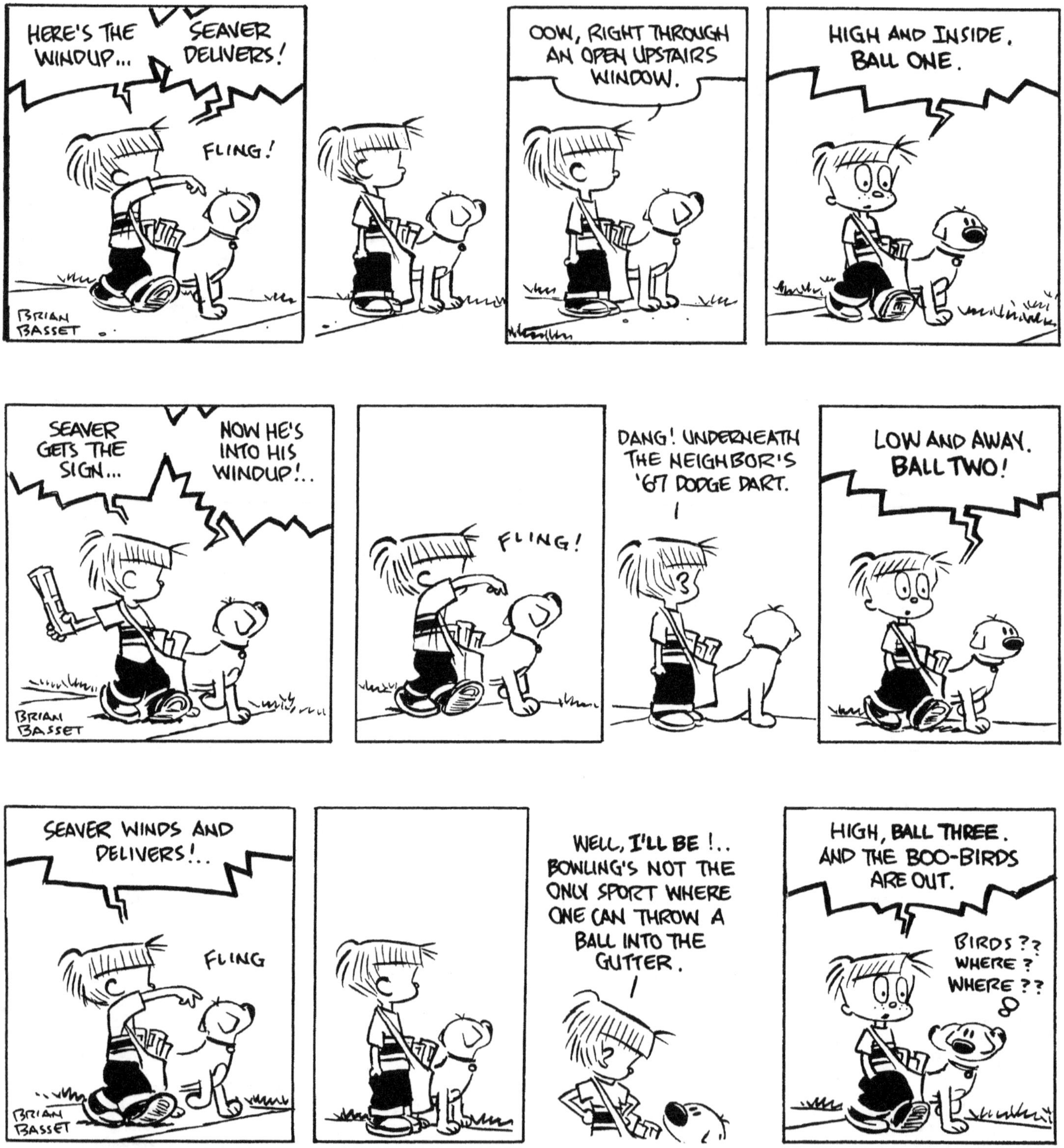
HERE'S THE WINDUP...
SEAVER DELIVERS!
FLING!
BRIAN BASSET
OOW, RIGHT THROUGH AN OPEN UPSTAIRS WINDOW.
HIGH AND INSIDE. BALL ONE.
SEAVER GETS THE SIGN...
NOW HE'S INTO HIS WINDUP!..
BRIAN BASSET
FLING!
DANG! UNDERNEATH THE NEIGHBOR'S '67 DODGE DART.
LOW AND AWAY. BALL TWO!
SEAVER WINDS AND DELIVERS!..
FLING
BRIAN BASSET
WELL, I'LL BE!.. BOWLING'S NOT THE ONLY SPORT WHERE ONE CAN THROW A BALL INTO THE GUTTER.
HIGH, BALL THREE. AND THE BOO-BIRDS ARE OUT.
BIRDS?? WHERE? WHERE??

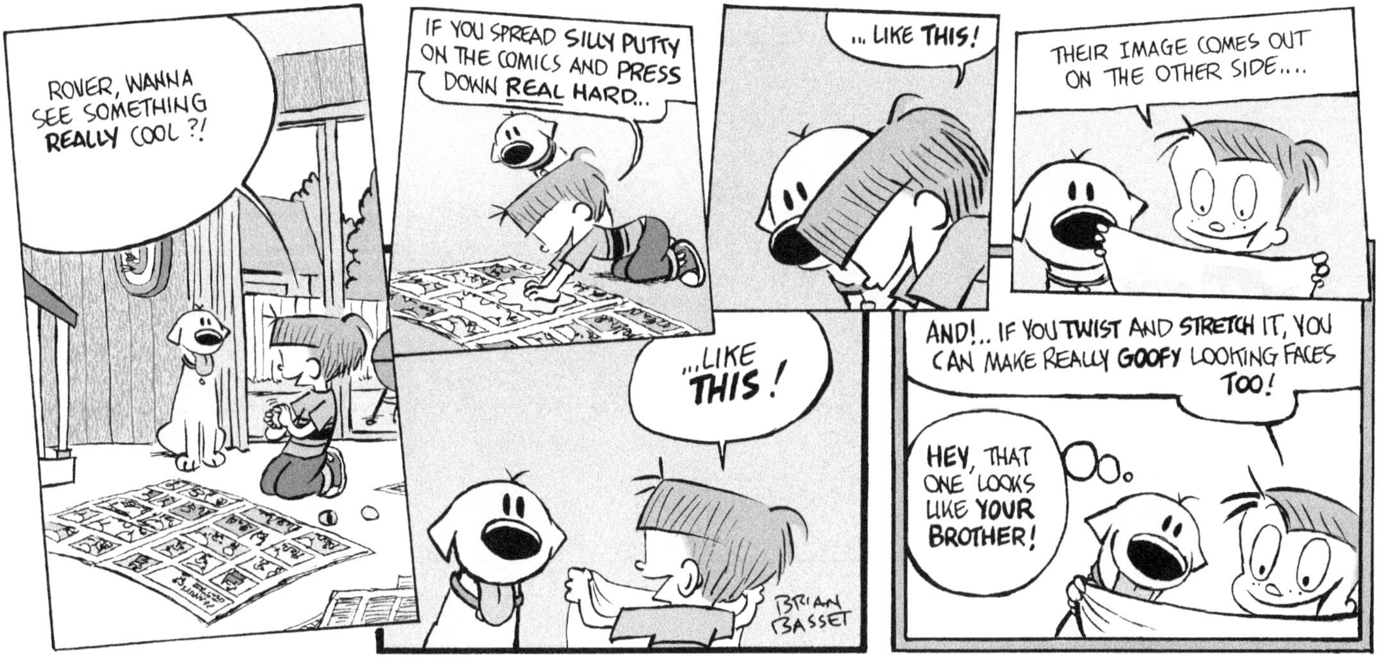
ROVER, WANNA SEE SOMETHING REALLY COOL ?!
IF YOU SPREAD SILLY PUTTY ON THE COMICS AND PRESS DOWN REAL HARD...
... LIKE THIS!
...LIKE THIS!
THEIR IMAGE COMES OUT ON THE OTHER SIDE....
AND!.. IF YOU TWIST AND STRETCH IT, YOU CAN MAKE REALLY GOOFY LOOKING FACES TOO!
HEY, THAT ONE LOOKS LIKE YOUR BROTHER!
BRIAN BASSET

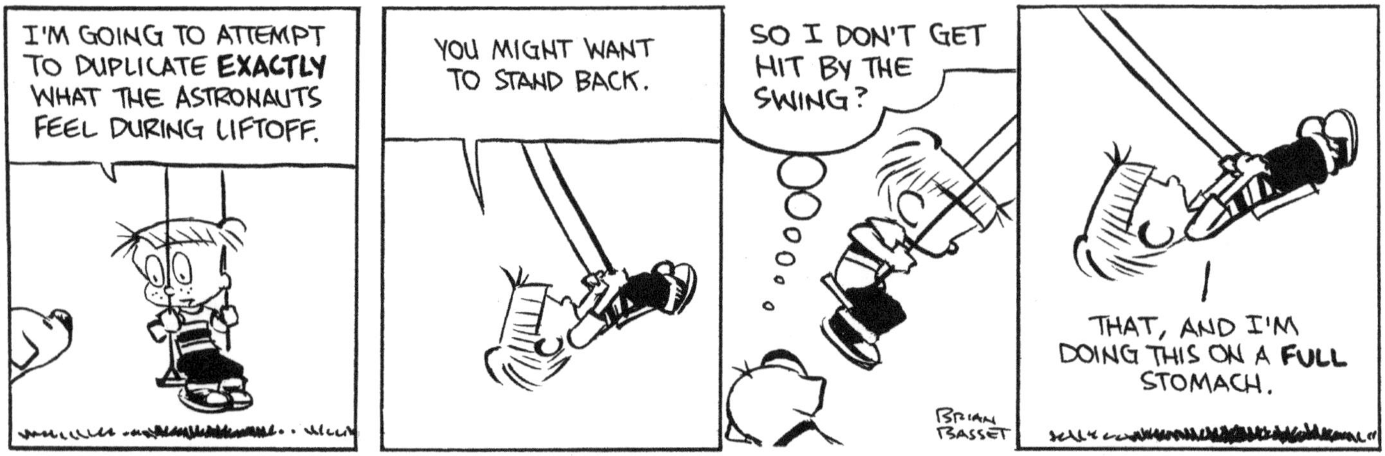
I'M GOING TO ATTEMPT TO DUPLICATE **EXACTLY** WHAT THE ASTRONAUTS FEEL DURING LIFTOFF.
YOU MIGHT WANT TO STAND BACK.
SO I DON'T GET HIT BY THE SWING?
THAT, AND I'M DOING THIS ON A **FULL** STOMACH.
BRIAN BASSET

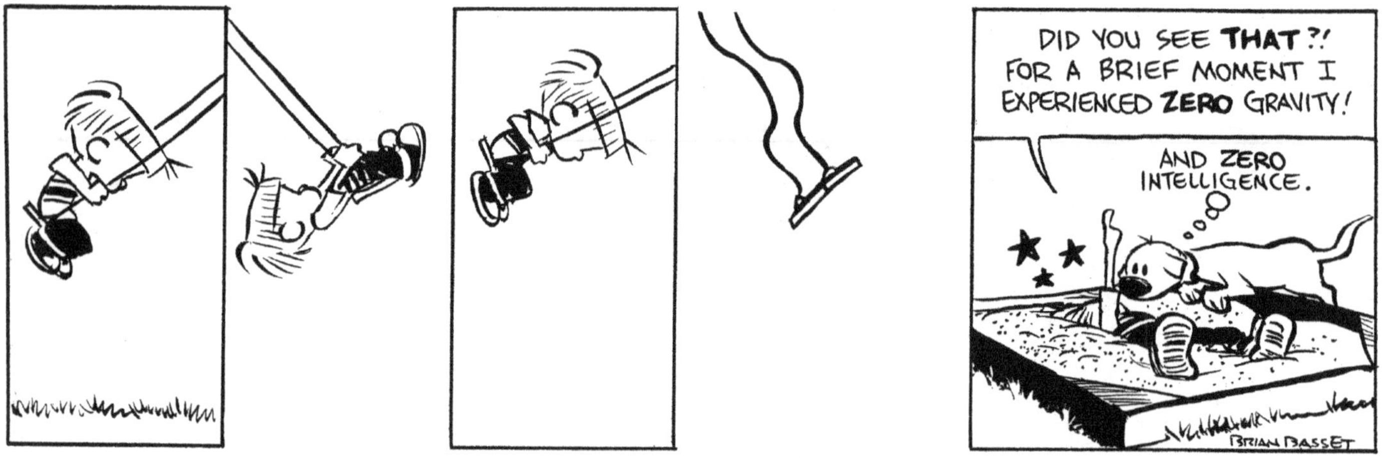
DID YOU SEE **THAT**?! FOR A BRIEF MOMENT I EXPERIENCED **ZERO** GRAVITY!
AND **ZERO** INTELLIGENCE.
BRIAN BASSET

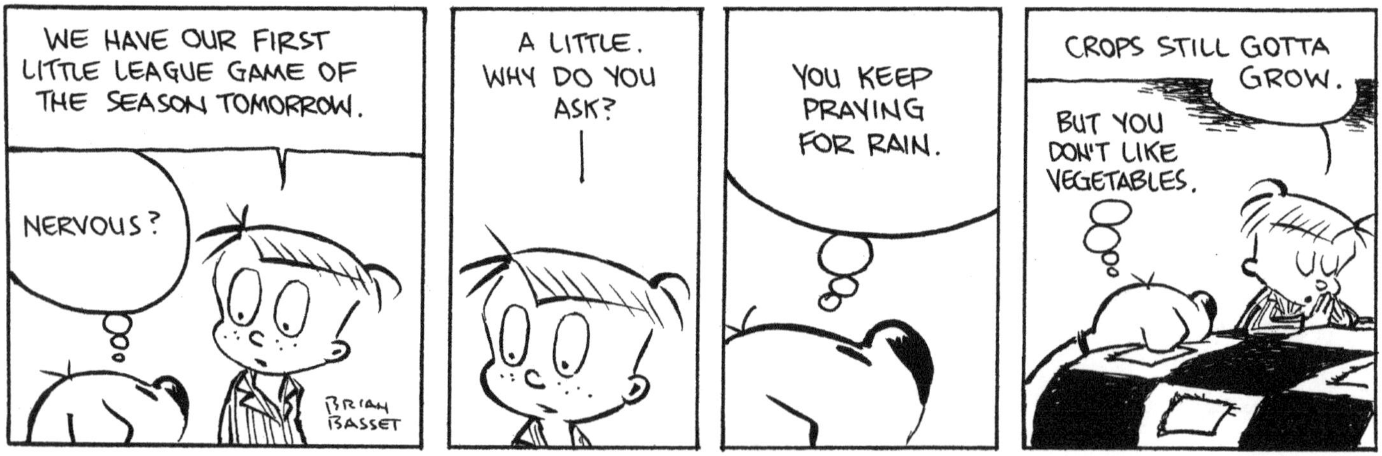
WE HAVE OUR FIRST LITTLE LEAGUE GAME OF THE SEASON TOMORROW.
NERVOUS?
BRIAN BASSET
A LITTLE. WHY DO YOU ASK?
YOU KEEP PRAYING FOR RAIN.
CROPS STILL GOTTA GROW.
BUT YOU DON'T LIKE VEGETABLES.

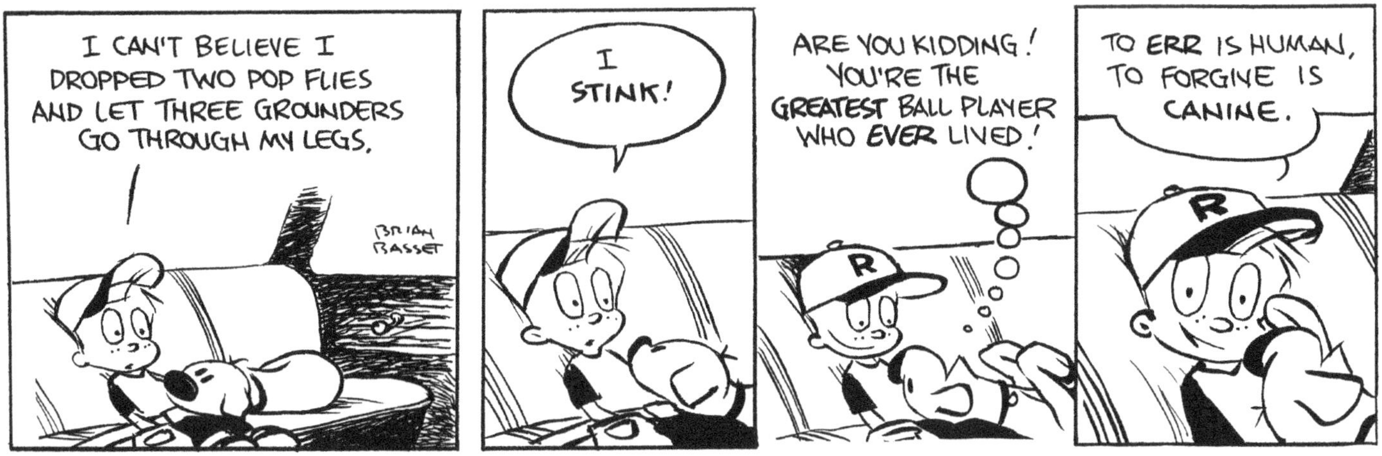
I CAN'T BELIEVE I DROPPED TWO POP FLIES AND LET THREE GROUNDERS GO THROUGH MY LEGS.
BRIAN BASSET
I STINK!
ARE YOU KIDDING! YOU'RE THE GREATEST BALL PLAYER WHO EVER LIVED!
TO ERR IS HUMAN, TO FORGIVE IS CANINE.

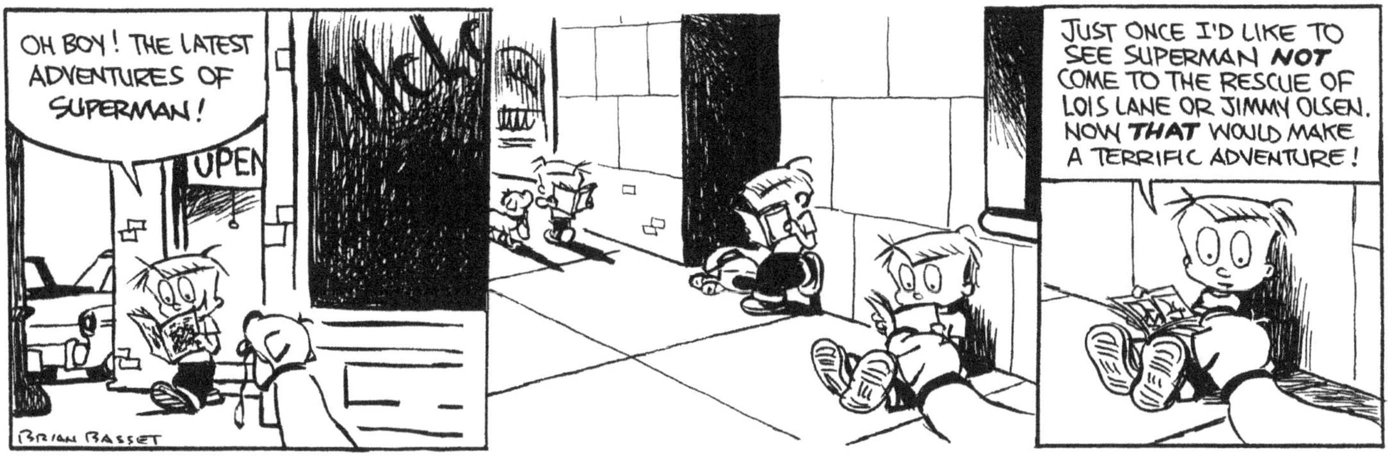
OH BOY! THE LATEST ADVENTURES OF SUPERMAN!
OPEN
BRIAN BASSET
JUST ONCE I'D LIKE TO SEE SUPERMAN NOT COME TO THE RESCUE OF LOIS LANE OR JIMMY OLSEN. NOW THAT WOULD MAKE A TERRIFIC ADVENTURE!

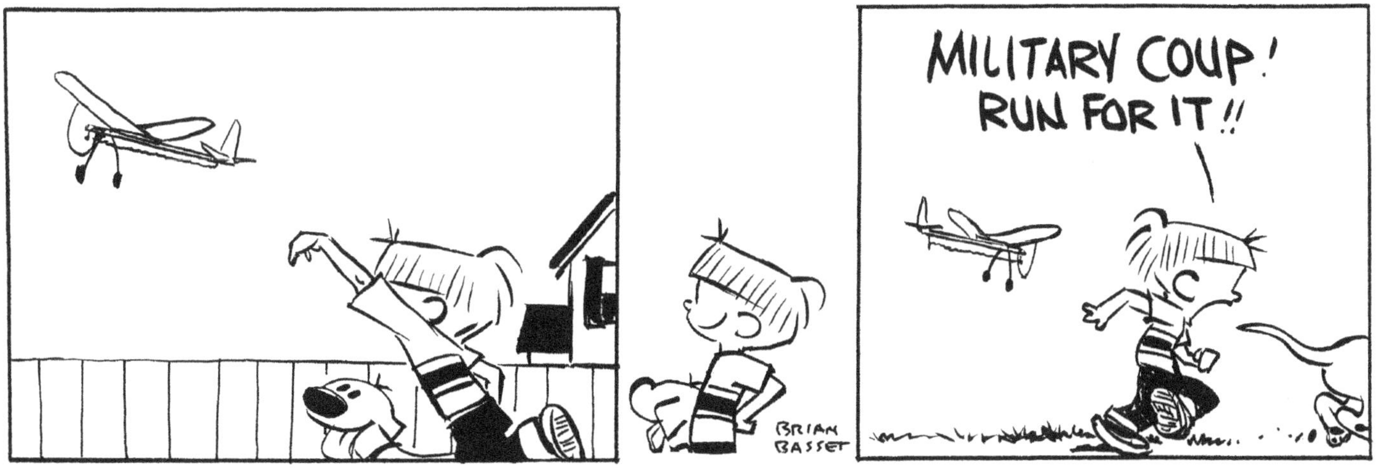
BRIAN BASSET
MILITARY COUP! RUN FOR IT!!

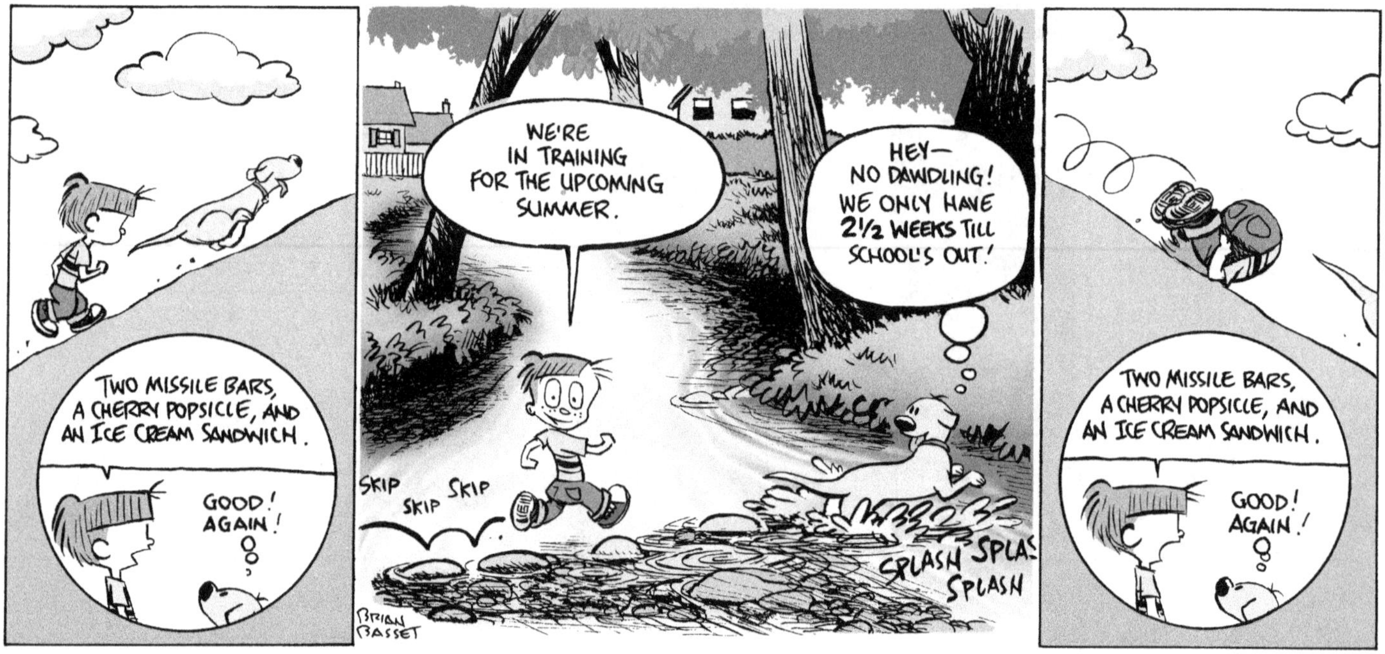
TWO MISSILE BARS, A CHERRY POPSICLE, AND AN ICE CREAM SANDWICH.
GOOD! AGAIN!
WE'RE IN TRAINING FOR THE UPCOMING SUMMER.
HEY— NO DAWDLING! WE ONLY HAVE 2 1/2 WEEKS TILL SCHOOL'S OUT!
SKIP SKIP SKIP
SPLASH SPLASH SPLASH
BRIAN BASSET
TWO MISSILE BARS, A CHERRY POPSICLE, AND AN ICE CREAM SANDWICH.
GOOD! AGAIN!

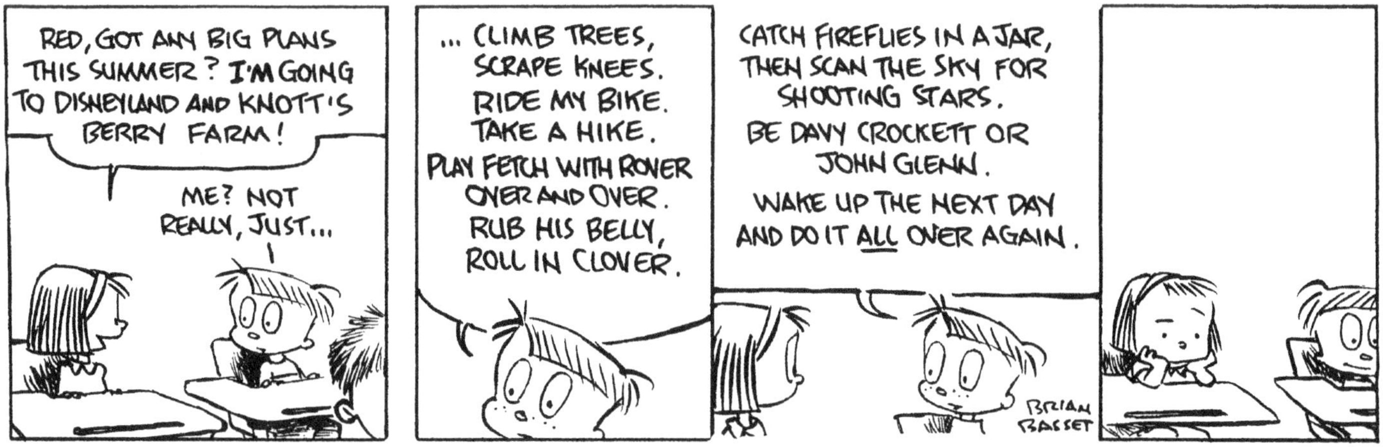
RED, GOT ANY BIG PLANS THIS SUMMER? I'M GOING TO DISNEYLAND AND KNOTT'S BERRY FARM!
ME? NOT REALLY, JUST...
... CLIMB TREES, SCRAPE KNEES. RIDE MY BIKE. TAKE A HIKE. PLAY FETCH WITH ROVER OVER AND OVER. RUB HIS BELLY, ROLL IN CLOVER.
CATCH FIREFLIES IN A JAR, THEN SCAN THE SKY FOR SHOOTING STARS. BE DAVY CROCKETT OR JOHN GLENN. WAKE UP THE NEXT DAY AND DO IT ALL OVER AGAIN.
BRIAN BASSET

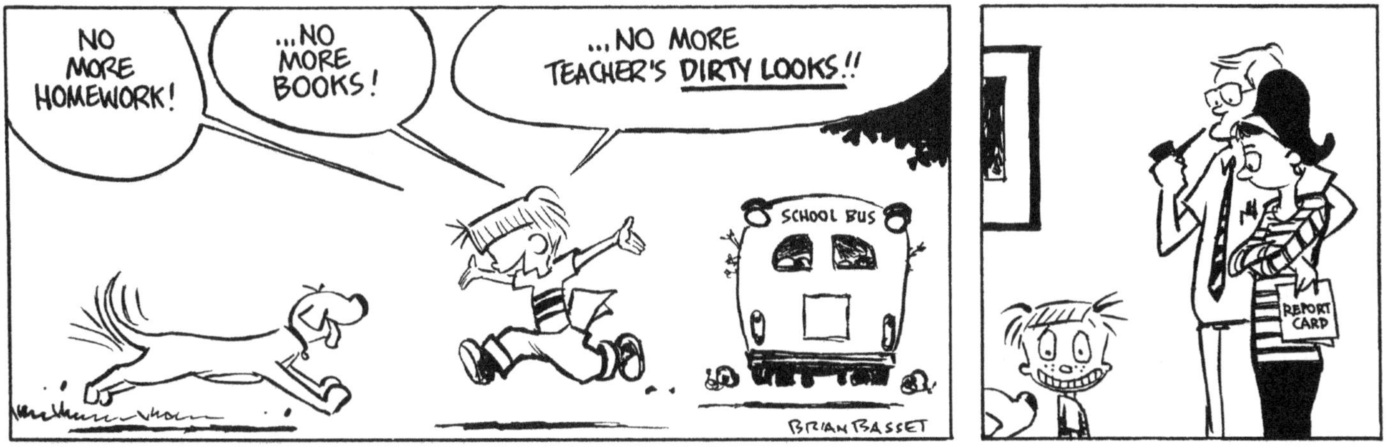
NO MORE HOMEWORK!
...NO MORE BOOKS!
...NO MORE TEACHER'S DIRTY LOOKS!!
SCHOOL BUS
BRIAN BASSET
REPORT CARD

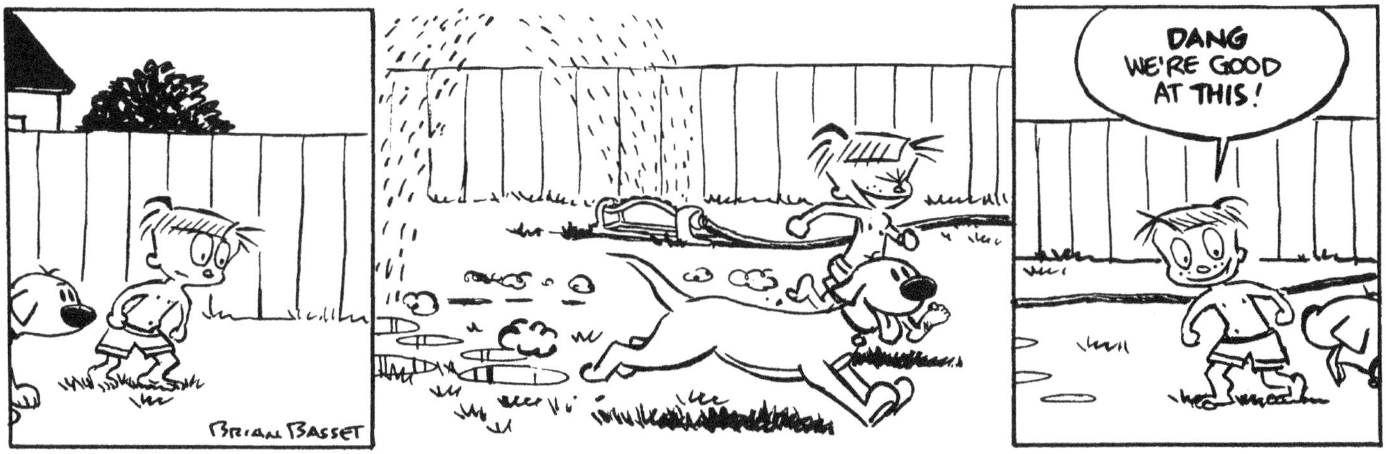
BRIAN BASSET
DANG WE'RE GOOD AT THIS!

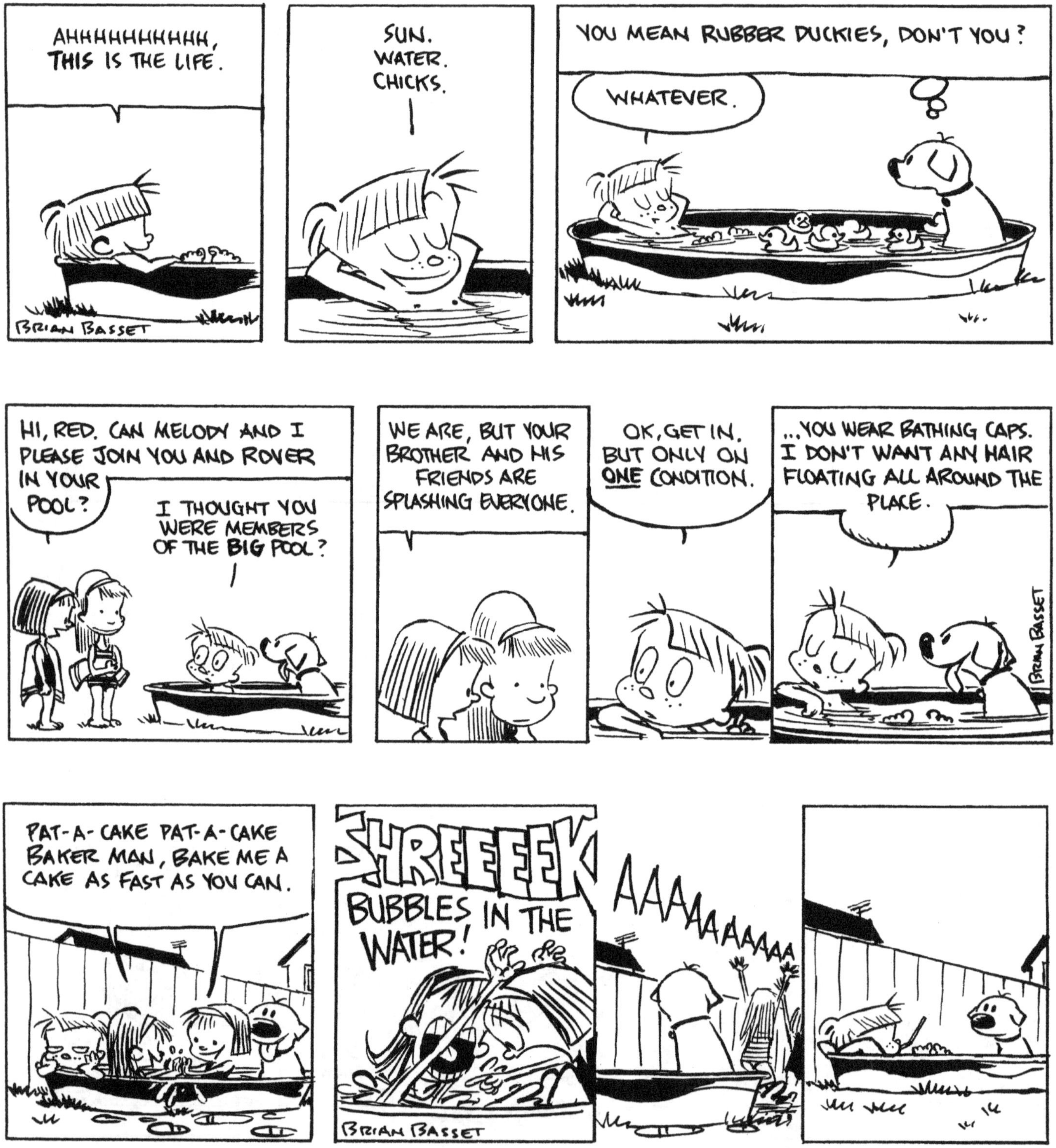
AHHHHHHHHHH, THIS IS THE LIFE.
BRIAN BASSET
SUN. WATER. CHICKS.
YOU MEAN RUBBER DUCKIES, DON'T YOU?
WHATEVER.
HI, RED. CAN MELODY AND I PLEASE JOIN YOU AND ROVER IN YOUR POOL?
I THOUGHT YOU WERE MEMBERS OF THE BIG POOL?
WE ARE, BUT YOUR BROTHER AND HIS FRIENDS ARE SPLASHING EVERYONE.
OK, GET IN, BUT ONLY ON ONE CONDITION.
...YOU WEAR BATHING CAPS. I DON'T WANT ANY HAIR FLOATING ALL AROUND THE PLACE.
BRIAN BASSET
PAT-A-CAKE PAT-A-CAKE BAKER MAN, BAKE ME A CAKE AS FAST AS YOU CAN.
SHREEEEK
BUBBLES IN THE WATER!
BRIAN BASSET
AAAAAAAAAAA

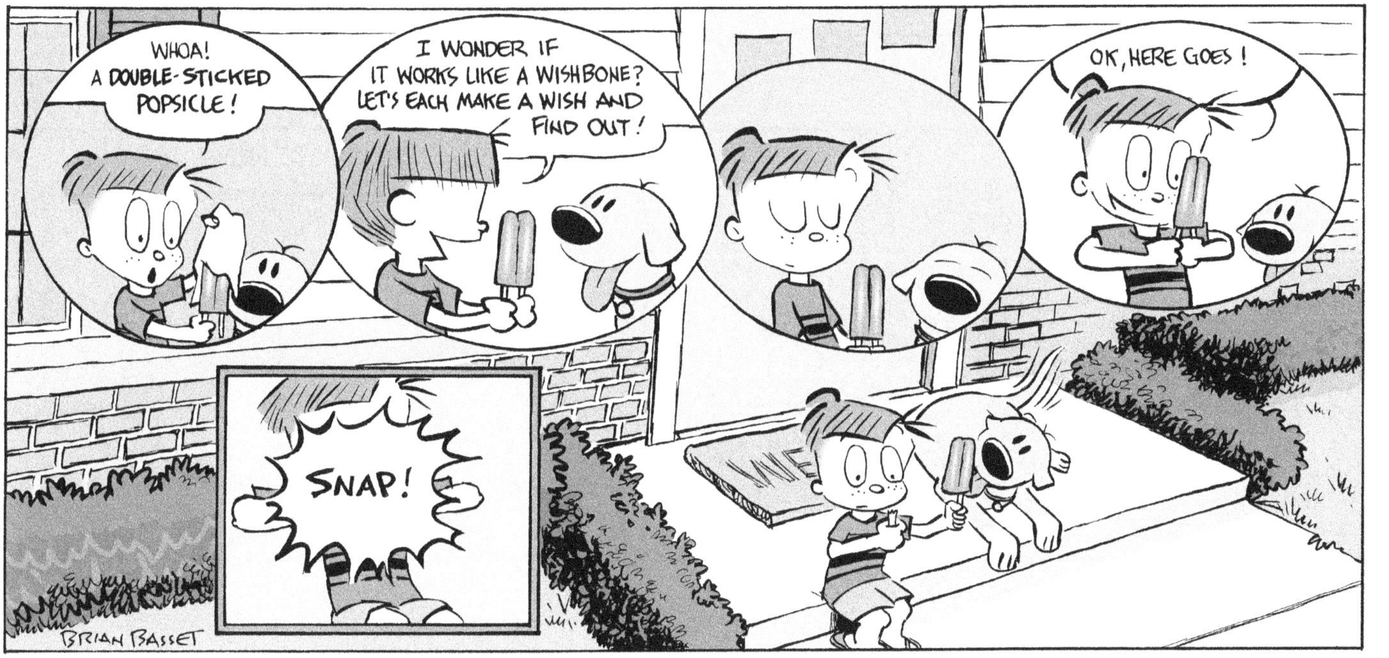
WHOA! A DOUBLE-STICKED POPSICLE!
I WONDER IF IT WORKS LIKE A WISHBONE? LET'S EACH MAKE A WISH AND FIND OUT!
OK, HERE GOES!
SNAP!
BRIAN BASSET

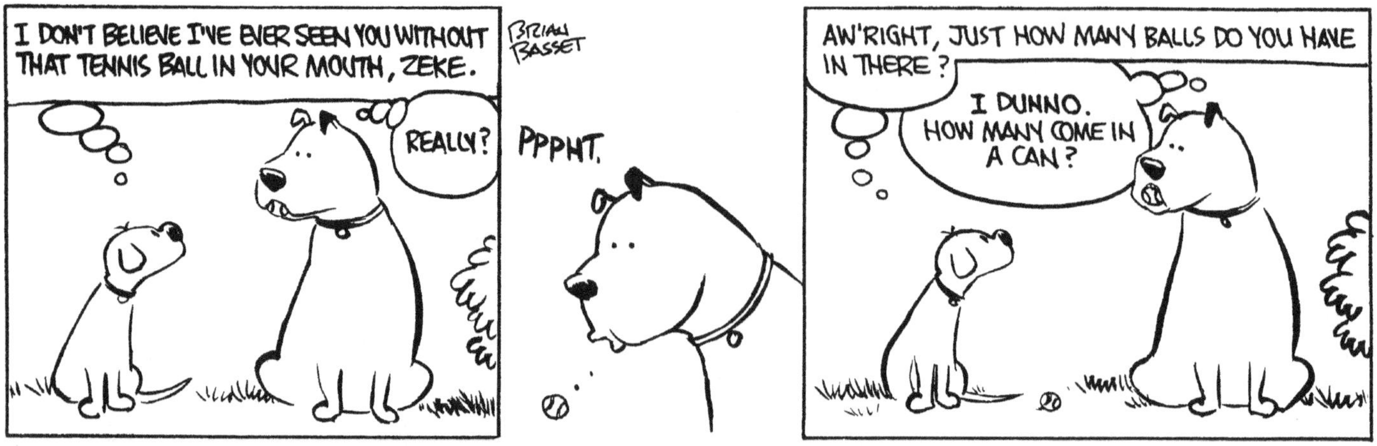
BRIAN BASSET
I DON'T BELIEVE I'VE EVER SEEN YOU WITHOUT THAT TENNIS BALL IN YOUR MOUTH, ZEKE.
REALLY?
PPPHT.
AW'RIGHT, JUST HOW MANY BALLS DO YOU HAVE IN THERE?
I DUNNO. HOW MANY COME IN A CAN?

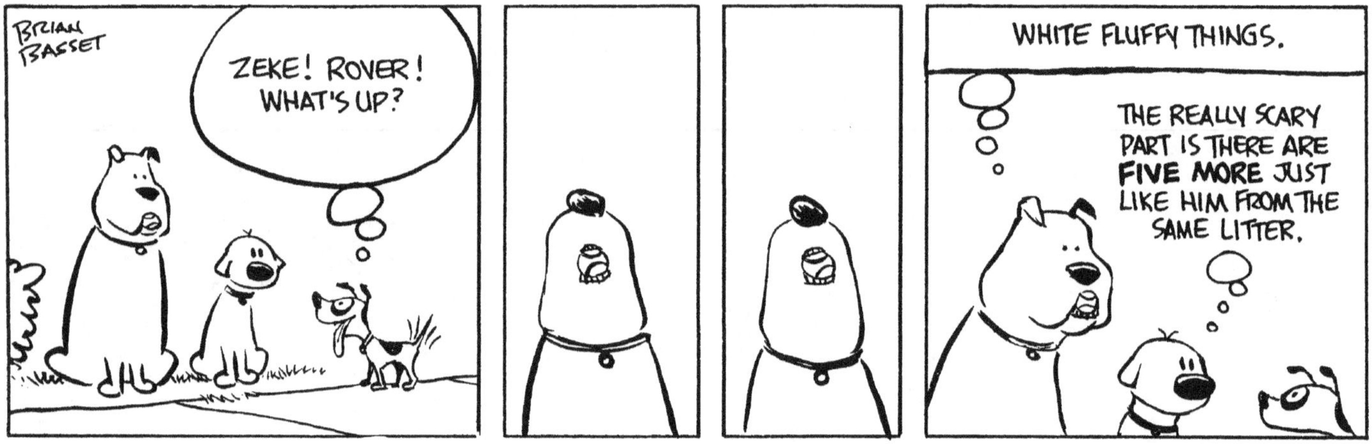
BRIAN BASSET
ZEKE! ROVER! WHAT'S UP?
WHITE FLUFFY THINGS.
THE REALLY SCARY PART IS THERE ARE **FIVE MORE** JUST LIKE HIM FROM THE SAME LITTER.

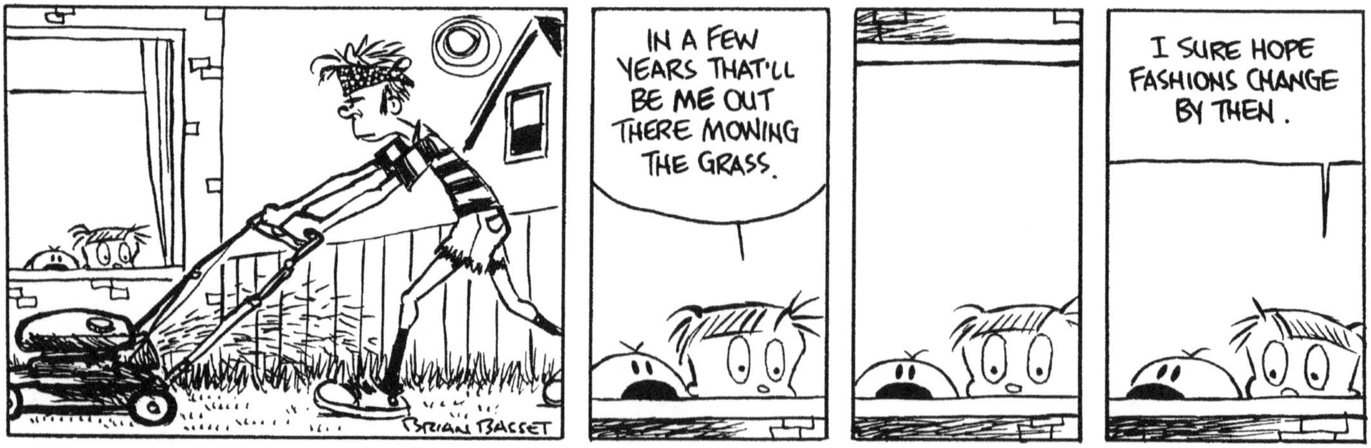
BRIAN BASSET
IN A FEW YEARS THAT'LL BE ME OUT THERE MOWING THE GRASS.
I SURE HOPE FASHIONS CHANGE BY THEN.

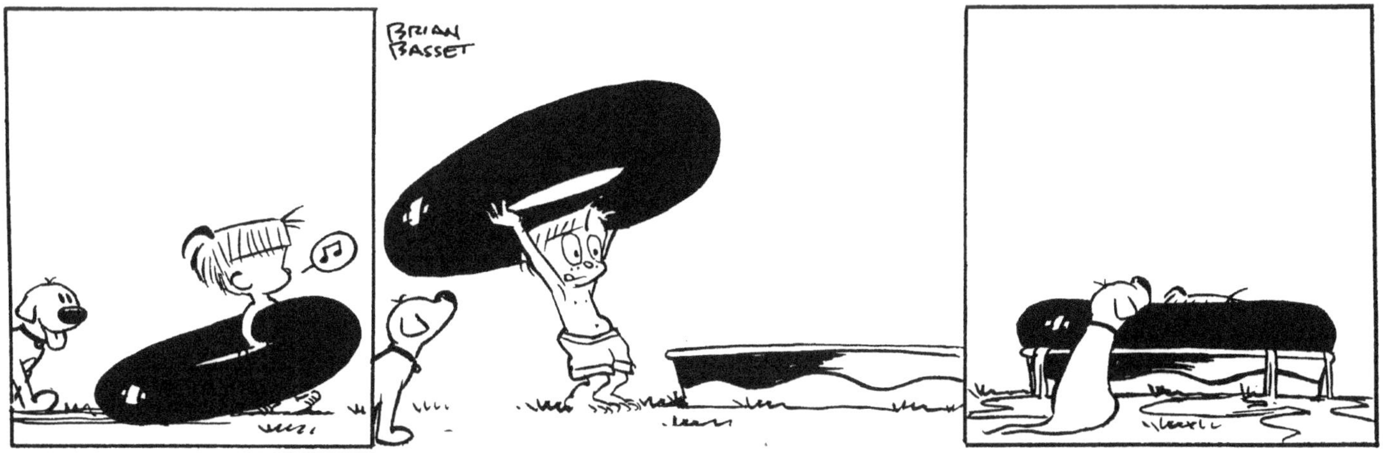
BRIAN BASSET

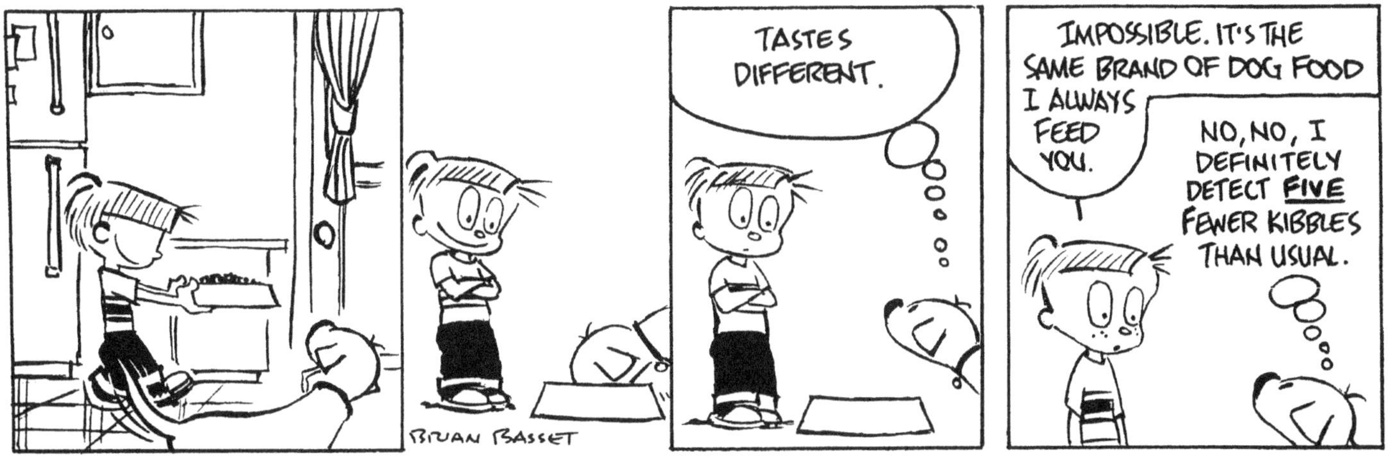
TASTES DIFFERENT.
IMPOSSIBLE. IT'S THE SAME BRAND OF DOG FOOD I ALWAYS FEED YOU.
NO, NO, I DEFINITELY DETECT **FIVE** FEWER KIBBLES THAN USUAL.
BRIAN BASSET

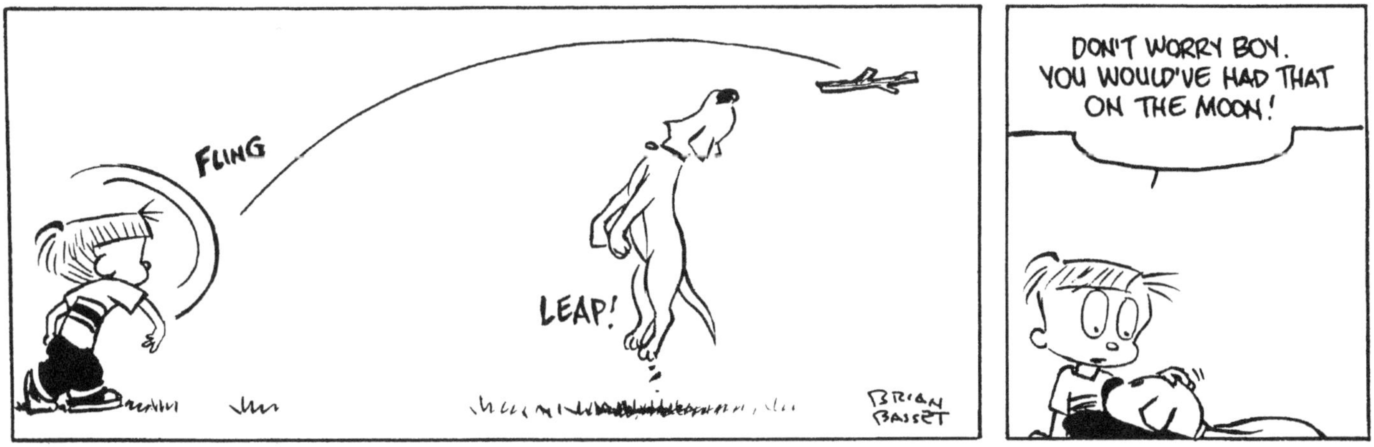
FLING
LEAP!
BRIAN BASSET
DON'T WORRY BOY. YOU WOULD'VE HAD THAT ON THE MOON!

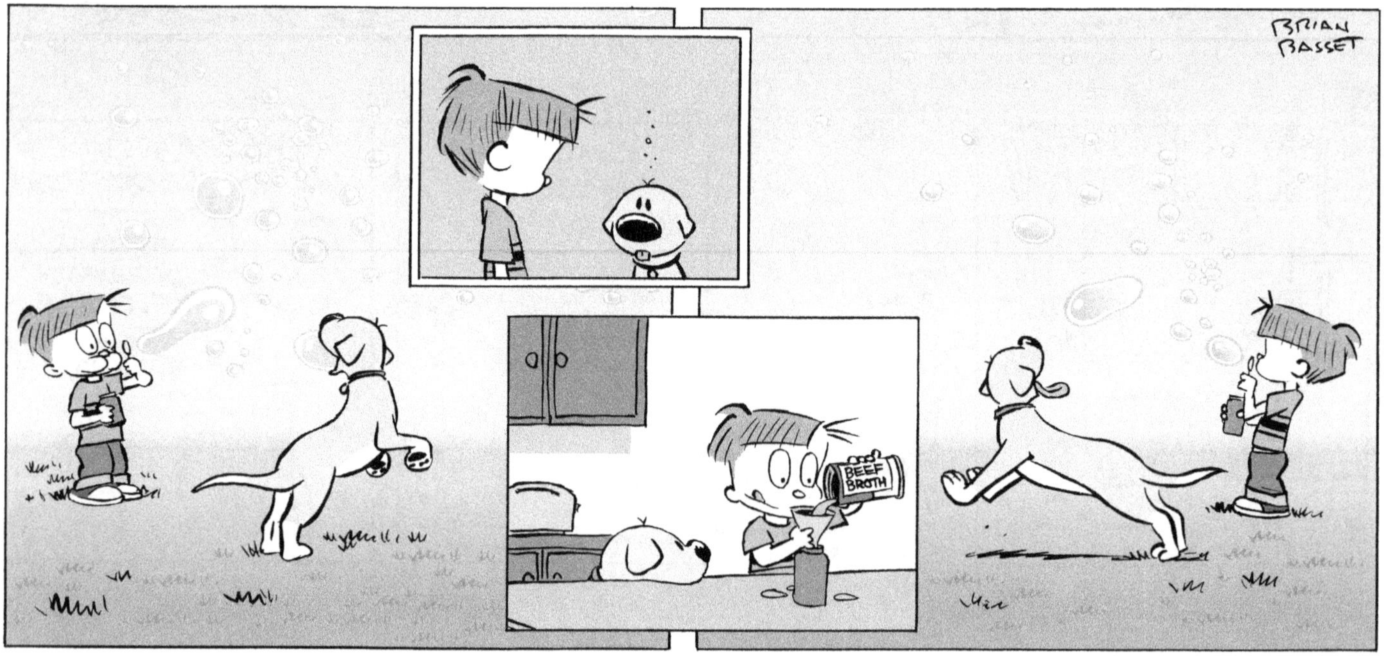
BRIAN BASSET
BEEF BROTH

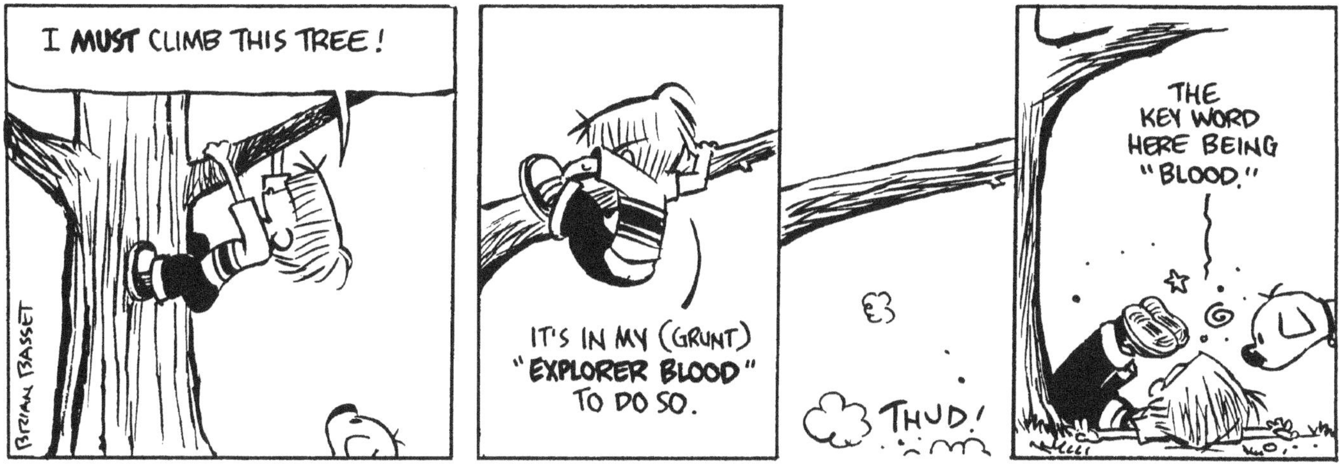
I MUST CLIMB THIS TREE!
BRIAN BASSET
IT'S IN MY (GRUNT) "EXPLORER BLOOD" TO DO SO.
THUD!
THE KEY WORD HERE BEING "BLOOD."

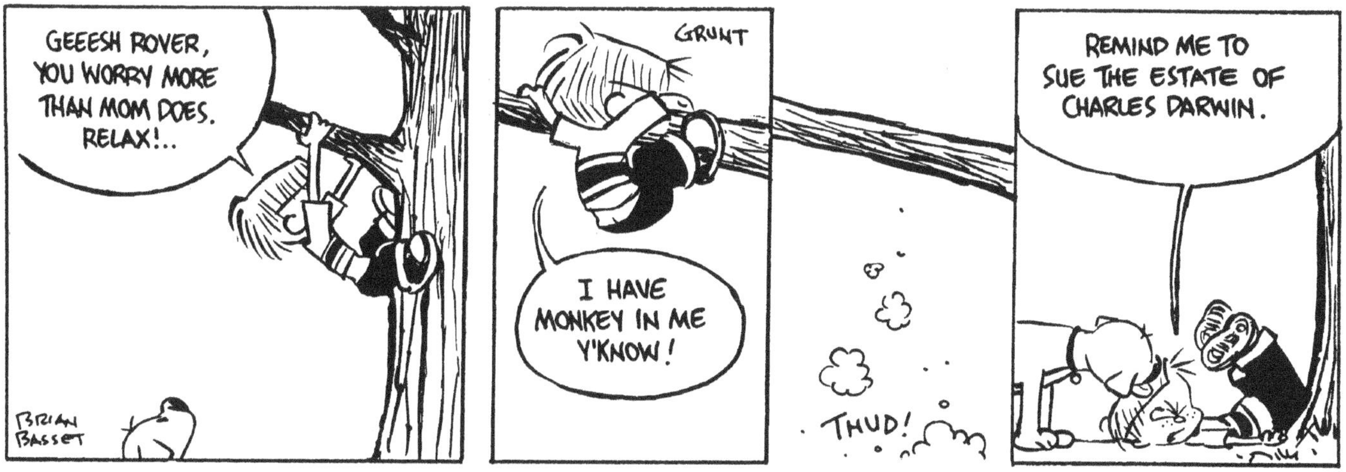
GEEESH ROVER, YOU WORRY MORE THAN MOM DOES. RELAX!..
BRIAN BASSET
GRUNT
I HAVE MONKEY IN ME Y'KNOW!
THUD!
REMIND ME TO SUE THE ESTATE OF CHARLES DARWIN.

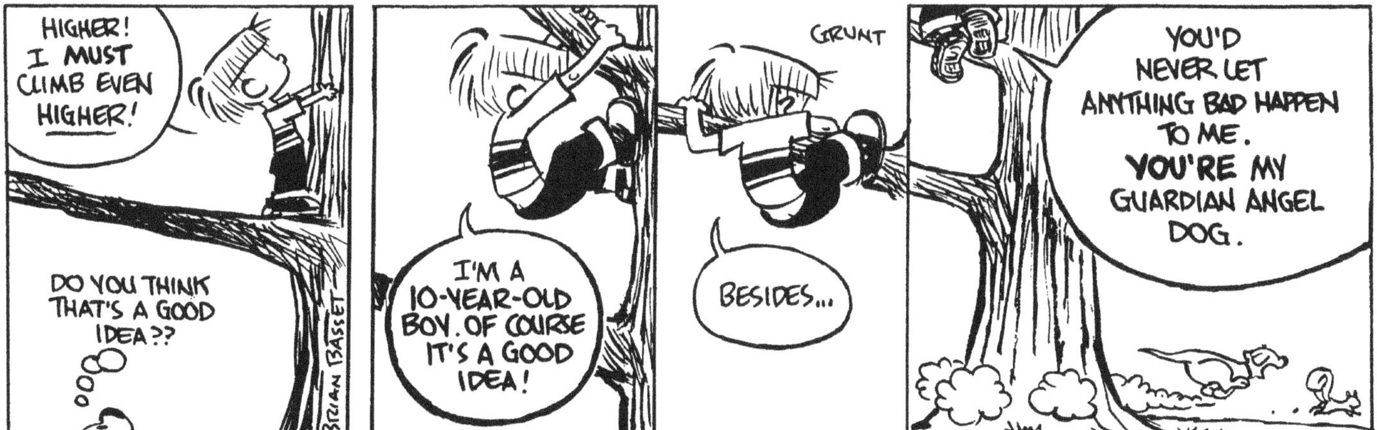
HIGHER! I MUST CLIMB EVEN HIGHER!
DO YOU THINK THAT'S A GOOD IDEA??
BRIAN BASSET
I'M A 10-YEAR-OLD BOY. OF COURSE IT'S A GOOD IDEA!
GRUNT
BESIDES...
YOU'D NEVER LET ANYTHING BAD HAPPEN TO ME. YOU'RE MY GUARDIAN ANGEL DOG.

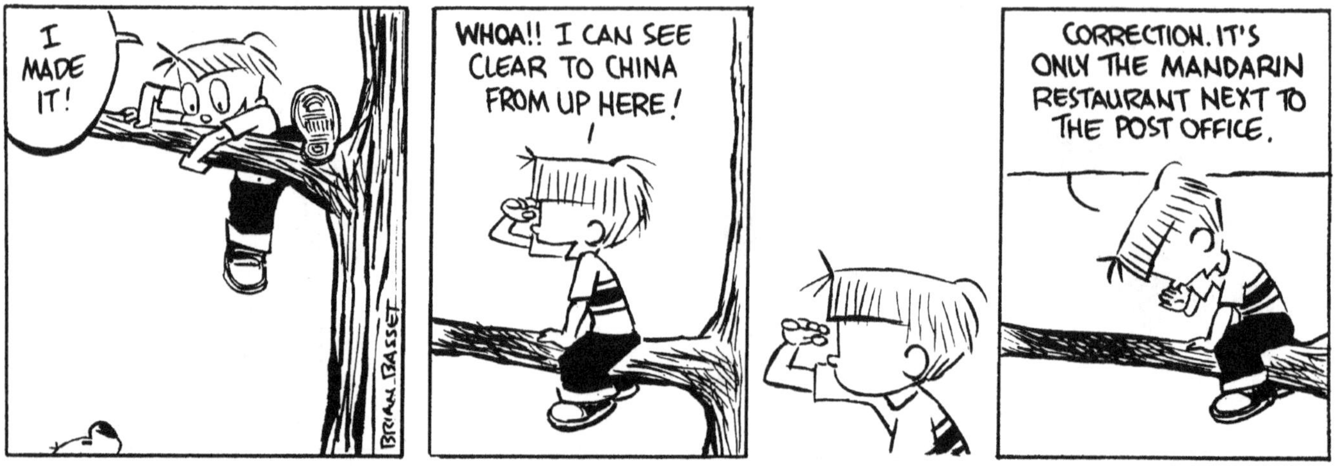
I MADE IT!
BRIAN BASSET
WHOA!! I CAN SEE CLEAR TO CHINA FROM UP HERE!
CORRECTION. IT'S ONLY THE MANDARIN RESTAURANT NEXT TO THE POST OFFICE.

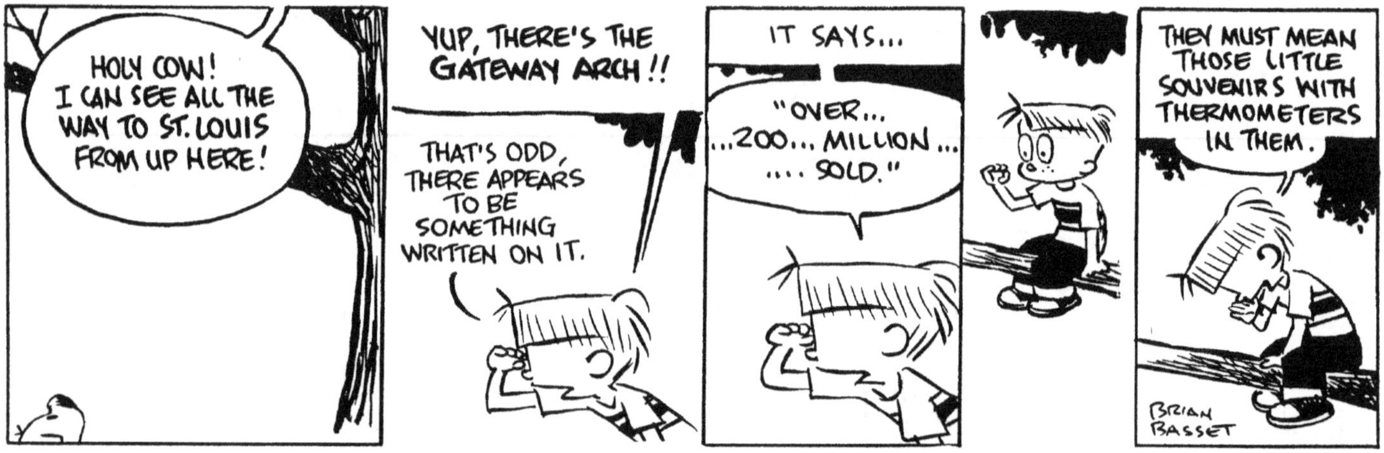
HOLY COW! I CAN SEE ALL THE WAY TO ST. LOUIS FROM UP HERE!
YUP, THERE'S THE GATEWAY ARCH!!
THAT'S ODD, THERE APPEARS TO BE SOMETHING WRITTEN ON IT.
IT SAYS...
"OVER... ...200... MILLION... .... SOLD."
THEY MUST MEAN THOSE LITTLE SOUVENIRS WITH THERMOMETERS IN THEM.
BRIAN BASSET

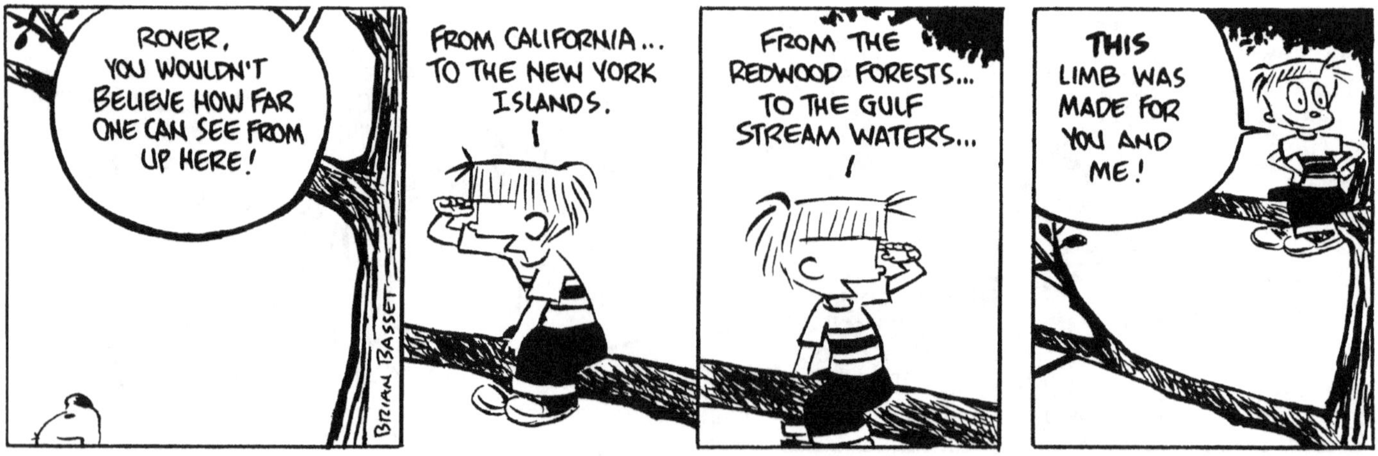
ROVER, YOU WOULDN'T BELIEVE HOW FAR ONE CAN SEE FROM UP HERE!
BRIAN BASSET
FROM CALIFORNIA... TO THE NEW YORK ISLANDS.
FROM THE REDWOOD FORESTS... TO THE GULF STREAM WATERS...
THIS LIMB WAS MADE FOR YOU AND ME!

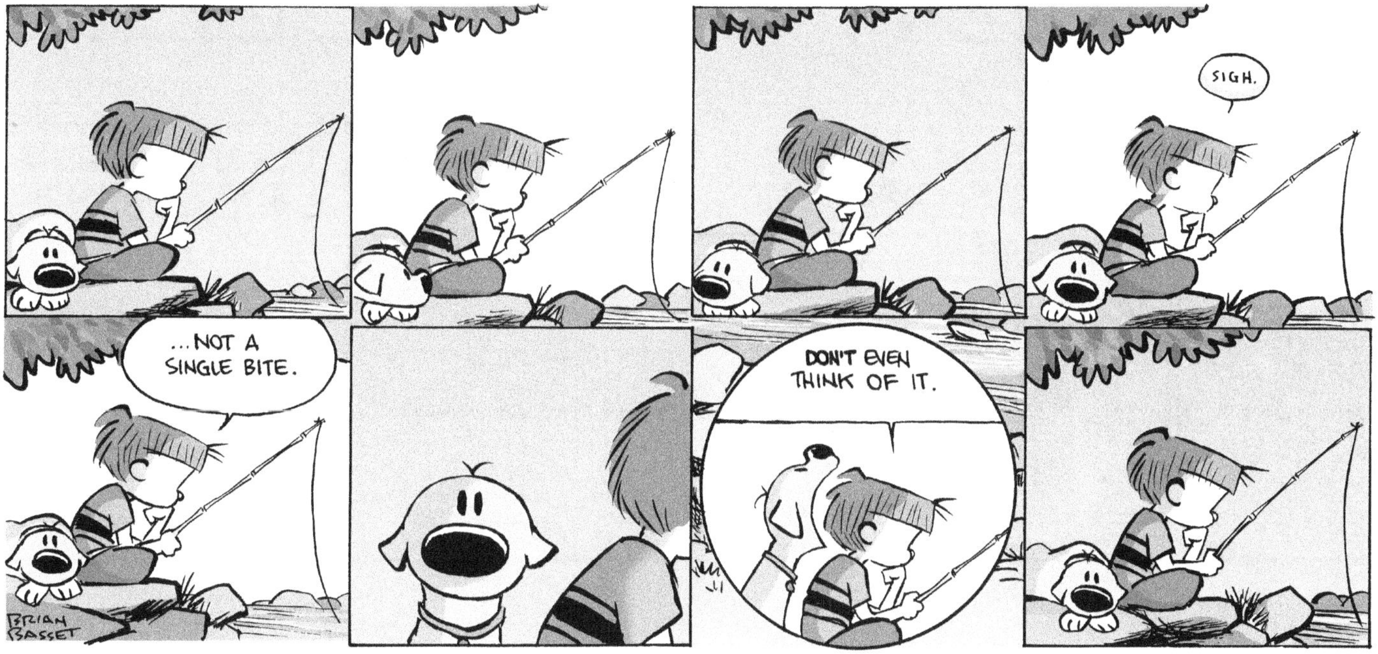
SIGH.
...NOT A SINGLE BITE.
DON'T EVEN THINK OF IT.
BRIAN BASSET

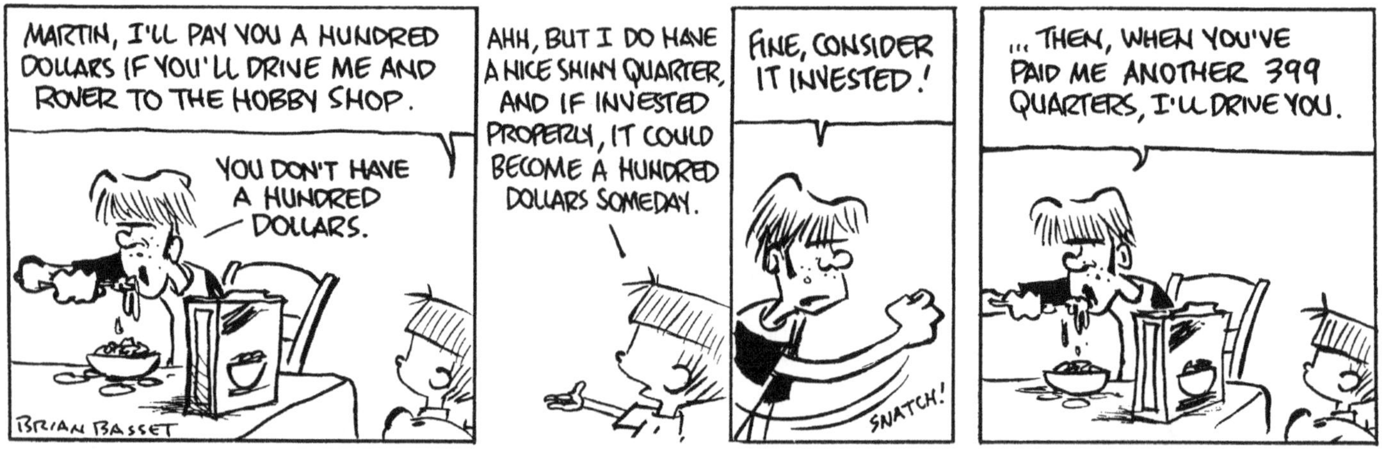
MARTIN, I'LL PAY YOU A HUNDRED DOLLARS IF YOU'LL DRIVE ME AND ROVER TO THE HOBBY SHOP.
YOU DON'T HAVE A HUNDRED DOLLARS.
BRIAN BASSET
AHH, BUT I DO HAVE A NICE SHINY QUARTER, AND IF INVESTED PROPERLY, IT COULD BECOME A HUNDRED DOLLARS SOMEDAY.
FINE, CONSIDER IT INVESTED!
SNATCH!
... THEN, WHEN YOU'VE PAID ME ANOTHER 399 QUARTERS, I'LL DRIVE YOU.

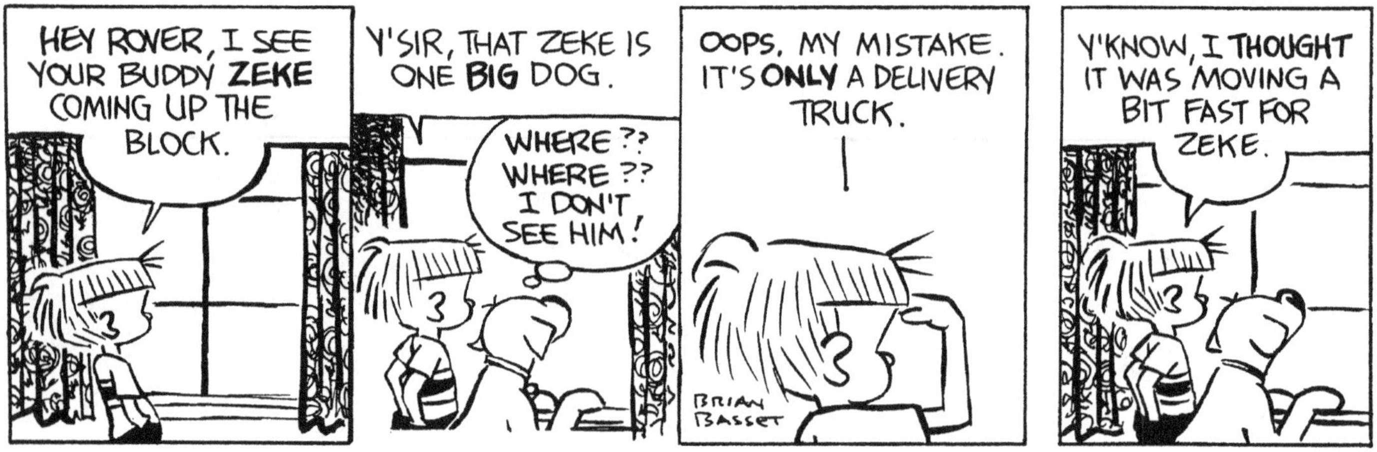
HEY ROVER, I SEE YOUR BUDDY ZEKE COMING UP THE BLOCK.
Y'SIR, THAT ZEKE IS ONE BIG DOG.
WHERE?? WHERE?? I DON'T SEE HIM!
OOPS. MY MISTAKE. IT'S ONLY A DELIVERY TRUCK.
BRIAN BASSET
Y'KNOW, I THOUGHT IT WAS MOVING A BIT FAST FOR ZEKE.

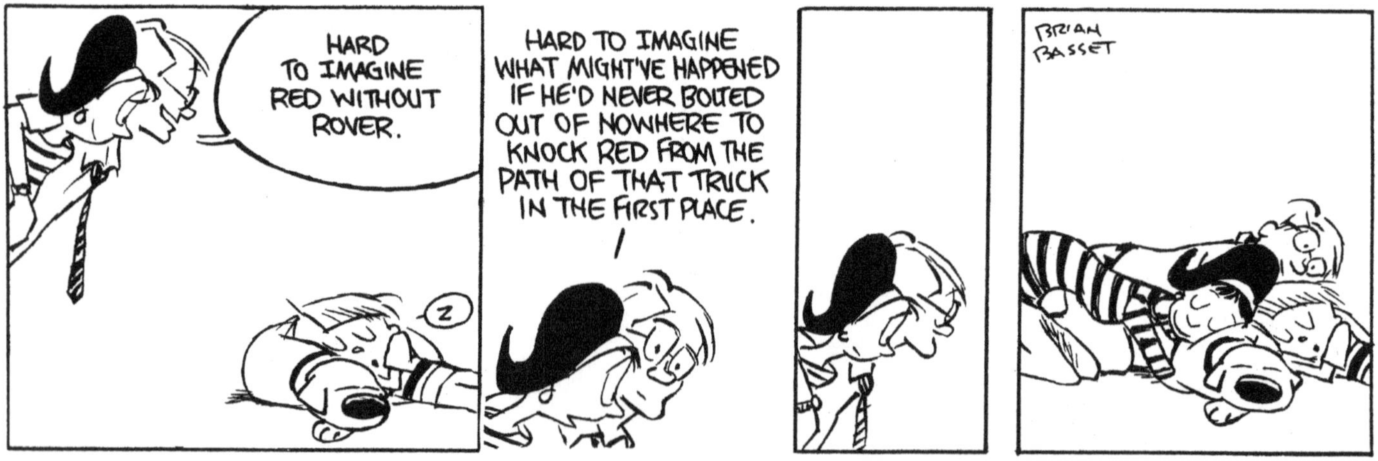
HARD TO IMAGINE RED WITHOUT ROVER.
Z
HARD TO IMAGINE WHAT MIGHT'VE HAPPENED IF HE'D NEVER BOLTED OUT OF NOWHERE TO KNOCK RED FROM THE PATH OF THAT TRUCK IN THE FIRST PLACE.
BRIAN BASSET

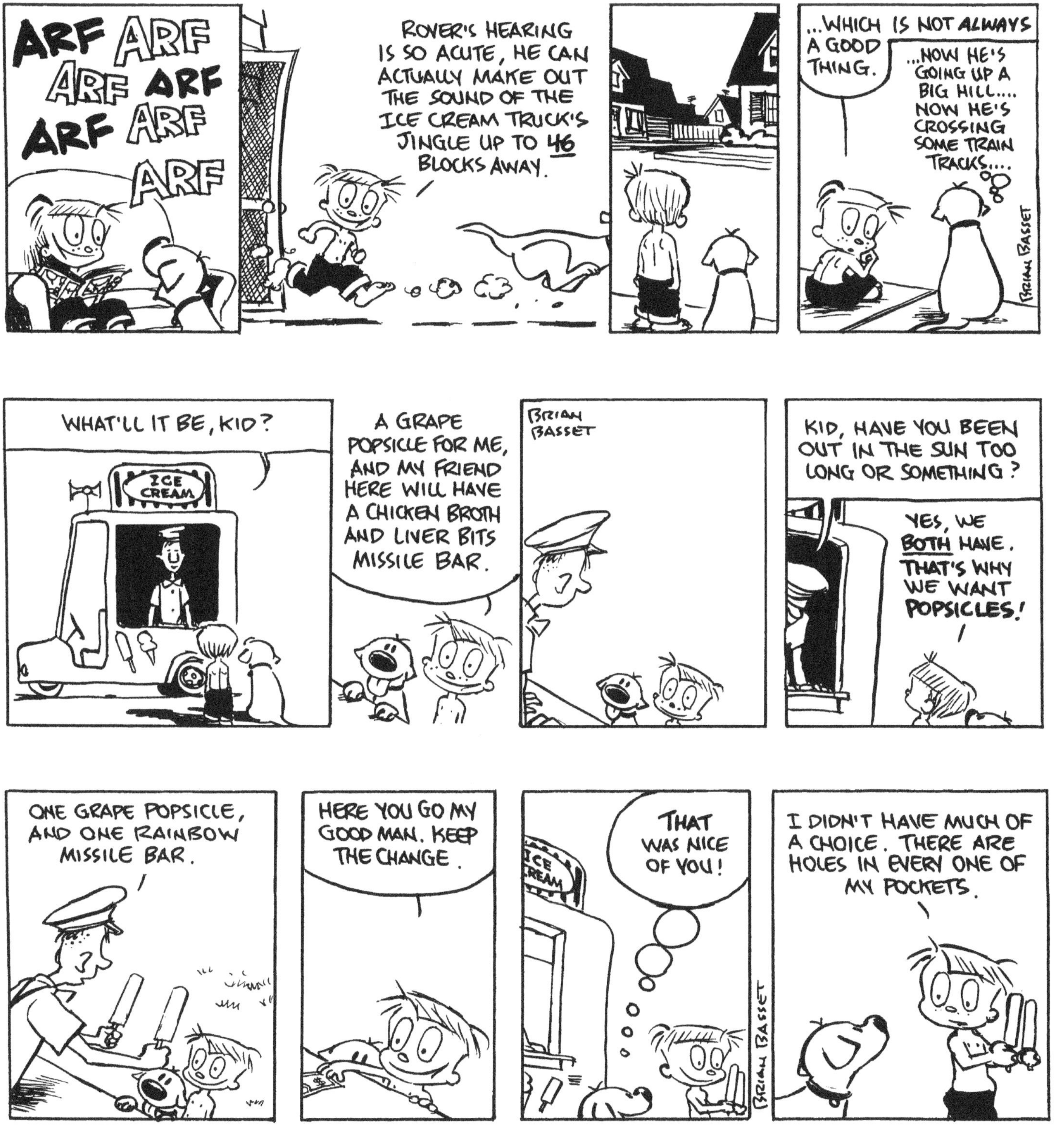
ARF ARF ARF ARF ARF ARF ARF
ROVER'S HEARING IS SO ACUTE, HE CAN ACTUALLY MAKE OUT THE SOUND OF THE ICE CREAM TRUCK'S JINGLE UP TO 46 BLOCKS AWAY.
...WHICH IS NOT ALWAYS A GOOD THING.
...NOW HE'S GOING UP A BIG HILL.... NOW HE'S CROSSING SOME TRAIN TRACKS....
BRIAN BASSET
WHAT'LL IT BE, KID?
ICE CREAM
A GRAPE POPSICLE FOR ME, AND MY FRIEND HERE WILL HAVE A CHICKEN BROTH AND LIVER BITS MISSILE BAR.
BRIAN BASSET
KID, HAVE YOU BEEN OUT IN THE SUN TOO LONG OR SOMETHING?
YES, WE BOTH HAVE. THAT'S WHY WE WANT POPSICLES!
ONE GRAPE POPSICLE, AND ONE RAINBOW MISSILE BAR.
HERE YOU GO MY GOOD MAN. KEEP THE CHANGE.
ICE CREAM
THAT WAS NICE OF YOU!
BRIAN BASSET
I DIDN'T HAVE MUCH OF A CHOICE. THERE ARE HOLES IN EVERY ONE OF MY POCKETS.

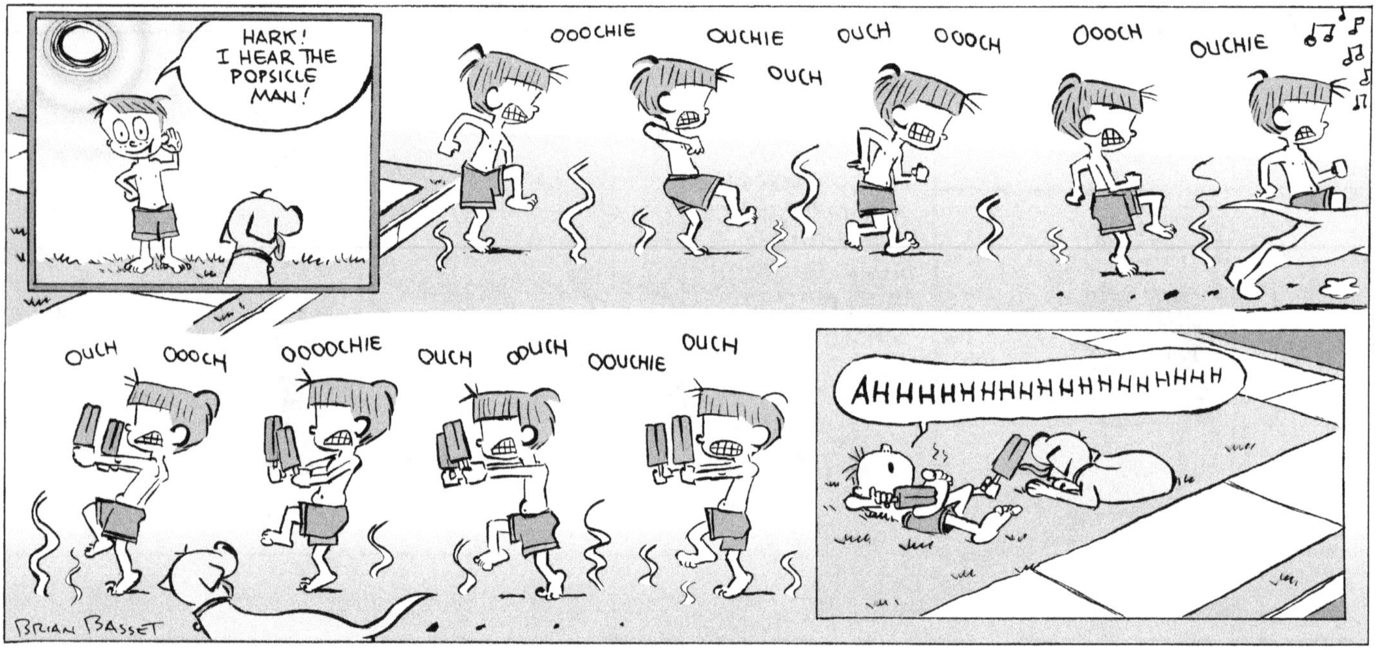
HARK! I HEAR THE POPSICLE MAN!
OOOCHIE
OUCHIE
OUCH
OUCH
OOOCH
OOOCH
OUCHIE
OUCH
OOOCH
OOOOCHIE
OUCH
OOUCH
OOUCHIE
OUCH
AHHHHHHHHHHHHHHHHH
BRIAN BASSET

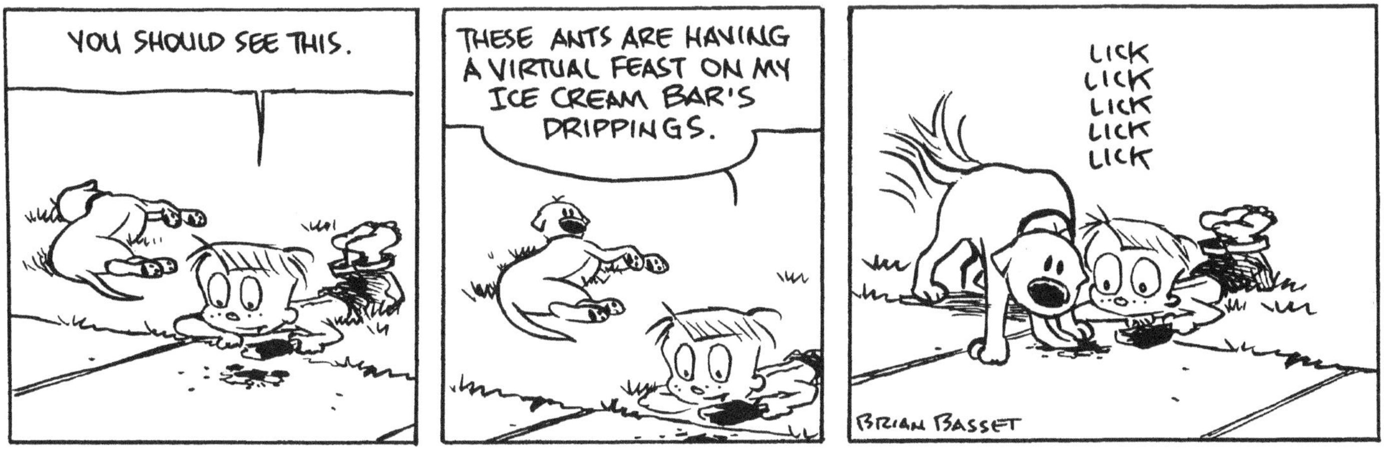
YOU SHOULD SEE THIS.
THESE ANTS ARE HAVING A VIRTUAL FEAST ON MY ICE CREAM BAR'S DRIPPINGS.
LICK LICK LICK LICK LICK
BRIAN BASSET

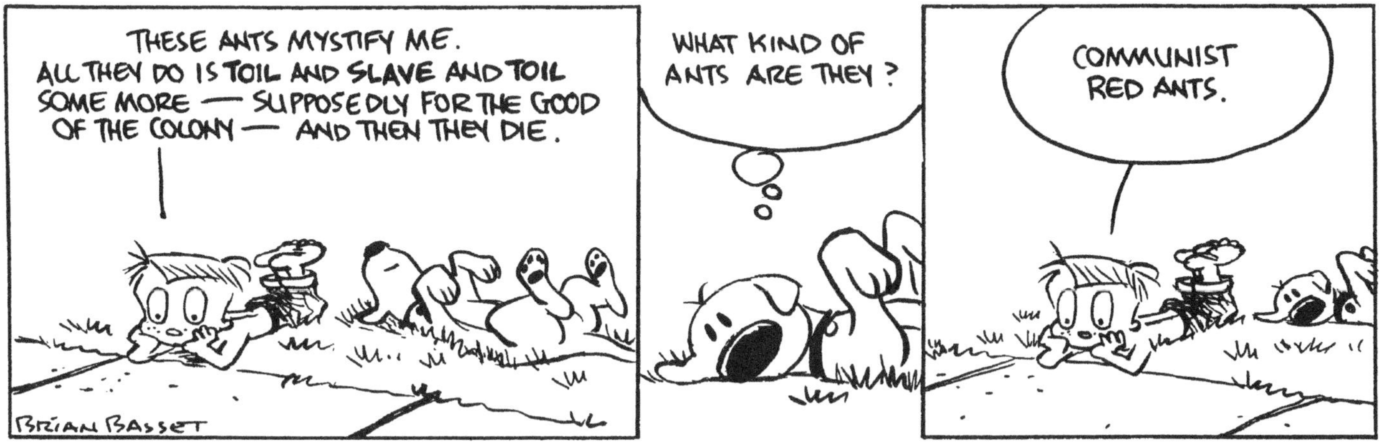
THESE ANTS MYSTIFY ME. ALL THEY DO IS TOIL AND SLAVE AND TOIL SOME MORE — SUPPOSEDLY FOR THE GOOD OF THE COLONY — AND THEN THEY DIE.
BRIAN BASSET
WHAT KIND OF ANTS ARE THEY?
COMMUNIST RED ANTS.

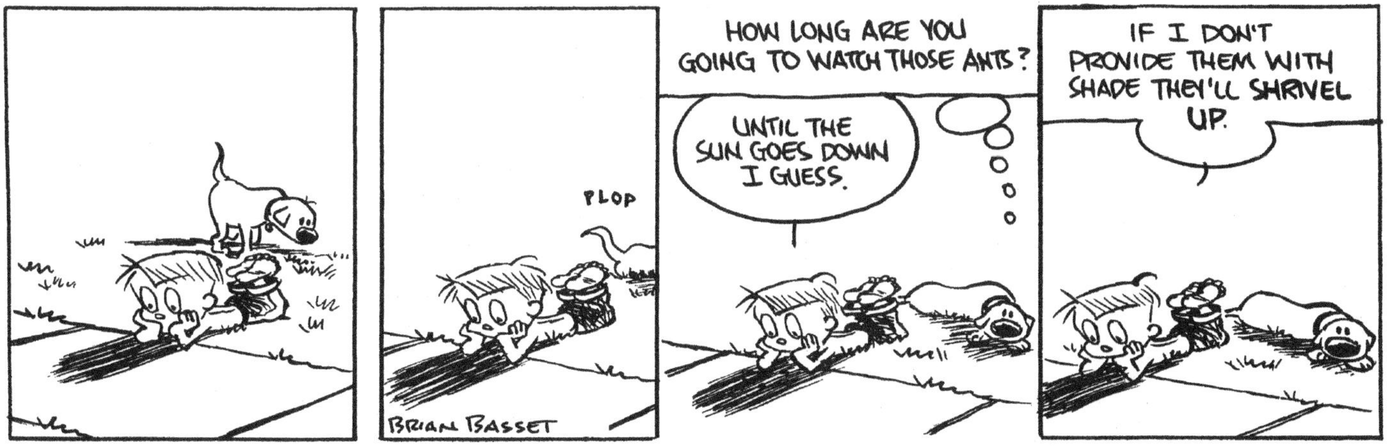
PLOP
BRIAN BASSET
HOW LONG ARE YOU GOING TO WATCH THOSE ANTS?
UNTIL THE SUN GOES DOWN I GUESS.
IF I DON'T PROVIDE THEM WITH SHADE THEY'LL SHRIVEL UP.

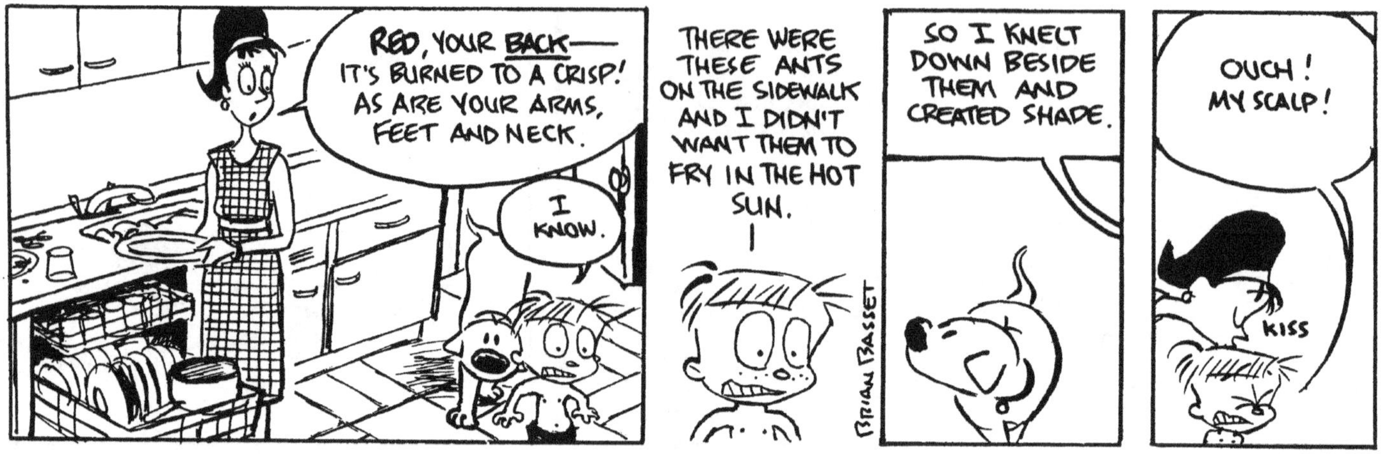
RED, YOUR BACK— IT'S BURNED TO A CRISP! AS ARE YOUR ARMS, FEET AND NECK.
I KNOW.
THERE WERE THESE ANTS ON THE SIDEWALK AND I DIDN'T WANT THEM TO FRY IN THE HOT SUN.
BRIAN BASSET
SO I KNELT DOWN BESIDE THEM AND CREATED SHADE.
OUCH! MY SCALP!
KISS

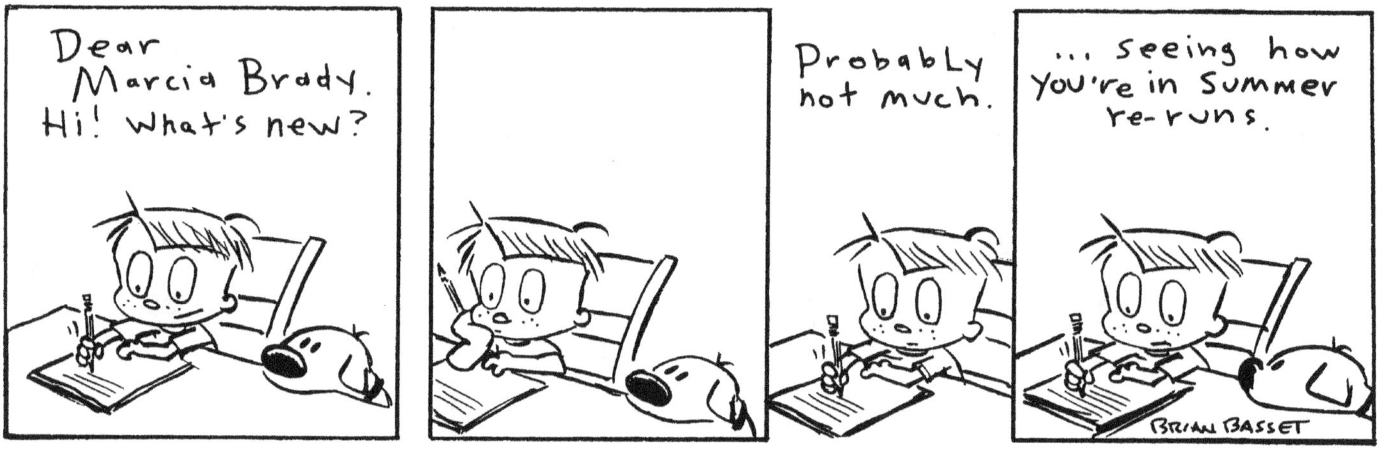
Dear Marcia Brady. Hi! What's new?
Probably not much.
... seeing how you're in Summer re-runs.
BRIAN BASSET

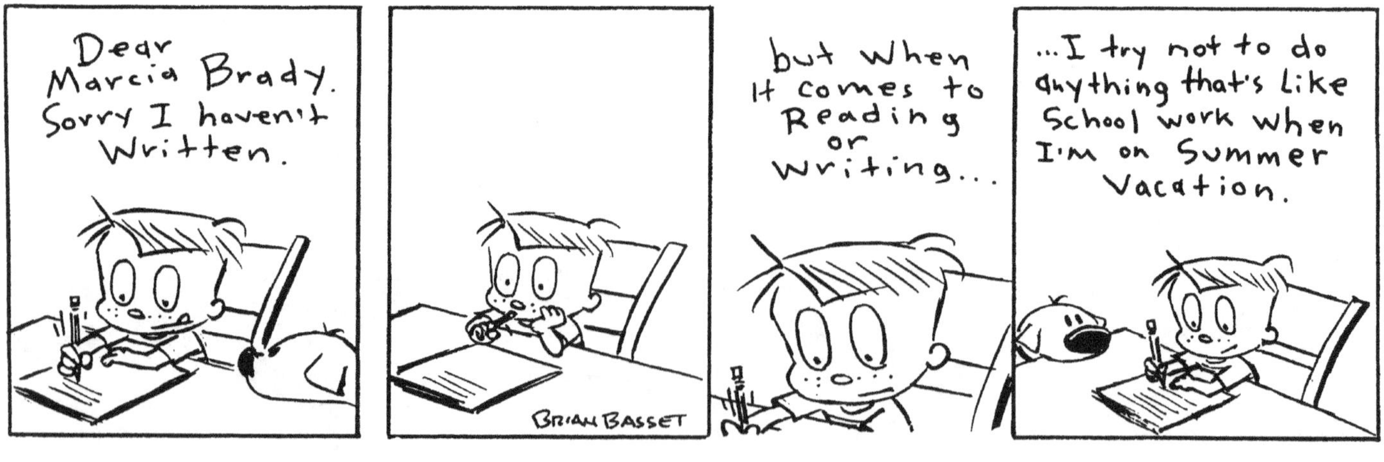
Dear Marcia Brady. Sorry I haven't Written.
BRIAN BASSET
but When It comes to Reading or Writing...
...I try not to do anything that's Like School work when I'm on Summer Vacation.

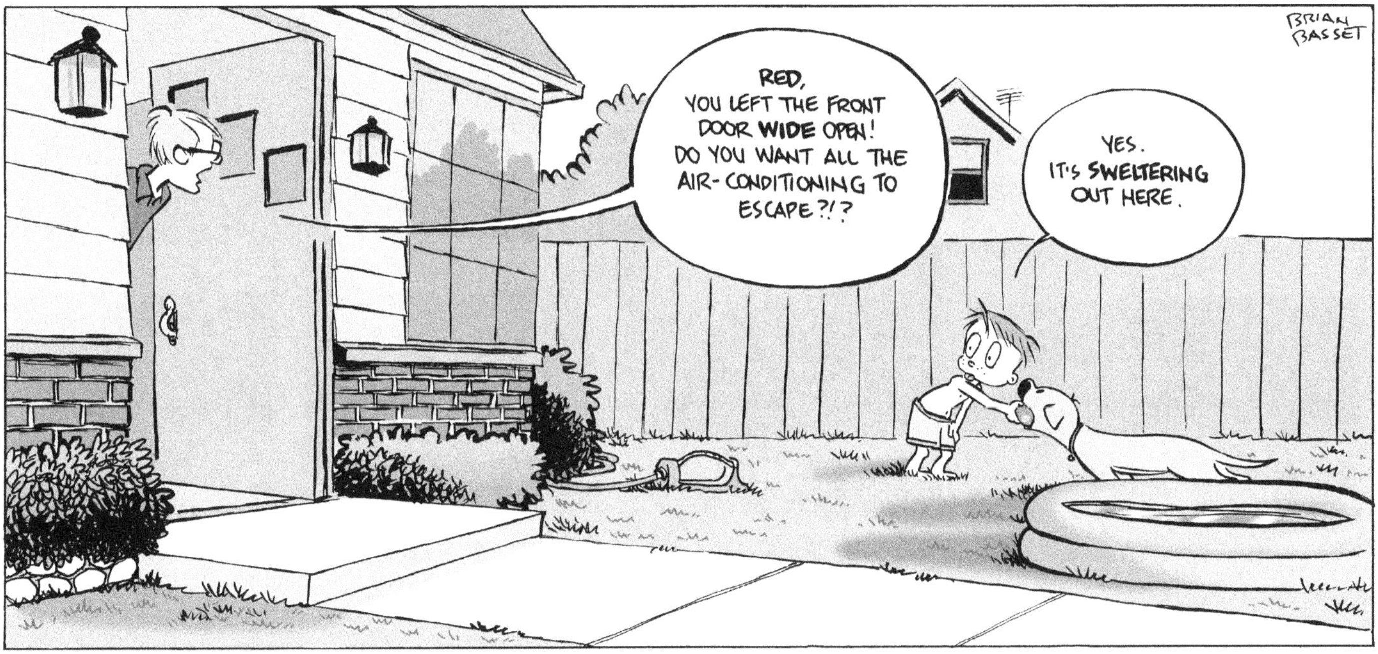
BRIAN BASSET
RED, YOU LEFT THE FRONT DOOR WIDE OPEN! DO YOU WANT ALL THE AIR-CONDITIONING TO ESCAPE?!?
YES. IT'S SWELTERING OUT HERE.

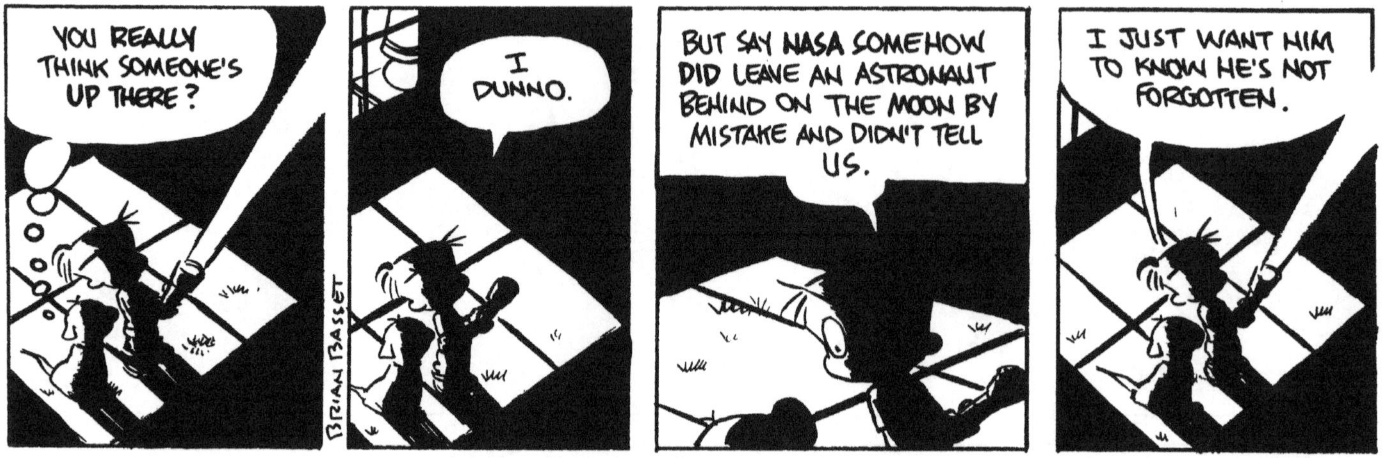
YOU REALLY THINK SOMEONE'S UP THERE?
I DUNNO.
BUT SAY NASA SOMEHOW DID LEAVE AN ASTRONAUT BEHIND ON THE MOON BY MISTAKE AND DIDN'T TELL US.
I JUST WANT HIM TO KNOW HE'S NOT FORGOTTEN.
BRIAN BASSET

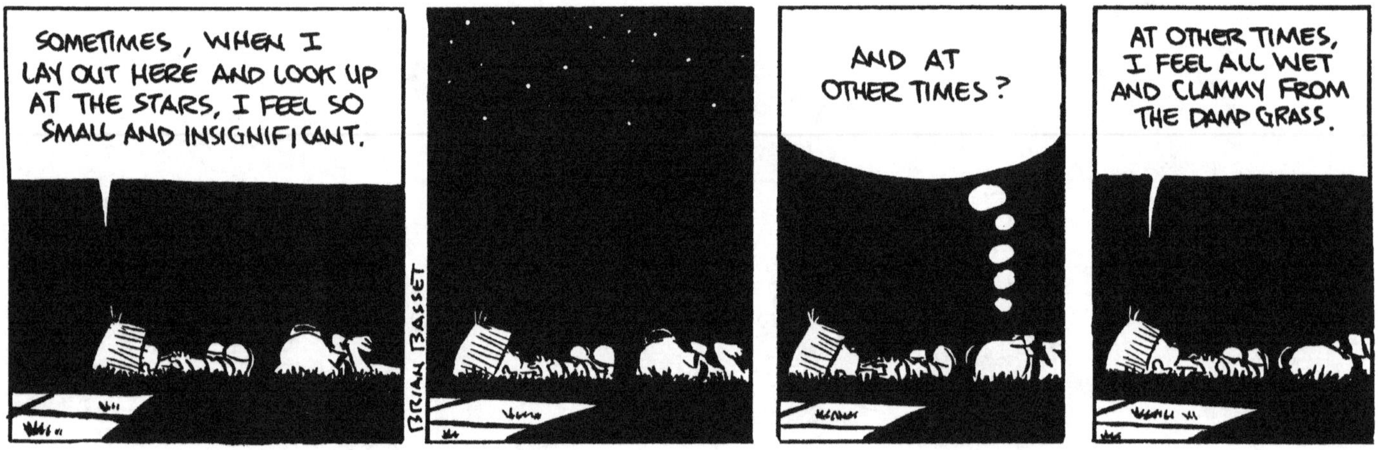
SOMETIMES, WHEN I LAY OUT HERE AND LOOK UP AT THE STARS, I FEEL SO SMALL AND INSIGNIFICANT.
AND AT OTHER TIMES?
AT OTHER TIMES, I FEEL ALL WET AND CLAMMY FROM THE DAMP GRASS.
BRIAN BASSET

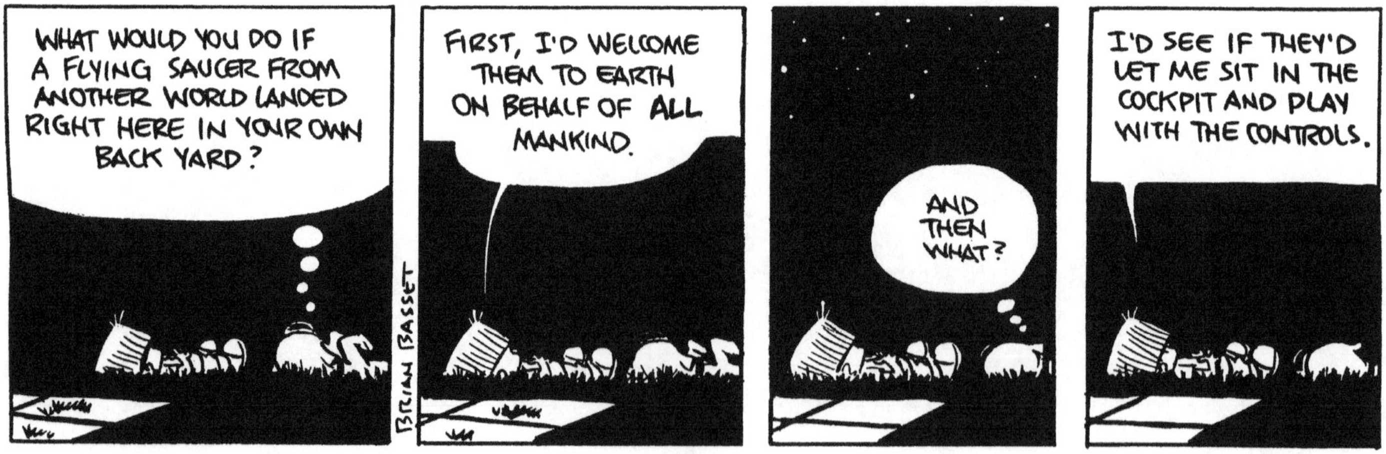
WHAT WOULD YOU DO IF A FLYING SAUCER FROM ANOTHER WORLD LANDED RIGHT HERE IN YOUR OWN BACK YARD?
FIRST, I'D WELCOME THEM TO EARTH ON BEHALF OF ALL MANKIND.
AND THEN WHAT?
I'D SEE IF THEY'D LET ME SIT IN THE COCKPIT AND PLAY WITH THE CONTROLS.
BRIAN BASSET

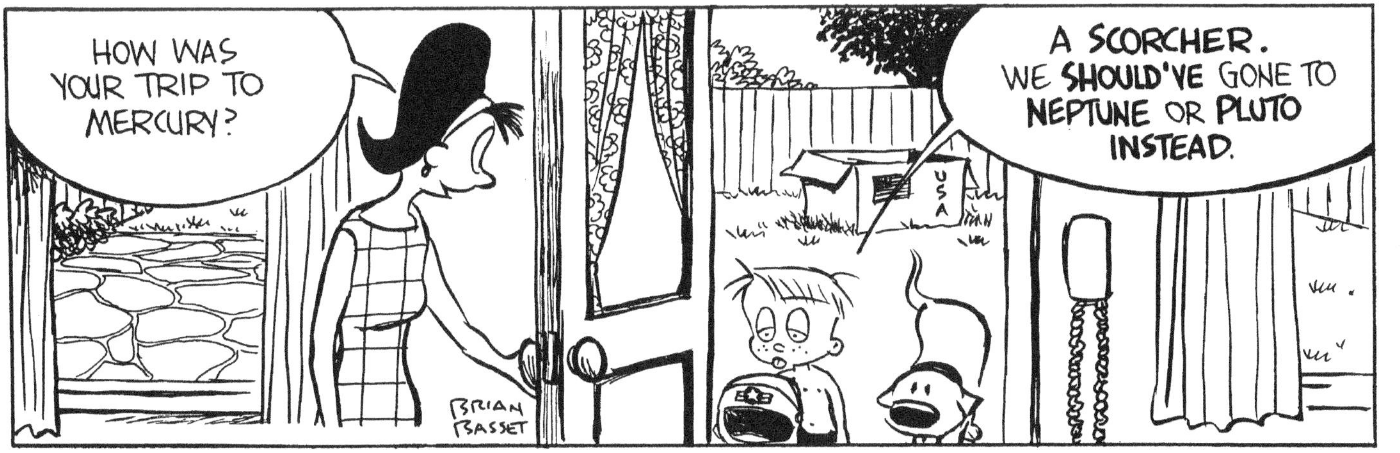
HOW WAS YOUR TRIP TO MERCURY?
A SCORCHER. WE SHOULD'VE GONE TO NEPTUNE OR PLUTO INSTEAD.
BRIAN BASSET

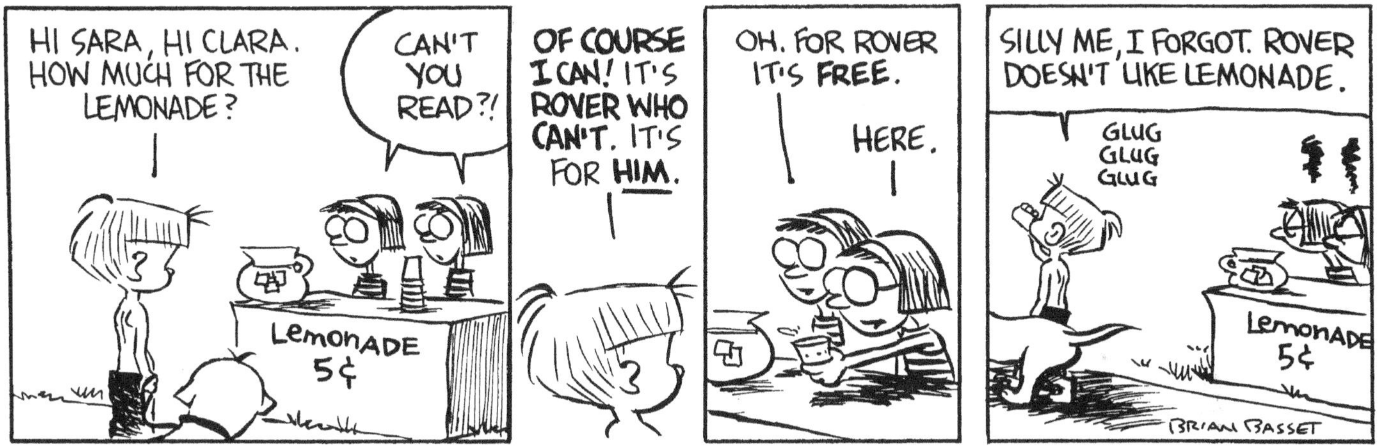
HI SARA, HI CLARA. HOW MUCH FOR THE LEMONADE?
CAN'T YOU READ?!
LEMONADE 5¢
OF COURSE I CAN! IT'S ROVER WHO CAN'T. IT'S FOR HIM.
OH. FOR ROVER IT'S FREE.
HERE.
SILLY ME, I FORGOT. ROVER DOESN'T LIKE LEMONADE.
GLUG GLUG GLUG
LEMONADE 5¢
BRIAN BASSET

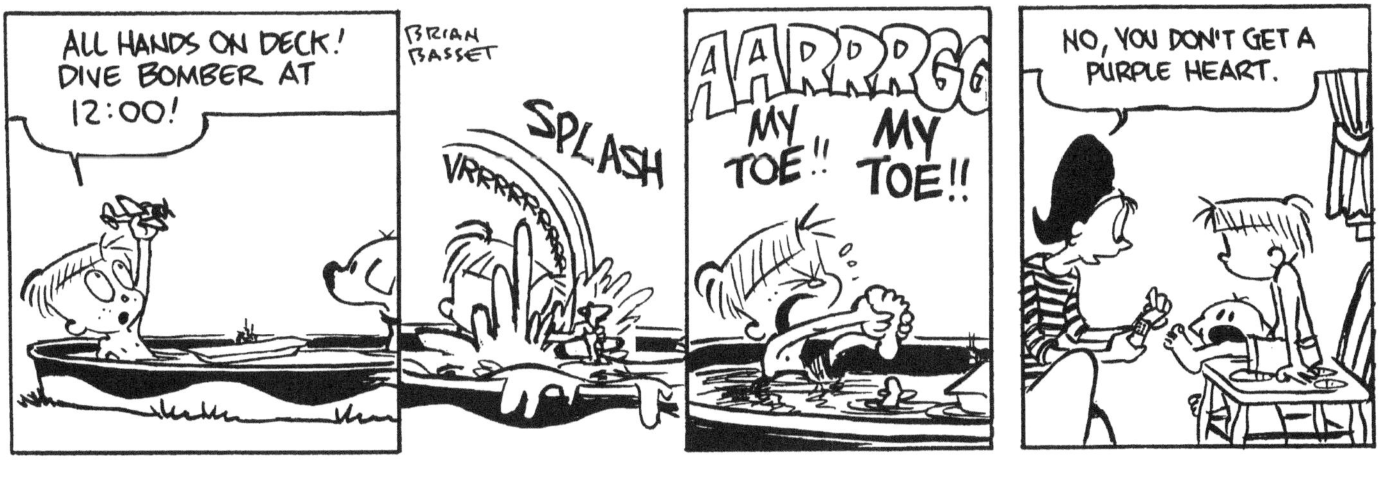
ALL HANDS ON DECK! DIVE BOMBER AT 12:00!
BRIAN BASSET
SPLASH
VRRRRRRRRR
AARRRGG
MY TOE!!
MY TOE!!
NO, YOU DON'T GET A PURPLE HEART.

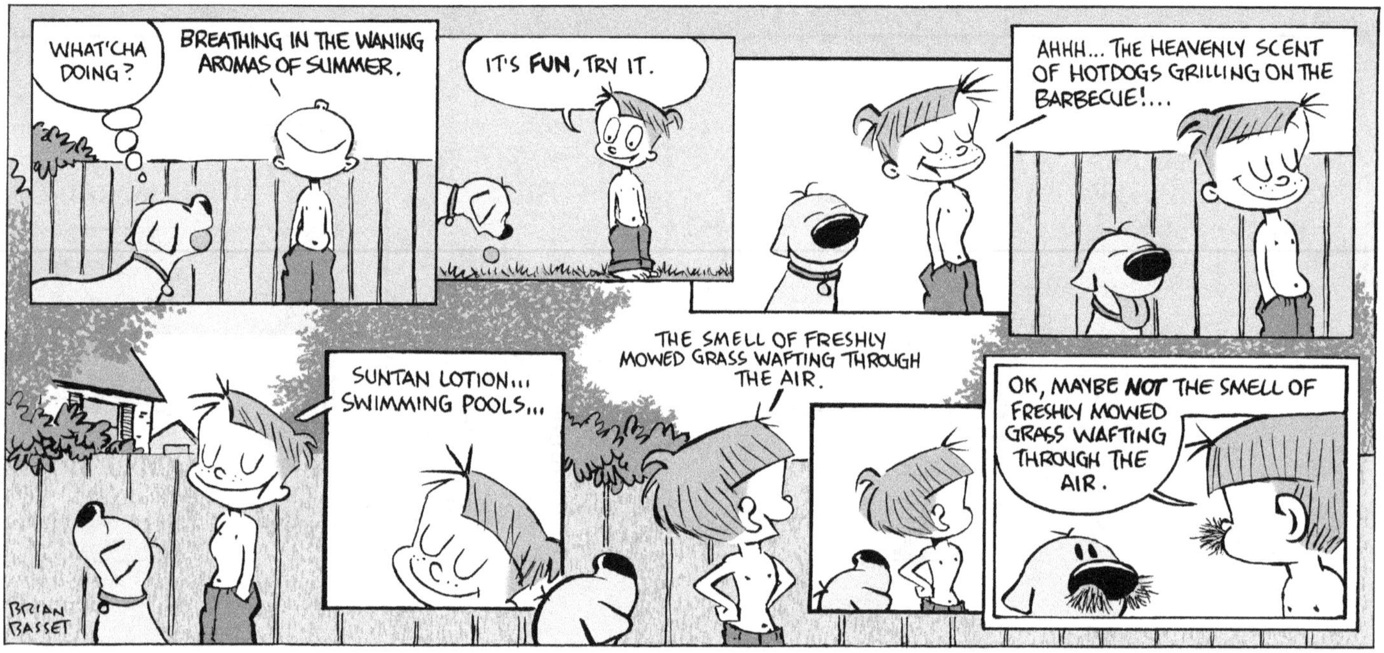
WHAT'CHA DOING?
BREATHING IN THE WANING AROMAS OF SUMMER.
IT'S **FUN**, TRY IT.
AHHH... THE HEAVENLY SCENT OF HOTDOGS GRILLING ON THE BARBECUE!...
SUNTAN LOTION... SWIMMING POOLS...
THE SMELL OF FRESHLY MOWED GRASS WAFTING THROUGH THE AIR.
OK, MAYBE **NOT** THE SMELL OF FRESHLY MOWED GRASS WAFTING THROUGH THE AIR.
BRIAN BASSET

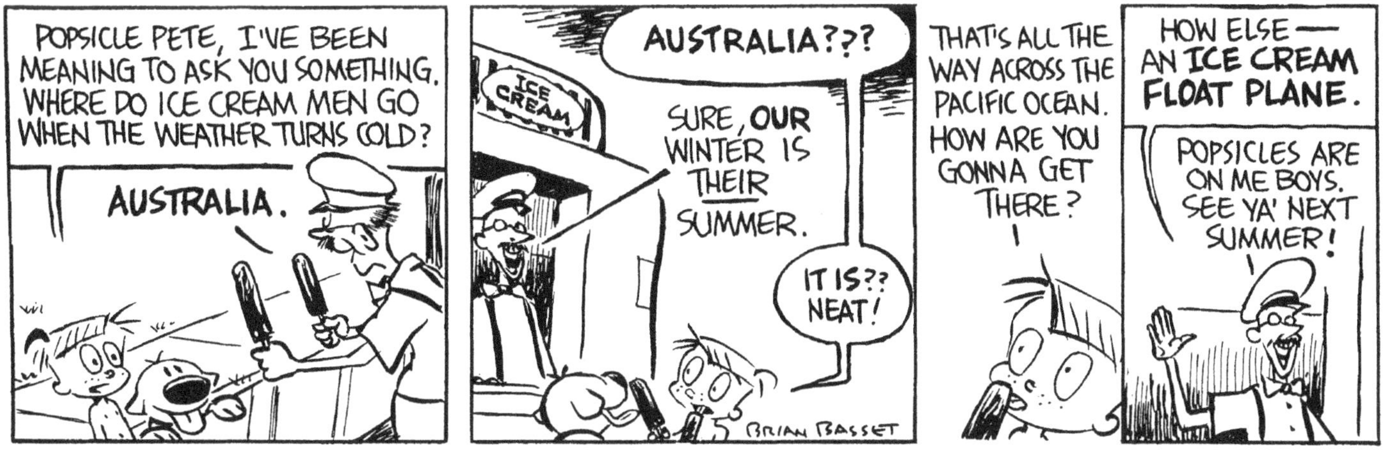
POPSICLE PETE, I'VE BEEN MEANING TO ASK YOU SOMETHING. WHERE DO ICE CREAM MEN GO WHEN THE WEATHER TURNS COLD?
AUSTRALIA.
AUSTRALIA???
ICE CREAM
SURE, **OUR** WINTER IS THEIR SUMMER.
IT IS?? NEAT!
BRIAN BASSET
THAT'S ALL THE WAY ACROSS THE PACIFIC OCEAN. HOW ARE YOU GONNA GET THERE?
HOW ELSE— AN **ICE CREAM FLOAT PLANE**.
POPSICLES ARE ON ME BOYS. SEE YA' NEXT SUMMER!

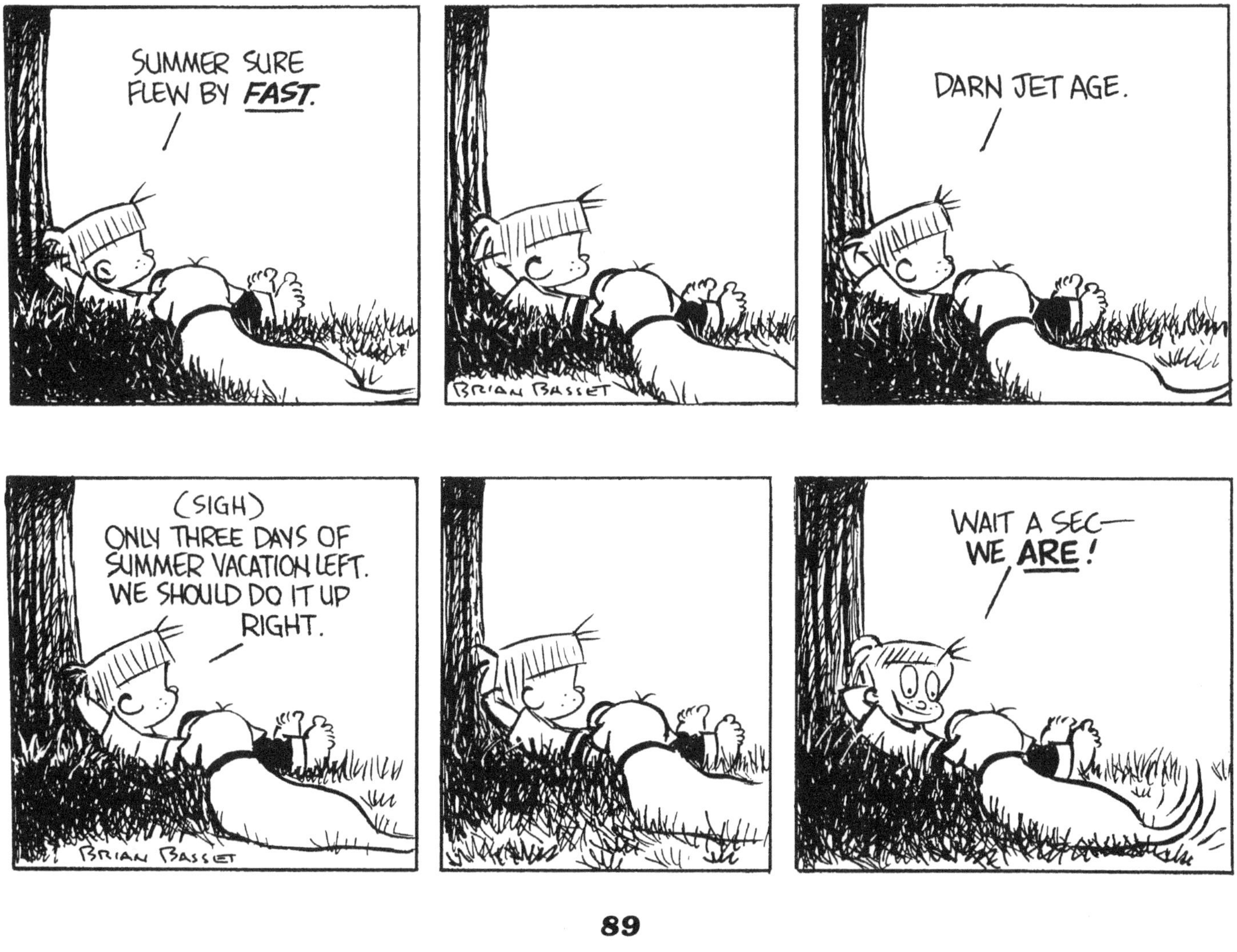
SUMMER SURE FLEW BY ***FAST.***
BRIAN BASSET
DARN JET AGE.
(SIGH) ONLY THREE DAYS OF SUMMER VACATION LEFT. WE SHOULD DO IT UP RIGHT.
BRIAN BASSET
WAIT A SEC— WE **ARE**!

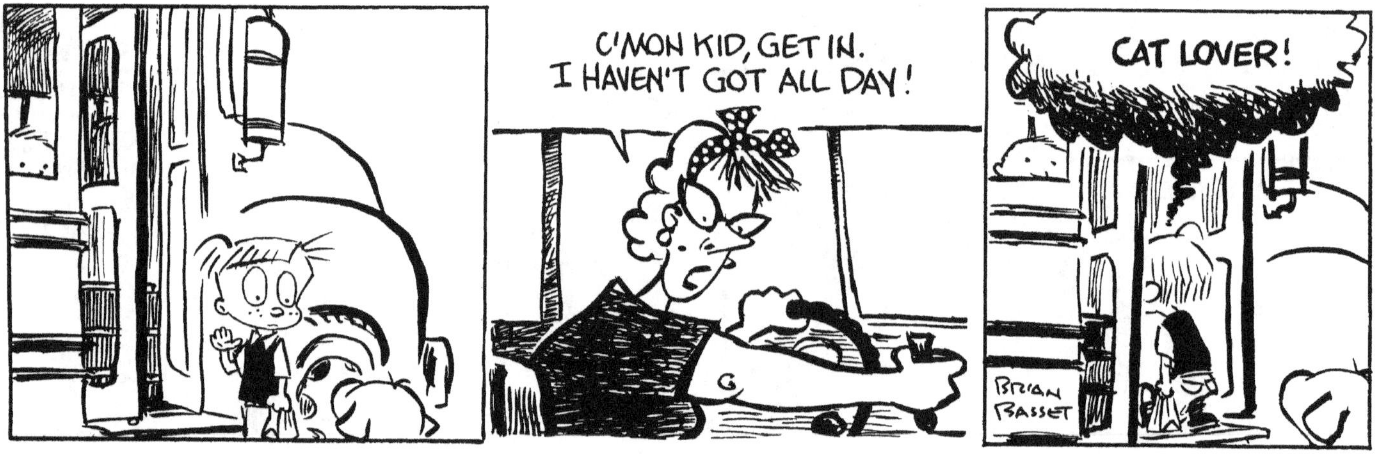
C'MON KID, GET IN.
I HAVEN'T GOT ALL DAY!
CAT LOVER!
BRIAN BASSET

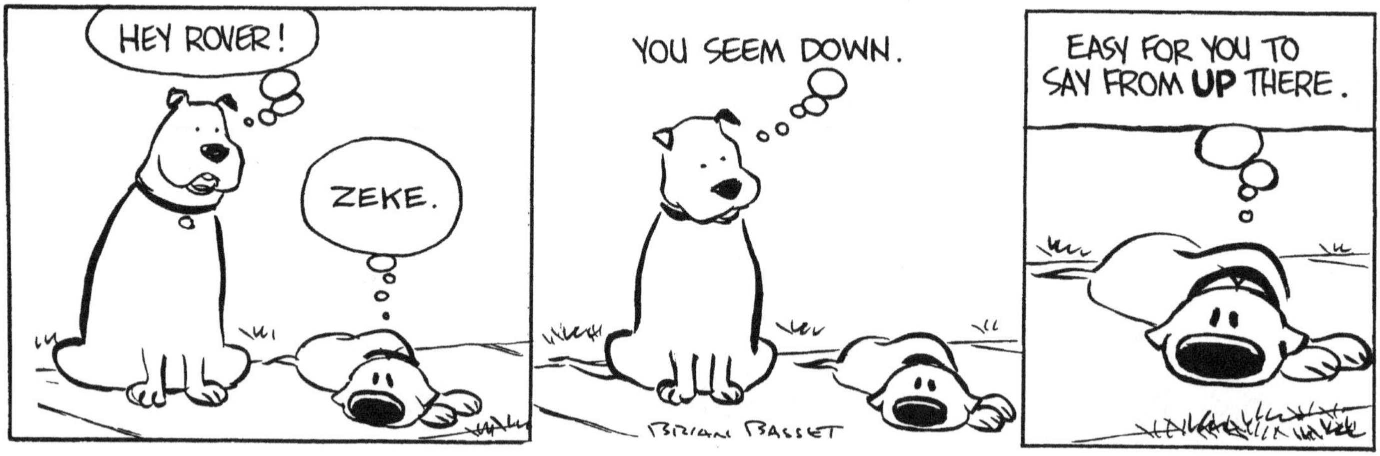
HEY ROVER!
ZEKE.
YOU SEEM DOWN.
EASY FOR YOU TO SAY FROM **UP** THERE.
BRIAN BASSET

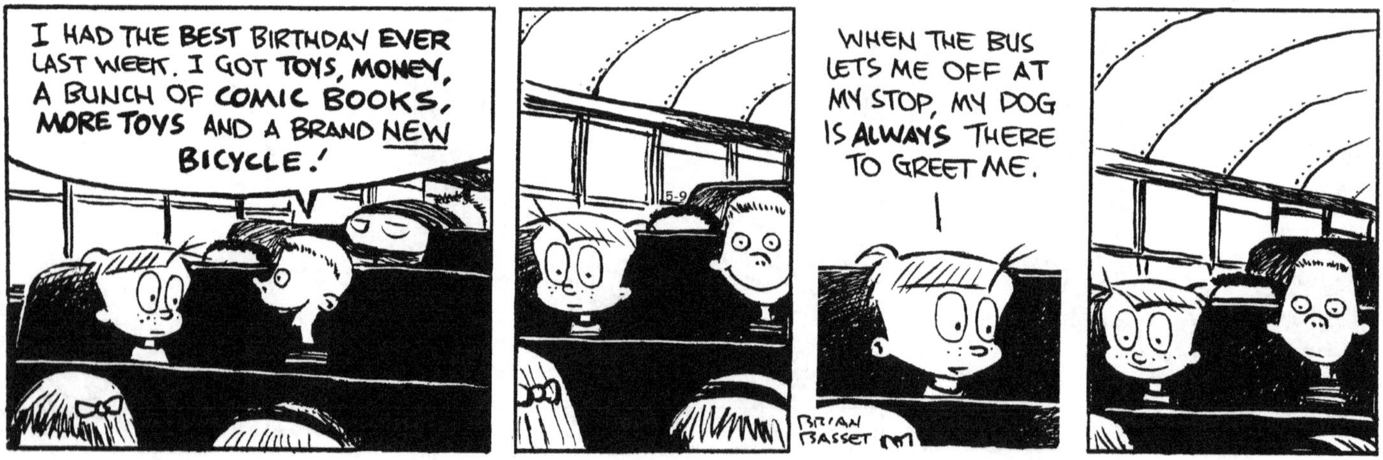
I HAD THE **BEST** BIRTHDAY **EVER** LAST WEEK. I GOT **TOYS**, **MONEY**, A BUNCH OF **COMIC BOOKS**, **MORE TOYS** AND A BRAND NEW **BICYCLE**!
WHEN THE BUS LETS ME OFF AT MY STOP, MY DOG IS **ALWAYS** THERE TO GREET ME.
BRIAN BASSET

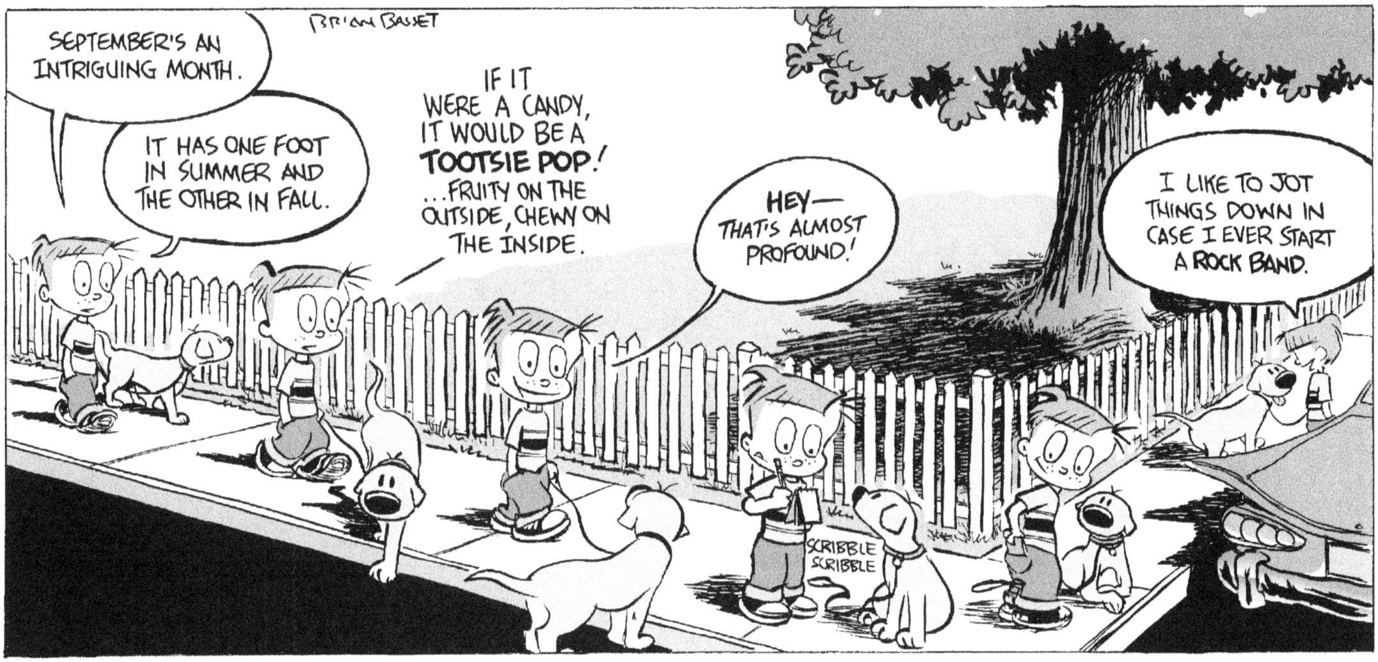
BRIAN BASSET
SEPTEMBER'S AN INTRIGUING MONTH.
IT HAS ONE FOOT IN SUMMER AND THE OTHER IN FALL.
IF IT WERE A CANDY, IT WOULD BE A TOOTSIE POP! ...FRUITY ON THE OUTSIDE, CHEWY ON THE INSIDE.
HEY— THAT'S ALMOST PROFOUND!
SCRIBBLE SCRIBBLE
I LIKE TO JOT THINGS DOWN IN CASE I EVER START A ROCK BAND.

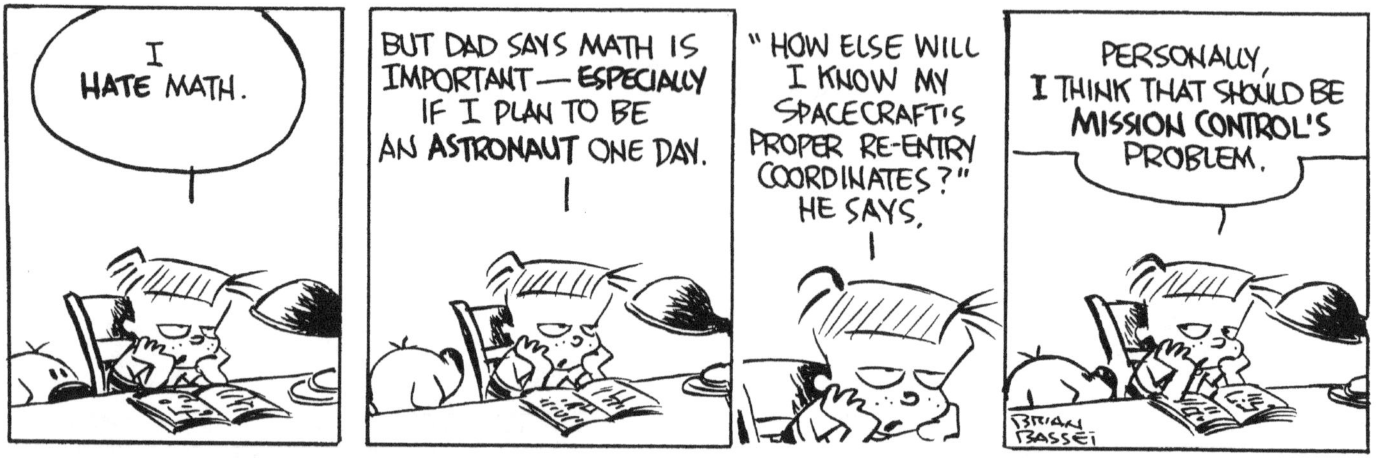
I HATE MATH.
BUT DAD SAYS MATH IS IMPORTANT — ESPECIALLY IF I PLAN TO BE AN ASTRONAUT ONE DAY.
"HOW ELSE WILL I KNOW MY SPACECRAFT'S PROPER RE-ENTRY COORDINATES?" HE SAYS.
PERSONALLY, I THINK THAT SHOULD BE MISSION CONTROL'S PROBLEM.
BRIAN BASSET

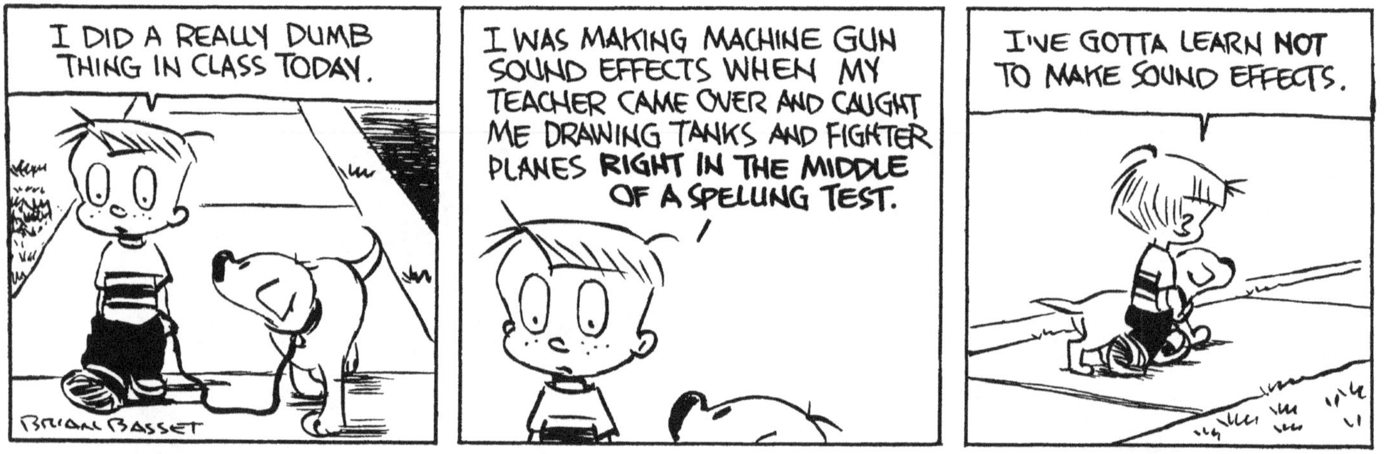
I DID A REALLY DUMB THING IN CLASS TODAY.
BRIAN BASSET
I WAS MAKING MACHINE GUN SOUND EFFECTS WHEN MY TEACHER CAME OVER AND CAUGHT ME DRAWING TANKS AND FIGHTER PLANES RIGHT IN THE MIDDLE OF A SPELLING TEST.
I'VE GOTTA LEARN NOT TO MAKE SOUND EFFECTS.

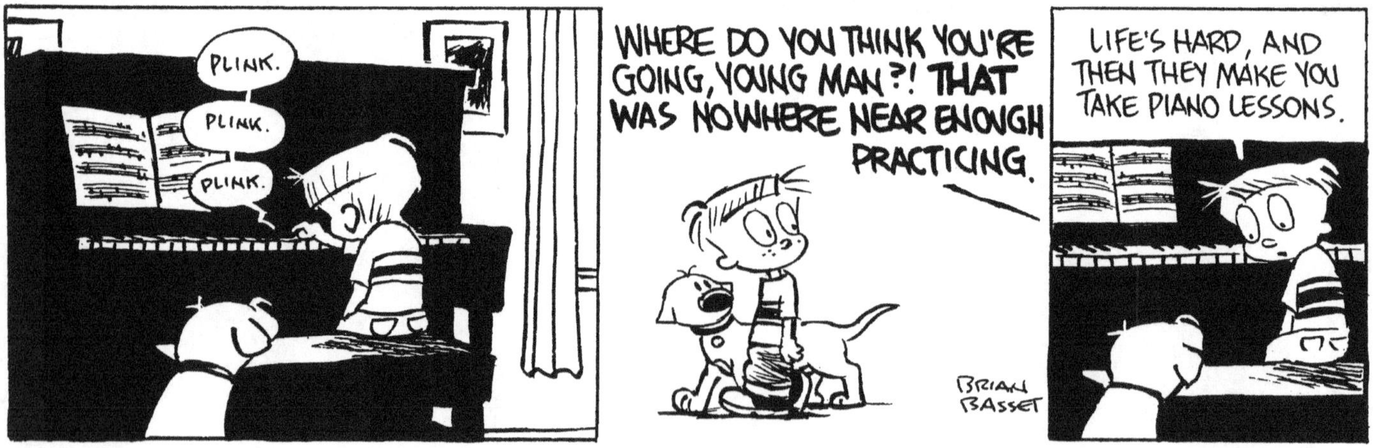
PLINK.
PLINK.
PLINK.
WHERE DO YOU THINK YOU'RE GOING, YOUNG MAN?! THAT WAS NOWHERE NEAR ENOUGH PRACTICING.
BRIAN BASSET
LIFE'S HARD, AND THEN THEY MAKE YOU TAKE PIANO LESSONS.

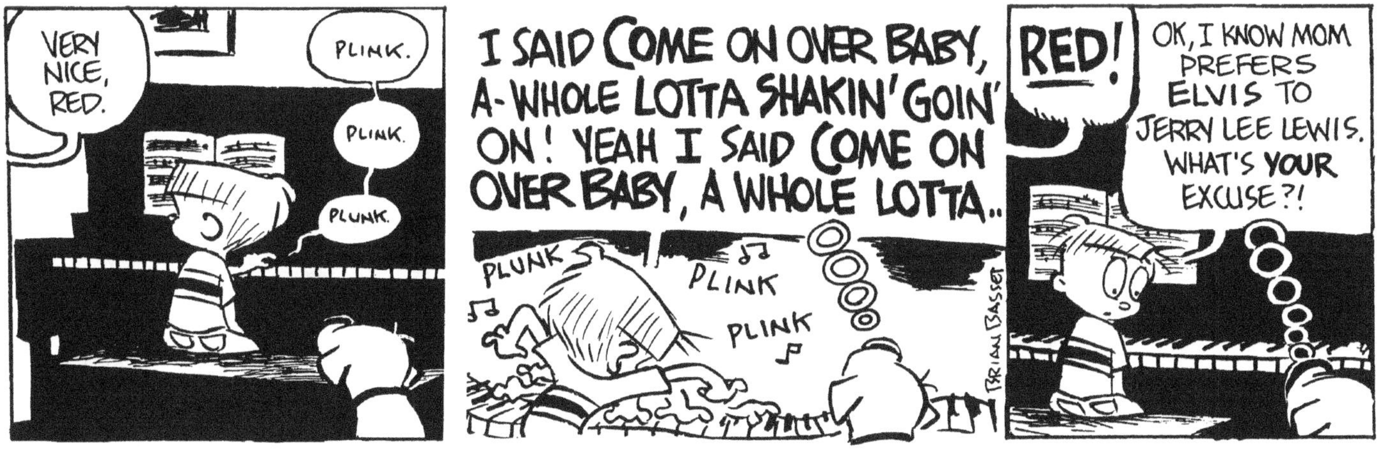
VERY NICE, RED.
PLINK.
PLINK.
PLINK.
I SAID COME ON OVER BABY, A-WHOLE LOTTA SHAKIN' GOIN' ON! YEAH I SAID COME ON OVER BABY, A WHOLE LOTTA..
PLUNK
PLINK
PLINK
BRIAN BASSET
RED!
OK, I KNOW MOM PREFERS ELVIS TO JERRY LEE LEWIS. WHAT'S YOUR EXCUSE?!

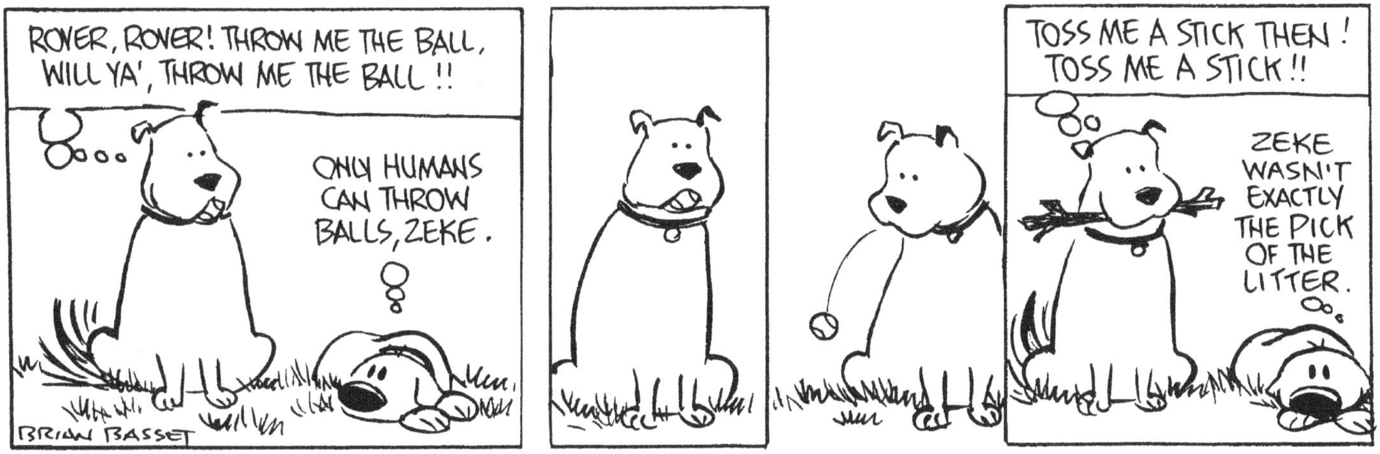
ROVER, ROVER! THROW ME THE BALL, WILL YA', THROW ME THE BALL!!
ONLY HUMANS CAN THROW BALLS, ZEKE.
BRIAN BASSET
TOSS ME A STICK THEN! TOSS ME A STICK!!
ZEKE WASN'T EXACTLY THE PICK OF THE LITTER.

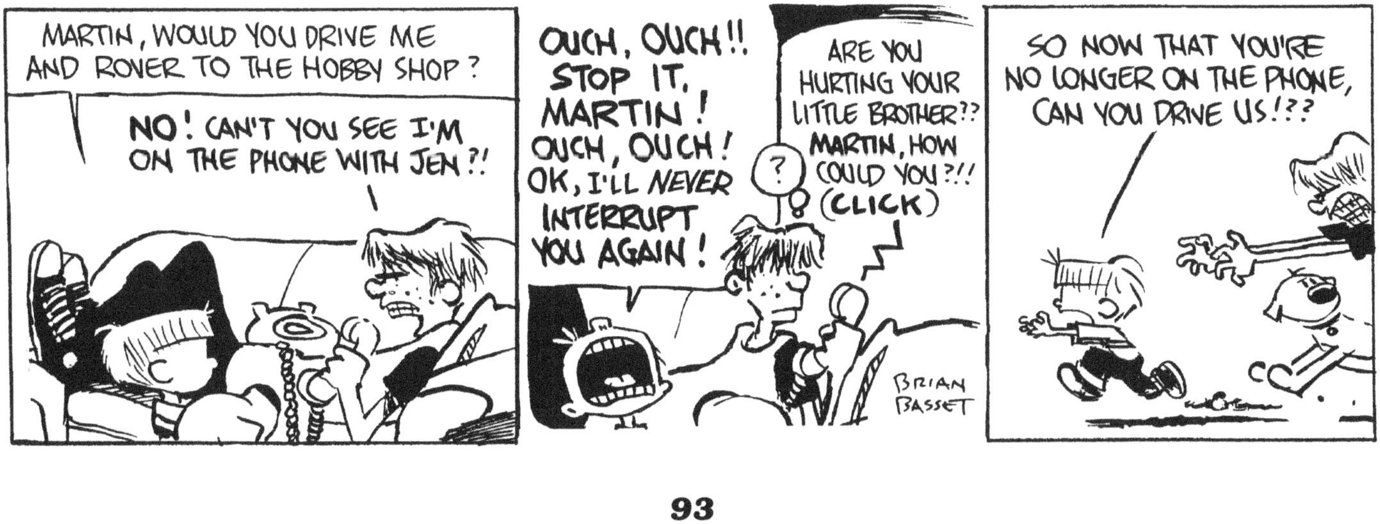
MARTIN, WOULD YOU DRIVE ME AND ROVER TO THE HOBBY SHOP?
NO! CAN'T YOU SEE I'M ON THE PHONE WITH JEN?!
OUCH, OUCH!! STOP IT, MARTIN! OUCH, OUCH! OK, I'LL NEVER INTERRUPT YOU AGAIN!
?
ARE YOU HURTING YOUR LITTLE BROTHER?? MARTIN, HOW COULD YOU?!! (CLICK)
BRIAN BASSET
SO NOW THAT YOU'RE NO LONGER ON THE PHONE, CAN YOU DRIVE US!??

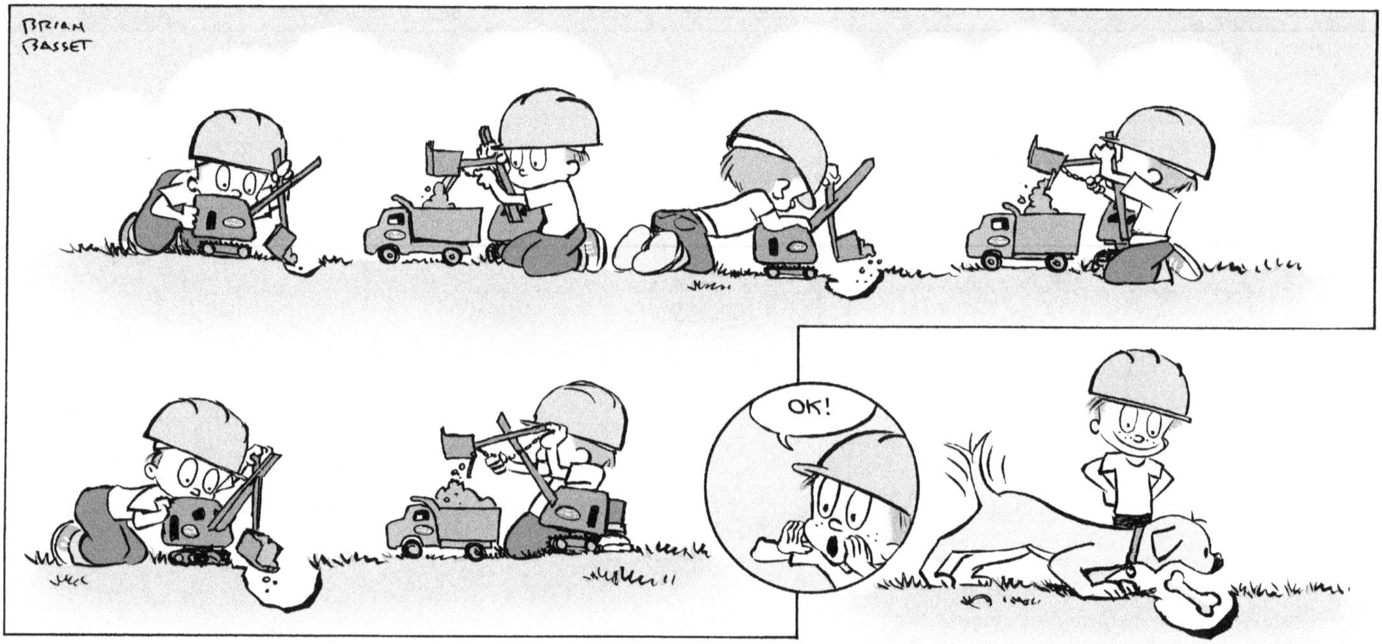
BRIAN BASSET
OK!

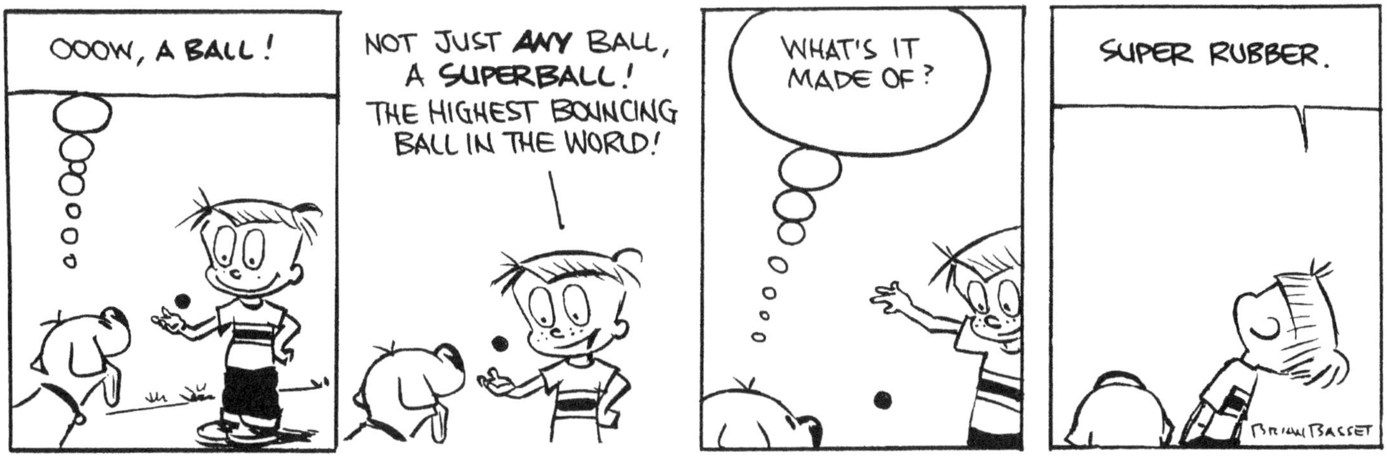
OOOW, A BALL!
NOT JUST ANY BALL, A SUPERBALL! THE HIGHEST BOUNCING BALL IN THE WORLD!
WHAT'S IT MADE OF?
SUPER RUBBER.
BRIAN BASSET

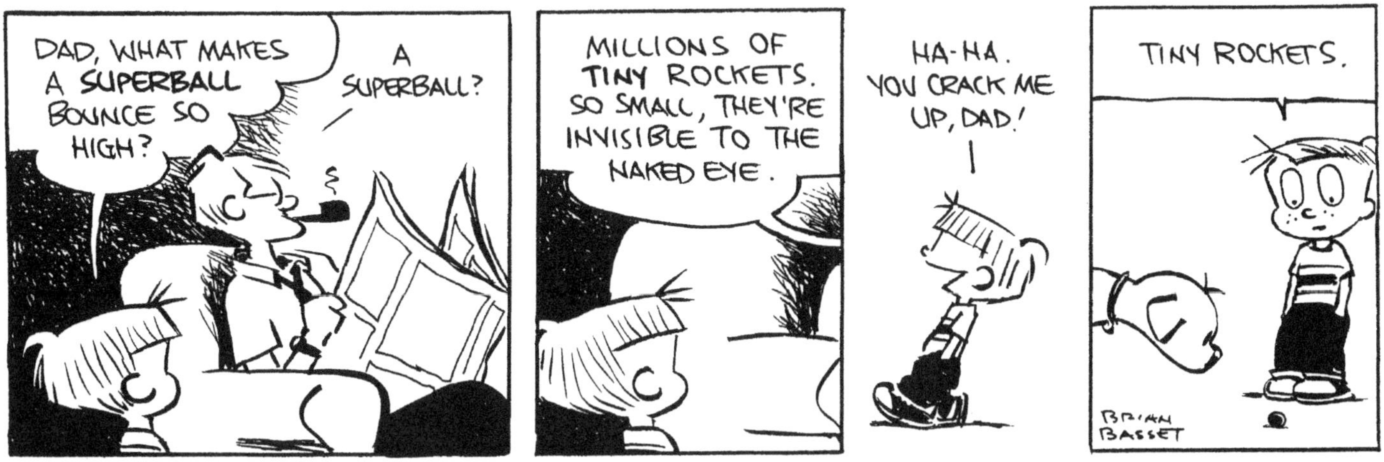
DAD, WHAT MAKES A SUPERBALL BOUNCE SO HIGH?
A SUPERBALL?
MILLIONS OF TINY ROCKETS. SO SMALL, THEY'RE INVISIBLE TO THE NAKED EYE.
HA-HA. YOU CRACK ME UP, DAD!
TINY ROCKETS.
BRIAN BASSET

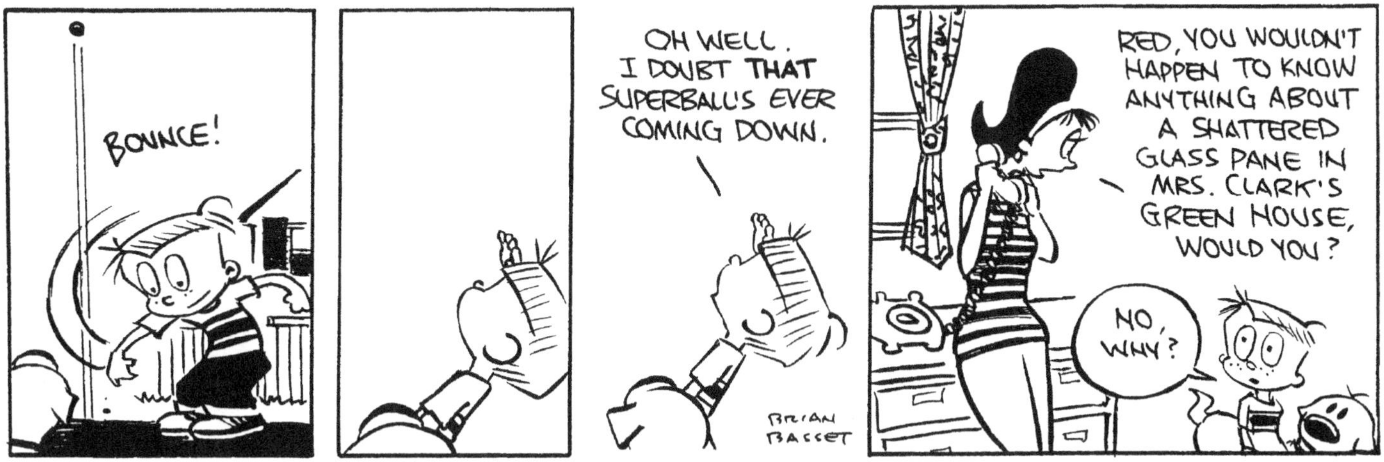
BOUNCE!
OH WELL. I DOUBT THAT SUPERBALL'S EVER COMING DOWN.
BRIAN BASSET
RED, YOU WOULDN'T HAPPEN TO KNOW ANYTHING ABOUT A SHATTERED GLASS PANE IN MRS. CLARK'S GREEN HOUSE, WOULD YOU?
NO, WHY?

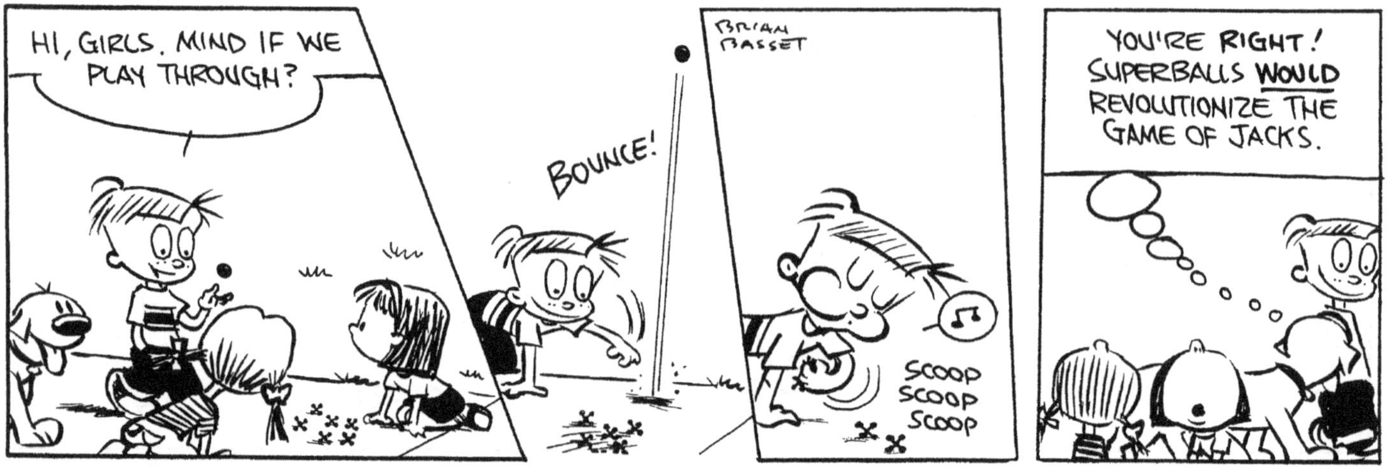
HI, GIRLS. MIND IF WE PLAY THROUGH?
BOUNCE!
BRIAN BASSET
SCOOP SCOOP SCOOP
YOU'RE RIGHT! SUPERBALLS WOULD REVOLUTIONIZE THE GAME OF JACKS.

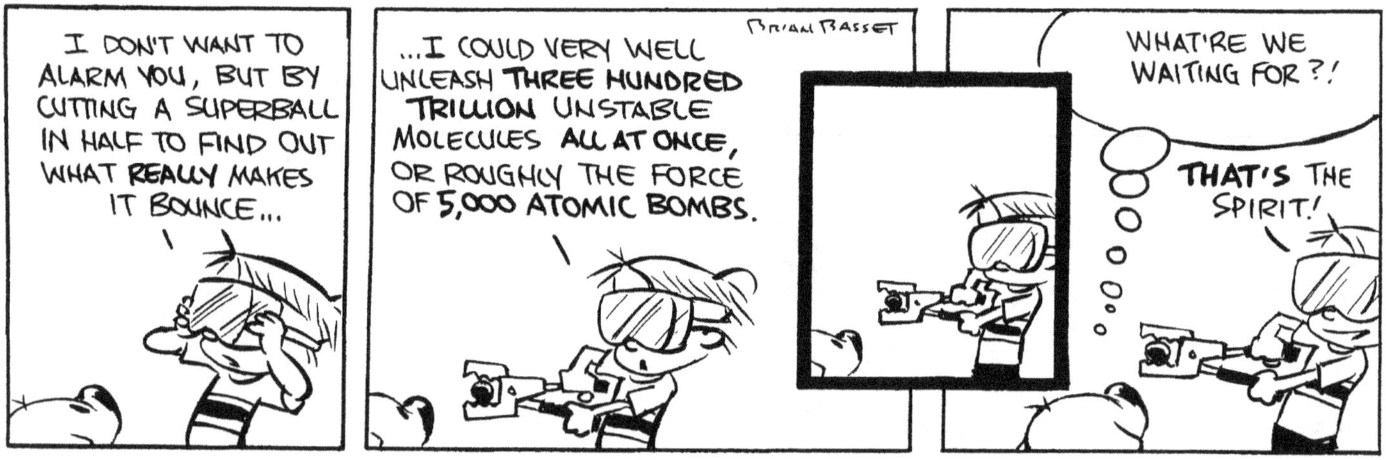
I DON'T WANT TO ALARM YOU, BUT BY CUTTING A SUPERBALL IN HALF TO FIND OUT WHAT REALLY MAKES IT BOUNCE...
BRIAN BASSET
...I COULD VERY WELL UNLEASH THREE HUNDRED TRILLION UNSTABLE MOLECULES ALL AT ONCE, OR ROUGHLY THE FORCE OF 5,000 ATOMIC BOMBS.
WHAT'RE WE WAITING FOR?!
THAT'S THE SPIRIT!

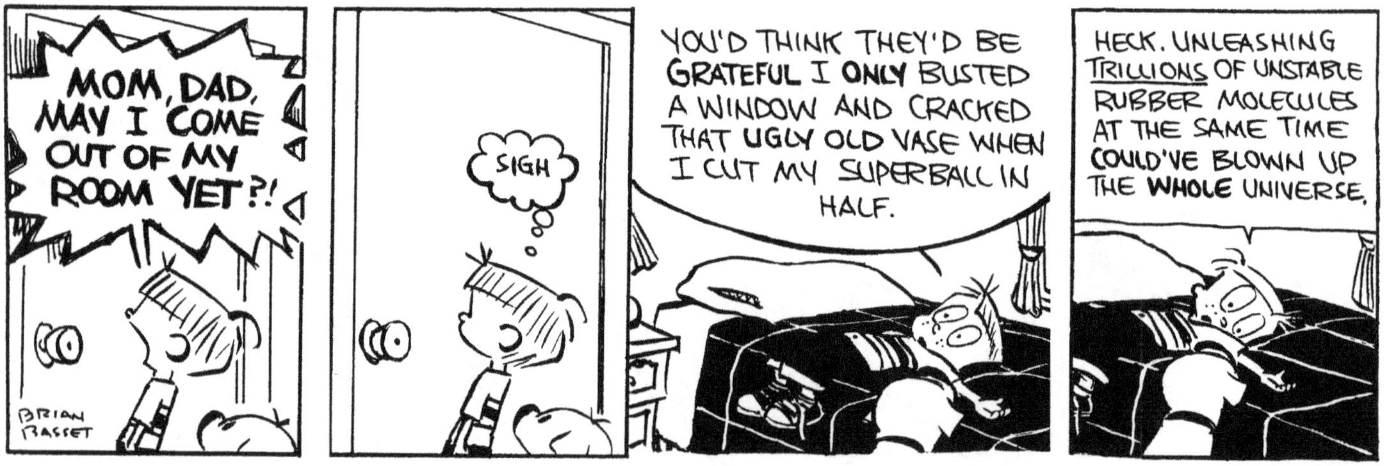
MOM, DAD, MAY I COME OUT OF MY ROOM YET?!
BRIAN BASSET
SIGH
YOU'D THINK THEY'D BE GRATEFUL I ONLY BUSTED A WINDOW AND CRACKED THAT UGLY OLD VASE WHEN I CUT MY SUPERBALL IN HALF.
HECK. UNLEASHING TRILLIONS OF UNSTABLE RUBBER MOLECULES AT THE SAME TIME COULD'VE BLOWN UP THE WHOLE UNIVERSE.

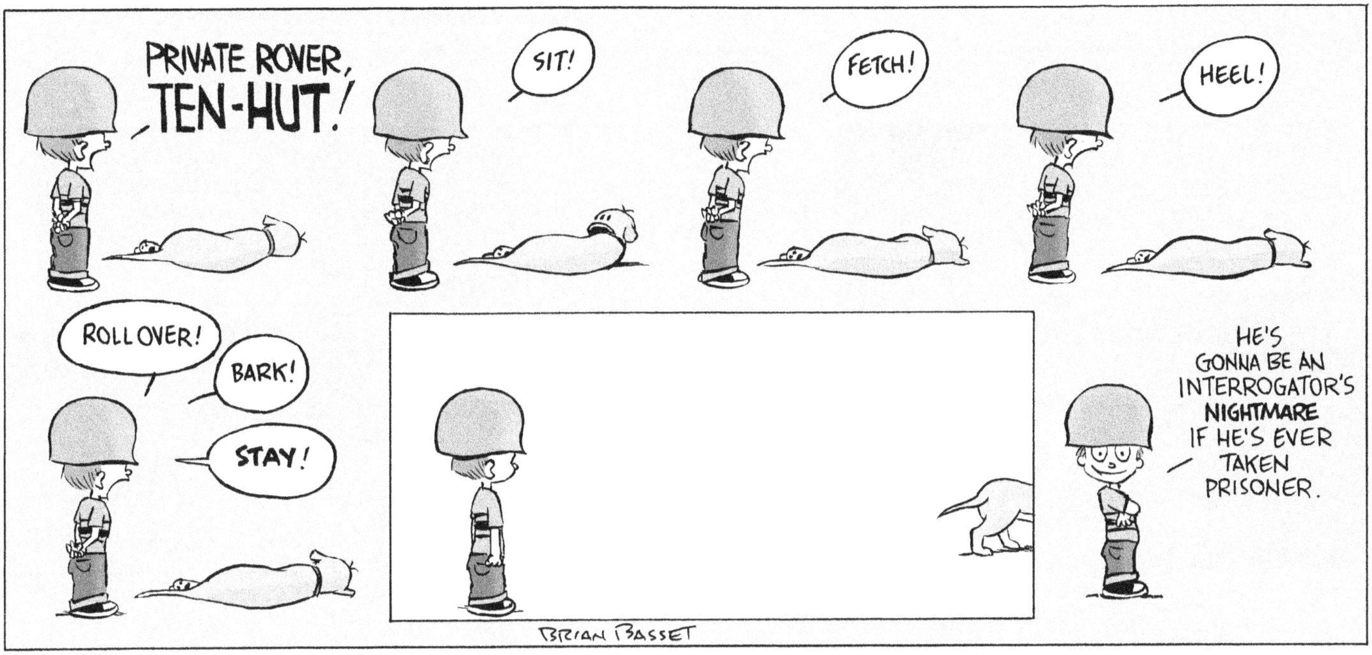
PRIVATE ROVER, TEN-HUT!
SIT!
FETCH!
HEEL!
ROLL OVER!
BARK!
STAY!
HE'S GONNA BE AN INTERROGATOR'S **NIGHTMARE** IF HE'S EVER TAKEN PRISONER.
BRIAN BASSET

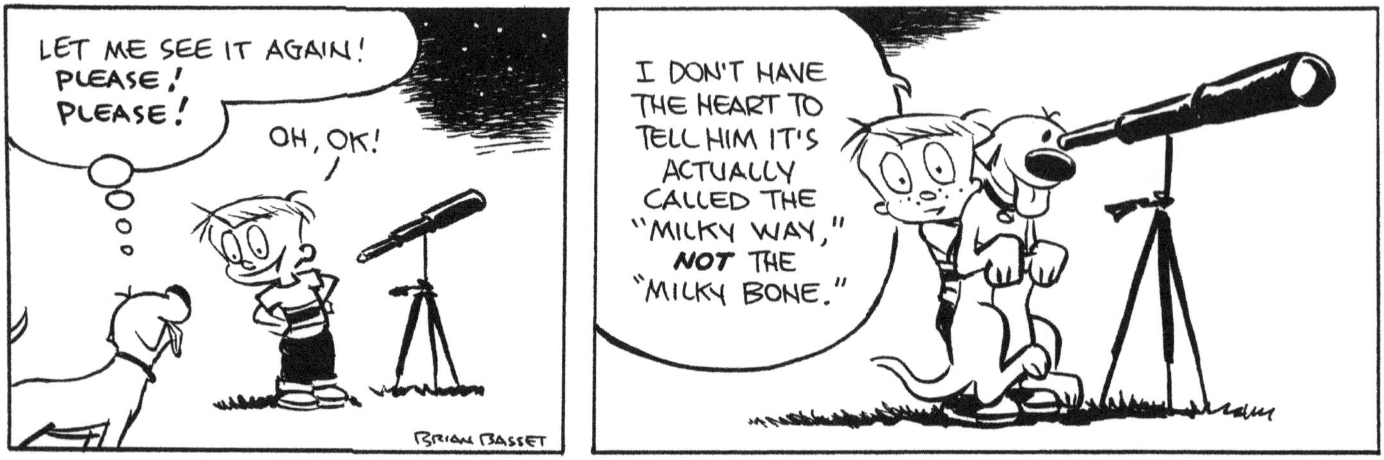
LET ME SEE IT AGAIN! PLEASE! PLEASE!
OH, OK!
BRIAN BASSET
I DON'T HAVE THE HEART TO TELL HIM IT'S ACTUALLY CALLED THE "MILKY WAY," NOT THE "MILKY BONE."

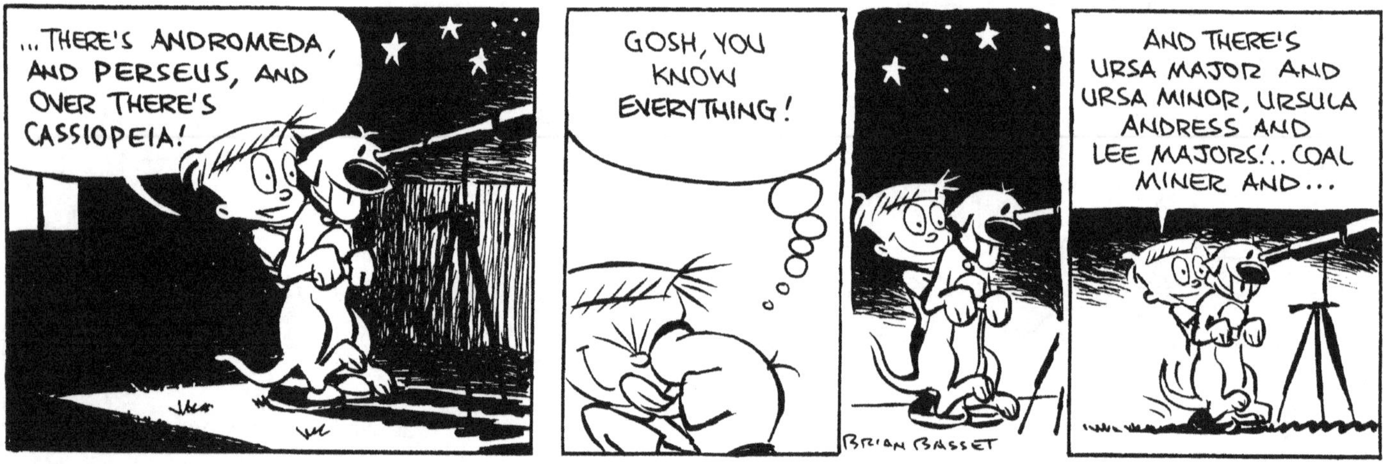
...THERE'S ANDROMEDA, AND PERSEUS, AND OVER THERE'S CASSIOPEIA!
GOSH, YOU KNOW EVERYTHING!
BRIAN BASSET
AND THERE'S URSA MAJOR AND URSA MINOR, URSULA ANDRESS AND LEE MAJORS!.. COAL MINER AND...

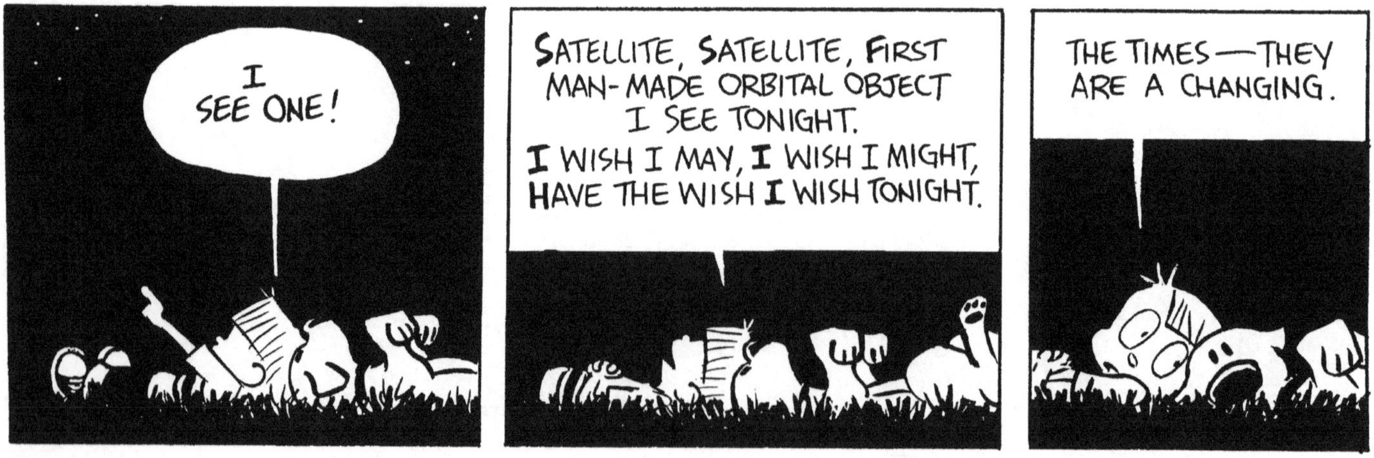
I SEE ONE!
SATELLITE, SATELLITE, FIRST MAN-MADE ORBITAL OBJECT I SEE TONIGHT.
I WISH I MAY, I WISH I MIGHT, HAVE THE WISH I WISH TONIGHT.
THE TIMES—THEY ARE A CHANGING.

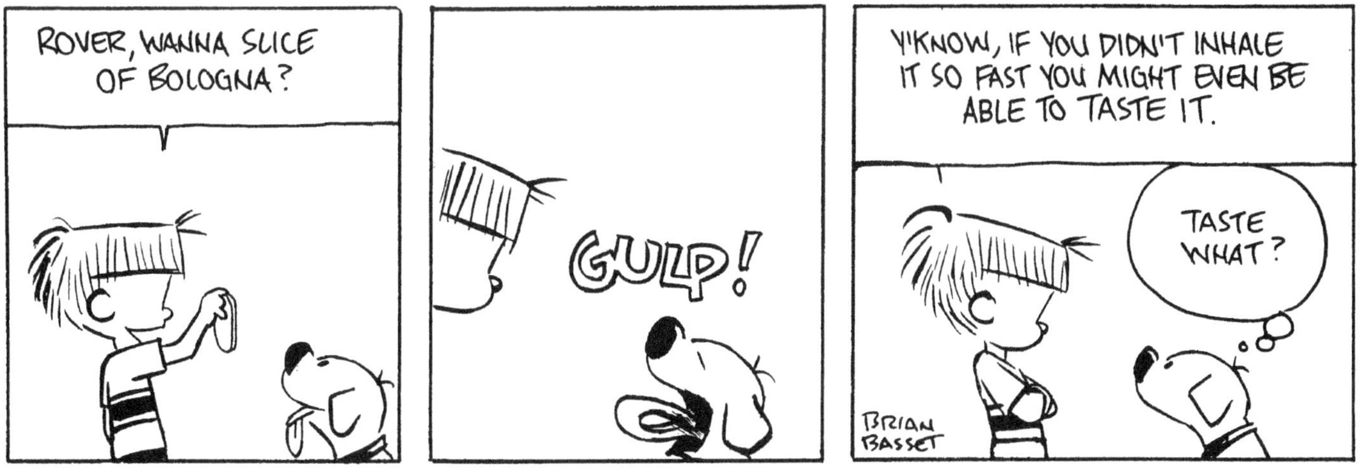
ROVER, WANNA SLICE OF BOLOGNA?
GULP!
Y'KNOW, IF YOU DIDN'T INHALE IT SO FAST YOU MIGHT EVEN BE ABLE TO TASTE IT.
TASTE WHAT?
BRIAN BASSET

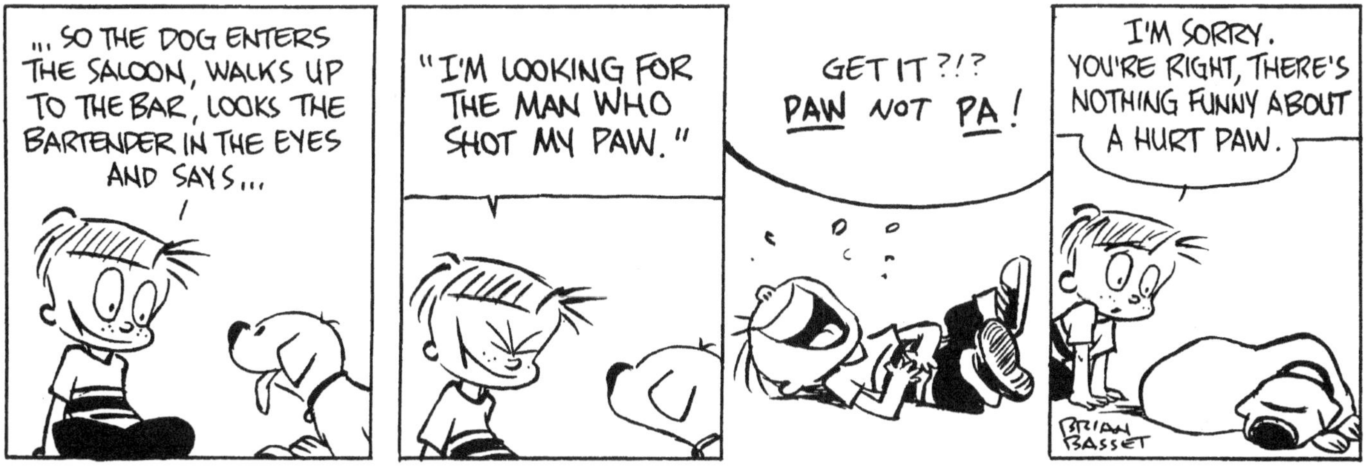
... SO THE DOG ENTERS THE SALOON, WALKS UP TO THE BAR, LOOKS THE BARTENDER IN THE EYES AND SAYS...
"I'M LOOKING FOR THE MAN WHO SHOT MY PAW."
GET IT?!? PAW NOT PA!
I'M SORRY. YOU'RE RIGHT, THERE'S NOTHING FUNNY ABOUT A HURT PAW.
BRIAN BASSET

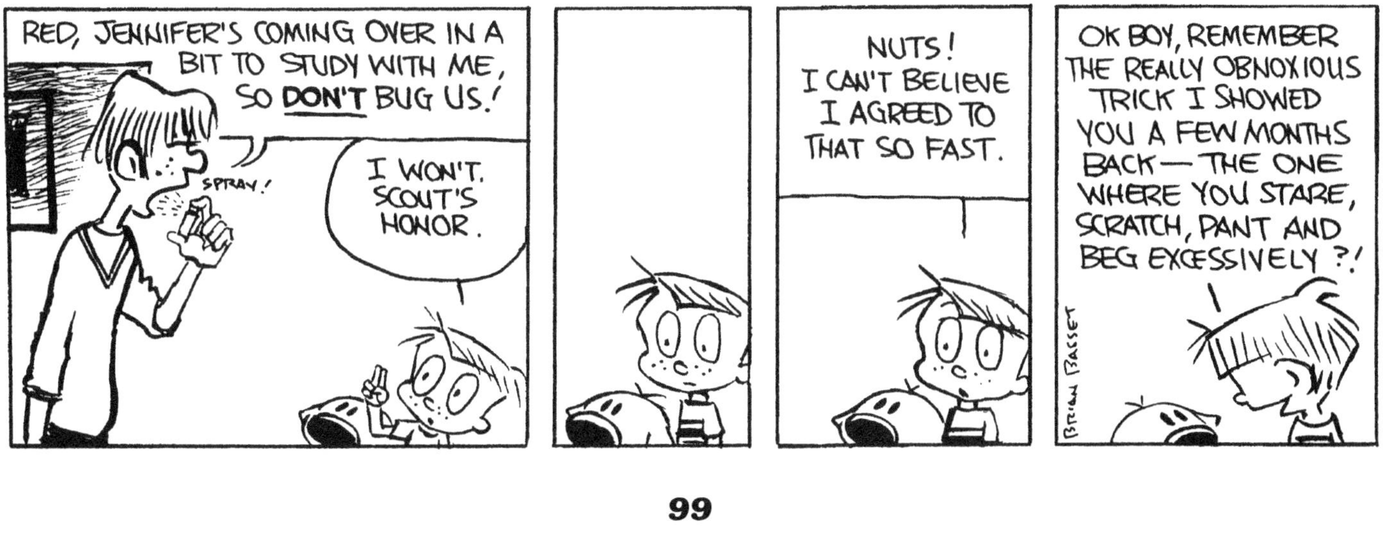
RED, JENNIFER'S COMING OVER IN A BIT TO STUDY WITH ME, SO DON'T BUG US!
SPRAY!
I WON'T. SCOUT'S HONOR.
NUTS! I CAN'T BELIEVE I AGREED TO THAT SO FAST.
OK BOY, REMEMBER THE REALLY OBNOXIOUS TRICK I SHOWED YOU A FEW MONTHS BACK — THE ONE WHERE YOU STARE, SCRATCH, PANT AND BEG EXCESSIVELY?!
BRIAN BASSET

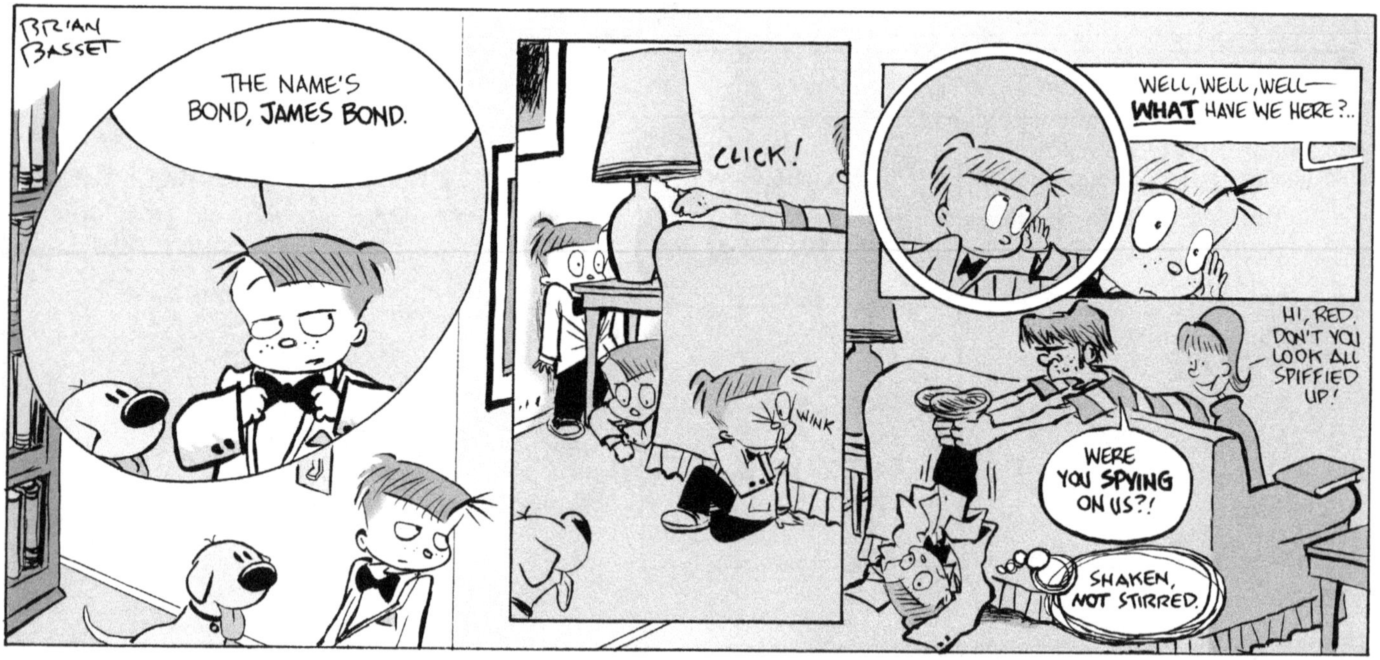
BRIAN BASSET
THE NAME'S BOND, JAMES BOND.
CLICK!
WINK
WELL, WELL, WELL— WHAT HAVE WE HERE?..
HI, RED. DON'T YOU LOOK ALL SPIFFIED UP!
WERE YOU SPYING ON US?!
SHAKEN, NOT STIRRED.

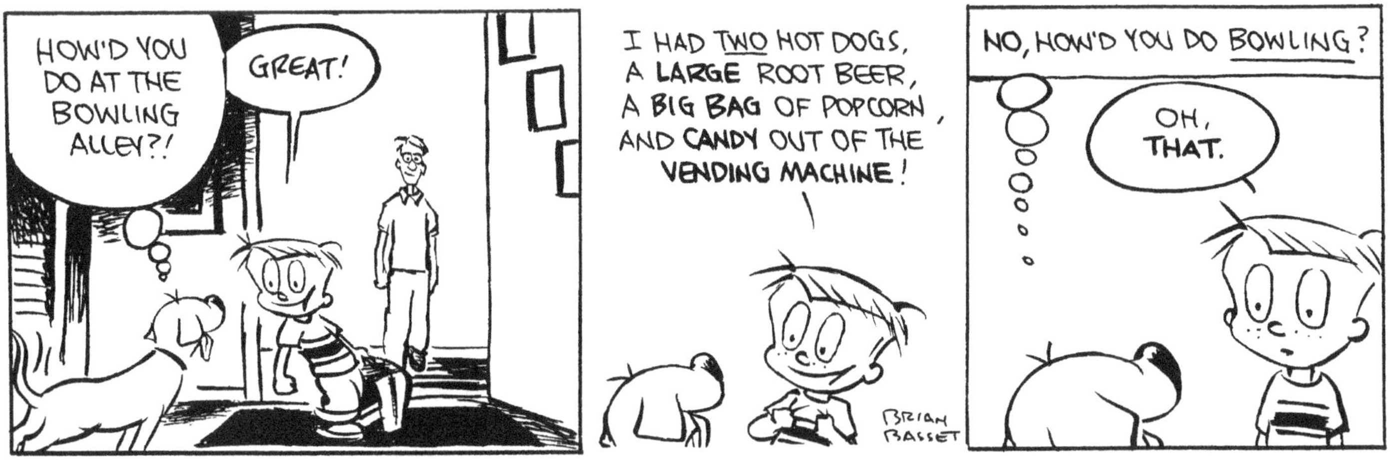
HOW'D YOU DO AT THE BOWLING ALLEY?!
GREAT!
I HAD TWO HOT DOGS, A LARGE ROOT BEER, A BIG BAG OF POPCORN, AND CANDY OUT OF THE VENDING MACHINE!
BRIAN BASSET
NO, HOW'D YOU DO BOWLING?
OH, THAT.

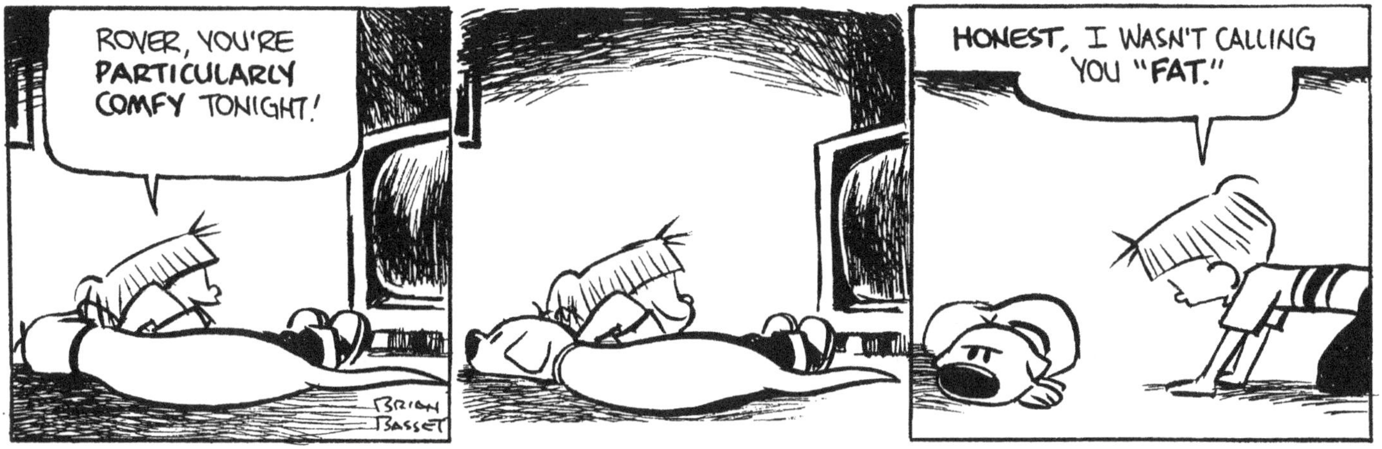
ROVER, YOU'RE PARTICULARLY COMFY TONIGHT!
BRIAN BASSET
HONEST, I WASN'T CALLING YOU "FAT."

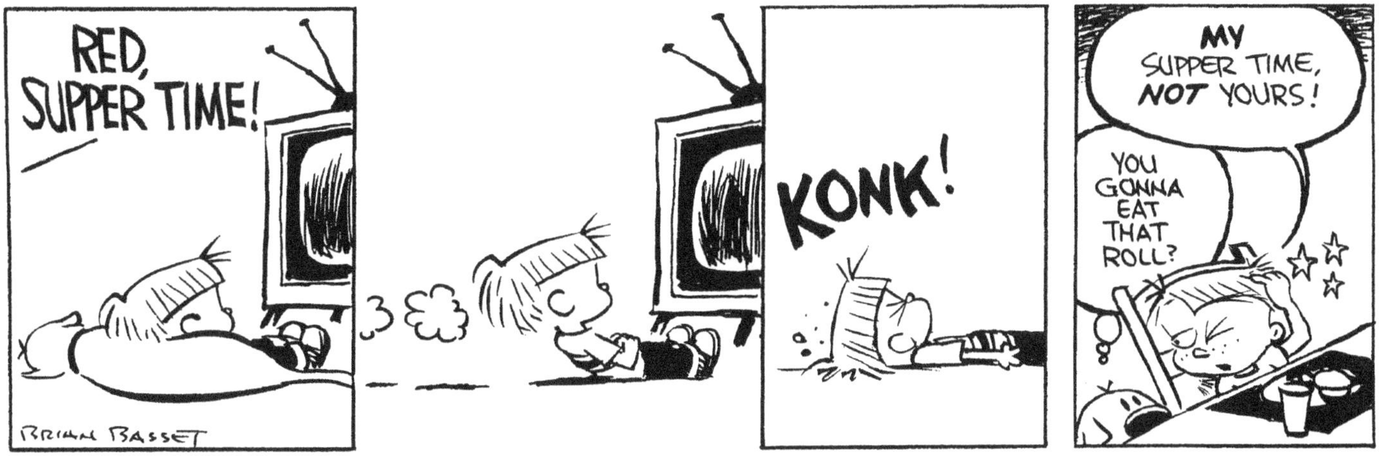
RED, SUPPER TIME!
BRIAN BASSET
KONK!
YOU GONNA EAT THAT ROLL?
MY SUPPER TIME, NOT YOURS!

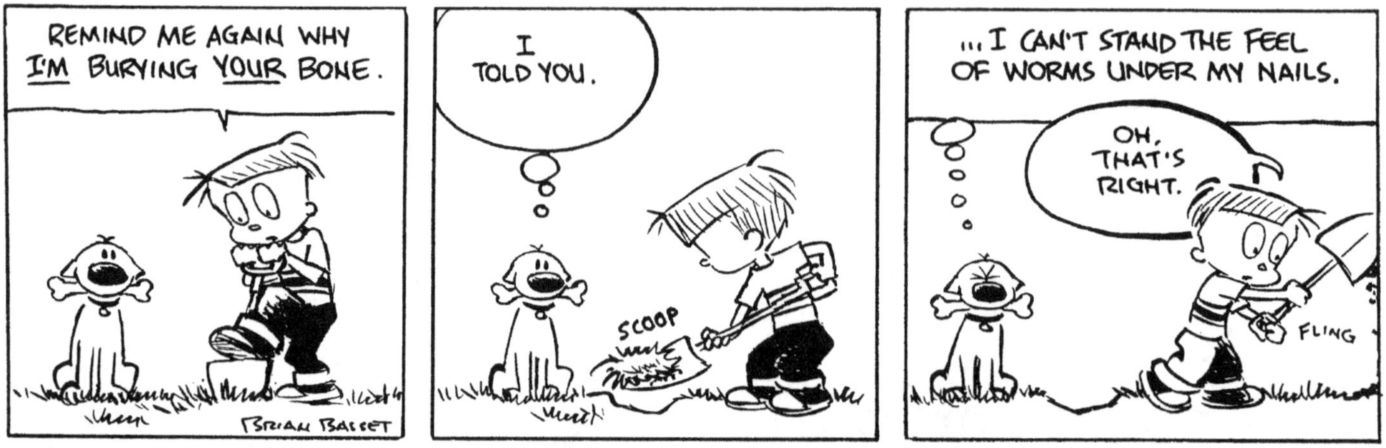
REMIND ME AGAIN WHY I'M BURYING YOUR BONE.
BRIAN BASSET
I TOLD YOU.
SCOOP
... I CAN'T STAND THE FEEL OF WORMS UNDER MY NAILS.
OH, THAT'S RIGHT.
FLING

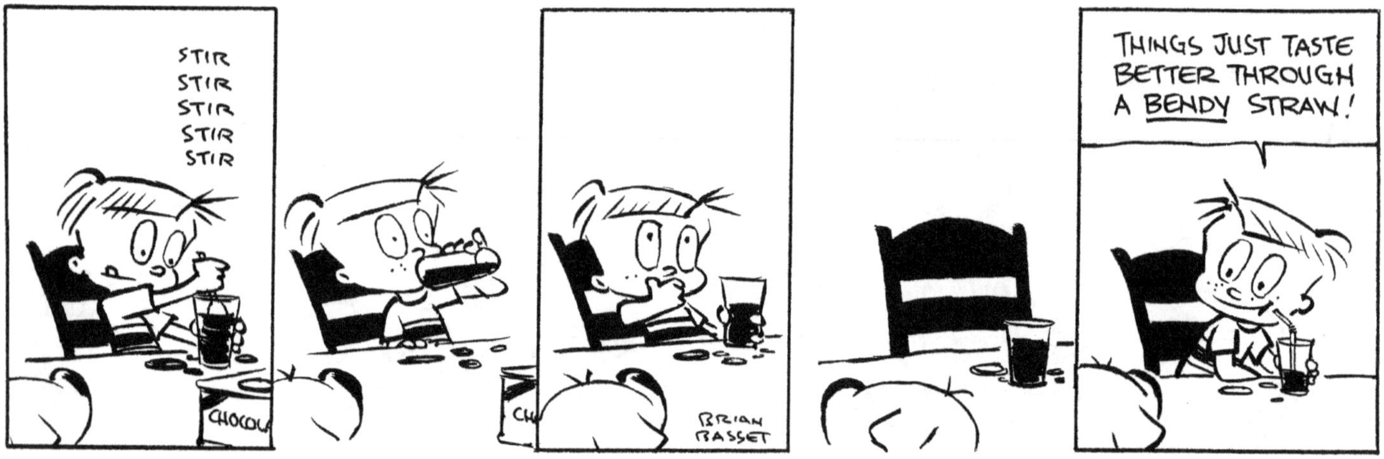
STIR STIR STIR STIR STIR
BRIAN BASSET
THINGS JUST TASTE BETTER THROUGH A BENDY STRAW!

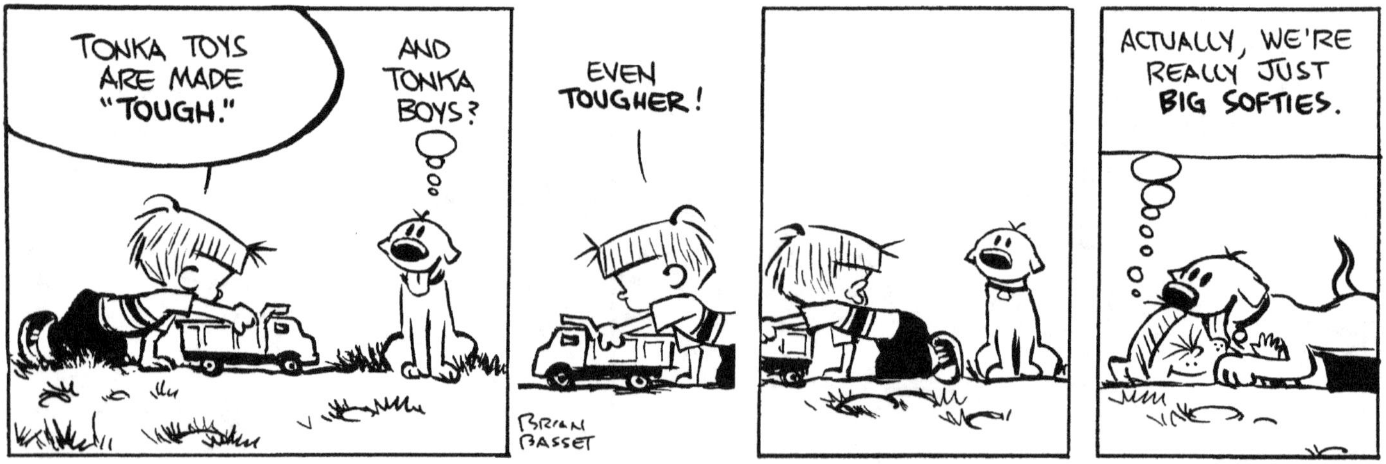
TONKA TOYS ARE MADE "TOUGH."
AND TONKA BOYS?
EVEN TOUGHER!
BRIAN BASSET
ACTUALLY, WE'RE REALLY JUST BIG SOFTIES.

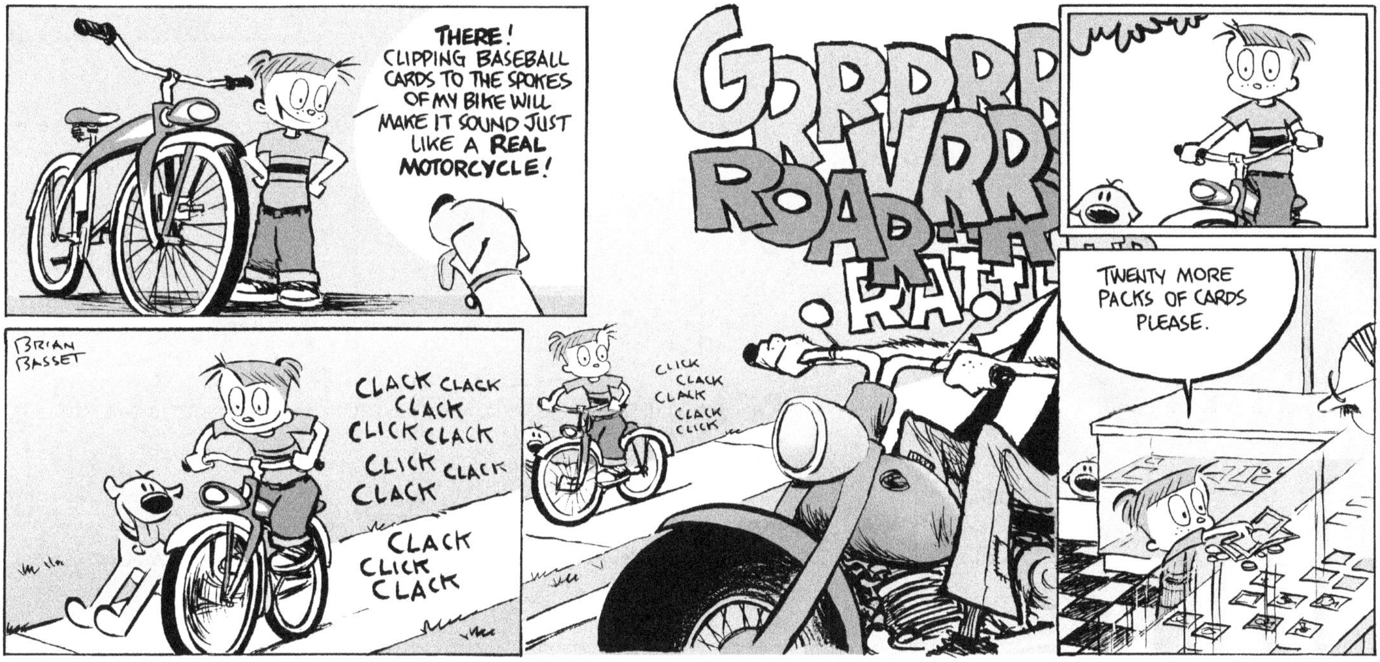
THERE! CLIPPING BASEBALL CARDS TO THE SPOKES OF MY BIKE WILL MAKE IT SOUND JUST LIKE A REAL MOTORCYCLE!
BRIAN BASSET
CLACK CLACK CLACK CLICK CLACK CLICK CLACK CLACK
CLACK CLICK CLACK
CLICK CLACK CLACK CLACK CLICK
GRRRRR
VRRR
ROAR
RATT
TWENTY MORE PACKS OF CARDS PLEASE.

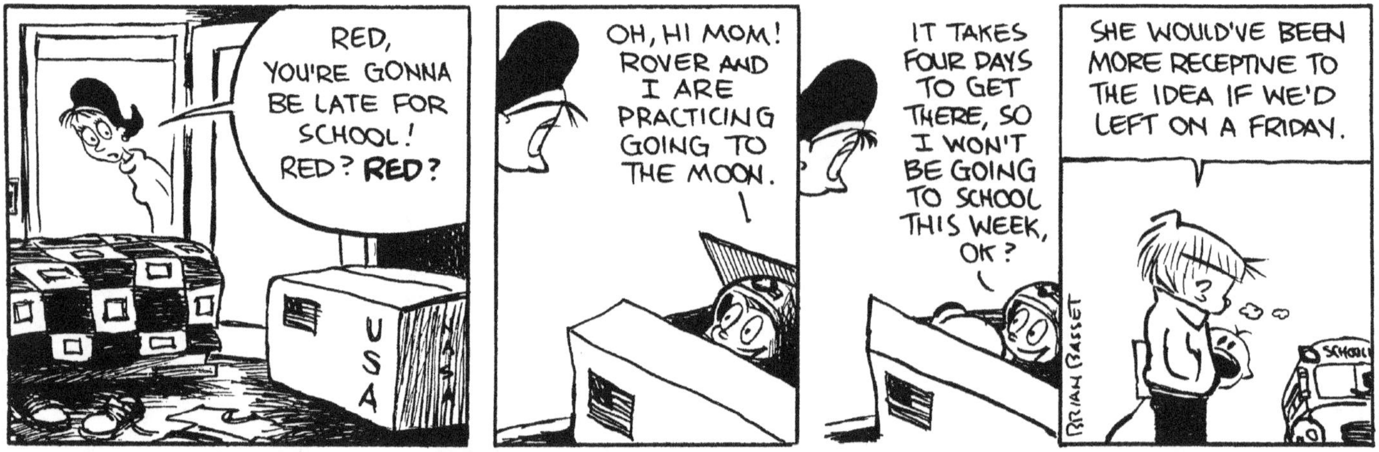
RED, YOU'RE GONNA BE LATE FOR SCHOOL! RED? RED?
OH, HI MOM! ROVER AND I ARE PRACTICING GOING TO THE MOON.
IT TAKES FOUR DAYS TO GET THERE, SO I WON'T BE GOING TO SCHOOL THIS WEEK, OK?
SHE WOULD'VE BEEN MORE RECEPTIVE TO THE IDEA IF WE'D LEFT ON A FRIDAY.
SCHOOL
BRIAN BASSET

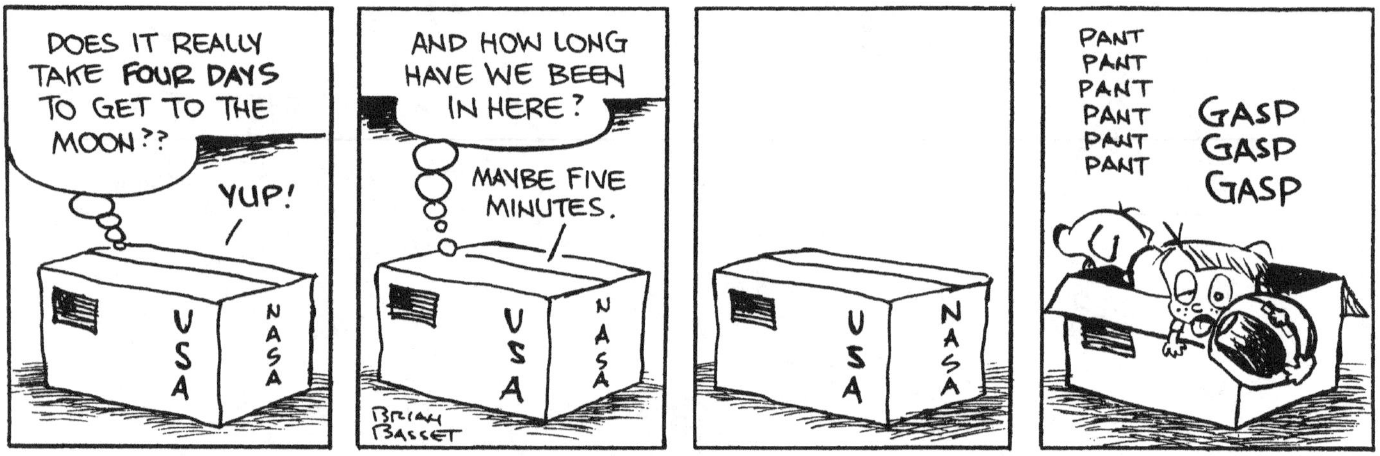
DOES IT REALLY TAKE FOUR DAYS TO GET TO THE MOON??
YUP!
USA
NASA
AND HOW LONG HAVE WE BEEN IN HERE?
MAYBE FIVE MINUTES.
BRIAN BASSET
PANT PANT PANT PANT PANT PANT
GASP GASP GASP

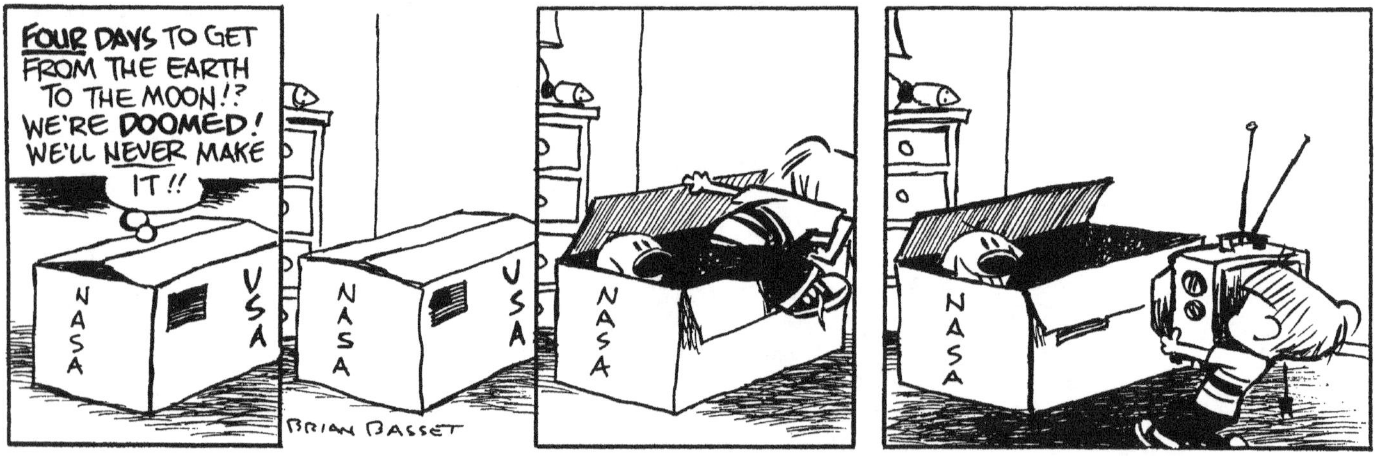
FOUR DAYS TO GET FROM THE EARTH TO THE MOON!? WE'RE DOOMED! WE'LL NEVER MAKE IT!!
NASA
USA
BRIAN BASSET

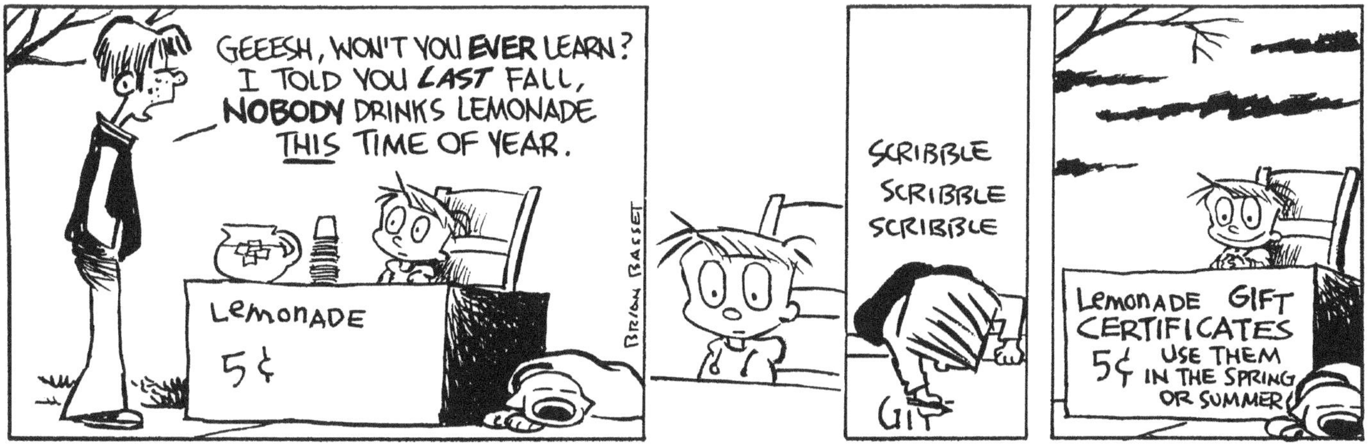
GEEESH, WON'T YOU EVER LEARN? I TOLD YOU LAST FALL, NOBODY DRINKS LEMONADE THIS TIME OF YEAR.
LEMONADE 5¢
BRIAN BASSET
SCRIBBLE SCRIBBLE SCRIBBLE
GIFT
LEMONADE GIFT CERTIFICATES 5¢ USE THEM IN THE SPRING OR SUMMER

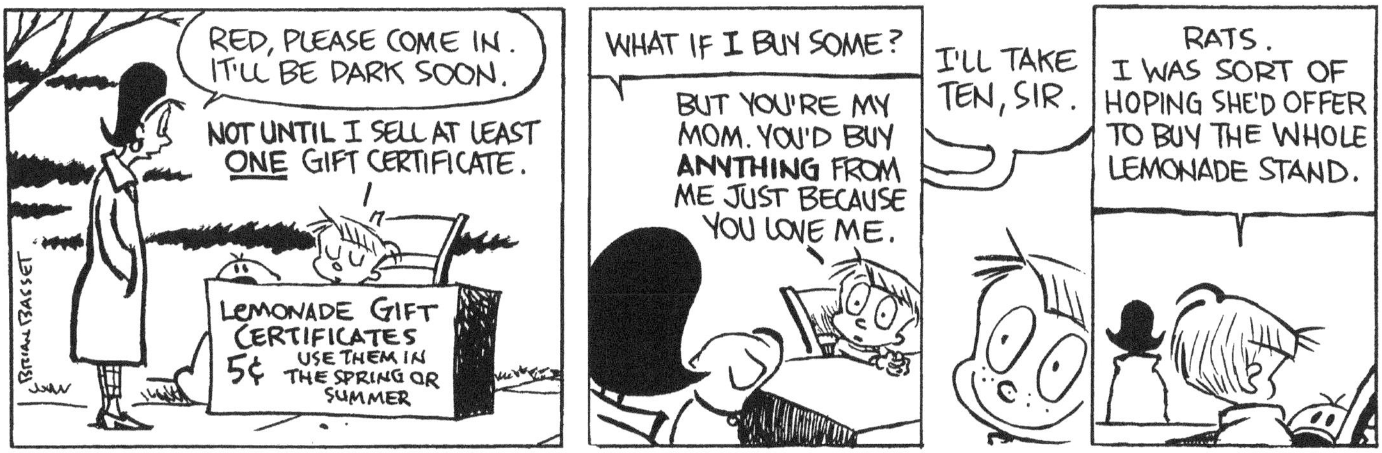
RED, PLEASE COME IN. IT'LL BE DARK SOON.
NOT UNTIL I SELL AT LEAST ONE GIFT CERTIFICATE.
BRIAN BASSET
LEMONADE GIFT CERTIFICATES 5¢ USE THEM IN THE SPRING OR SUMMER
WHAT IF I BUY SOME?
BUT YOU'RE MY MOM. YOU'D BUY ANYTHING FROM ME JUST BECAUSE YOU LOVE ME.
I'LL TAKE TEN, SIR.
RATS. I WAS SORT OF HOPING SHE'D OFFER TO BUY THE WHOLE LEMONADE STAND.

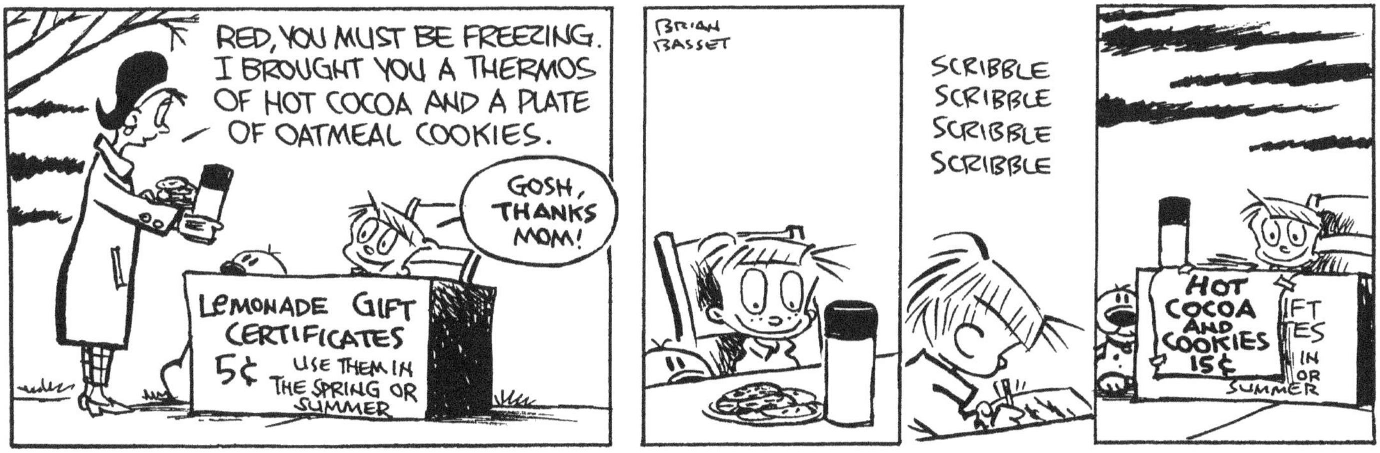
RED, YOU MUST BE FREEZING. I BROUGHT YOU A THERMOS OF HOT COCOA AND A PLATE OF OATMEAL COOKIES.
GOSH, THANKS MOM!
LEMONADE GIFT CERTIFICATES 5¢ USE THEM IN THE SPRING OR SUMMER
BRIAN BASSET
SCRIBBLE SCRIBBLE SCRIBBLE SCRIBBLE
HOT COCOA AND COOKIES 15¢

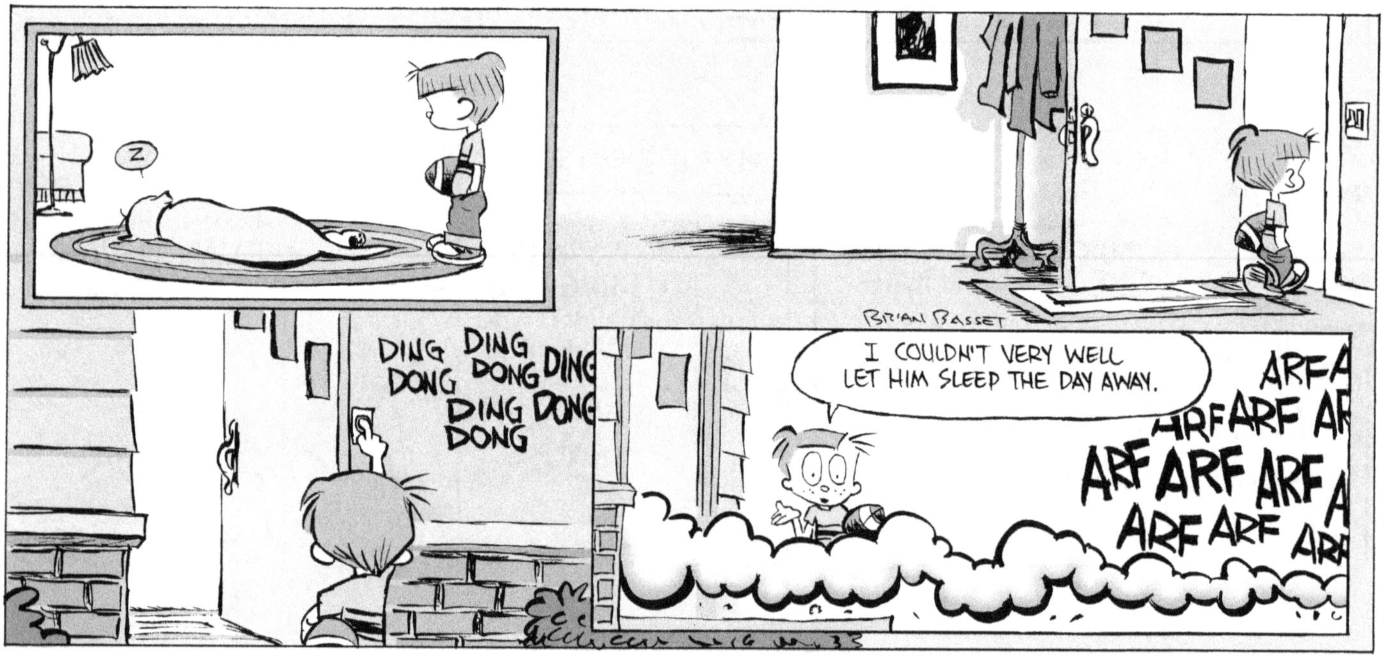
Z
BRIAN BASSET
DING DONG DING DONG DING DING DONG DONG
I COULDN'T VERY WELL LET HIM SLEEP THE DAY AWAY.
ARF ARF ARF ARF ARF ARF ARF ARF ARF ARF ARF ARF

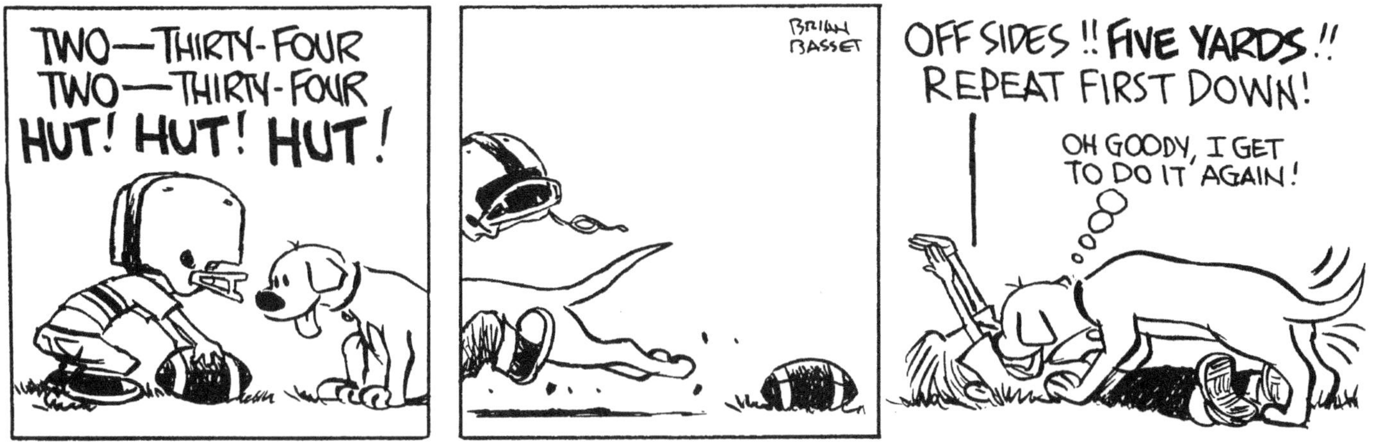
TWO—THIRTY-FOUR
TWO—THIRTY-FOUR
HUT! HUT! HUT!
BRIAN BASSET
OFF SIDES !! FIVE YARDS !!
REPEAT FIRST DOWN!
OH GOODY, I GET TO DO IT AGAIN!

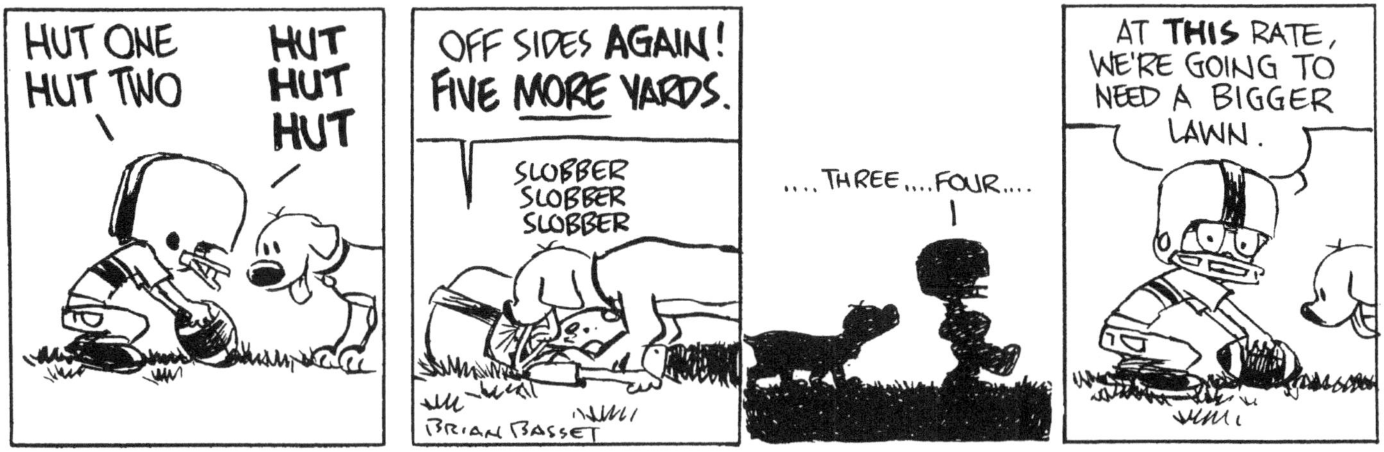
HUT ONE
HUT TWO
HUT
HUT
HUT
OFF SIDES AGAIN!
FIVE MORE YARDS.
SLOBBER
SLOBBER
SLOBBER
BRIAN BASSET
....THREE....FOUR....
AT THIS RATE, WE'RE GOING TO NEED A BIGGER LAWN.

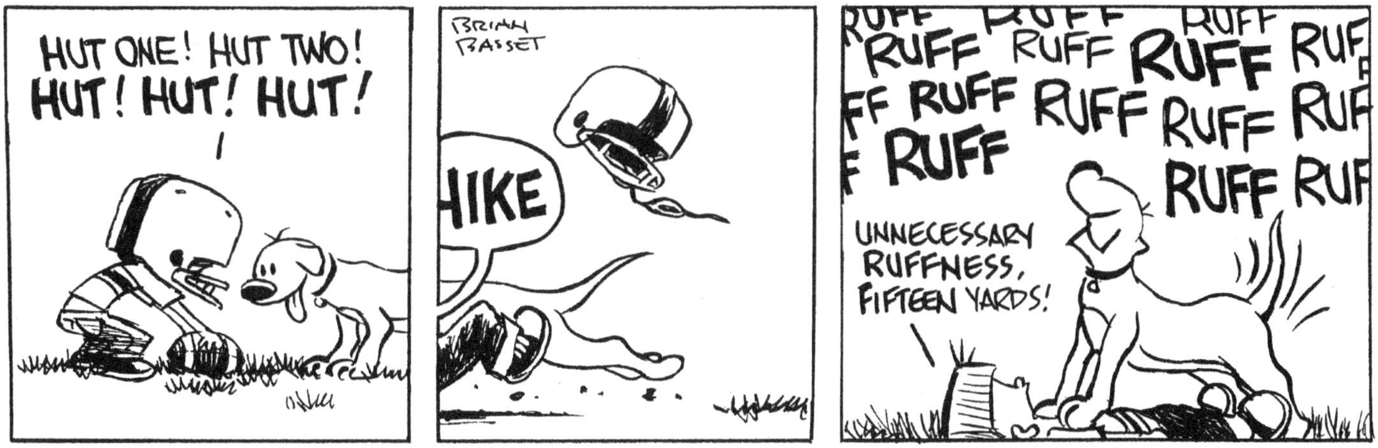
HUT ONE! HUT TWO!
HUT! HUT! HUT!
BRIAN BASSET
HIKE
RUFF RUFF RUFF RUFF
RUFF RUFF RUFF RUFF
RUFF
RUFF RUFF
UNNECESSARY RUFFNESS, FIFTEEN YARDS!

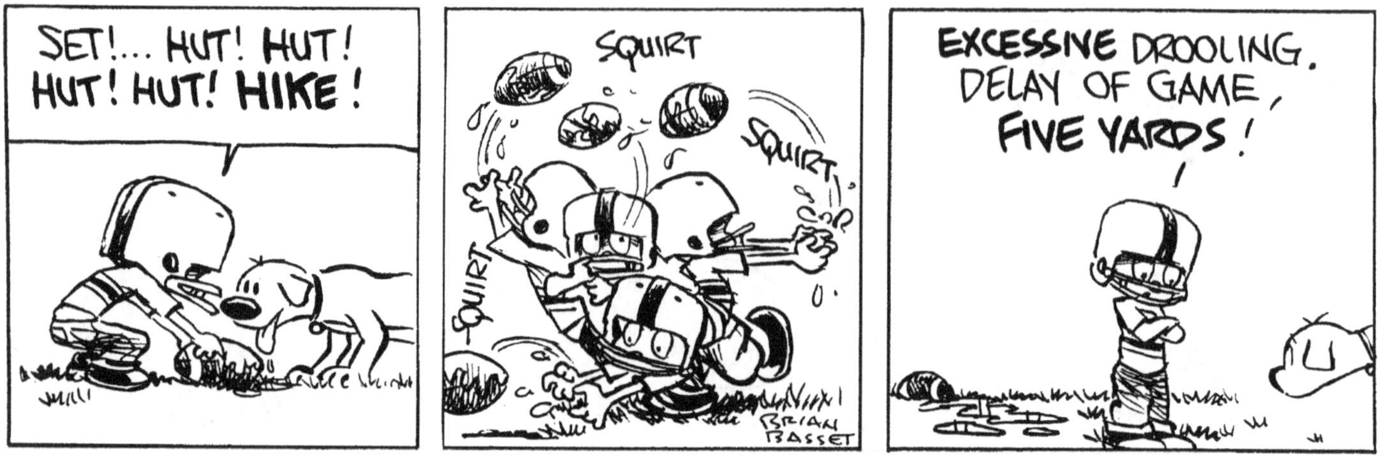
SET!... HUT! HUT! HUT! HUT! HIKE!
SQUIRT
SQUIRT
SQUIRT
BRIAN BASSET
EXCESSIVE DROOLING. DELAY OF GAME, FIVE YARDS!

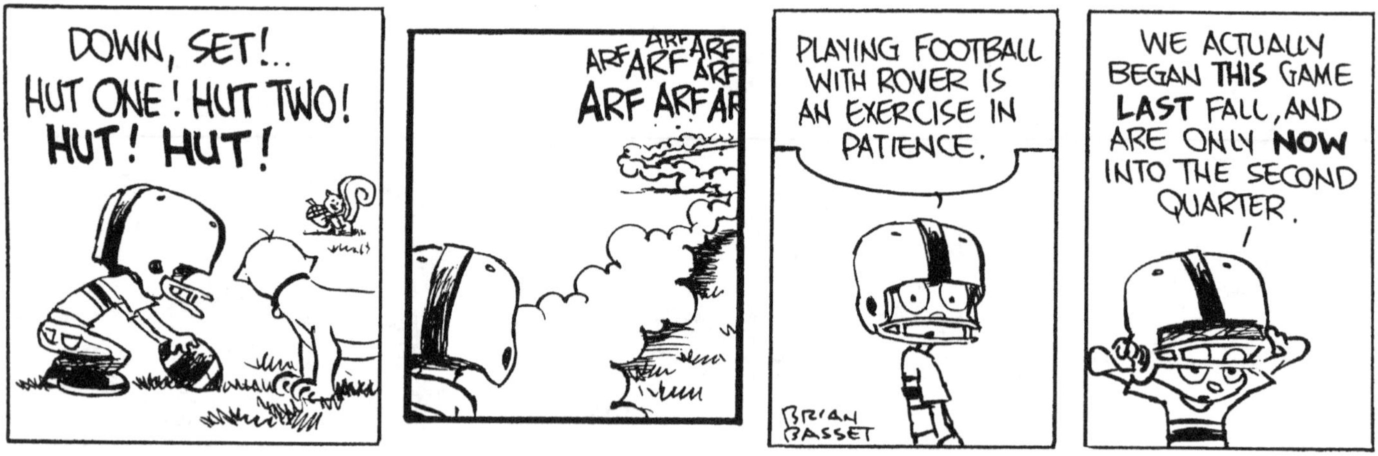
DOWN, SET!.. HUT ONE! HUT TWO! HUT! HUT!
ARF ARF ARF ARF ARF
PLAYING FOOTBALL WITH ROVER IS AN EXERCISE IN PATIENCE.
BRIAN BASSET
WE ACTUALLY BEGAN THIS GAME LAST FALL, AND ARE ONLY NOW INTO THE SECOND QUARTER.

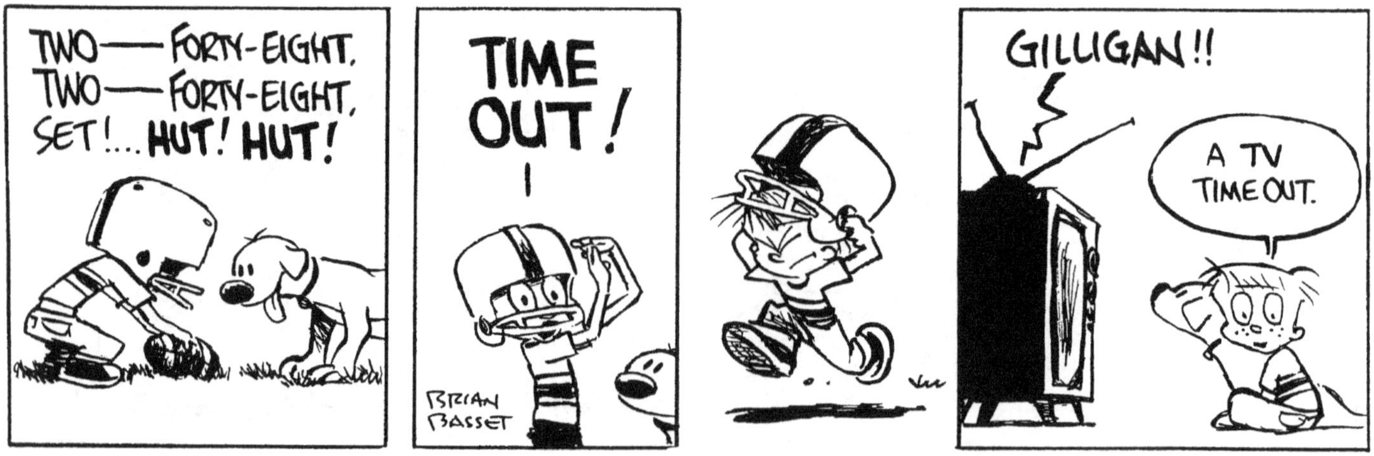
TWO— FORTY-EIGHT. TWO— FORTY-EIGHT. SET!... HUT! HUT!
TIME OUT!
BRIAN BASSET
GILLIGAN!!
A TV TIME OUT.

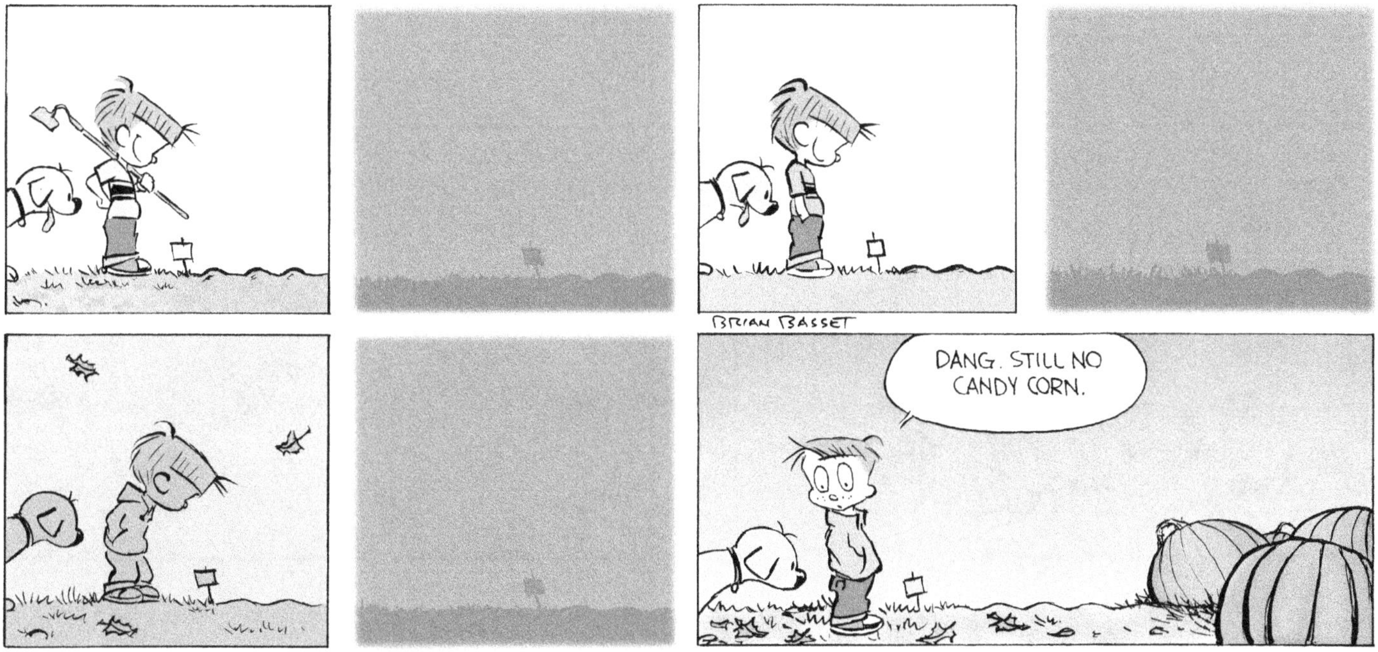
BRIAN BASSET
DANG. STILL NO CANDY CORN.

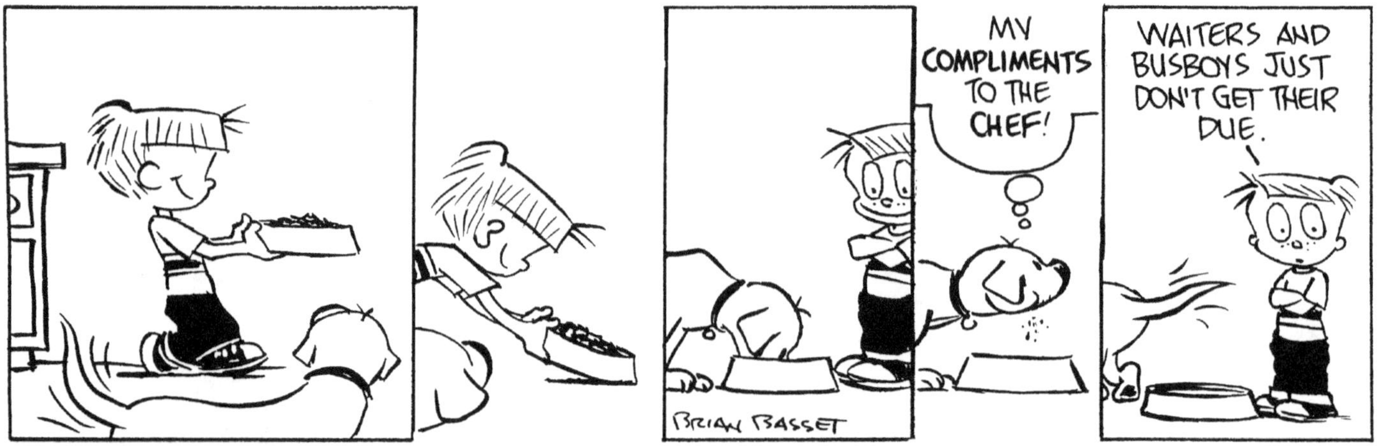
MY COMPLIMENTS TO THE CHEF!
WAITERS AND BUSBOYS JUST DON'T GET THEIR DUE.
BRIAN BASSET

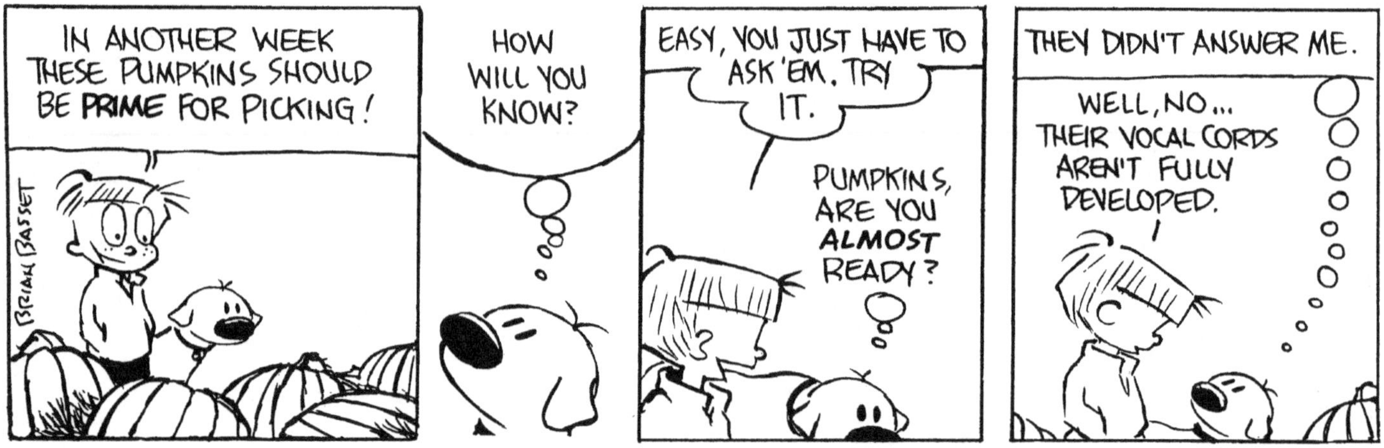
IN ANOTHER WEEK THESE PUMPKINS SHOULD BE PRIME FOR PICKING!
BRIAN BASSET
HOW WILL YOU KNOW?
EASY, YOU JUST HAVE TO ASK 'EM. TRY IT.
PUMPKINS, ARE YOU ALMOST READY?
THEY DIDN'T ANSWER ME.
WELL, NO... THEIR VOCAL CORDS AREN'T FULLY DEVELOPED.

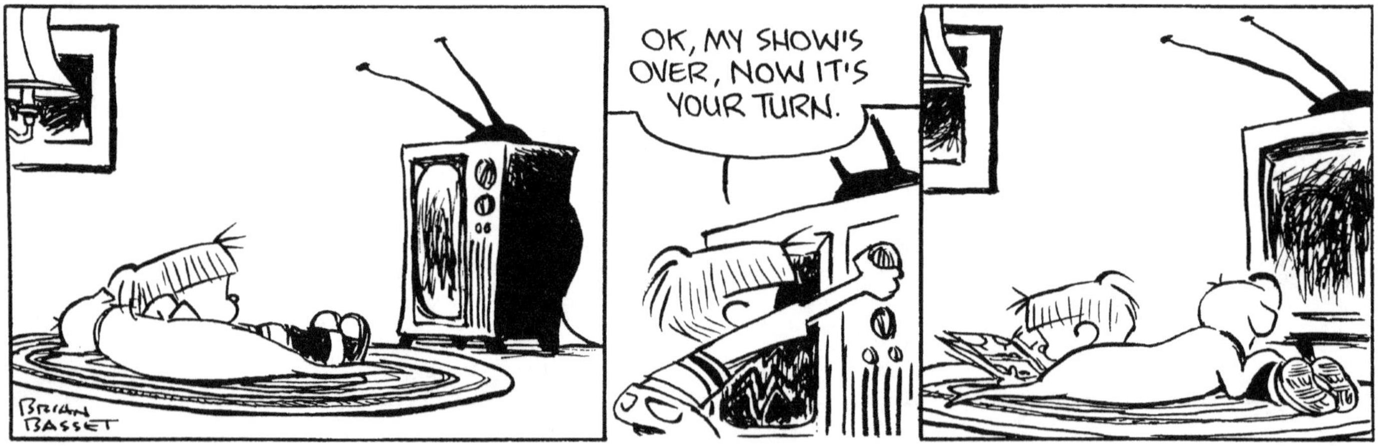
BRIAN BASSET
OK, MY SHOW'S OVER, NOW IT'S YOUR TURN.

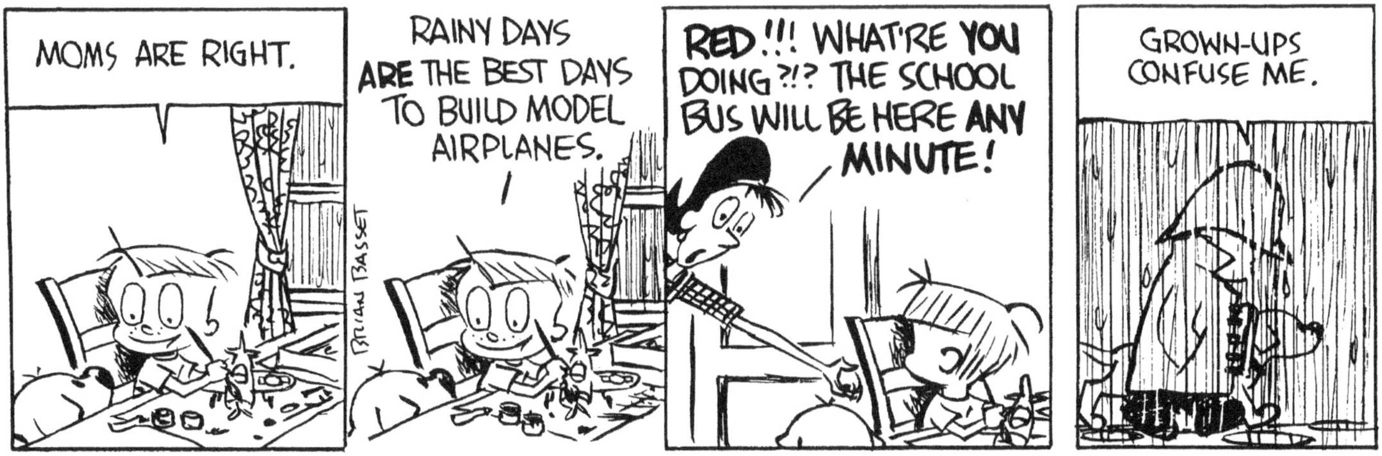
MOMS ARE RIGHT.
BRIAN BASSET
RAINY DAYS **ARE** THE BEST DAYS TO BUILD MODEL AIRPLANES.
RED!!! WHAT'RE **YOU** DOING?!? THE SCHOOL BUS WILL BE HERE **ANY MINUTE**!
GROWN-UPS CONFUSE ME.

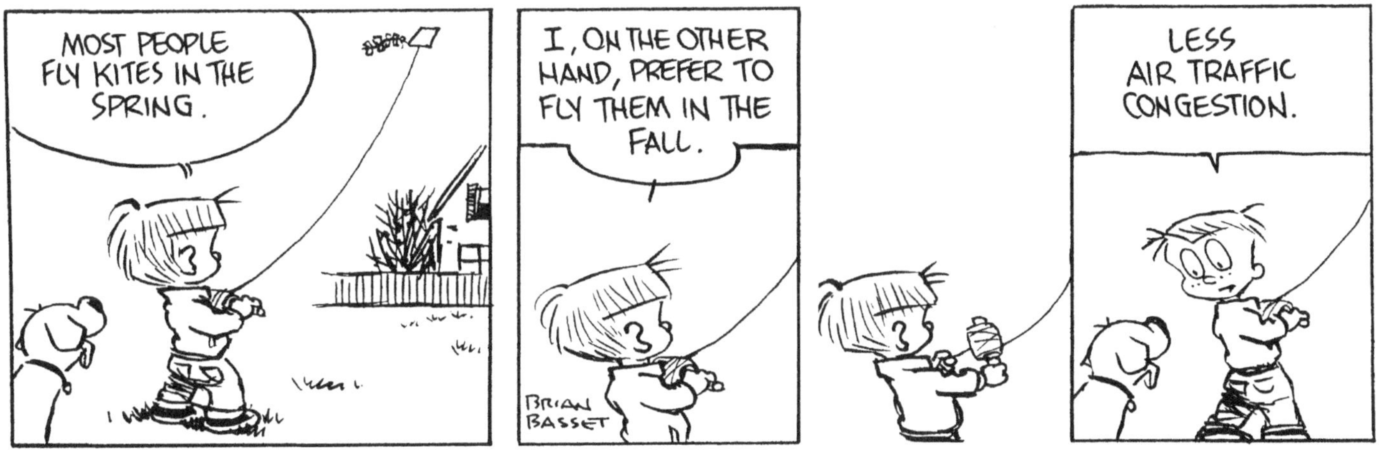
MOST PEOPLE FLY KITES IN THE SPRING.
I, ON THE OTHER HAND, PREFER TO FLY THEM IN THE FALL.
BRIAN BASSET
LESS AIR TRAFFIC CONGESTION.

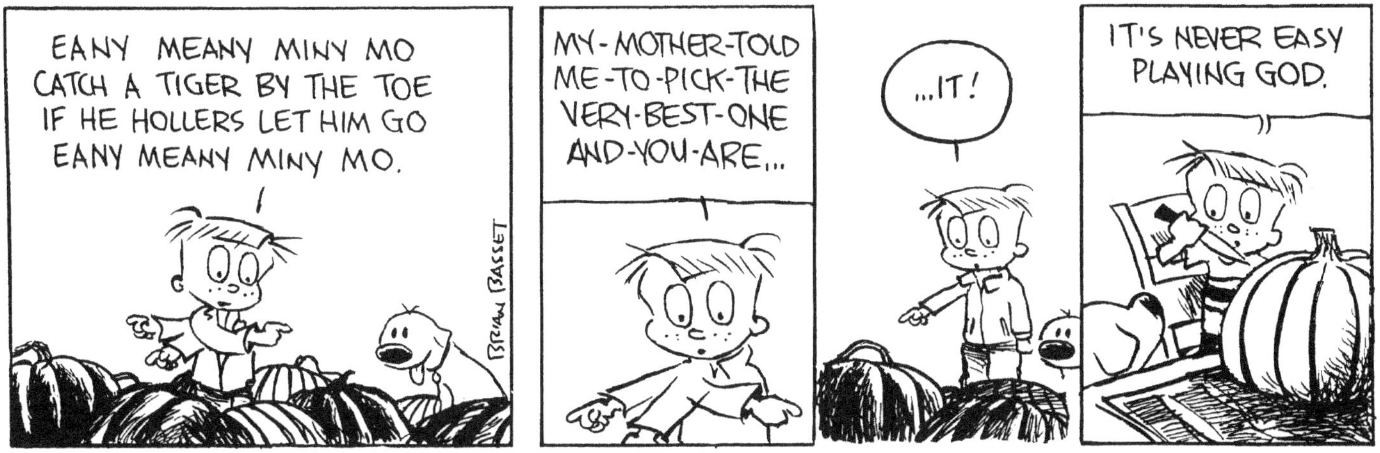
EANY MEANY MINY MO
CATCH A TIGER BY THE TOE
IF HE HOLLERS LET HIM GO
EANY MEANY MINY MO.
BRIAN BASSET
MY-MOTHER-TOLD ME-TO-PICK-THE VERY-BEST-ONE AND-YOU-ARE...
...IT!
IT'S NEVER EASY PLAYING GOD.

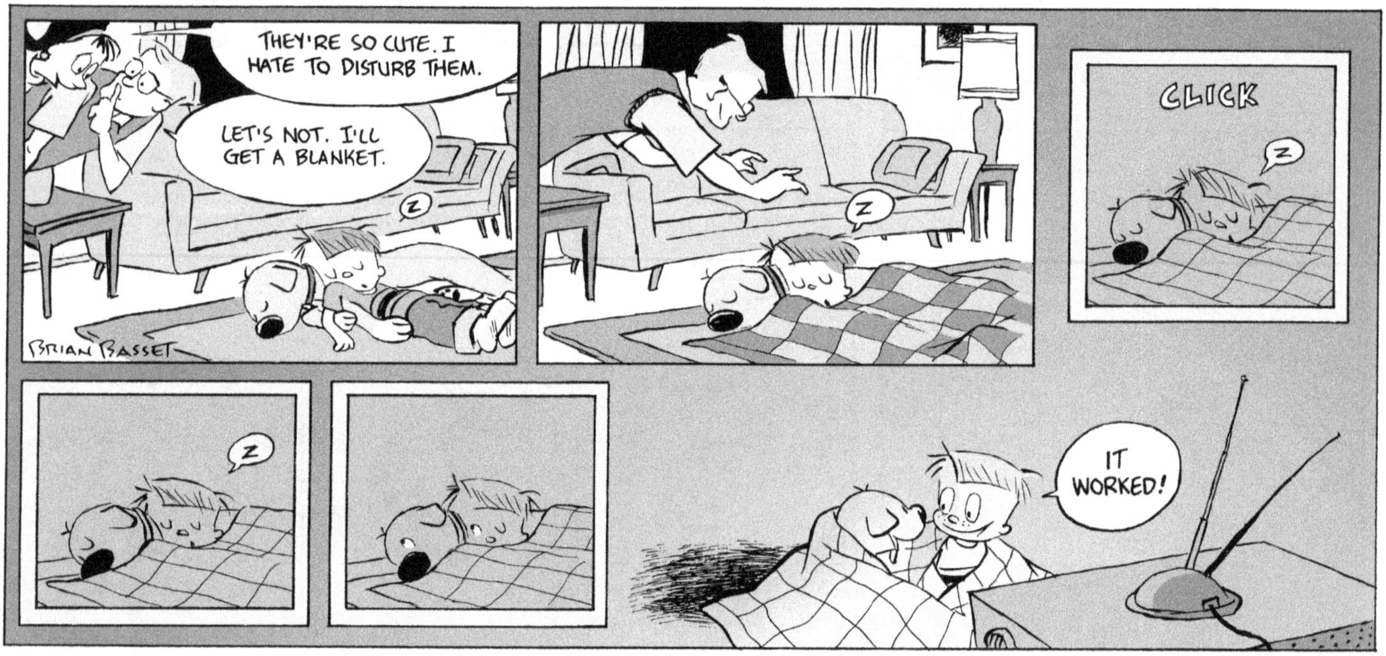
THEY'RE SO CUTE. I HATE TO DISTURB THEM.
LET'S NOT. I'LL GET A BLANKET.
Z
BRIAN BASSET
Z
CLICK
Z
Z
IT WORKED!

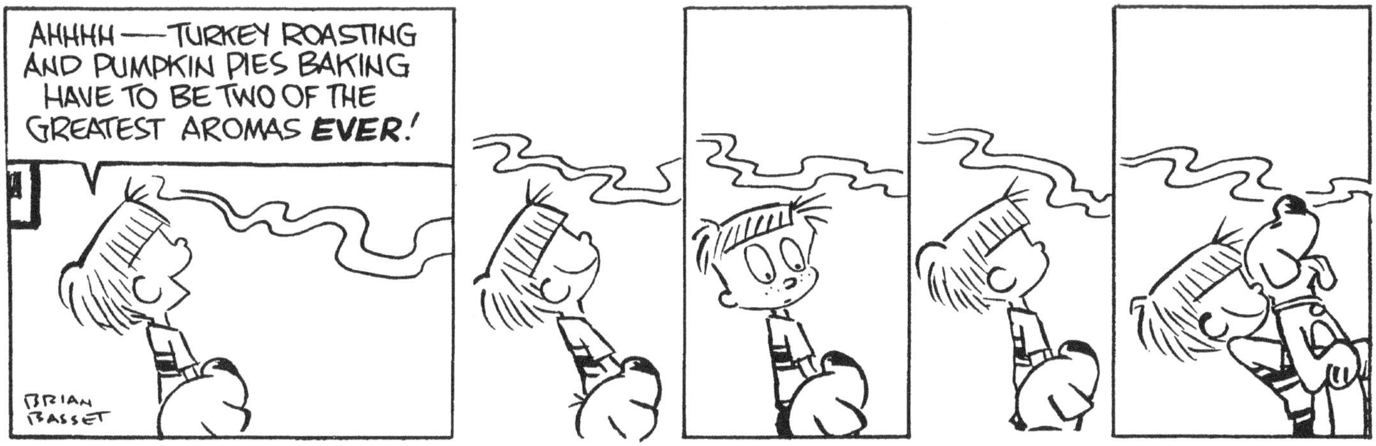
AHHHH — TURKEY ROASTING AND PUMPKIN PIES BAKING HAVE TO BE TWO OF THE GREATEST AROMAS **EVER**!
BRIAN BASSET

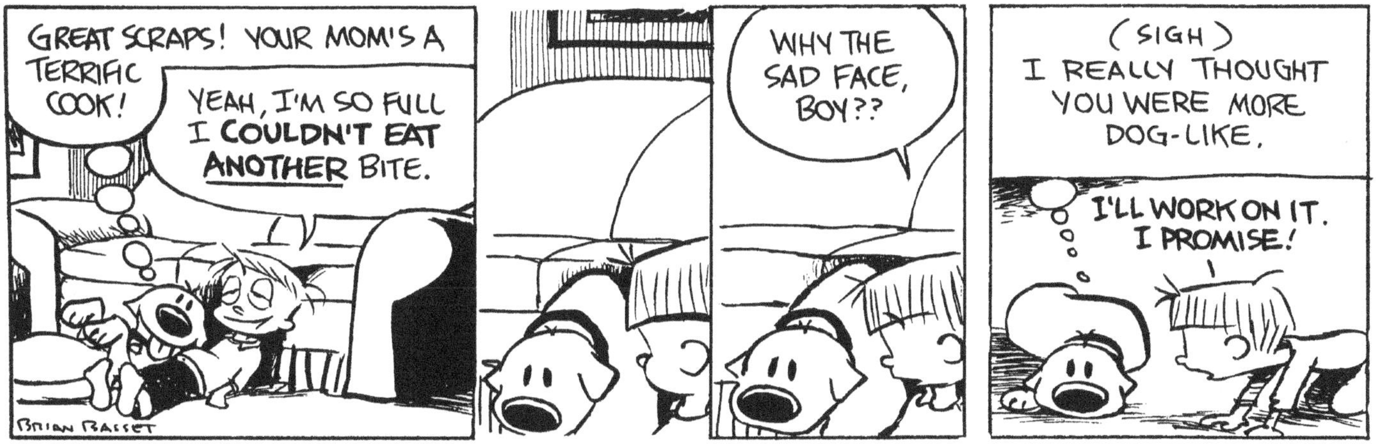
GREAT SCRAPS! YOUR MOM'S A TERRIFIC COOK!
YEAH, I'M SO FULL I **COULDN'T EAT ANOTHER** BITE.
BRIAN BASSET
WHY THE SAD FACE, BOY??
(SIGH) I REALLY THOUGHT YOU WERE MORE DOG-LIKE.
I'LL WORK ON IT. I PROMISE!

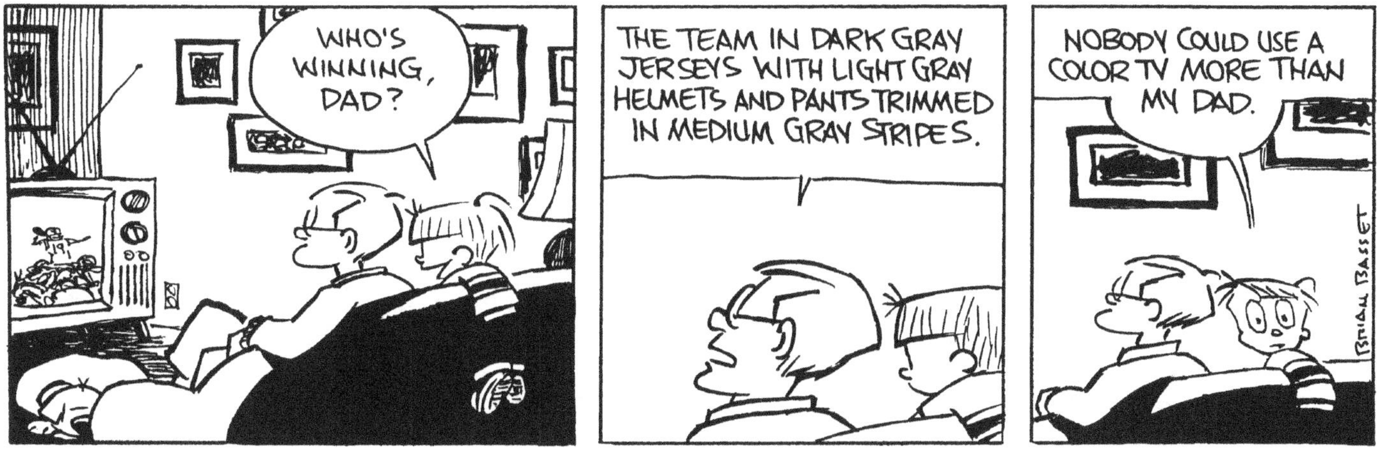
WHO'S WINNING, DAD?
THE TEAM IN DARK GRAY JERSEYS WITH LIGHT GRAY HELMETS AND PANTS TRIMMED IN MEDIUM GRAY STRIPES.
NOBODY COULD USE A COLOR TV MORE THAN MY DAD.
BRIAN BASSET

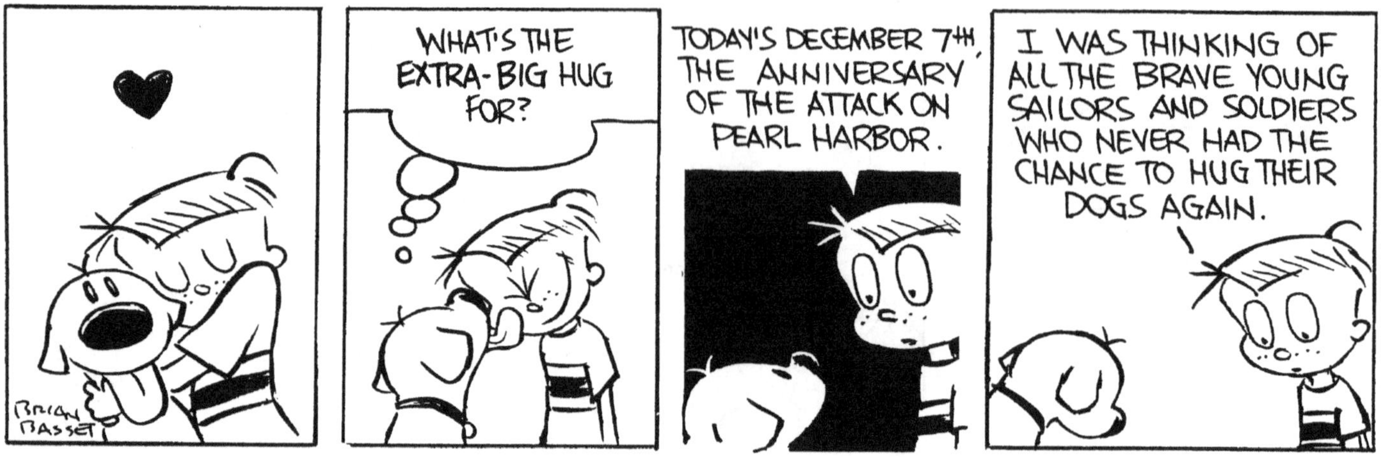
BRIAN BASSET
WHAT'S THE EXTRA-BIG HUG FOR?
TODAY'S DECEMBER 7TH, THE ANNIVERSARY OF THE ATTACK ON PEARL HARBOR.
I WAS THINKING OF ALL THE BRAVE YOUNG SAILORS AND SOLDIERS WHO NEVER HAD THE CHANCE TO HUG THEIR DOGS AGAIN.

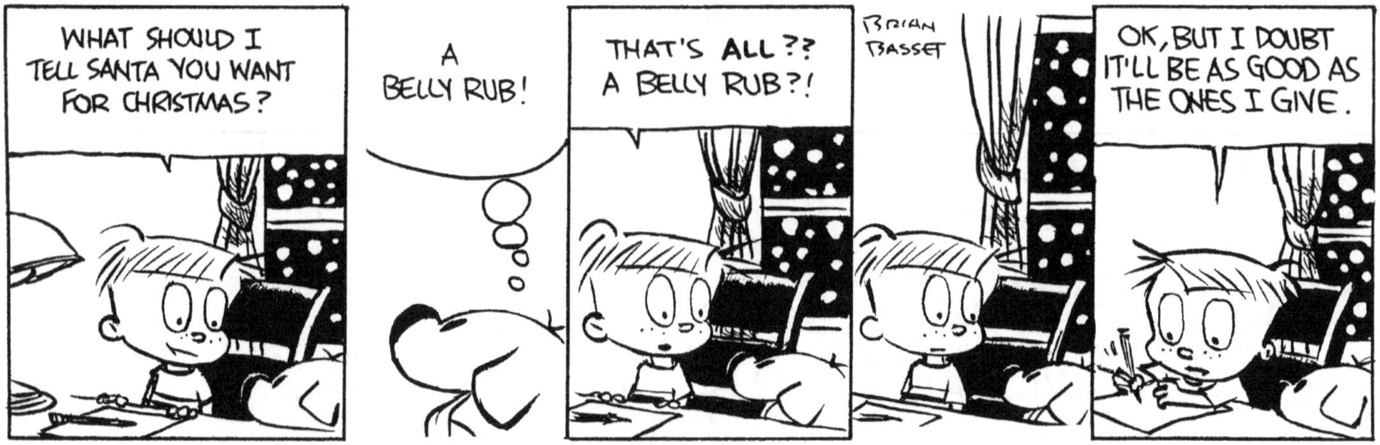
WHAT SHOULD I TELL SANTA YOU WANT FOR CHRISTMAS?
A BELLY RUB!
THAT'S **ALL**?? A BELLY RUB?!
BRIAN BASSET
OK, BUT I DOUBT IT'LL BE AS GOOD AS THE ONES I GIVE.

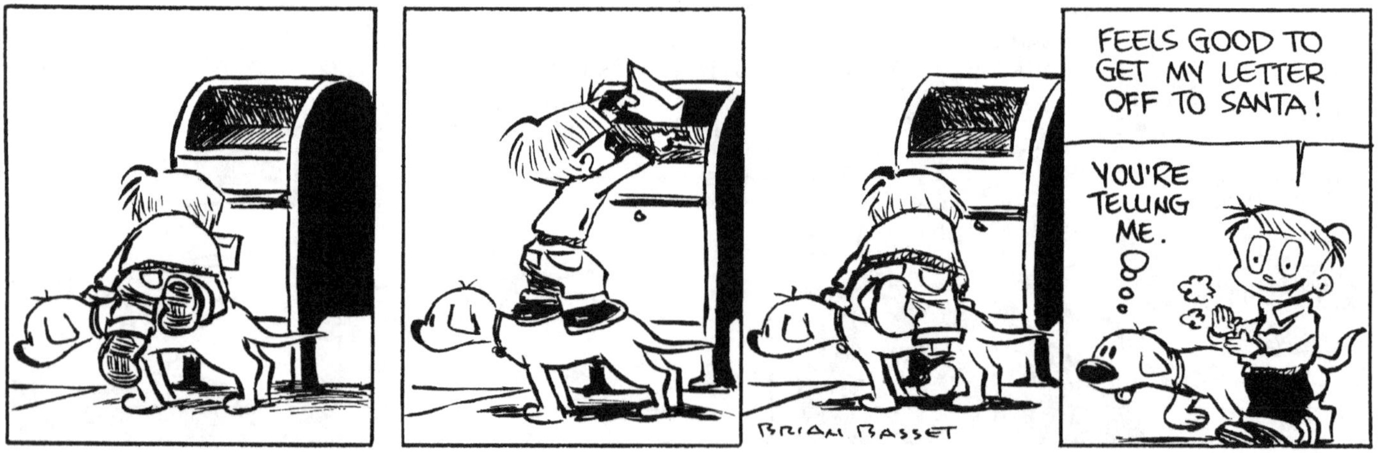
BRIAN BASSET
FEELS GOOD TO GET MY LETTER OFF TO SANTA!
YOU'RE TELLING ME.

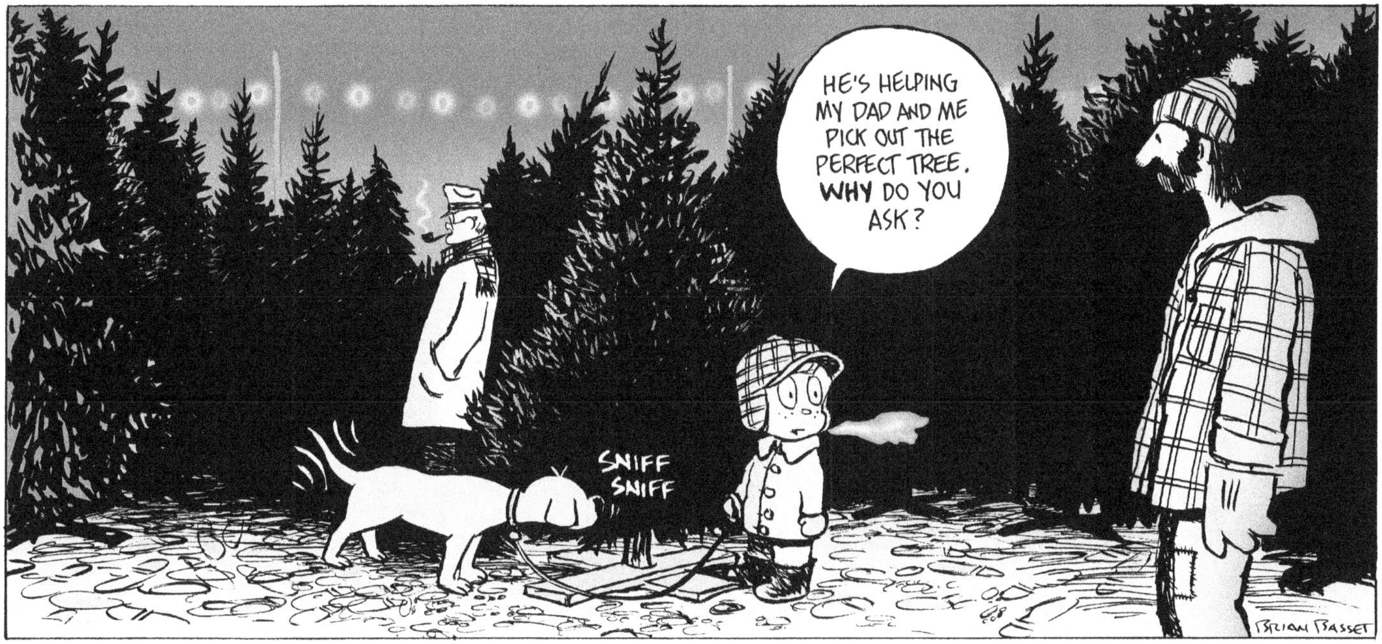
HE'S HELPING MY DAD AND ME PICK OUT THE PERFECT TREE. WHY DO YOU ASK?
SNIFF SNIFF
BRIAN BASSET

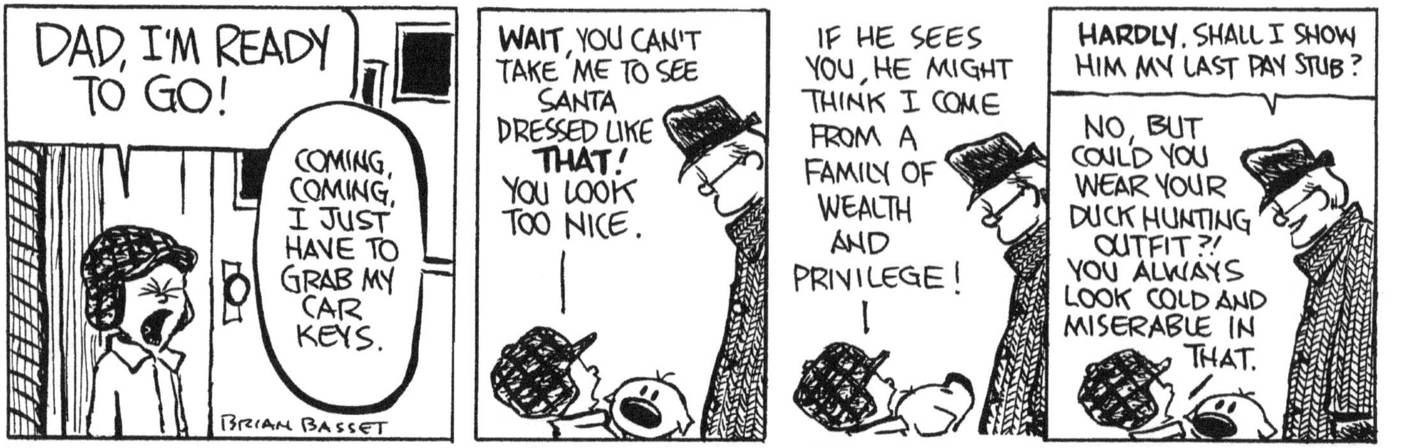
DAD, I'M READY TO GO!
COMING, COMING, I JUST HAVE TO GRAB MY CAR KEYS.
BRIAN BASSET
WAIT, YOU CAN'T TAKE ME TO SEE SANTA DRESSED LIKE THAT! YOU LOOK TOO NICE.
IF HE SEES YOU, HE MIGHT THINK I COME FROM A FAMILY OF WEALTH AND PRIVILEGE!
HARDLY. SHALL I SHOW HIM MY LAST PAY STUB?
NO, BUT COULD YOU WEAR YOUR DUCK HUNTING OUTFIT?! YOU ALWAYS LOOK COLD AND MISERABLE IN THAT.

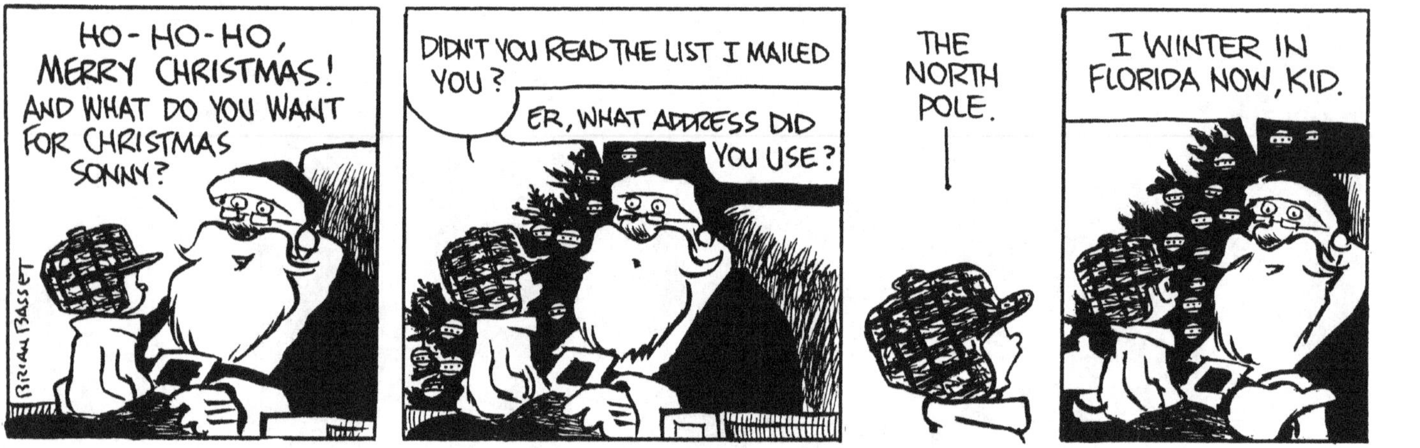
HO-HO-HO, MERRY CHRISTMAS! AND WHAT DO YOU WANT FOR CHRISTMAS SONNY?
BRIAN BASSET
DIDN'T YOU READ THE LIST I MAILED YOU?
ER, WHAT ADDRESS DID YOU USE?
THE NORTH POLE.
I WINTER IN FLORIDA NOW, KID.

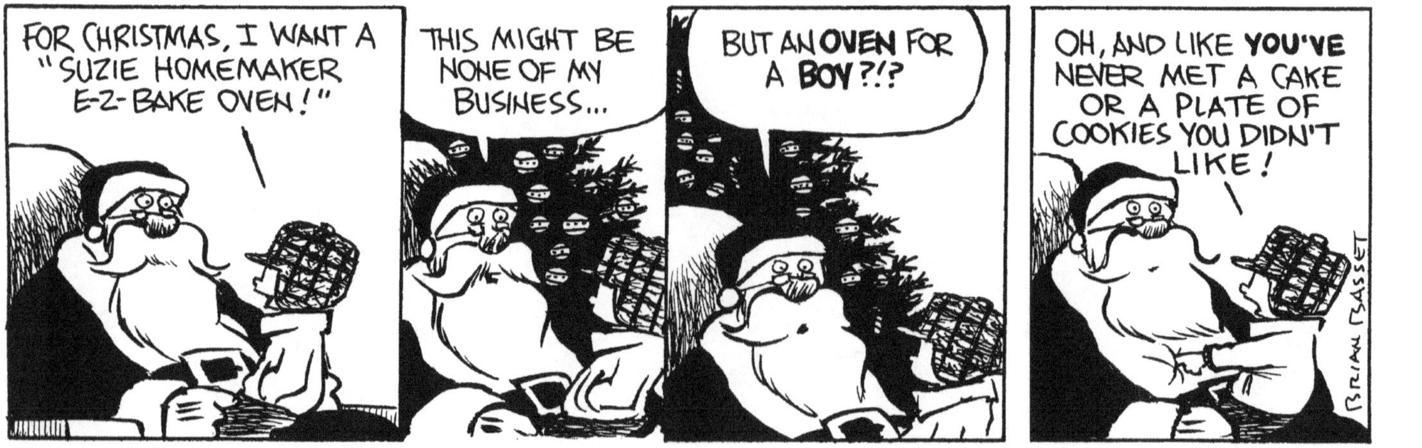
FOR CHRISTMAS, I WANT A "SUZIE HOMEMAKER E-Z-BAKE OVEN!"
THIS MIGHT BE NONE OF MY BUSINESS...
BUT AN OVEN FOR A BOY?!?
OH, AND LIKE YOU'VE NEVER MET A CAKE OR A PLATE OF COOKIES YOU DIDN'T LIKE!
BRIAN BASSET

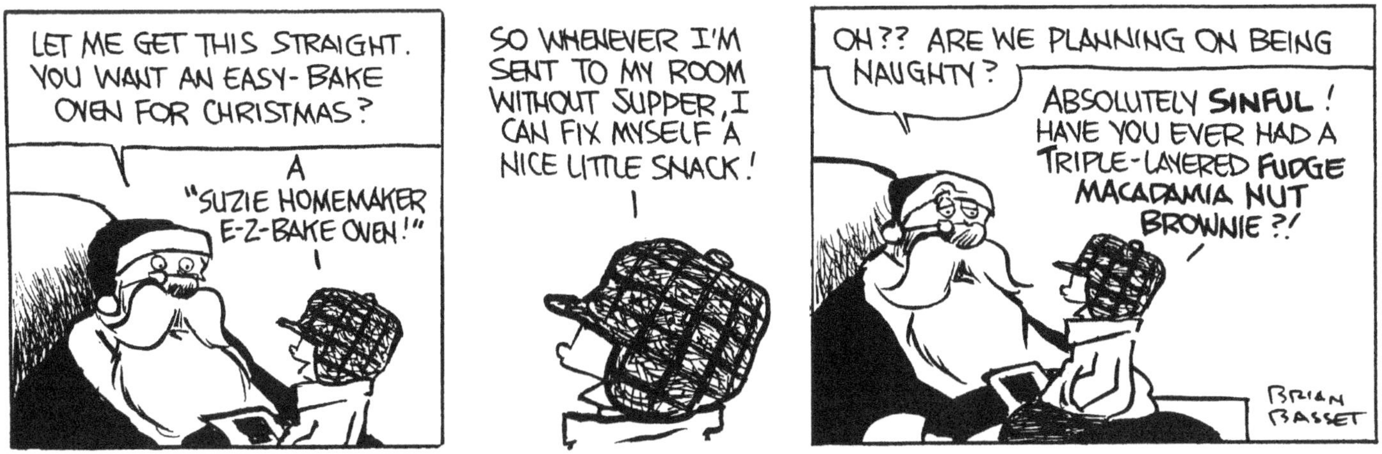
LET ME GET THIS STRAIGHT. YOU WANT AN EASY-BAKE OVEN FOR CHRISTMAS?
A "SUZIE HOMEMAKER E-Z-BAKE OVEN!"
SO WHENEVER I'M SENT TO MY ROOM WITHOUT SUPPER, I CAN FIX MYSELF A NICE LITTLE SNACK!
OH?? ARE WE PLANNING ON BEING NAUGHTY?
ABSOLUTELY SINFUL! HAVE YOU EVER HAD A TRIPLE-LAYERED FUDGE MACADAMIA NUT BROWNIE?!
BRIAN BASSET

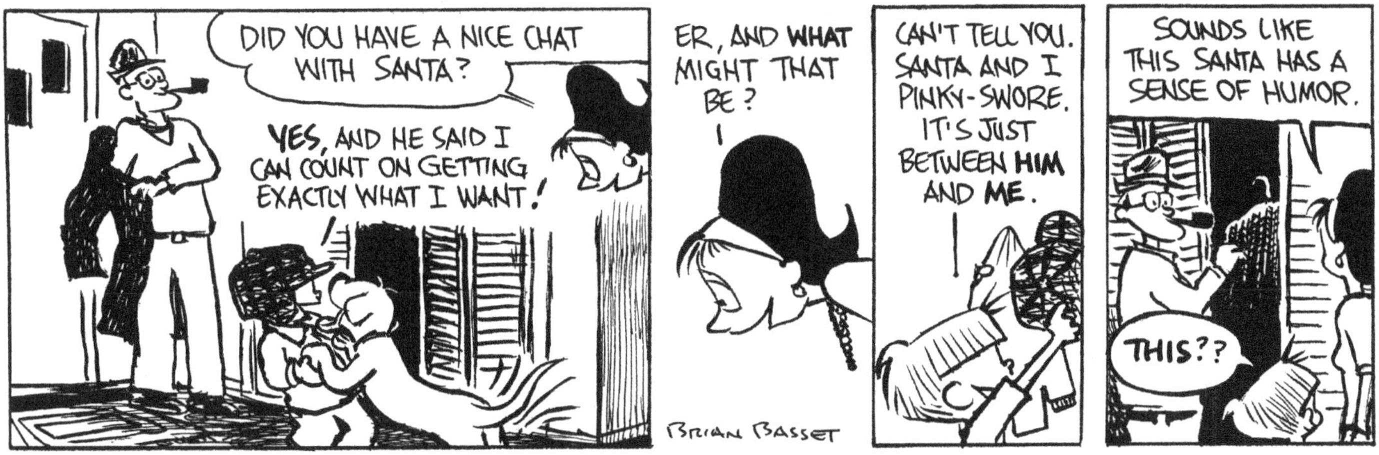
DID YOU HAVE A NICE CHAT WITH SANTA?
YES, AND HE SAID I CAN COUNT ON GETTING EXACTLY WHAT I WANT!
ER, AND WHAT MIGHT THAT BE?
BRIAN BASSET
CAN'T TELL YOU. SANTA AND I PINKY-SWORE. IT'S JUST BETWEEN HIM AND ME.
SOUNDS LIKE THIS SANTA HAS A SENSE OF HUMOR.
THIS??

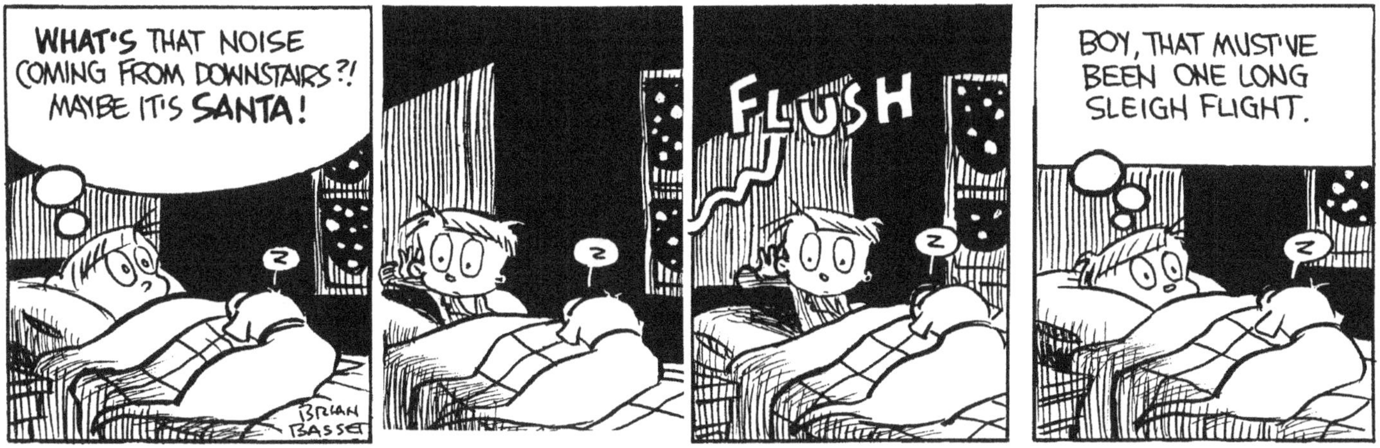
WHAT'S THAT NOISE COMING FROM DOWNSTAIRS?! MAYBE IT'S SANTA!
Z
BRIAN BASSET
FLUSH
BOY, THAT MUST'VE BEEN ONE LONG SLEIGH FLIGHT.

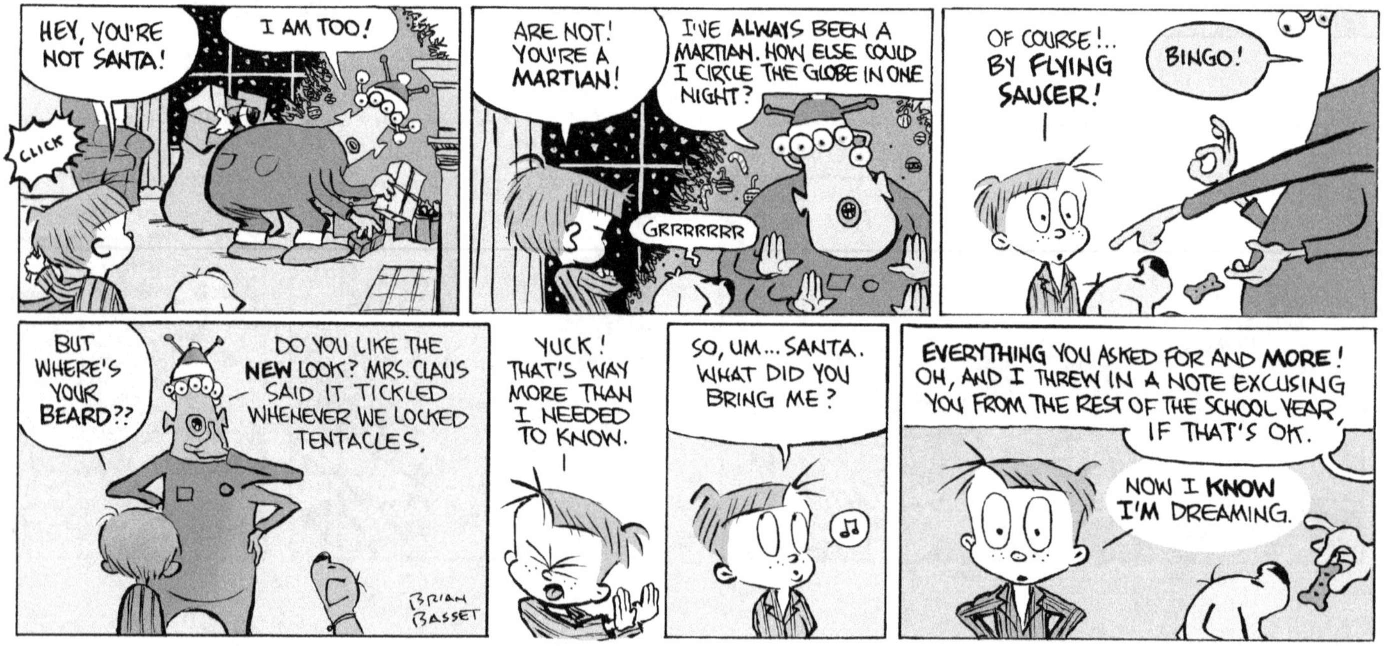
HEY, YOU'RE NOT SANTA!
I AM TOO!
CLICK
ARE NOT! YOU'RE A MARTIAN!
I'VE ALWAYS BEEN A MARTIAN. HOW ELSE COULD I CIRCLE THE GLOBE IN ONE NIGHT?
GRRRRRRR
OF COURSE!.. BY FLYING SAUCER!
BINGO!
BUT WHERE'S YOUR BEARD??
DO YOU LIKE THE NEW LOOK? MRS. CLAUS SAID IT TICKLED WHENEVER WE LOCKED TENTACLES.
BRIAN BASSET
YUCK! THAT'S WAY MORE THAN I NEEDED TO KNOW.
SO, UM... SANTA. WHAT DID YOU BRING ME?
EVERYTHING YOU ASKED FOR AND MORE! OH, AND I THREW IN A NOTE EXCUSING YOU FROM THE REST OF THE SCHOOL YEAR, IF THAT'S OK.
NOW I KNOW I'M DREAMING.

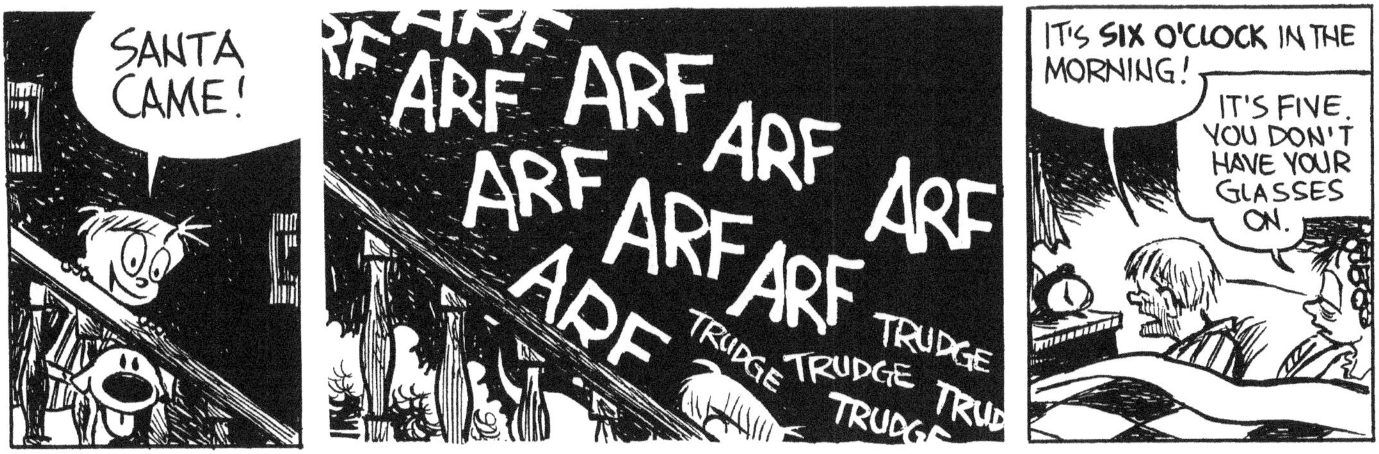
SANTA CAME!
ARF ARF ARF ARF ARF ARF ARF ARF ARF ARF ARF
TRUDGE TRUDGE TRUDGE TRUDGE TRUD TRUDGE
IT'S **SIX O'CLOCK** IN THE MORNING!
IT'S FIVE. YOU DON'T HAVE YOUR GLASSES ON.

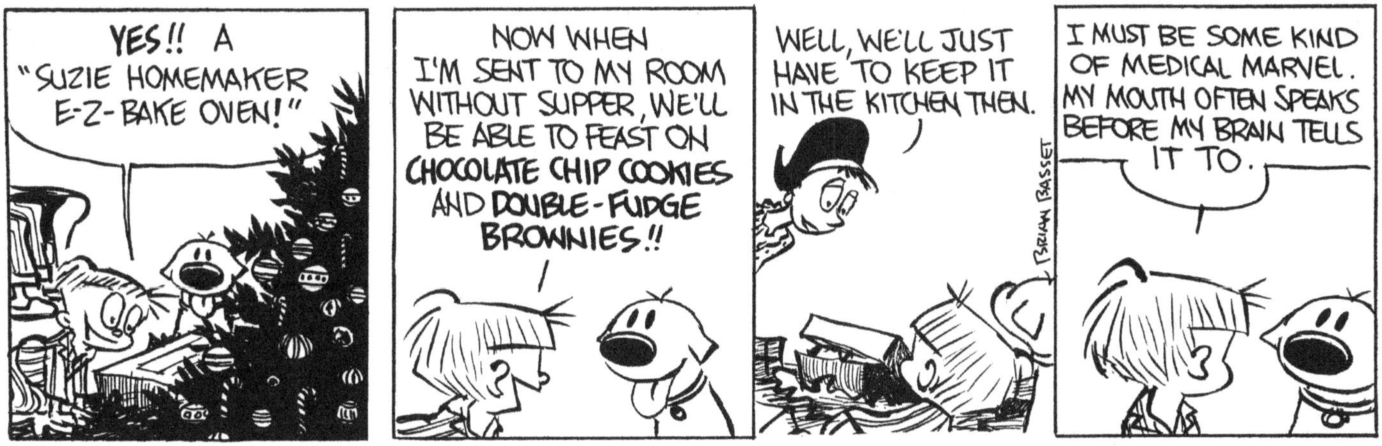
YES!! A "SUZIE HOMEMAKER E-Z-BAKE OVEN!"
NOW WHEN I'M SENT TO MY ROOM WITHOUT SUPPER, WE'LL BE ABLE TO FEAST ON **CHOCOLATE CHIP COOKIES** AND **DOUBLE-FUDGE BROWNIES!!**
WELL, WE'LL JUST HAVE TO KEEP IT IN THE KITCHEN THEN.
BRIAN BASSET
I MUST BE SOME KIND OF MEDICAL MARVEL. MY MOUTH OFTEN SPEAKS BEFORE MY BRAIN TELLS IT TO.

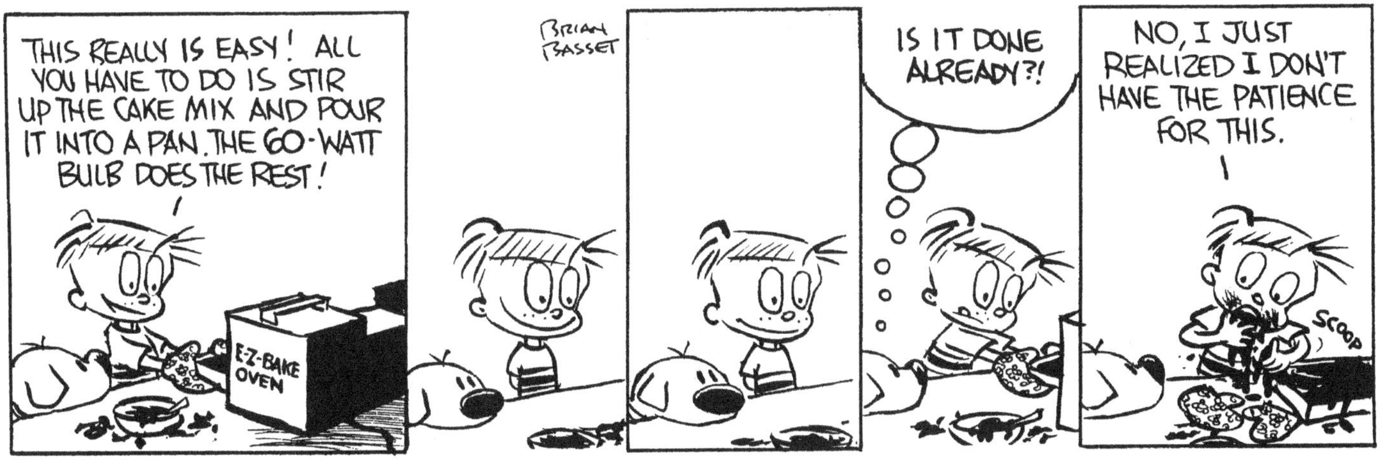
THIS REALLY IS EASY! ALL YOU HAVE TO DO IS STIR UP THE CAKE MIX AND POUR IT INTO A PAN. THE 60-WATT BULB DOES THE REST!
E-Z-BAKE OVEN
BRIAN BASSET
IS IT DONE ALREADY?!
NO, I JUST REALIZED I DON'T HAVE THE PATIENCE FOR THIS.
SCOOP

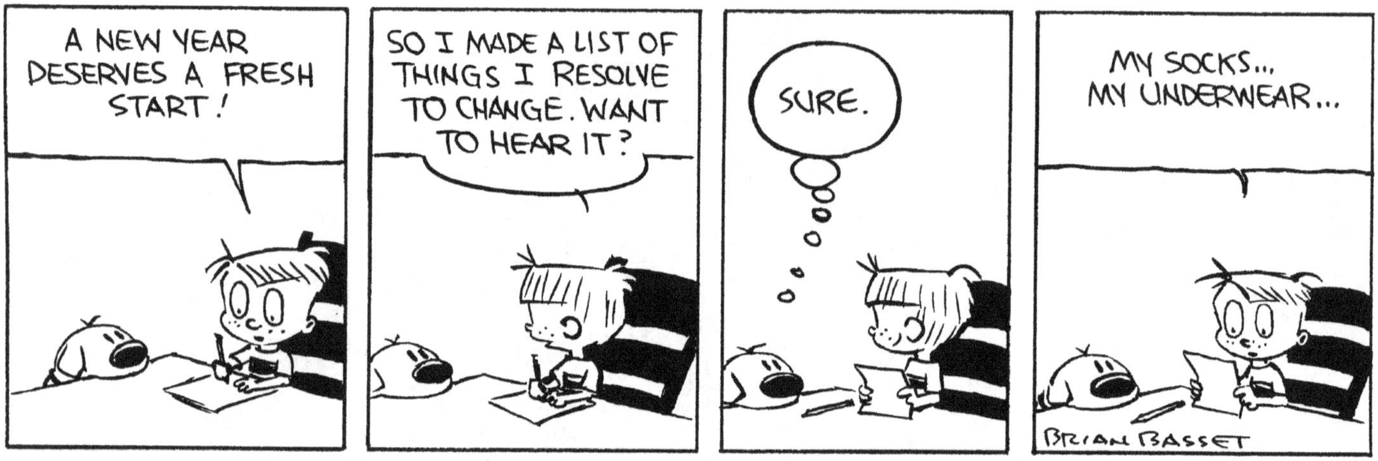
A NEW YEAR DESERVES A FRESH START!
SO I MADE A LIST OF THINGS I RESOLVE TO CHANGE. WANT TO HEAR IT?
SURE.
MY SOCKS... MY UNDERWEAR...
BRIAN BASSET

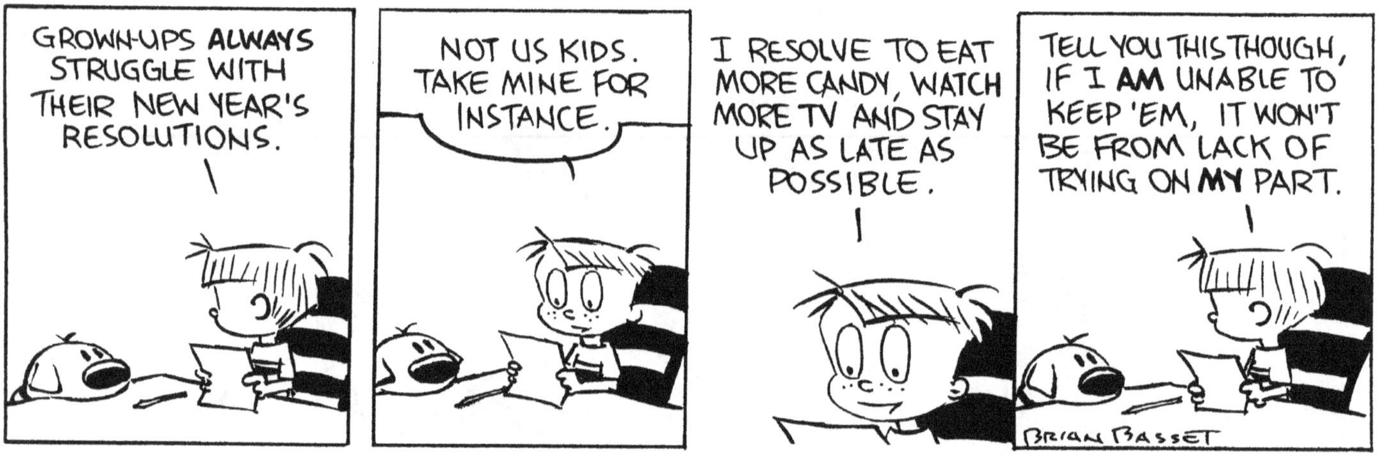
GROWN-UPS **ALWAYS** STRUGGLE WITH THEIR NEW YEAR'S RESOLUTIONS.
NOT US KIDS. TAKE MINE FOR INSTANCE.
I RESOLVE TO EAT MORE CANDY, WATCH MORE TV AND STAY UP AS LATE AS POSSIBLE.
TELL YOU THIS THOUGH, IF I **AM** UNABLE TO KEEP 'EM, IT WON'T BE FROM LACK OF TRYING ON **MY** PART.
BRIAN BASSET

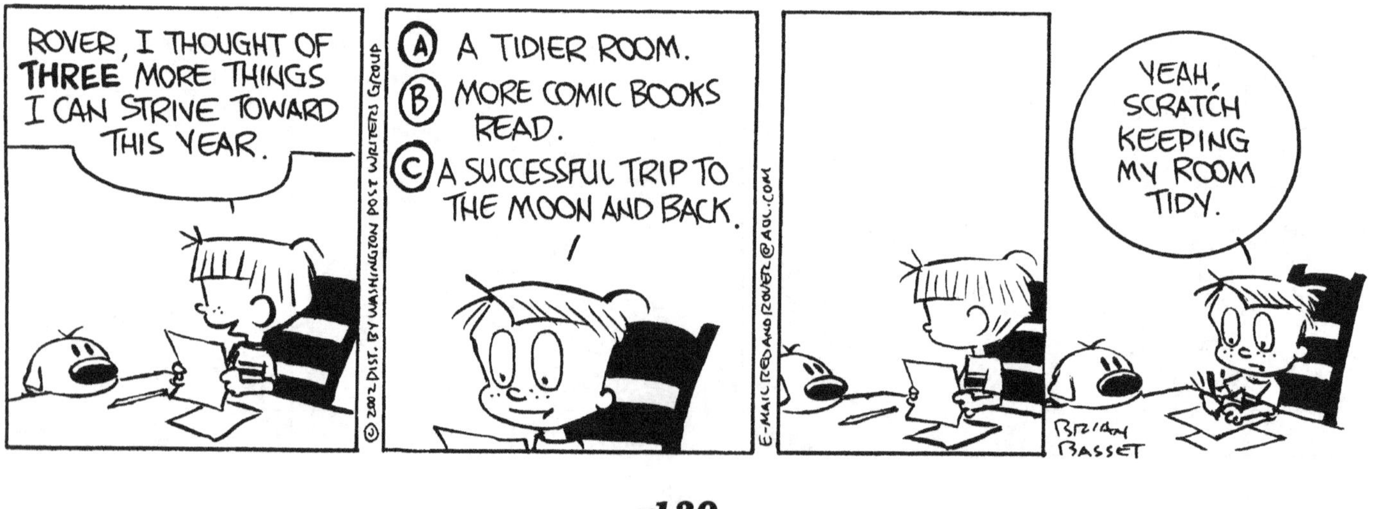
ROVER, I THOUGHT OF **THREE** MORE THINGS I CAN STRIVE TOWARD THIS YEAR.
© 2002 DIST. BY WASHINGTON POST WRITERS GROUP
(A) A TIDIER ROOM.
(B) MORE COMIC BOOKS READ.
(C) A SUCCESSFUL TRIP TO THE MOON AND BACK.
E-MAIL REDANDROVER@AOL.COM
YEAH, SCRATCH KEEPING MY ROOM TIDY.
BRIAN BASSET

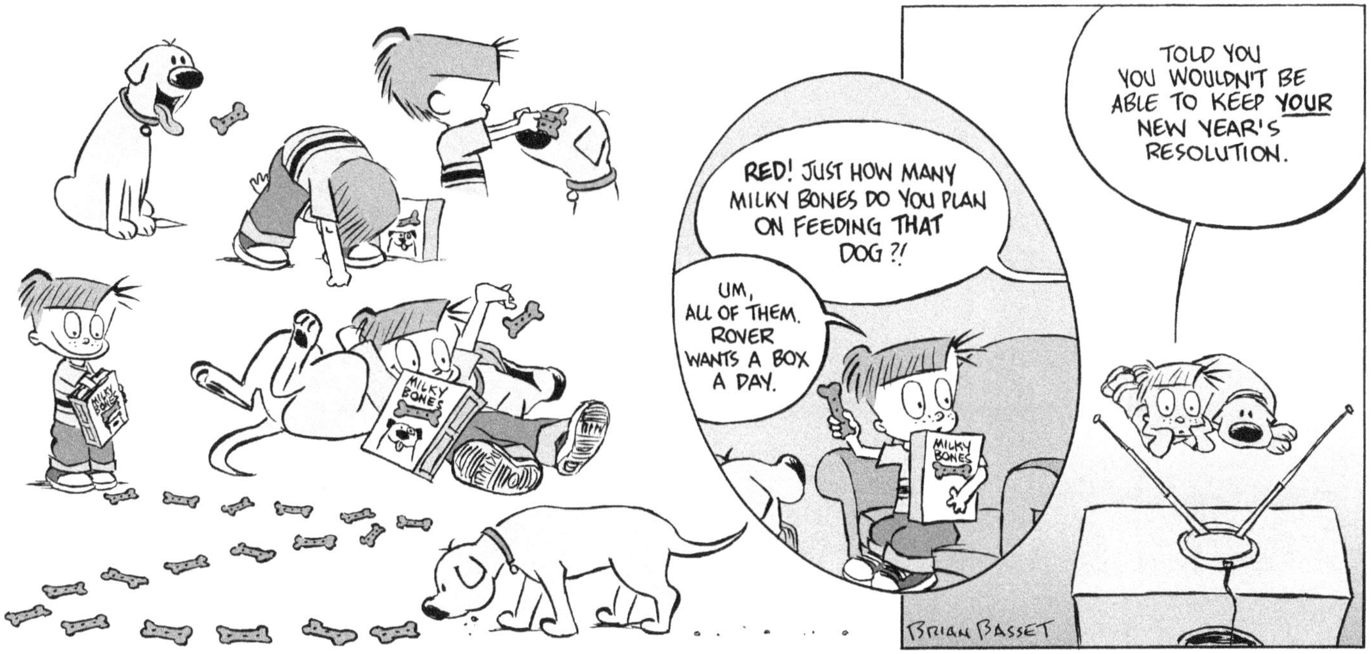
MILKY BONES
RED! JUST HOW MANY MILKY BONES DO YOU PLAN ON FEEDING THAT DOG ?!
UM, ALL OF THEM. ROVER WANTS A BOX A DAY.
TOLD YOU YOU WOULDN'T BE ABLE TO KEEP YOUR NEW YEAR'S RESOLUTION.
BRIAN BASSET

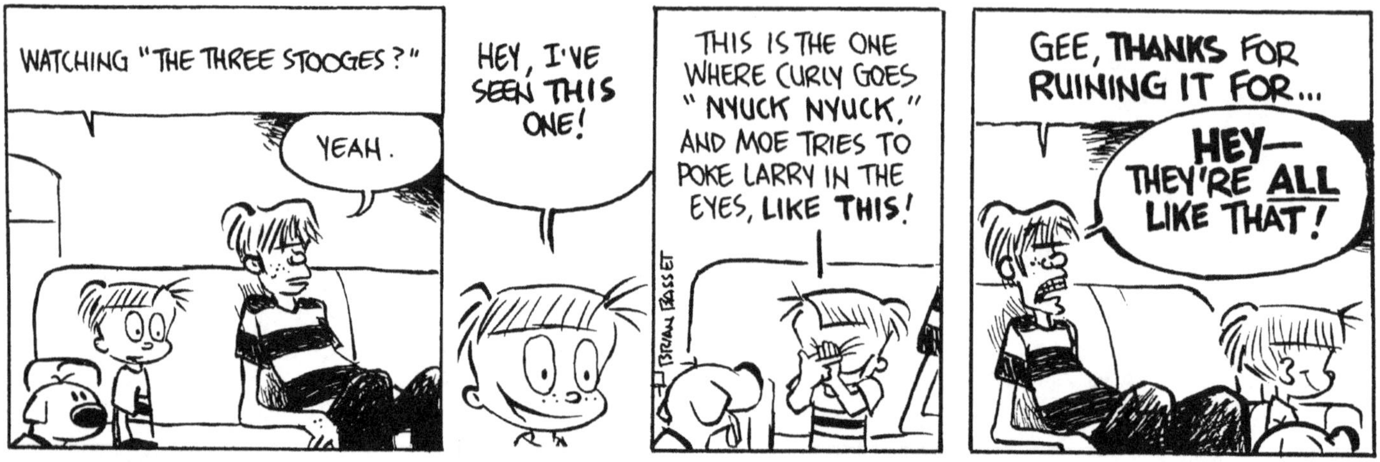
WATCHING "THE THREE STOOGES?"
YEAH.
HEY, I'VE SEEN THIS ONE!
THIS IS THE ONE WHERE CURLY GOES "NYUCK NYUCK," AND MOE TRIES TO POKE LARRY IN THE EYES, LIKE THIS!
BRIAN BASSET
GEE, THANKS FOR RUINING IT FOR...
HEY— THEY'RE ALL LIKE THAT!

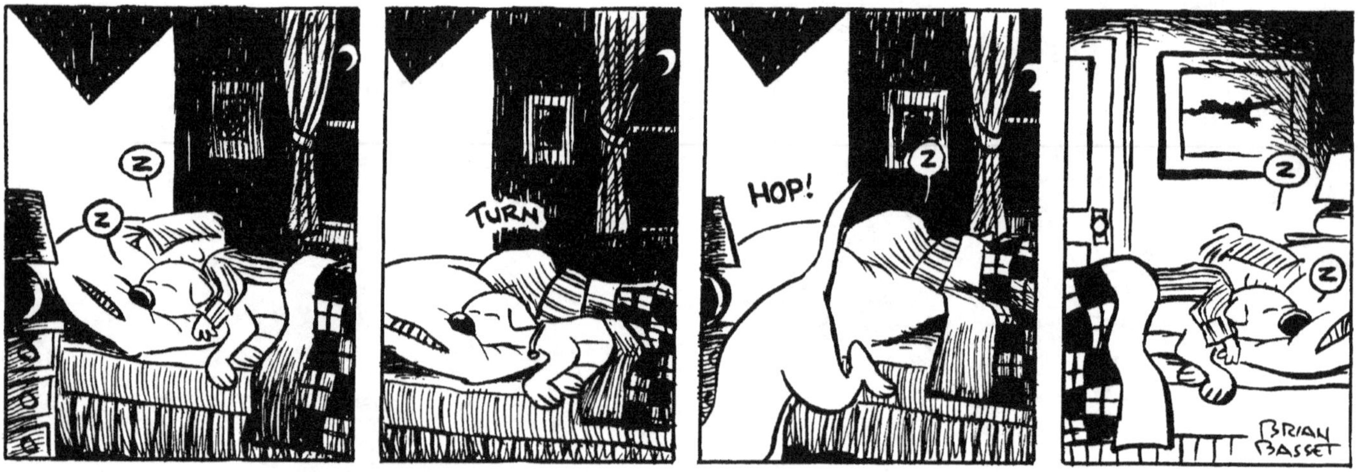
Z
Z
TURN
HOP!
Z
Z
Z
BRIAN BASSET

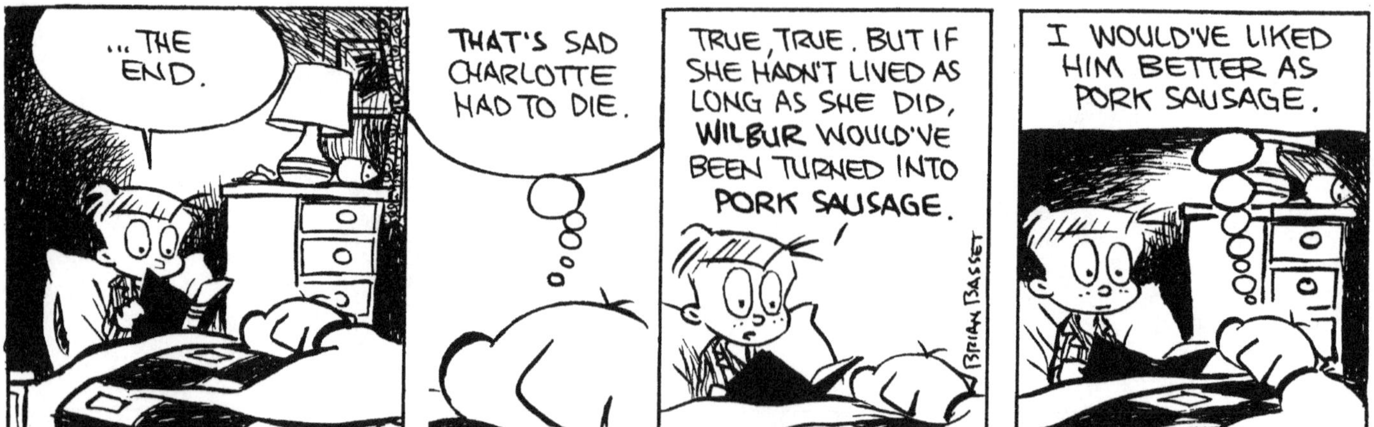
...THE END.
THAT'S SAD CHARLOTTE HAD TO DIE.
TRUE, TRUE. BUT IF SHE HADN'T LIVED AS LONG AS SHE DID, WILBUR WOULD'VE BEEN TURNED INTO PORK SAUSAGE.
BRIAN BASSET
I WOULD'VE LIKED HIM BETTER AS PORK SAUSAGE.

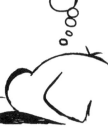

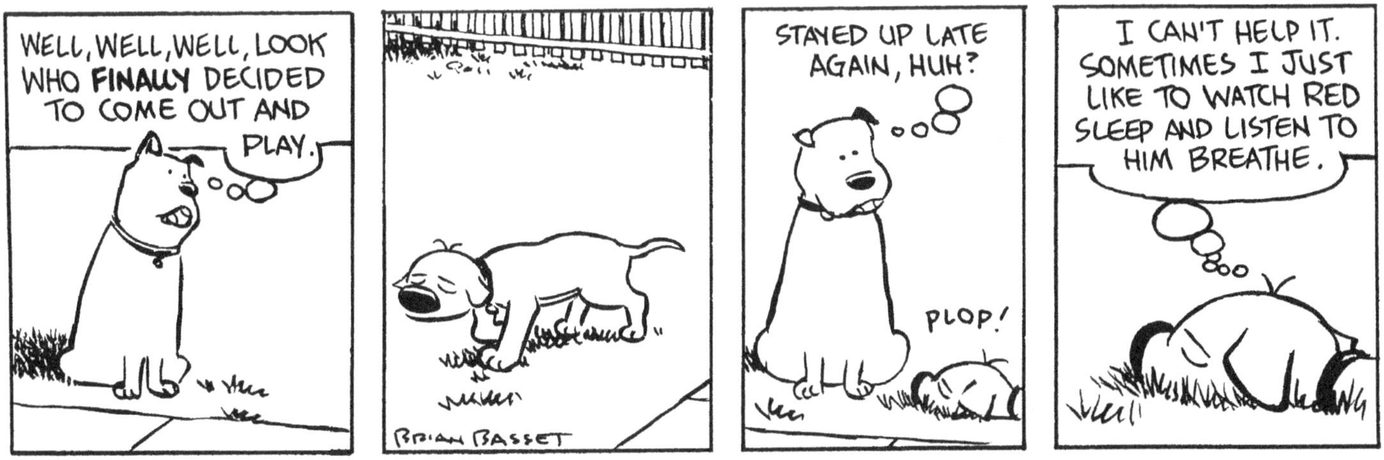
WELL, WELL, WELL, LOOK WHO FINALLY DECIDED TO COME OUT AND PLAY.
BRIAN BASSET
STAYED UP LATE AGAIN, HUH?
PLOP!
I CAN'T HELP IT. SOMETIMES I JUST LIKE TO WATCH RED SLEEP AND LISTEN TO HIM BREATHE.

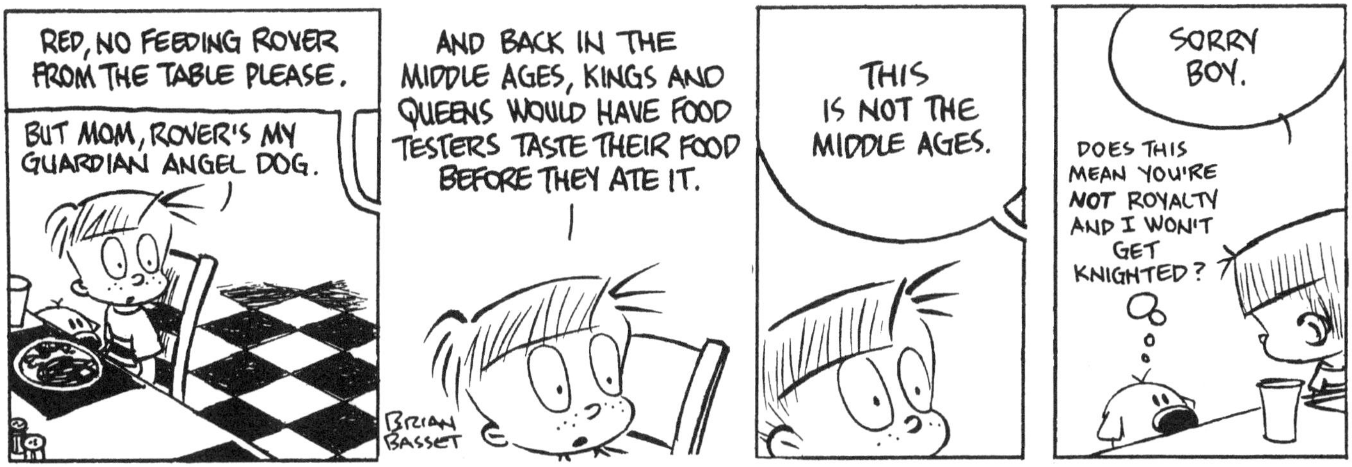
RED, NO FEEDING ROVER FROM THE TABLE PLEASE.
BUT MOM, ROVER'S MY GUARDIAN ANGEL DOG.
AND BACK IN THE MIDDLE AGES, KINGS AND QUEENS WOULD HAVE FOOD TESTERS TASTE THEIR FOOD BEFORE THEY ATE IT.
BRIAN BASSET
THIS IS NOT THE MIDDLE AGES.
SORRY BOY.
DOES THIS MEAN YOU'RE NOT ROYALTY AND I WON'T GET KNIGHTED?

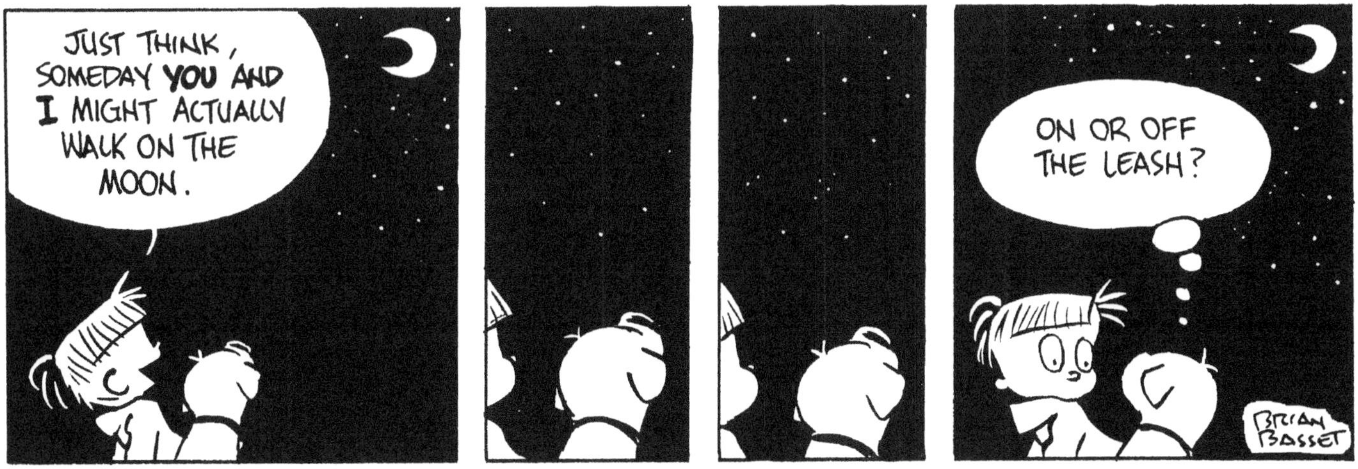
JUST THINK, SOMEDAY YOU AND I MIGHT ACTUALLY WALK ON THE MOON.
ON OR OFF THE LEASH?
BRIAN BASSET

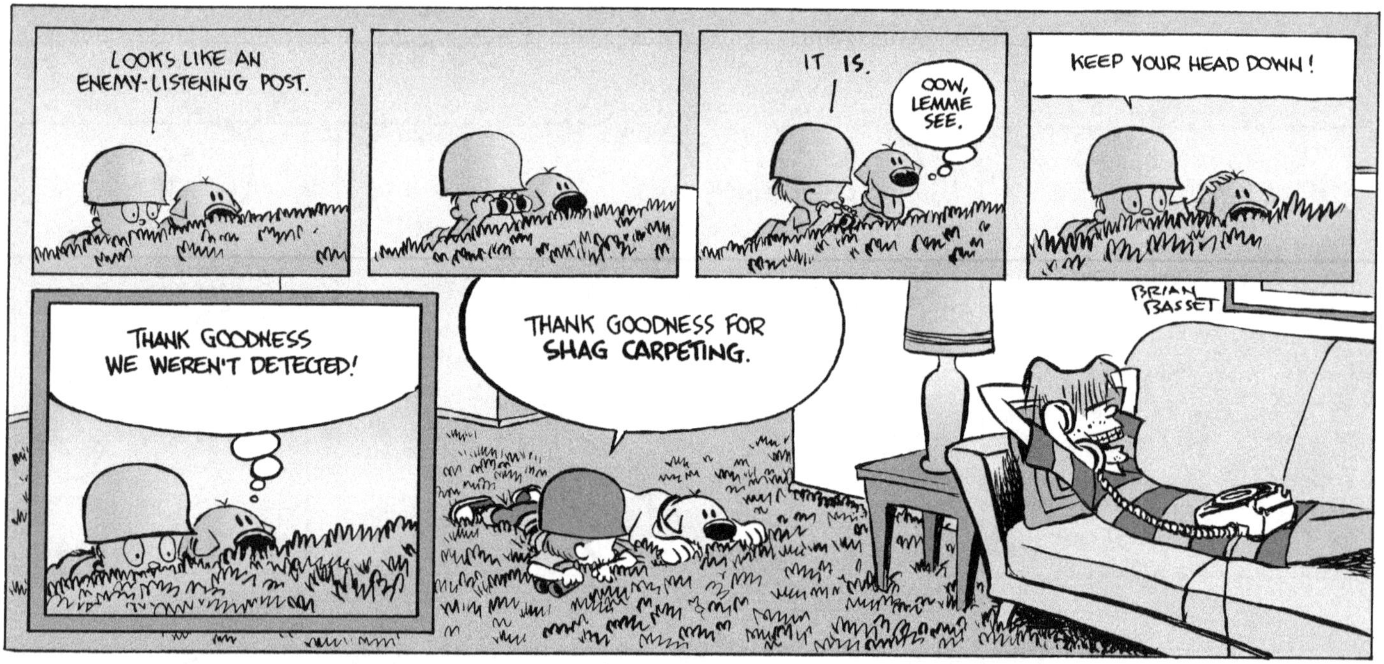
LOOKS LIKE AN ENEMY-LISTENING POST.
IT IS.
OOW, LEMME SEE.
KEEP YOUR HEAD DOWN!
BRIAN BASSET
THANK GOODNESS WE WEREN'T DETECTED!
THANK GOODNESS FOR SHAG CARPETING.

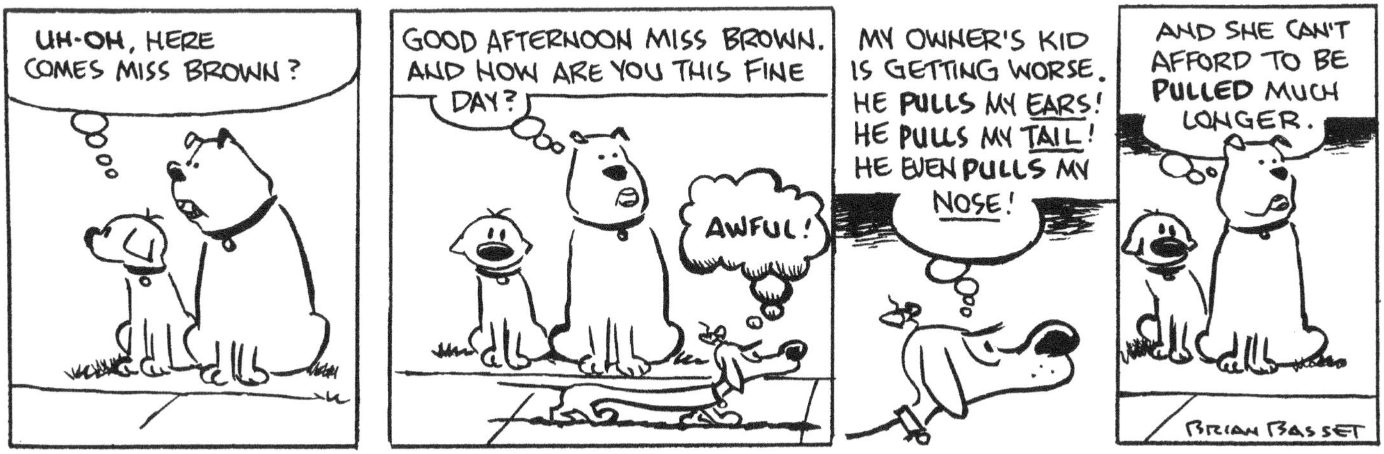
UH-OH, HERE COMES MISS BROWN?
GOOD AFTERNOON MISS BROWN. AND HOW ARE YOU THIS FINE DAY?
AWFUL!
MY OWNER'S KID IS GETTING WORSE. HE PULLS MY EARS! HE PULLS MY TAIL! HE EVEN PULLS MY NOSE!
AND SHE CAN'T AFFORD TO BE PULLED MUCH LONGER.
BRIAN BASSET

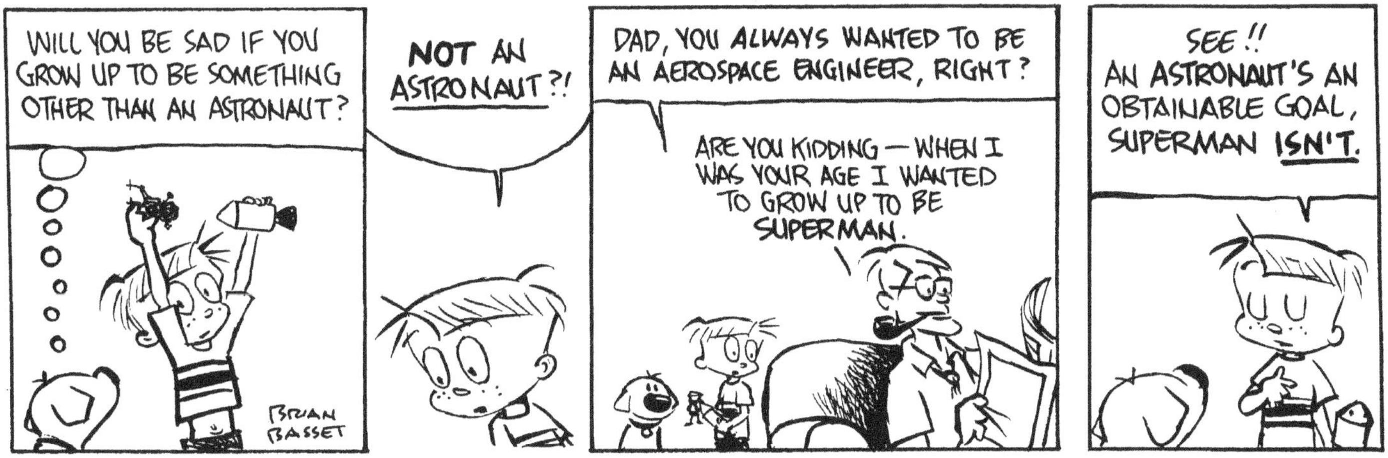
WILL YOU BE SAD IF YOU GROW UP TO BE SOMETHING OTHER THAN AN ASTRONAUT?
BRIAN BASSET
NOT AN ASTRONAUT?!
DAD, YOU ALWAYS WANTED TO BE AN AEROSPACE ENGINEER, RIGHT?
ARE YOU KIDDING — WHEN I WAS YOUR AGE I WANTED TO GROW UP TO BE SUPERMAN.
SEE!! AN ASTRONAUT'S AN OBTAINABLE GOAL, SUPERMAN ISN'T.

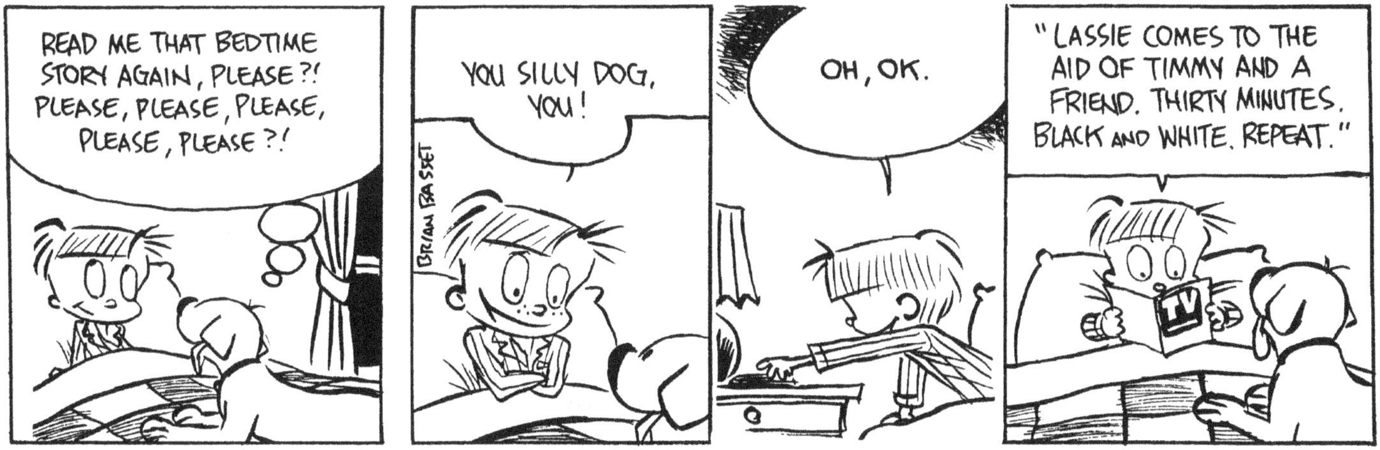
READ ME THAT BEDTIME STORY AGAIN, PLEASE?! PLEASE, PLEASE, PLEASE, PLEASE, PLEASE?!
YOU SILLY DOG, YOU!
BRIAN BASSET
OH, OK.
"LASSIE COMES TO THE AID OF TIMMY AND A FRIEND. THIRTY MINUTES. BLACK AND WHITE. REPEAT."

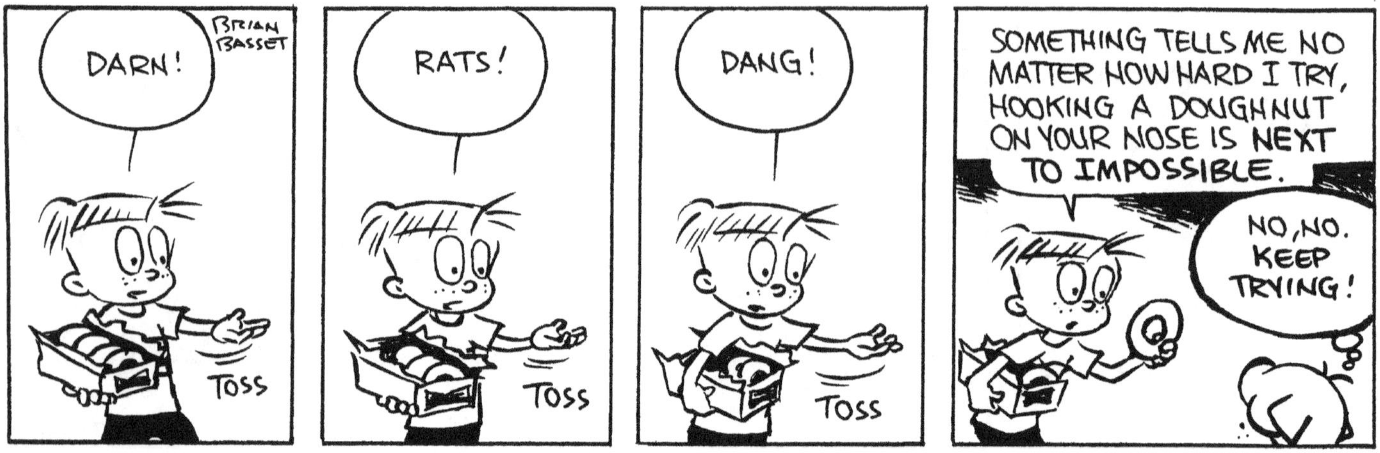
BRIAN BASSET
DARN!
TOSS
RATS!
TOSS
DANG!
TOSS
SOMETHING TELLS ME NO MATTER HOW HARD I TRY, HOOKING A DOUGHNUT ON YOUR NOSE IS NEXT TO IMPOSSIBLE.
NO, NO. KEEP TRYING!

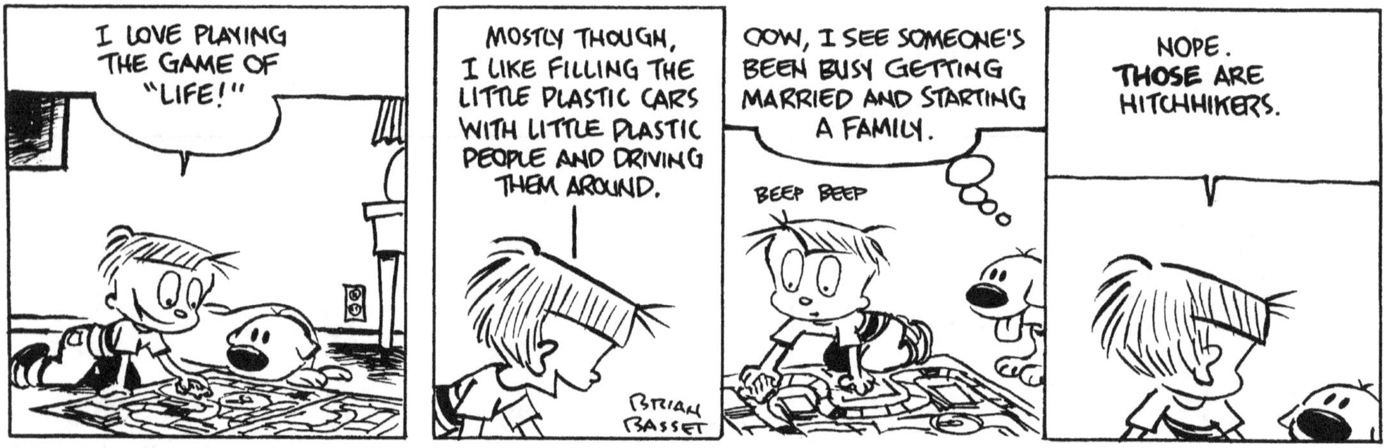
I LOVE PLAYING THE GAME OF "LIFE!"
MOSTLY THOUGH, I LIKE FILLING THE LITTLE PLASTIC CARS WITH LITTLE PLASTIC PEOPLE AND DRIVING THEM AROUND.
BRIAN BASSET
OOW, I SEE SOMEONE'S BEEN BUSY GETTING MARRIED AND STARTING A FAMILY.
BEEP BEEP
NOPE. THOSE ARE HITCHHIKERS.

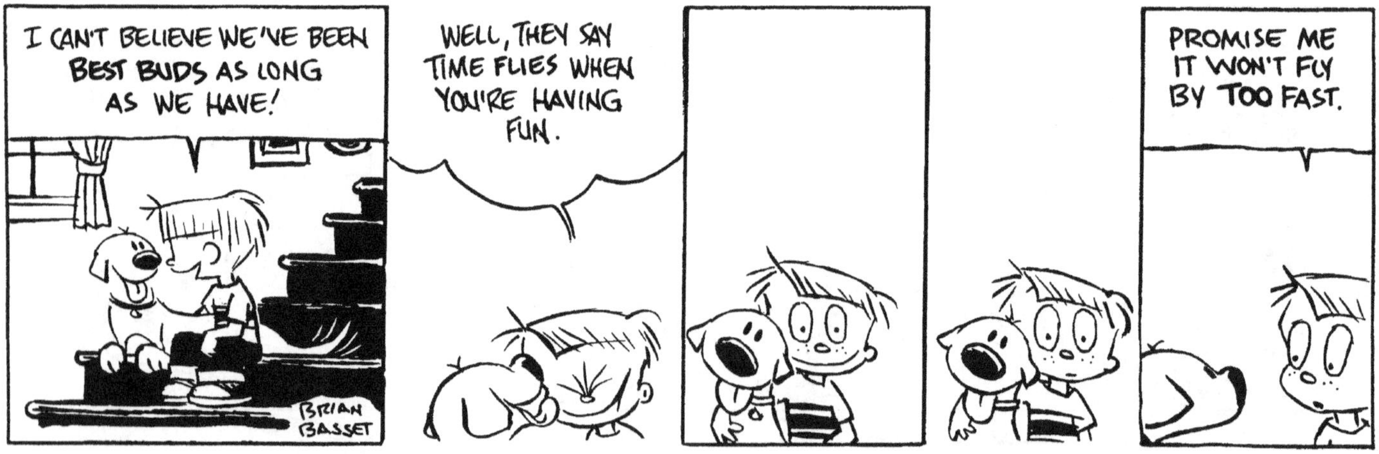
I CAN'T BELIEVE WE'VE BEEN BEST BUDS AS LONG AS WE HAVE!
BRIAN BASSET
WELL, THEY SAY TIME FLIES WHEN YOU'RE HAVING FUN.
PROMISE ME IT WON'T FLY BY TOO FAST.

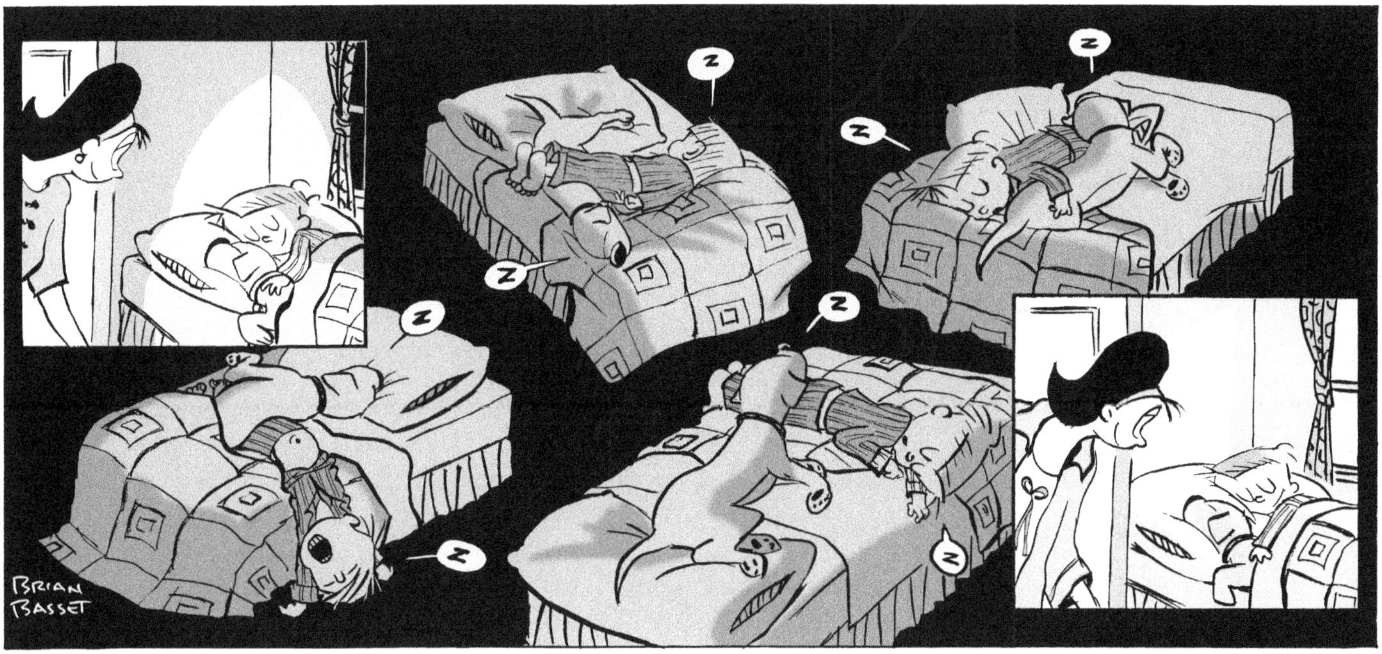
Z
Z
Z
Z
Z
Z
Z
Z
BRIAN BASSET

The End

CPSIA information can be obtained
at www.ICGtesting.com
Printed in the USA
BVHW051225051218
534845BV00024B/1421